SOURCES FOR *WORLD IN THE MAKING*

SOURCES FOR
WORLD IN THE MAKING

A Global History

VOLUME I to 1500

BONNIE G. SMITH
RUTGERS UNIVERSITY

MARC VAN DE MIEROOP
COLUMBIA UNIVERSITY

RICHARD VON GLAHN
UNIVERSITY OF CALIFORNIA, LOS ANGELES

KRIS LANE
TULANE UNIVERSITY

NEW YORK   OXFORD
OXFORD UNIVERSITY PRESS

Oxford University Press is a department of the University of Oxford.
It furthers the University's objective of excellence in research, scholarship,
and education by publishing worldwide. Oxford is a registered trade mark of
Oxford University Press in the UK and certain other countries.

Published in the United States of America by Oxford University Press
198 Madison Avenue, New York, NY 10016, United States of America.

For titles covered by Section 112 of the US Higher Education
Opportunity Act, please visit www.oup.com/us/he for the latest
information about pricing and alternate formats.

Library of Congress Cataloging-in-Publication Data

Names: Smith, Bonnie G., 1940- author. | Smith, Bonnie G., 1940- World in the
    making.
Title: Sources for world in the making : a global history / Bonnie G. Smith,
    Rutgers University, Marc Van de Mieroop, Columbia University, Richard von
    Glahn, University of California, Los Angeles, Kris Lane, Tulane University.
Description: New York : Oxford University Press, [2019] | Includes
    bibliographical references.
Identifiers: LCCN 2018013216 (print) | LCCN 2018015988 (ebook) | ISBN
    9780190849351 (Volume 1 Ebook) | ISBN 9780190849368 (Volume 2 Ebook) |
    ISBN 9780190849337 (volume 1 print) | ISBN 9780190849344 (volume 2 print)
Subjects: LCSH: World history—Sources.
Classification: LCC D21 (ebook) | LCC D21 .S625 2019 (print) | DDC 909—dc23
LC record available at https://lccn.loc.gov/2018013216

9 8 7 6 5
Printed by Marquis, Canada

CONTENTS

PREFACE

Designed to accompany *World in the Making: A Global History, Sources for World in the Making* reflects the textbook's integrated and multidimensional approach to the global past. We, the authors of *World in the Making*, have carefully selected sources that complement the topics and themes in each chapter of the textbook and that will spark students' interest. The documents in this collection buttress our belief that world history can best be taught by emphasizing the crossroads of human interaction. For example, the *Florentine Codex* and *Codex Mendoza* (Documents 15.1 and 15.2) were produced at a crossroads at which learned local people in New Spain and priests from Spain itself came together to create documents recording everyday life and religious observances of the Aztec people. Persian manuscript illuminations (Document 14.4) reflect the influence of Chinese paintings that circulated throughout Asia during the Mongol era. Other crossroads appear as political exchanges and disputes, such as letters concerning diplomatic marriages among Babylonian and Egyptian royalty (Document 2.3) and Cold War confrontations in Chapter 27. These documents reinforce our theme of exchange, contestation, encounters, and other points of cross-cultural and transnational contact. We present these themes in conjunction with political, social, cultural, and economic aspects of past experience so that students will understand what it means to live in global history.

We have selected sources representing not only the pivotal moments and world-changing actors of the global past but also the lives and thoughts of ordinary people—another major theme of *World in the Making*. We "people" this document's reader with the songs, diaries, and expressions of outrage and support in politics from across social classes and from across the globe. Document 22.1, for example, presents Enlightenment values from the perspective of a glassworker, and Chapter 24 provides diary excerpts written by an Indian soldier—himself a colonial subject—serving in the British army during the Boxer Rebellion. We set these in a world historical context to show the ways in which people have contributed to the global past despite appearing to some as being outside world history. Indeed, we integrate ordinary folks with major actors because world history only comes alive in the stories of people who experienced the global past.

Documents come in all forms, and we have attempted to give students a sense of their variety by including letters, epics, memoirs, religious and political texts, travel accounts, ethnographic evidence, and much more. To underscore the importance of images in historical analysis, we provide a range of visual documents throughout, from an Indus Valley clay tablet to Cold War–era advertisements. These sources engage students' visual proclivities, while the accompanying pedagogy helps guide their analysis of visual details and prompts reflection on their historical significance. To give students access to periods and peoples for which there are few, if any, written records, we have occasionally included alternative documents. For example, Chapter 1 includes later sources on evolution to supplement the textbook's discussion of human origins. Such sources will help generate discussion of what a document is, how evidence is constituted through the development of new knowledge and techniques, and what nonhistorians can teach us about the past.

PEDAGOGICAL FEATURES

Contextualization, evaluation, and synthesis are fundamental skills needed by all students of history, and we aimed to make this documents reader a place where students can find tools for historical thinking and where the instructor will have access to an array of devices to help develop the analytical skills of students. Each chapter therefore opens with an introductory paragraph that provides a broad overview of the chapter's themes, and then individual document headnotes set each source within a more specific historical context. At the end of each document or set of documents are questions to guide students in examining the evidence, probing students to review their understanding of a document's content, and encouraging analysis of deeper issues. Finally, we want students to be able to assess the significance of the documents within the context of larger global developments. A set of Making Connections questions at the end of each chapter invites students to trace similarities and differences among documents as they set them in the context of the chapter's overall themes. We have also defined unfamiliar terms and concepts throughout the collection to aid students' comprehension of the sources.

Again, emphasizing the individual voices of people—grand and humble—the Contrasting Views feature (seven are included in this volume) presents differing perspectives on a development, issue, or event and encourages students' synthesis of multiple sources. In Chapter 4, students encounter contrasting opinions about the value of democracy in ancient Greece, and in Chapter 21 the pros and cons of Spanish activity in the Americas in the sixteenth and seventeenth centuries—discussions that we still have today and that students love to participate in. Chapter 23 presents differing viewpoints on the Industrial Revolution from people living at the time, many of them participants in the developments of that period.

Given the demands of reading primary sources from distant times and places, we have done our best to select documents that speak to a range of students with a variety of skill levels, even as we aim for balanced coverage within the chapters. Overall, our goal is to build into the classroom experience both familiarity with the methods of historians and student proficiency in the historical method. Through grouping documents as the basis of their own narrative, students learn how historians synthesize their findings into a coherent account. Thus, we believe that these selections can serve as the foundation for students to act as historians in small-group activities, writing assignments, and classroom debates. We recognize that this is a tall order in the face of the enormity of world history, but we fervently hope that the selections and teaching aids in *Sources for World in the Making* benefit you and your students.

ACKNOWLEDGMENTS

In compiling *Sources for World in the Making*, the author team has tapped the extensive expertise of the editors and staff at Oxford University Press who helped us every step of the way. Our editor, Charles Cavaliere, kept us on task and disciplined our efforts. Editorial assistant Katie Tunkavige prepared the manuscript and oversaw clearing permissions. Our sincere thanks are offered to them as well as to Phil Scott, who oversaw production. We are grateful for this stellar team. Bonnie Smith also thanks Molly Giblin, Courtney Doucette, and Donald R. Kelley for their contributions, large and small.

INTRODUCTION FOR STUDENTS

WHY STUDY PRIMARY SOURCES?

If events of the past are to be understood simply as matters of fact, why do historians disagree about them? Can't they just give us the facts and let us interpret them? Can't they just tell us the objective truth about what happened? Many believe that the historian, like the archaeologist digging up a broken pot, simply has to recover the pieces and put them back together. History in this view is the piecing together of an uncontested, objective past, a reconstruction composed of facts and dates.

Yet, as any archaeologist or historian knows, a reassembled pot is not a story, much less a history, and telling one—explaining the pot's historical significance—requires careful attention to context as well as asking many questions. Where was the pot buried? How was it broken? What did it contain? Who might have made it? Who might have owned it? How old is it? The questions may go on and on, but the point is that the pot, even when reconstructed, does not explain itself. Properly telling its story, its *history*, is not a simple and straightforward task. Historians, like archaeologists, try to answer as many questions as they can about their evidence. Historians use the term *primary sources* to refer to evidence produced as close to the events in question as possible. At best, primary sources are firsthand descriptions or eyewitness accounts.

Imagine that someone studying the pot in question came across a text in an archive or a library that described the use of pots in the same area from which the pot had been excavated. Suppose that several hundred years ago a traveler wrote an account of a visit to the region and remarked that women there made special pots for the drinking of a beverage considered sacred, and that these pots were customarily smashed following royal weddings. Does this eyewitness account then explain the broken pot that the archaeologist found and pieced together? It is a tantalizing clue, to be sure, but many questions remain. Does the archaeologist's pot match those in the written description, or is the travel narrative too vague to make such a determination? Does the pot contain any residue that might link it to the sacred beverage mentioned by the traveler? Was it found in the right location for such a ritual smashing, or was it discovered in a household trash dump?

In this case a written primary source, the usual raw material of historians, would seem to provide the smoking gun, or definitive explanation, for the archaeologist. But as helpful as it may be, the text, like the pot, is not self-explanatory; it must be thoroughly examined before any conclusions can be drawn. First, the document is itself a physical object, an artifact like the archaeologist's pot. Historians first evaluate the document's age and the context of its production. What is its form? Is this a copy, a translation, or an original manuscript? Or is it a forgery? Inadequate evaluation of primary sources as artifacts, that is, testing their veracity at the most basic or "forensic" level, can lead to wildly inaccurate historical claims.

Second, the primary source text is often a narrative: an attempt to record an event or experience based on an individual's perception and memory, which are often colored by his or her own biases and beliefs. The traveler's account, though clearly valuable in some way, is limited by these and other constraints, including the traveler's abilities to convey lived experience in written form—that is to say, the writer's ability as a writer. The more we examine this seemingly objective, firsthand description, the more subjective, or specific to this individual, it appears.

The contents of the traveler's account are as subject to doubt, or at least close scrutiny, as testimony provided by an eyewitness in a criminal trial. Even when an objective sequence of events such as in an armed robbery occurs, not everyone sees, much less remembers—or *narrates*—the same thing. This is not to say that the traveler's account cannot be trusted at all simply because it is subjective, or fallible, but rather that its claims must be analyzed carefully before we deploy them in our historical narrative, our legalistic "case" about the smashed pot. We must evaluate the source to determine how plausible the traveler's account is. Evaluating the account's plausibility—and therefore its utility and limitations as evidence in our quest for the historical significance of the pot—requires formulating and answering questions similar to those raised by the archaeologist. Who was the writer of the account? Who was the intended audience? Are there other accounts that might be consulted to verify the writer's claims in this instance? Are other works by this writer known to be trustworthy? Does the date of the narrative roughly match the date assigned to the pot in question, or was it written so much later—or so much earlier—that it could not possibly relate to the same thing?

What about our traveler's perspective on a foreign culture, seeing it and reporting on it as an outsider? Is the traveler's account biased or distorted by personal opinion or prejudice? Or is it simply mistaken, prone to error or poor observation? The traveler may have witnessed an event such as the breaking of a pot, but how is the historian to know if the pot was broken for ritual purposes, as the traveler claimed? Did this breaking take place after a royal wedding, as the traveler "testified," or had the preceding ritual actually been a reenactment of some other union, perhaps between two deities? The fact of the broken pot seems indisputable, inasmuch as it is mentioned in the account and was discovered by the archaeologist, but the reason for its breaking remains uncertain. Perhaps the archaeologist's pot simply collapsed under the weight of the earth that covered it.

Imagine that the historian then happened on a book by an ethnographer who lived among the descendants of the group studied by the archaeologist, and in it there was a description of ritual pot breaking following royal wedding ceremonies. Would this ethnographic evidence at last provide the necessary proof to close the case? Perhaps, but the historian would still have to ask more questions. In essence, can recent ethnographic sources be considered primary when used as evidence for much earlier practices or beliefs? This remains a vexing question for many world historians seeking to explain the actions of past cultures that lack a written tradition.

This may seem a tiresome exercise with only a small payoff, but by combining the variety of evidence and approaches, we have come closer to understanding some small part of this past foreign culture that may have otherwise escaped our notice. We can do this only by rigorously interrogating all kinds of sources. Even the most explicit texts cannot entirely speak for themselves.

INTERPRETING PRIMARY SOURCES

Primary sources express a point of view, or perspective, and are therefore always subject to interpretation. Beyond verification and classification, then, the historian must examine primary sources with a detective's eye for telling details or turns of phrase, searching for clues as to the author's purpose. Is the author making an argument, or is the author simply relaying information with nothing at stake? Is he or she writing to impress some authority or to defame a rival? Interpreting texts written by individuals who openly display their opinions or biases may seem straightforward, and sometimes it is, but what can we make of primary sources whose biases or assumptions are concealed, or were created at times and places so different from our own that they are difficult to identify?

A classic example is the law code, such as "The Placard of the People's Instructions" (Document 14.3), which was composed in late-medieval China. Such codes, especially when read by foreigners like us, far removed from those who wrote them in space and time, often reveal the differences between their cultural assumptions and ours. Again, asking the right questions brings us to a closer understanding of the context in which the document was created. In this case, what constituted a crime, and what was considered a just punishment? Was the placard issued by those in power in response to a credible threat, or did it reflect some wider consensus? Ultimately, historians must "unpack" the source for clues into what it can reveal about the people and period in question. When possible, historians try to assemble as broad a range of sources as possible, including those that contradict each other. When interpreted in light of many other sources from the period, the Chinese placard may make a great deal more sense. Like the reassembled pot, it may not remain such a mystery.

History, then, is not the recovery of a single, uncontested narrative of the past. It is instead an ongoing conversation about the past, a conversation constantly enriched—and occasionally revolutionized—by new evidence and new perspectives. As students of history, we must continue to challenge or improve on accepted or "master" narratives of the past by searching for new evidence and examining it with rigor. To put it another way, we should make a habit of questioning authority, not for the sake of defiance, but rather with the intention of improving our knowledge.

The good historian, like the good detective, follows every promising lead, knowing many will be dead ends. When a historian or detective is trying to solve a thorny problem, or answer a tough question, one good lead trumps a thousand bad ones. The good historian must also be willing to confront and reveal his or her own biases, assumptions, and tastes. What is your personal point of view, and how have you arrived at it? What aspects of the human past and what kinds of primary sources do you find most compelling, and why? The great conversation that is history has plenty of space for you to enter in and make an original contribution. Your perspective counts.

SOURCES IN WORLD HISTORY

As the example of the broken pot suggests, world history presents special challenges, especially in cases in which written sources are rare, but it also presents many opportunities. The study of world history, like that of large regions such as East Asia, western Europe, or Latin America, remains largely reliant on written sources, but by its very global nature it demands incorporation of other types of evidence. This includes material objects, archaeological findings, ethnographic fieldwork, oral interviews, linguistic studies, photographs, video recordings, DNA analysis, and much else. It may even be useful to think in terms of an all-encompassing global archive that includes everything touched by or relevant to humans.

This is casting an awfully wide net, so it should be kept in mind that the broader academic discipline of history has traditionally focused on evaluating and interpreting written primary sources, be they inscriptions, law codes, letters, memoirs, censuses, or chronicles. Anything written is fair game for historians. As we have seen, what makes a written source useful depends in large part on what questions we ask of it. We must interrogate not only its contents but also the context of its production and the aims of its writer or writers.

When sources have been produced by outsiders, as in the case of our traveler's account mentioned earlier, we must work hard to assess what is valuable for our purposes and what is the product of the writer's prejudices, ignorance, or emotional state. In world history it is especially important not to discard such obviously biased sources simply because we find them offensive. Instead we must ask what led the writer to think in such a way. Is the source's overall validity completely compromised by prejudice, or might it still contain useful observations? Or might it be useful only in the study of prejudiced outsiders and their views on the culture at hand? As mentioned earlier, other sources in world history may be puzzling to us because they derive from a radically foreign perspective or worldview. Insiders, then, can be as difficult to understand as outsiders. Harder, but of key importance, is asking how such worldviews fit into our larger model of world history. What does this one source about a single group of people mean in the larger scheme of things?

Some of the questions generated by world history are small and regionally specific. For example, we may want to know when the Dutch conquered Southeast Asia's Banda Islands and took over the global trade in nutmeg. A variety of published primary sources can be readily consulted and compared, and a quite specific answer given. But world history also lends itself to much larger questions, most of them not easily answered in such a definitive, *Jeopardy!*-style way. For example: How does the early-modern transatlantic slave trade compare with other slave trades in world history? Addressing such a big question requires quantifying the various slave trades we know about and can document with some assurance, then comparing them and an-swering various subsidiary questions. Such big and often comparative questions are what most compel world historians writing today, and they are what make world his-tory such a vibrant and exciting field.

Although no collection of documents can encompass the vast global archive, *Sources for World in the Making* aims to present global history on a more human scale, giving pride of place to individual voices—to people telling their stories. You will encounter tradi-tional documents such as law codes, chronicles, court histories, and literary works, as well as less familiar ones such as textiles and oracle bone fragments. You will also be exposed to a rich variety of perspectives, from influential figures to lesser known local and personal voices that nonetheless shed light on larger, global concerns.

Think of these documents as your chance to "overhear" the ideas and expressions of people who lived in the past. By examining a document, you are now in closer touch with the reality of a past that is indeed in many ways a foreign country and filled with total strangers. Because of this strangeness, you, the apprentice–historian, need to have knowl-edge not only of these sources but also of the conditions in which the original speakers and authors lived and acted. The chapter introductions and document headnotes in this sourcebook, along with the *World in the Making* textbook, provide this context. Some of these sources will strike a chord with you and others will not. The master narrative you create in reading them in tandem with the *World in the Making* textbook will be your own, the product of your conversation with the global past.

The Ancient World, from Human Origins to 500 C.E.

CHAPTER 1

Peopling the World,
to 4000 B.C.E.

Writing, a technology that appeared first in ancient Southwest Asia some 5,000 years ago, did not exist for most of the four million years that humans and their hominid ancestors have inhabited the earth. Although written documents usually provide the primary source material for historical research, historians have no access to written accounts for the so-called prehistoric periods discussed in this chapter. For the earliest periods of world history, historians must rely on a variety of other evidence, especially the physical remains of early humans and their ancestors, and the materials these humans left behind, including their art. This evidence often derives from more than one discipline, and opinions vary on how to interpret discoveries and data in light of different techniques and approaches. Moreover, some humans maintained lifestyles that resembled those of prehistory when others already wrote, and we can use descriptions of these lifestyles in our historical reconstructions as well.

The documents presented here primarily include writings that discuss how scholars discover and interpret evidence about the earliest aspects of human existence. The first pair of readings, Document 1.1, reveals how interpretations of the course of human evolution have changed based on new technology that allows analysis of DNA. Descriptions of key fossil finds make up the second document set, Document 1.2. Document 1.3 presents a modern attempt to understand Paleolithic artwork. Document 1.4, an observation on a relatively recent hunter-gatherer society, assists scholars' understanding of hunter-gatherers of the distant past.

1.1   THEORIES OF HUMAN EVOLUTION

Charles Darwin, *The Descent of Man, and Selection in Relation to Sex* (1871)

The study of the evolutionary progressions that led to the development of the human species experienced a major breakthrough in the work of Charles Darwin (1809–1882), whose writings dealt with the evolution of all natural species and their adaptation to circumstances that promote the survival of a group. Darwin did not specifically address the issue of hominid development, but in his work *The Descent of Man, and Selection in Relation to Sex* he proposed that humans were related to other animals. He argued that there are elements in human physiognomy that no longer have a useful function but survived from earlier animal species in which they were important. Although Darwin's work is a century and a half old and new evidence and approaches to the study of human evolution have emerged more recently, his writings still form the intellectual basis for the entire study of this topic.

The main conclusion here arrived at, and now held by many naturalists who are well competent to form a sound judgment, is that man is descended from some less highly organised form. The grounds upon which this conclusion rests will never be shaken, for the close similarity between man and the lower animals in embryonic development, as well as in innumerable points of structure and constitution, both of high and of the most trifling importance—the rudiments which he retains and the abnormal reversions to which he is occasionally liable—are facts which cannot be disputed. They have long been known, but until recently they told us nothing with respect to the origin of man. Now when viewed by the light of our knowledge of the whole organic world, their meaning is unmistakable. The great principle of evolution stands up clear and firm when these groups of facts are considered in connection with others, such as the mutual affinities of the members of the same group, their geographical distribution in past and present times, and their geological succession. It is incredible that all these facts should speak falsely. He who is not content to look, like a savage, at the phenomena of nature as disconnected can not any longer believe that man is the work of a separate act of creation. He will be forced to admit that the close resemblance of the embryo of man to that, for instance, of a dog—the construction of his skull, limbs, and whole frame on the same plan with that of other mammals, independently of the uses to which the parts may be put—the occasional reappearance of various structures, for instance, of several muscles, which man does not normally possess but which are common to the Quadrumana[1]—and a crowd of analogous facts—all point in the plainest manner to the conclusion that man is the co-descendant with other mammals of a common progenitor.

We have seen that man incessantly presents individual differences in all parts of his body and in his mental faculties. These differences or variations seem to be induced by the same general causes, and to obey the same laws as with the lower animals. In both cases similar laws of inheritance prevail. Man tends to increase at a greater rate than his means of subsistence; consequently he is occasionally subjected to a severe struggle for existence, and natural selection will have effected whatever lies within its scope. A succession of strongly-marked variations of a similar nature are by no means requisite; slight fluctuating differences in the individual suffice for

[1] **Quadrumana:** A primate group with four "hands"—that is, with feet that are shaped the same way as their hands.

Charles Darwin, *The Origin of Species by Means of Natural Selection; or, The Preservation of Favored Races in the Struggle for Life* and *The Descent of Man, and Selection in Relation to Sex* (New York: Modern Library, 1936), 909–911.

the work of natural selection; not that we have any reason to suppose that in the same species, all parts of the organization tend to vary to the same degree. We may feel assured that the inherited effects of the long-continued use or disuse of parts will have done much in the same direction with natural selection. Modifications formerly of importance, though no longer of any special use, are long-inherited. When one part is modified, other parts change through the principle of correlation, of which we have instances in many curious cases of correlated monstrosities. Something may be attributed to the direct and definite action of the surrounding conditions of life, such as abundant food, heat or moisture; and lastly, many characters of slight physiological importance, some indeed of considerable importance, have been gained through sexual selection. . . .

Through the means just specified, aided perhaps by others as yet undiscovered, man has been raised to his present state. But since he attained to the rank of manhood, he has diverged into distinct races, or as they may be more fitly called, sub-species. Some of these, such as the Negro and European, are so distinct that, if specimens had been brought to a naturalist without any further information, they would undoubtedly have been considered by him as good and true species. Nevertheless all the races agree in so many unimportant details of structure and in so many mental peculiarities, that these can be accounted for only through inheritance from a common progenitor; and a progenitor thus characterised would probably deserve to rank as man.

It must not be supposed that the divergence of each race from the other races, and of all from a common stock, can be traced back to any one pair of progenitors. On the contrary, at every stage in the process of modification, all the individuals which were in any way best fitted for their conditions of life, though in different degrees, would have survived in greater numbers than the less well-fitted. The process would have been like that followed by man, when he does not intentionally select particular individuals, but breeds from all the superior individuals and neglects the inferior. He thus slowly but surely modifies his stock, and unconsciously forms a new strain.

Rick Groleau, *Tracing Ancestry with MtDNA* (2002)

Darwin's approach dominated the study of human evolution until the late twentieth century, when the analysis of DNA provided a means to investigate the genetic relationship between human beings all over the world. Of the various types of DNA, mitochondrial DNA has been especially useful. The research requires a wide-ranging collection of data and an analysis with the help of computers, but its principles are straightforward and its results have contributed much to the study of the origins of the human species and human migration. The article included here provides a clear explanation of the new research method and its conclusions.

In 1987, three scientists announced in the journal *Nature* that they had found a common ancestor to us all, a woman who lived in Africa 200,000 years ago. She was given the name "Eve," which was great for capturing attention, though somewhat misleading, as the name at once brought to mind the biblical Eve and with it the mistaken notion that the ancestor was the first of our species—the woman from whom all humankind descended.

The "Eve" in question was actually the most recent common ancestor through matrilineal descent of all humans living today. That is, all people alive today can trace some of their genetic heritage through their mothers back to this one woman. The scientists hypothesized this ancient woman's existence by looking within the cells of living people and analyzing short loops of genetic code known as mitochondrial DNA, or mtDNA for short. In recent years, scientists have used mtDNA to trace the evolution and migration of human species, including when the common ancestor to modern humans and Neanderthals lived—though there has been considerable debate over the validity and value of the findings.

Rick Groleau, "Tracing Ancestry with mtDNA," NOVA Online, WGBH, January 2002, http://www.pbs.org/wgbh/nova/neanderthals/mtdna.html.

Nuclear DNA versus Mitochondrial DNA

When someone mentions human DNA, what do you think of? If you know a little about the topic, perhaps you think of the 46 chromosomes that inhabit the nucleus of almost every cell that comprises your body. These chromosomes hold the vast bulk of genetic information that you've inherited from your parents.

Outside the nucleus, but still within the cell, lie mitochondria. Mitochondria are tiny structures that help cells in a number of ways, including producing the energy that cells need. Each mitochondrion — there are about 1,700 in every human cell — includes an identical loop of DNA about 16,000 base pairs long containing 37 genes. In contrast, nuclear DNA consists of three billion base pairs and an estimated 70,000 genes. (This estimate has been revised upward several times since the announcement that the human genome had been decoded, and likely will be again.)

Inheriting mtDNA

Whenever an egg cell is fertilized, nuclear chromosomes from a sperm cell enter the egg and combine with the egg's nuclear DNA, producing a mixture of both parents' genetic code. The mtDNA from the sperm cell, however, is left behind, outside of the egg cell.

So the fertilized egg contains a mixture of the father and mother's nuclear DNA and an exact copy of the mother's mtDNA, but none of the father's mtDNA. The result is that mtDNA is passed on only along the maternal line. This means that all of the mtDNA in the cells of a person's body are copies of his or her mother's mtDNA, and all of the mother's mtDNA is a copy of her mother's, and so on. No matter how far back you go, mtDNA is always inherited only from the mother.

If you went back six generations in your own family tree, you'd see that your nuclear DNA is inherited from 32 men and 32 women.[1] Your mtDNA,

on the other hand, would have come from only one of those 32 women.

Defining Mitochondrial Ancestors

Let's get back to "Eve." The ancestor referred to in the 1987 *Nature* article can be more precisely stated as "the most recent common ancestor through matrilineal descent of all humans living today." In other words, she is the most recent person from whom everyone now living on Earth has inherited his or her mtDNA. This certainly does not mean that she is the ancestral mother of all who came after her; during her time and even before her time there were many women and men who contributed to the nuclear genes we now carry. It also does not mean that the mtDNA originated with this "Eve"; she and her contemporaries also had their own "most recent common ancestor through matrilineal descent," a woman who lived even further into the past who passed on her mtDNA to everyone living during "Eve's" time. (We get our mtDNA from that same, older ancestor. She's just not, to us, the *most recent* common ancestor.)

So what about all of the mtDNA of the other women who lived during "Eve's" time? What happened to it? Simply this: Somewhere between now and then, they had female descendants who had only sons (or no children). When this happened, the passing on of their mtDNA halted.

Finding Mitochondrial Ancestors

Even though everyone on Earth living today has inherited his or her mtDNA from one person who lived long ago, our mtDNA is not exactly alike. Random mutations have altered the genetic code over the millennia. But these mutations are organized, in a way. For example, let's say that 10,000 years after the most recent common ancestor, one of the mtDNA branches experienced a mutation. From that point on, that line of mtDNA would include that alteration. Another branch might experience a mutation in a different location. This alteration would also be passed on. What we would eventually end up with are some descendants who have mtDNA that is exactly or very much like that of

---

[1] Unless two or more of those 64 married each other and bore children from which you are descended. For example, your great-great-grandfather on your mother's side might have married and had children with your great-great-grandmother on your father's side. In that case, the number of your ancestors in this example would drop to 63. [Original note.]

some people's, somewhat like that of others, and less like that of yet others. By looking at the similarities and differences of the mtDNA of all of these individuals, researchers could try to reconstruct where the branching took place.

This is what some researchers have done. For the original 1987 *Nature* article, the three authors (Rebecca Cann, Mark Stoneking, and Allan Wilson) looked at the mtDNA of 147 people from continents around the world (though for Africans, they relied on African Americans[2]). Later, with the help of a computer program, they put together a sort of family tree, grouping those with the most similar DNA together, then grouping the groups, and then grouping the groups of groups. The tree they ended up with showed that one of the two primary branches consisted only of African mtDNA and that the other branch consisted of mtDNA from all over the world, including Africa. From this, they inferred that the most recent common mtDNA ancestor was an African woman.[3]

Dating Mitochondrial Ancestors

The three researchers went even further—they estimated the age of the ancestor. To get the estimate, they made the assumption that the random mutations occurred at a steady rate. And since they now had an idea of how much the mtDNA had changed from the ancestor's, all they needed was the mutation rate to determine the age of the ancestor. For instance, if they took the mutation rate to be one in every 1,000 years and knew that there was a difference of 10 mutations between the mtDNA of people living today and the mtDNA of an ancestor

who lived long ago, then they could infer that the ancestor lived 10,000 years ago.

Cann, Stoneking, and Wilson estimated the mutation rate by looking at the mtDNA of groups of people whose ancestors migrated to areas at known times. One group was Australian aborigines, whose ancestors moved to the island-continent as then-calculated 30,000 years ago.[4] Since the three then knew how long it took for that group's mtDNA to diverge as well as how much it diverged, they determined the mutation rate. Using this rate, they determined that the most recent common ancestor lived 140,000 to 290,000 years ago (which they roughly averaged to 200,000 years ago). That was back in 1987. Since then, researchers have updated the estimate to 120,000 to 150,000 years ago. However, the margin for error for this estimate and the previous one are significant—when all of the variables are taken into account, the current range is more like 50,000 to 500,000.

Neanderthals and mtDNA

Finding out about our most recent common ancestor relies solely on inferences from the mtDNA of people living today. What if we could actually compare our mtDNA with mtDNA of a distant ancestor? This, in fact, has been done, with mtDNA from the bones of Neanderthals. Comparing mtDNA of these Neanderthals to mtDNA of living people from various continents, researchers have found that the Neanderthals' mtDNA is not more closely related to that of people from any one continent over another. This was an unwelcome finding for anthropologists who believe that there was some interbreeding between Neanderthals and early modern humans living in Europe (which might have helped to explain why modern Europeans possess some Neanderthal-like features); these particular anthropologists instead would have expected the Neanderthals' mtDNA to be more similar to that of modern Europeans than to that of other peoples. Moreover, the researchers determined that the common ancestor to Neanderthals and modern

---

[2] Although the original study was criticized for using African Americans instead of native Africans, a subsequent study in which the researchers used mtDNA from native Africans came up with similar results. [Original note.]

[3] Other researchers later showed that the computer program could come up with other variations of the tree, some of which did not place an African at the root of the tree. This study, then, cannot be viewed as definitive proof that the ancestor lived in Africa. However, it does still suggest that humans originated in Africa, a hypothesis that other, more recent studies support. [Original note.]

[4] The date for the migration to Australia is now estimated to be 50,000 to 60,000 years ago. [Original note.]

Homo sapiens lived as long as 500,000 years ago, well before the most recent common mtDNA ancestor of modern humans. This suggests (though it does not prove) that Neanderthals went extinct without contributing to the gene pool of any modern humans.

Final Note

There are many variables that can affect the mutation rate of mtDNA, including even the possibility that mtDNA is not always inherited strictly through maternal lines. In fact, recent studies show that paternal mtDNA can on rare occasions enter an egg during fertilization and alter the maternal mtDNA through recombination. Such recombination would drastically affect the mutation rate and throw off date estimates.

Not surprisingly, there is currently a heated debate over the value of "mitochondrial Eve" — especially between history-hunting geneticists and some fossil-finding paleoanthropologists. According to these anthropologists, even if we could accurately gauge the age of the ancestor, that knowledge is meaningless because all she really is is the woman whose mtDNA did not die out due to random lineage extinctions. Furthermore, her status as the most recent common ancestor doesn't mean that she and her contemporaries were any different from their ancestors. (Remember, she and all of her contemporaries had their own mitochondrial Eve.)

Perhaps the most valuable finding regarding the "most recent common ancestor" is that she probably lived in Africa — a finding that supports the most popular theories about the worldwide spread of hominids.

Examining the Evidence

1. Although Darwin and modern DNA analysis use very different evidence, they share certain basic principles of interpretation. What are these shared principles?
2. Methods and theories of scientific investigation are rooted in the cultural and technological contexts of their time. Can you describe these contexts for the two approaches described here?
3. According to these documents, is race important for categorizing humans? Why or why not?

1.2 FINDING FOSSILS

Donald C. Johanson and Maitland A. Edey, *Lucy: The Beginnings of Humankind* (1981)

Because ancestors of the modern human species no longer exist, paleontologists have to rely on fossils to determine what their physical characteristics might have been when they were alive. The bones have survived in unusual circumstances, and many finds are accidental. Every fossil can change the existing opinions of the development of human ancestry, and new finds continue to be made, some of which are especially important for the study of human evolution. The passage reproduced here is a popularized account of Donald C. Johanson and Tom Gray's 1974 unearthing of Lucy, the earliest relatively well-preserved example of *Australopithecus afarensis*, in the Afar Valley in modern Ethiopia. The find changed ideas about when human ancestors started to walk upright, and accounts of this nature have made Lucy one of the most famous human fossils in existence.

Some people are good at finding fossils. Others are hopelessly bad at it. It's a matter of practice, of training your eye to see what you need to see.

Donald C. Johanson and Maitland A. Edey, *Lucy: The Beginnings of Humankind* (New York: Simon and Schuster, 1981; New York: Warner Books, 1982), 15–18. Citations refer to the Warner Books edition.

I will never be as good as some of the Afar people. They spend all their time wandering around in the rocks and sand. They have to be sharp-eyed; their lives depend on it. Anything the least bit unusual they notice. One quick educated look at all those stones and pebbles, and they'll spot a couple of things a person not acquainted with the desert would miss.

Tom and I surveyed for a couple of hours. It was now close to noon, and the temperature was approaching 110. We hadn't found much: a few teeth of the small extinct horse *Hipparion*; part of the skull of an extinct pig; some antelope molars; a bit of a monkey jaw. We had large collections of all these things already, but Tom insisted on taking these also as added pieces in the overall jigsaw puzzle of what went where.

I've had it," said Tom. "When do we head back to camp?"

"Right now. But let's go back this way and survey the bottom of that little gully over there."

The gully in question was just over the crest of the rise where we had been working all morning. It had been thoroughly checked out at least twice before by other workers, who had found nothing interesting. Nevertheless, conscious of the "lucky" feeling that had been with me since I woke, I decided to make that small final detour. There was virtually no bone in the gully. But as we turned to leave, I noticed something lying on the ground partway up the slope.

"That's a bit of hominid arm," I said.

"Can't be. It's too small. Has to be a monkey of some kind."

We knelt to examine it.

"Much too small," said Gray again.

I shook my head. "Hominid."

"What makes you so sure?" he said.

"That piece right next to your hand. That's hominid too."

"Jesus Christ," said Gray. He picked it up. It was the back of a small skull. A few feet away was part of a femur: a thighbone. "Jesus Christ," he said again. We stood up, and began to see other bits of bone on the slope: a couple of vertebrae, part of a pelvis — all of them hominid. An unbelievable, impermissible thought flickered through my mind. Suppose all

these fitted together? Could they be parts of a single, extremely primitive skeleton? No such skeleton had ever been found anywhere.

"Look at that," said Gray. "Ribs."

A single individual?

"I can't believe it," I said. "I just can't believe it."

"By God, you'd better believe it!" said Gray. "Here it is. Right here!" His voice went up into a howl. I joined him. In that 110-degree heat we began jumping up and down. With nobody to share our feelings, we hugged each other, sweaty and smelly, howling and hugging in the heat-shimmering gravel, the small brown remains of what now seemed almost certain to be parts of a single hominid skeleton lying all around us.

"We've got to stop jumping around," I finally said. "We may step on something. Also, we've got to make sure."

"Aren't you sure, for Christ's sake?"

"I mean, suppose we find two left legs. There may be several individuals here, all mixed up. Let's play it cool until we can come back and make absolutely sure that it all fits together."

We collected a couple of pieces of jaw, marked the spot exactly and got into the blistering Land-Rover for the run back to camp. On the way we picked up two expedition geologists who were loaded down with rock samples they had been gathering.

"Something big," Gray kept saying to them. "Something big, something *big*."

"Cool it," I said.

But about a quarter of a mile from camp, Gray could not cool it. He pressed his thumb on the Land-Rover's horn, and the long blast brought a scurry of scientists who had been bathing in the river.

"We've got it," he yelled. "Oh, Jesus, we've got it. We've got The Whole Thing!"

That afternoon everyone in camp was at the gully, sectioning off the site and preparing for a massive collecting job that ultimately took three weeks. When it was done we recovered several hundred pieces of bone (many of them fragments) representing about forty percent of the skeleton of a single individual. Tom's and my original hunch had been right. There was no bone duplication.

But a single individual of what? On preliminary examination it was very hard to say, for nothing quite like it had ever been discovered. The camp was rocking with excitement. That first night we never went to bed at all. We talked and talked. We drank beer after beer. There was a tape recorder in the camp, and a tape of the Beatles song "Lucy in the Sky with Diamonds" went belting out into the night sky, and was played at full volume over and over again out of sheer exuberance. At some point during the unforgettable evening — I no longer remember exactly when — the new fossil picked up the name of Lucy, and has been so known ever since, although its proper name — its acquisition number in the Hadar collection — is AL 288-1.

Jamie Shreeve, *Oldest Skeleton of Human Ancestor Found* (2009)

This passage from *National Geographic Magazine* reports on research that was about to be published in much more technical detail in the journal *Science*. It describes the find conditions and analysis of a skeleton of the *Ardipithecus ramidus* species, predating Lucy by more than a million years but recovered in the same part of eastern Africa in which Lucy was found, which forced a fundamental reinterpretation of the development of some basic human characteristics, such as bipedalism

Move Over, Lucy. And Kiss the Missing Link Goodbye

Scientists today announced the discovery of the oldest fossil skeleton of a human ancestor. The find reveals that our forebears underwent a previously unknown stage of evolution more than a million years before Lucy, the iconic early human ancestor specimen that walked the Earth 3.2 million years ago.

The centerpiece of a treasure trove of new fossils, the skeleton — assigned to a species called *Ardipithecus ramidus* — belonged to a small-brained, 110-pound (50-kilogram) female nicknamed "Ardi."

The fossil puts to rest the notion, popular since Darwin's time, that a chimpanzee-like missing link — resembling something between humans and today's apes — would eventually be found at the root of the human family tree. Indeed, the new evidence suggests that the study of chimpanzee anatomy and behavior — long used to infer the nature of the earliest human ancestors — is largely irrelevant to understanding our beginnings.

Ardi instead shows an unexpected mix of advanced characteristics and of primitive traits seen in much older apes that were unlike chimps or gorillas. As such, the skeleton offers a window on what the last common ancestor of humans and living apes might have been like.

Announced at joint press conferences in Washington, D.C., and Addis Ababa, Ethiopia, the analysis of the *Ardipithecus ramidus* bones will be published in a collection of papers tomorrow in a special edition of the journal *Science*, along with an avalanche of supporting materials published online.

"This find is far more important than Lucy," said Alan Walker, a paleontologist from Pennsylvania State University who was not part of the research. "It shows that the last common ancestor with chimps didn't look like a chimp, or a human, or some funny thing in between."

Ardi Surrounded by Family

The *Ardipithecus ramidus* fossils were discovered in Ethiopia's harsh Afar desert at a site called Aramis in the Middle Awash region, just 46 miles (74 kilometers) from where Lucy's species, *Australopithecus afarensis*, was found in 1974. Radiometric dating of two layers of volcanic ash that tightly sandwiched the fossil deposits revealed that Ardi lived 4.4 million years ago.

Older hominid fossils have been uncovered, including a skull from Chad at least six million years old and some more fragmentary, slightly younger remains from Kenya and nearby in the Middle Awash.

While important, however, none of those earlier fossils are nearly as revealing as the newly announced remains, which in addition to Ardi's partial skeleton include bones representing at least 36 other individuals.

"All of a sudden you've got fingers and toes and arms and legs and heads and teeth," said Tim White

---

Jamie Shreeve, "Oldest Skeleton of Human Ancestor Found," *National Geographic Magazine*, October 1, 2009.

of the University of California, Berkeley, who co-directed the work with Berhane Asfaw, a paleoanthropologist and former director of the National Museum of Ethiopia, and Giday WoldeGabriel, a geologist at Los Alamos National Laboratory in New Mexico.

"That allows you to do something you can't do with isolated specimens," White said. "It allows you to do biology."

Ardi's Weird Way of Moving

The biggest surprise about *Ardipithecus*'s biology is its bizarre means of moving about.

All previously known hominids — members of our ancestral lineage — walked upright on two legs, like us. But Ardi's feet, pelvis, legs, and hands suggest she was a biped on the ground but a quadruped when moving about in the trees.

Her big toe, for instance, splays out from her foot like an ape's, the better to grasp tree limbs. Unlike a chimpanzee foot, however, *Ardipithecus*'s contains a special small bone inside a tendon, passed down from more primitive ancestors, that keeps the divergent toe more rigid. Combined with modifications to the other toes, the bone would have helped Ardi walk bipedally on the ground, though less efficiently than later hominids like Lucy. The bone was lost in the lineages of chimps and gorillas.

According to the researchers, the pelvis shows a similar mosaic of traits. The large flaring bones of the upper pelvis were positioned so that Ardi could walk on two legs without lurching from side to side like a chimp. But the lower pelvis was built like an ape's, to accommodate huge hind limb muscles used in climbing.

Even in the trees, Ardi was nothing like a modern ape, the researchers say. Modern chimps and gorillas have evolved limb anatomy specialized to climbing vertically up tree trunks, hanging and swinging from branches, and knuckle-walking on the ground.

While these behaviors require very rigid wrist bones, for instance, the wrists and finger joints of *Ardipithecus* were highly flexible. As a result Ardi would have walked on her palms as she moved about in the trees — more like some primitive fossil apes than like chimps and gorillas.

"What Ardi tells us is there was this vast intermediate stage in our evolution that nobody knew about," said Owen Lovejoy, an anatomist at Kent State University in Ohio, who analyzed Ardi's bones below the neck. "It changes everything."

Against All Odds, Ardi Emerges

The first, fragmentary specimens of *Ardipithecus* were found at Aramis in 1992 and published in 1994. The skeleton announced today was discovered that same year and excavated with the bones of the other individuals over the next three field seasons. But it took 15 years before the research team could fully analyze and publish the skeleton, because the fossils were in such bad shape.

After Ardi died, her remains apparently were trampled down into mud by hippos and other passing herbivores. Millions of years later, erosion brought the badly crushed and distorted bones back to the surface.

They were so fragile they would turn to dust at a touch. To save the precious fragments, White and colleagues removed the fossils along with their surrounding rock. Then, in a lab in Addis, the researchers carefully tweaked out the bones from the rocky matrix using a needle under a microscope, proceeding "millimeter by submillimeter," as the team puts it in *Science*. This process alone took several years.

Pieces of the crushed skull were then CT-scanned and digitally fit back together by Gen Suwa, a paleoanthropologist at the University of Tokyo.

In the end, the research team recovered more than 125 pieces of the skeleton, including much of the feet and virtually all of the hands — an extreme rarity among hominid fossils of any age, let alone one so very ancient.

"Finding this skeleton was more than luck," said White. "It was against all odds."

Ardi's World

The team also found some 6,000 animal fossils and other specimens that offer a picture of the world Ardi inhabited: a moist woodland very different from the region's current, parched landscape. In addition to antelope and monkey species associated with forests, the deposits contained forest-dwelling birds and seeds from fig and palm trees.

Wear patterns and isotopes in the hominid teeth suggest a diet that included fruits, nuts, and other forest foods.

If White and his team are right that Ardi walked upright as well as climbed trees, the environmental evidence would seem to strike the death knell for the "savanna hypothesis" — a long-standing notion that our ancestors first stood up in response to their move onto an open grassland environment.

Sex for Food

Some researchers, however, are unconvinced that *Ardipithecus* was quite so versatile.

"This is a fascinating skeleton, but based on what they present, the evidence for bipedality is limited at best," said William Jungers, an anatomist at Stony Brook University in New York State.

"Divergent big toes are associated with grasping, and this has one of the most divergent big toes you can imagine," Jungers said. "Why would an animal fully adapted to support its weight on its forelimbs in the trees elect to walk bipedally on the ground?"

One provocative answer to that question — originally proposed by Lovejoy in the early 1980s and refined now in light of the *Ardipithecus* discoveries — attributes the origin of bipedality to another trademark of humankind: monogamous sex.

Virtually all apes and monkeys, especially males, have long upper canine teeth — formidable weapons in fights for mating opportunities.

But *Ardipithecus* appears to have already embarked on a uniquely human evolutionary path, with canines reduced in size and dramatically "feminized" to a stubby, diamond shape, according to the researchers. Males and female specimens are also close to each other in body size.

Lovejoy sees these changes as part of an epochal shift in social behavior: Instead of fighting for access to females, a male *Ardipithecus* would supply a "targeted female" and her offspring with gathered foods and gain her sexual loyalty in return.

To keep up his end of the deal, a male needed to have his hands free to carry home the food. Bipedalism may have been a poor way for *Ardipithecus* to get around, but through its contribution to the "sex for food" contract, it would have been an excellent way to bear more offspring. And in evolution, of course, more offspring is the name of the game.

Two hundred thousand years after *Ardipithecus*, another species called *Australopithecus anamensis* appeared in the region. By most accounts, that species soon evolved into *Australopithecus afarensis*, with a slightly larger brain and a full commitment to a bipedal way of life. Then came early *Homo*, with its even bigger brain and budding tool use.

Did primitive *Ardipithecus* undergo some accelerated change in the 200,000 years between it and *Australopithecus* — and emerge as the ancestor of all later hominids? Or was *Ardipithecus* a relict species, carrying its quaint mosaic of primitive and advanced traits with it into extinction?

Study co-leader White sees nothing about the skeleton "that would exclude it from ancestral status." But he said more fossils would be needed to fully resolve the issue.

Stony Brook's Jungers added, "These finds are incredibly important, and given the state of preservation of the bones, what they did was nothing short of heroic.

But this is just the beginning of the story."

Examining the Evidence

1. In what physical environment do paleontologists discover fossil remains, and how does that environment affect the remains?
2. Why is it so important to discover complete skeletons?
3. Why is East Africa the source of so many important fossil finds?
4. What are the techniques used to recover fossil fragments?

1.3   INTERPRETING PALEOLITHIC ART

Georges Bataille, *A Meeting in Lascaux: Civilized Man Rediscovers the Man of Desire* (1953)

It was only after millions of years of human evolution that our ancestors began to create objects without practical purposes and for aesthetic pleasure only. These we can call works of art. The date of the first preserved piece of art is much debated, but it is clear that the *Homo sapiens* regularly created art objects starting some 40,000 years ago. Among the earliest remains are paintings inside rock caves, which are especially abundant in areas of modern France and Spain. One of the most famous examples is the French Lascaux cave, which four teenage boys discovered in 1940. The paintings probably date to approximately 17,000 years ago (the date is uncertain). How do we understand them in the absence of written comments from their creators? Scholars can base interpretations only on the images themselves and on their knowledge of the ancient cultures at the time of their creation. The passage presented here, originally published in the 1950s, is by the French philosopher Georges Bataille (1897–1962), whose writings explored eroticism, mysticism, and the irrational in all periods of human history. His works have become very influential in recent years.

After more than ten years, we are still far from having fully recognized the magnitude of the discovery of Lascaux. It goes without saying that these paintings are beautiful, they enchant everyone who sees them, and they allow us to feel closer to the earliest men. But, understandably, we find these expressions daunting. They are cold, and it may seem pretentious to discuss these cave paintings more passionately.

They are within the provinces of both science and desire. Would it be possible to discuss them the way Proust discussed Vermeer or Breton discussed Marcel Duchamp? Not only is it inappropriate to fall under their spell when near them, in the disorder of a visit, lacking the time to collect ourselves, but prehistorians also bid us to keep in mind what these apparitions meant to the men who animated them and who, unintentionally, bestowed them on us.

The anticipation and desire of these hunters, these carnivores who arranged these images on these rocks, and their unsophisticated magic ordained these beautiful animals to carry the promise of carnage and quarry. An appetite for meat? Undoubtedly. We cannot think that the prehistorians have misled us. It is their duty to define the abyss that separates us from these men living at the dawn of time. It was up to them to determine the meaning of these figures and to tell us how they differ from the paintings we love. The images before us are the mirrors of a long-standing dream that passion pursues within us.

In vain we sought our dreams in these figures, which were a response, as the dreams of children often are, to the cravings of hunger. In Lascaux, we are unable to feel that which makes us dissolve when we look at a painting by Leonardo da Vinci, that which dictates that we have only one, rather vapid and ungraspable, notion — similar to the dispersed diversity of the universe — of the painter and the landscape, of the painted face, and of this gaze that drinks it in. These hunters of the Dordogne would better understand a housewife from Sarlat[1] buying meat for lunch from a butcher shop than they would Leonardo da Vinci, or those drowned eyes intoxicated by his painting. They skillfully simplified their representations of animals, and the world is no less rich for the large appetizing beasts that populate these walls. The cave paintings of Lascaux are beautiful, and we marvel at their state of preservation, but they only announce their author's desire to eat. Prehistoric man painted them before hunting,

[1] **Sarlat:** A modern village near the Lascaux cave.

Georges Bataille, *The Cradle of Humanity: Prehistoric Art and Culture*, ed. Stuart Kendall, trans. Michelle Kendall and Stuart Kendall (New York: Zone Books, 2005), 81–85. Originally published in *Arts*, no. 423 (August 7–13, 1953).

believing that the possession of the painted figure would ensure the possession of the actual animal represented.

What can oppose the cry of joy which alone has the power to correspond to the sight that has been waiting for us for a million years in Lascaux?

What shatters this is the illusion that across such a long period of time—the mind cannot imagine anything more distant—I recognize someone who resembles me. It is myself in fact that I think I recognize, myself and the marvelous world linked to the power to dream, a power common to myself and the earliest man. I may be wary of a feeling that runs counter to the conclusions of scholars. Yet could I abandon it before science, which has the burden of proving its assertions, which has clearly demonstrated its inanity?

The opinion according to which the first men, close to the animals and burdened by the difficulties of material life, would have been on the level of the most primitive men of today often passes as a response to the objectivity of history. For a long time, science has seemed linked to the idea of continuous progress, passing from wild animals to primitive man, who was himself still savage, and then finally to the fully civilized man, which we are.

In any case, we can know nothing essential about Leonardo da Vinci if we are not familiar with his paintings. This said, it is not necessarily easier to know his paintings than the paintings of Lascaux; at minimum, we can distinguish but a question of degree from one case to the other. I am not saying the communication coming to us from so profoundly distant a place as Lascaux has the same force as if it came from a time nearer to our own. But this is not clear. The cave paintings would have great power if we were not intimidated by the summons to reduce them to a work of magic, to a practical, utilitarian meaning, to the flat meaning of this poetic term. The most cautious prehistorians agree on this: the meaning that prehistoric man gave his figures does not mean that the Lascaux paintings are not, unintentionally, works of art. But for us, what does a work of art mean when it, not being destined for our eyes, was not intended as a work of art by those who made it?

Even the most inept figurations would have been effective as a work of magic—at least if the intention to go further were not implied. An extremely powerful communicative quality, beyond the end point of pure magic, was nonetheless able to fulfill the shared passion of the painter and of all those anticipating the work. There was nothing more mysterious in such qualities than in the unrest that emanates from the violence of a tom-tom, which even affects whites. Nothing more unintelligible. On this level (but only within these limitations), science ultimately has nothing to say. It can still talk about the figures that represent our feelings and impressions, about the conditions or circumstances related to the creation of the image. The impression itself, on the other hand, is beyond its grasp. We are reduced to explaining that impression by directly reproducing its cause (the painting) or, however awkwardly, searching within the order of words, or sounds, for the sources that suggest it.

The uneasiness that paralyzes us as we stand before and consider the figures of Lascaux ultimately leaves us with a weak and disappointed feeling and seems to be in opposition to the force of the impression actually felt. What pushes us, past the initial moment, to see in these paintings a world of only an unfortunate sense of need—impenetrable to us—is linked to our inability to find a complete response to our desire in an animal world. In our eyes, it is just an incomplete world. The conditions and circumstances linked to our strongest impressions and feelings never imprison us within this animal depth. At a very young age, we learned to see *what is lacking* in the animal and to designate with the word "beast" those among us whose lack of reason made us ashamed. This meeting in a Dordogne cave, given to us unintentionally from the depths of time by these hunters, could be disappointing if very quickly we did not see, in the tests it imposes on us, a way to set ourselves free. We have to free ourselves from all the human foolishness that prevents us from rediscovering ourselves and from establishing the most seductive contact between the simplest and the most complex beings—from the earliest humans to the most contemporary. Ultimately, since a deep similarity brings us closer to our forefathers, it would be enough to detach ourselves through the most complete and focused thought from this careful construction that distances us from these men who seemed to be related to animals, and who—science teaches us—felt remorse when they killed the animals that would give them nourishment. Lascaux asks us to no longer deny *what we are.* We denigrate the animality that, through the men of these obscure caves, who hid their humanity beneath animal masks, we have not ceased to prolong. We cannot stop being human, and we cannot forgo a rationality that only knows the limits of reason. Yet just as our forefathers felt remorse for killing the animals they loved — and had to kill — we could, in Lascaux, feel shame for being, through reason, slaves to the work that we must pursue at any price. Thus the cry of joy I mentioned becomes more strange and straggled, more gay.

Examining the Evidence

1. How does Bataille characterize the prehistorian's role in explaining the significance of these early paintings?
2. According to Bataille, can we interpret Lascaux's art in the same way we do European paintings such as those of da Vinci and Vermeer?
3. How do you interpret the author's assertion that "Lascaux asks us to no longer deny *what we are*"?

1.4 ETHNOGRAPHY AS A SOURCE OF HISTORICAL RESEARCH

Albert F. Calvert, *The Aborigines of Western Australia* (1894)

Until recently, many cultures in world history did not leave written records behind, even in times when other cultures were producing many writings. However, literate people often described nonliterate cultures when they encountered them, and these descriptions can help us in trying to understand these cultures. What follows is a description written by a British traveler to Australia, where he observed the hunter-gatherer lifestyle, long abandoned in his own country. The author, Albert F. Calvert (1872–1946), was a mining engineer who surveyed western Australia for its mineral resources when the country was still a British colony. Critical of other accounts of indigenous people, he wrote down some of his experiences for an audience of Victorian Englishmen. Although he shows great sympathy for the Australians, he also demonstrates many of his own society's prejudices.

A Description of Aboriginal Hunting and Gathering

The sympathies of travellers have been much wasted upon Aborigines, on the score of a supposed scarcity of food. As a rule they have an abundance, although they may run a little short in the height of the rainy season, or when they are overcome with laziness in very hot weather. The following list of articles, forming the food of the West Australian, is from the journal: "Six sorts of kangaroo, twenty-nine sorts of fish, one kind of whale, two species of seal, wild dogs, three kinds of turtle, emus, wild turkeys, two species of opossum, eleven kinds of frogs, four kinds of fresh water shell fish, every sort of sea shell fish, except oysters, four kinds of edible grubs, eggs of birds and lizards, five animals of the rabbit class, eight sorts of snakes, seven sorts of iguanas, nine species of mice and rats, twenty-nine sorts of roots, seven kinds of fungis, four sorts of gum, two sorts of manna, two species of by-yu, or the nut of the zamia palm, two species of mesembry and themum, two kinds of small nuts, four sorts of wild fruit, besides the seeds of several plants." The above can hardly be called a starvation bill of fare, although, of course, it does not look very appetizing to the European.

The equipment of the Blackboy consists of his kiley (boomerang), hatchet, and dow-uk (a short heavy stick), which are stuck in his belt of opossum fur; also his different spears for war and

Albert F. Calvert, *The Aborigines of Western Australia* (London: Simpkin, Marshall, Hamilton, Kent, 1894), 24–29.

chase — which, with his throwing stick, he carries in his hand. In the colder parts of the continent he sometimes wears a warm kangaroo skin cloak. He also occasionally carries a wooden shield, curving inward at the ends.

The wife, who always follows her lord at a respectful distance, is usually in heavy marching order. A long stick is carried in her hand, and a bag on her shoulders, in the top of which is placed any child who cannot walk. The other contents of this useful receptacle are numerous and heterogeneous, comprising the stock-in-trade of the family.

There will be a flat stone to pound roots with, pieces of quartz for making spears and knives with, and larger stones for hatchets. Prepared cakes of gum for making and mending weapons. Kangaroo sinews for manufacture of spears, and to sew with. The shell of a mussel to cut hair with, different small stone-knives, pipe clay, red and yellow ochre. These are a few of her belongings; and she likewise carries spare skins for cloaks, &c., between the bag and her sorely tried back. The natives are very skilful hunters, and it is an interesting and beautiful spectacle to watch one of these swarthy savages on the trail, with bright eye, and swift noiseless footsteps. Sometimes they join in company for the chase, which if kangaroo are hunted is "Yowart-a-Kaipoon."[1] These public battues[2] are governed by certain rules. The invitation issues from the native owner of the soil, and the first spear which strikes determines whose property the game is to be, no matter how slight the wound. The animals are surrounded, and each man has his position assigned; then the circle gradually closes in on the terrified creatures, but few of which escape.

The native hunting cries are wild and strange, always commencing with a hard consonant, such as "Kau," or "Koo-ee." They are thus audible much further than our "Hullo" or "Ho," beginning as the latter do with a soft aspirate. Kangaroos are also caught in nets, and pitfalls, and the hunter will sometimes follow up their tracks until they are so weary as to be approachable. This latter mode requires the very highest class of skill and the greatest

endurance; for which reason only a few of the most renowned sportsmen can perform the feat.

So far as their cooking is concerned they cannot exactly be considered epicures. Sometimes they roast the kangaroo whole in a pit which they dig for the purpose; and occasionally cut it up and broil the portion piecemeal. The blood, entrails, and marrow are considered delicacies, and as such are reserved for the head men of the tribe.

Of their fishing, our native friends are justly somewhat proud. The captures are effected in three different ways; spearing, entrapping in a weir, and netting. In the first method they show marvellous skill, whether in rivers or the sea. They scarcely ever miss their aim. Regarding the weirs they shew considerable sagacity in hitting upon the exact place; of course constructing them at low water.

Probably the greatest joy which a coast Native knows is the discovery of a stranded whale upon his property. As a rule he is very greedy over his food, not being greatly given to sharing it with others. Such unusual abundance, however, changes his whole nature. He lights fires, and invites his friends from near and far.

Then, I am sorry to say, a most disgusting orgie sets in. The host and guests continue feasting for weeks, knowing no regular meal times but literally continually cutting, and for ever coming to the attack again. The revellers have been known to stay by the mammoth's carcase long after it has become quite putrid, and even it is etiquette to present each guest at parting with an evil-smelling chunk, to convey to absent friends, whose urgent private affairs have kept them away from the delicious banquet.

Adult wild dog is occasionally eaten for a change, but puppies are an ever-welcome treat. As the dog is, however, with the blacks, as among the whites, frequently trained up to be the slave of man, the pups are often spared; and revolting as it appears to our notions, — wet nursed by the women of the family. Australia being the land of contraries, black swans and so forth, we need not be, perhaps, too much surprised at this approach to a reversal of the history of Romulus and Remus.

Like the leading citizens in a well known city, the West Australian native is a great admirer of the luscious turtle, and are not surpassed by the New

---

[1] **Yowart-a-Kaipoon:** Encircling a kangaroo.

[2] **public battues:** The beating of woods and bushes to flush out game.

Yorkers in their appreciation of terrapin.[3] The latter they cook whole, shell and all, in the ashes; then removing the bottom shell, the upper one serves as a dish. Most delicious of all, however, is accounted the emu, and hence it follows that heavy penalties are pronounced, by the law-makers of the nation, against any one eating this bird but themselves. I think I remember having heard that any sturgeon, caught in the Thames, belongs to the Lord Mayor of London, which would be a parallel case.

Cockatoos are considered another great delicacy, and are often killed with the boomerang. To see this strange weapon swooping wildly among a flock of these birds, — spinning, and whirling and slaying, — is one of the oddest sights imaginable.

One of the dexterous feats which Sir George Grey recounts is the killing of a bird as it flies from the nest. Two men are engaged in it, one of whom, placing himself under the nest, transfixes the latter with a spear. As a rule the creature is only frightened or very slightly wounded, and is slain by the unerring dow-uk of the other hunter as it quits the tree.

In opossum hunting the savage climbs the tree, which he notches into footholds as he proceeds; then either smokes or prods the animal out of his hole, when he seizes it by the tail and dashes it to the ground — always careful, however, to avoid being bitten.

Frog catching, when the swamps are partly dried up, is usually the duty or pastime of the women. It is no easy task, however, for while poking about with their long sticks in the mud, they are almost devoured with flies and mosquitos. This is pretty rough on these poor, wild, dusky damsels of the Desert.

---

[3] **terrapin:** A small turtle.

Grubs, which are extremely palatable, are procured from the grass tree; and likewise in an excrescence of the wattle tree. They are eaten either raw or roasted, but seem to be greatly improved by cooking. I am told they have a nut-like flavour, but I never had the courage to sample them.

In addition to their culinary duties the women have to dig for the various roots they dress for their husbands, and they become very expert in this occupation. When found the roots are sometimes pounded and mixed with a kind of earth, and sometimes roasted plain.

The By-yu nut is also collected and eaten with relish, which proves the great difference which exists between the Australian and European stomach, for so violent a cathartic is this nut, that some of Captain Cook's crew who ate it nearly paid for their experience with their lives. There is, however, a pulp which encases the inner kernel, which, after certain preparation, can be used as an agreeable and nutritious article of food. Besides those I have glanced at there are innumerable other native dishes, products of the earth and of the chase, with which I will not trouble my courteous reader.

Examining the Evidence

1. How does the author compare Aboriginal to European habits?
2. Does his description include a value judgment? If so, how?
3. How does Calvert describe men's roles and those of women?
4. What conclusions can you draw about the Aboriginal diet from this description? What does the description tell us about the Aboriginal Australian decision not to use agriculture?

MAKING CONNECTIONS

1. Although the writings collected here are of a varied nature, they all show a similar relationship to their subject of investigation. Describe that relationship.
2. How do these documents display the signs of the time in which they were written?
3. How confident do you feel about relying on these interpretations as a means of understanding the distant past? Which approaches do you feel are the most and least reliable, and why?

CHAPTER 2

Temples and Palaces: Birth of the City, 5000–1200 B.C.E.

Soon after they invented writing, the peoples of ancient Mesopotamia and Egypt started to produce written records that describe many aspects of life and that provide insight into their beliefs and customs. The examples presented here show concerns with issues of justice, peaceful interaction with neighboring states, and death. From the very beginning, the authors used various formats to express their thoughts, including poetry, letters, and official inscriptions on stone monuments. Vast amounts of these records have been recovered by modern archaeologists, who continue to enrich the body of knowledge with new finds.

2.1   THE KING GUARANTEES JUSTICE IN THE LAND

Hammurabi of Babylon, *The Law Code of Hammurabi* (c. 1755 B.C.E.)

The presence of the king by far dominates the historical record of ancient Mesopotamia and Egypt, which often recounts his military deeds, always portrayed as victories. Kings boasted about accomplishments in other areas of life as well, as they sought to present themselves as good rulers who provided for their subjects. One crucial royal contribution to society was a system of justice, and the most elaborate early statement about this subject derives from the reign of Hammurabi (r. 1792–1750 B.C.E.) of Babylon in the eighteenth century B.C.E. Hammurabi is rightly famous for his so-called law code, which he had carved on a large stone monolith. The list of his laws is incorporated in a longer statement in which the king explains when and why he issued them.

Prologue

When the august god Anu, king of the Anunnaku deities, and the god Enlil, lord of heaven and earth, who determines the destinies of the land, allotted supreme power over all peoples to the god Marduk, the firstborn son of the god Ea, exalted him among the Igigu deities, named the city of Babylon with its august name and made it supreme within the regions of the world, and established for him within it eternal kingship whose foundations are as fixed as heaven and earth, at that time, the gods Anu and Enlil, for the enhancement of the well-being of the people, named me by my name: Hammurabi, the pious prince who venerates the gods, to make justice prevail in the land, to abolish the wicked and the evil, to prevent the strong from oppressing the weak, to rise like the sun-god Shamash over all humankind, to illuminate the land.

I am Hammurabi, the shepherd, selected by the god Enlil, he who heaps high abundance and plenty, who perfects every possible thing for the city Nippur, (the city known as) band-of-heaven-and-earth, the pious provider of the Ekur temple; the capable king, the restorer of the city Eridu, the purifier of the rites of the Eabzu temple; the onslaught of the four regions of the world, who magnifies the reputation of the city Babylon, who gladdens the heart of his divine lord Marduk, whose days are devoted to the Esagil temple; . . . .

Scion of Sumu-la-el, mighty heir of Sîn-muballit, eternal seed of royalty, mighty king, solar disk of the city of Babylon, who spreads light over the lands of Sumer and Akkad, king who makes the four regions obedient, favored of the goddess Ishtar, am I,

When the god Marduk commanded me to provide just ways for the people of the land (in order to obtain) appropriate behavior, I established truth and justice as the declaration of the land, I enhanced the well-being of the people.

At that time:

Laws

§ 1: If a man accuses another man and charges him with homicide but cannot bring proof against him, his accuser shall be killed. . . .

§ 159 If a man who has the ceremonial marriage prestation brought to the house of his father-in-law, and who gives the bridewealth [marriage payment], should have his attention diverted to another woman and declare to his father-in-law, "I will not marry your daughter," the father of the daughter shall take full legal possession of whatever had been brought to him.

§ 160 If a man has the ceremonial marriage prestation brought to the house of his father-in-law and gives the bridewealth, and the father of the daughter then declares, "I will not give my daughter to you," he shall return twofold everything that had been brought to him.

§ 161 If a man has the ceremonial marriage prestation brought to the house of his father-in-law and gives the bridewealth, and then his comrade slanders him (with the result that) his father-in-law declares to the one entitled to the wife, "You will

Martha T. Roth, *Law Collections from Mesopotamia and Asia Minor*, 2d ed. *Writings from the Ancient World*, vol. 6 (Atlanta: Society of Biblical Literature, 1995), 71–140.

not marry my daughter," he shall return twofold everything that has been brought to him; moreover, his comrade will not marry his (intended) wife.

§ 162 If a man marries a wife, she bears him children, and that woman then goes to her fate, her father shall have no claim to her dowry; her dowry belongs only to her children.

§ 163 If a man marries a wife but she does not provide him with children, and that woman goes to her fate — if his father-in-law then returns to him the bridewealth that that man brought to his father-in-law's house, her husband will have no claim to that woman's dowry; her dowry belongs only to her father's house.

§ 164 If his father-in-law should not return to him the bridewealth, he shall deduct the value of her bridewealth from her dowry and restore (the balance of) her dowry to her father's house. . . .

Epilogue

These are the just decisions which Hammurabi, the able king, has established and thereby has directed the land along the course of truth and the correct way of life. . . .

In order that the mighty not wrong the weak, to provide just ways for the waif and the widow, I have inscribed my precious pronouncements upon my stela and set it up before the statue of me, the king of justice, in the city of Babylon, the city which the gods Anu and Enlil have elevated, within the Esagil, the temple whose foundations are fixed as are heaven and earth, in order to render the judgments of the land, to give the verdicts of the land, and to provide just ways for the wronged. . . .

Let any wronged man who has a lawsuit come before the statue of me, the king of justice, and let him have my inscribed stela read aloud to him, thus may he hear my precious pronouncements and let my stela reveal the lawsuit for him; may he examine his case, may he calm his (troubled) heart, (and may he praise me) saying:

"Hammurabi, the lord, who is like a father and begetter to his people, submitted himself to the command of the god Marduk, his lord, and achieved victory for the god Marduk everywhere. He gladdened the heart of the god Marduk, his lord, and he secured the eternal well-being of the people and provided just ways for the land."

May he say thus, and may he pray for me with his whole heart before the gods Marduk, my lord, and Zarpanitu, my lady. May the protective spirits, the gods who enter the Esagil temple, and the very brickwork of the Esagil temple, make my daily portents auspicious before the gods Marduk, my lord, and Zarpanitu, my lady.

May any king who will appear in the land in the future, at any time, observe my pronouncements of justice that I inscribed upon my stela. May he not alter the judgments that I rendered and the verdicts that I gave, nor remove my engraved image. If that man has discernment, and is capable of providing just ways for his land, may he heed the pronouncements I inscribed upon my stela, may that stela reveal for him the traditions, the proper conduct, the judgments of the land that I rendered, the verdicts of the land that I gave and may he, too, provide just ways for all humankind in his care. May he render their judgments, may he give their verdicts, may he eradicate the wicked and the evil from his land, may he enhance the well-being of his people.

I am Hammurabi, king of justice, to whom the god Shamash has granted (insight into) the truth. My pronouncements are choice, and my achievements are unrivaled; they are meaningless only to the fool, but to the wise they are praiseworthy.

Examining the Evidence

1. What accomplishments does Hammurabi stress in the Prologue of his code? How does he portray himself as a beneficent ruler?

2. The laws appear in a sequence so that particular areas of life are explored in successive paragraphs. What is the logic behind the sequence given here?

3. What is the king's relationship to the gods? How do you think this prolonged relationship affected how the public received them?

4. What is the code's purpose, according to the Epilogue?

Advice to Egyptian Scribes (Thirteenth to Twelfth Centuries B.C.E.)

The cultures of ancient Mesopotamia and Egypt were the first in world history in which some people knew how to write, a skill that remained limited to very few individuals within each culture. The earliest writings include texts in which literate skills are praised and in which youngsters learning to write are encouraged to pursue the career of scribe both because of the importance of the work scribes do and because the life of a scribe was much better than that of others, such as soldiers and farmers. The short passages translated here are exercises that apprentice scribes had to copy in order to learn their skills. The copies we have date to the thirteenth and twelfth centuries B.C.E., but the texts may have been composed centuries earlier. They show how aware scribes were of their special status in society.

Reminder of the Scribe's Superior Status

The overseer of the record-keepers of the treasury of Pharaoh, Amunemone speaks to the scribe Pentawere. This letter is brought to you saying: I have been told that you have abandoned writing and that you reel about in pleasures, that you have given your attention to work in the fields, and that you have turned your back on hieroglyphs. Do you not remember the condition of the field hand in the face of the registration of the harvest-tax, the snake having taken away half of the grain and the hippopotamus having eaten the remainder? The mice are numerous in the field, the locust descends, and the cattle eat. The sparrows bring want to the field hand. The remainder which is [on] the threshing floor is finished, and it is for the thieves. Its value in copper is lost, and the yoke of oxen is dead from threshing and ploughing. The scribe has moored (at) the riverbank. He reckons the tax, with the attendants bearing staffs and the Nubians rods of palm.

They [say]: Give the grain! There is none. They beat [him] vigorously. He is bound and cast into the well. They beat [him], drowning [him] head first, while his wife is bound in his presence. His children are manacled; his neighbors have abandoned them and fled. Their grain is gathered. But a scribe, he is the taskmaster of everyone. There is [no] taxing of the work of the scribe. He does not have dues. So take note of this.

Advice to the Youthful Scribe

O scribe, do not be idle, do not be idle, or you shall be curbed straightway. Do not give your heart to pleasures, or you shall fail. Write with your hand, recite with your mouth, and converse with those more knowledgeable than you. Exercise the office of magistrate, and then you will find it [advantageous] in old age. Fortunate is a scribe skilled in his office, the possessor of (a good) upbringing. Persevere in action daily, and you will gain mastery over them. Do not spend a day of idleness or you shall be beaten. The youth has a back and he hearkens to the beating of him. Pay attention. Hearken to what I have said. You will find it advantageous. One teaches apes [to] dance, and one tames horses. One can place a kite[1] in a nest, and a falcon can be caught by the wings. Persevere in conversation. Do not be idle. Write. Do not feel distaste.

The Hardships of the Soldier's Life

What is it that you say they relate, that the soldier's is more pleasant than the scribe's (profession)? Come, let me tell you the condition of the soldier, that much castigated one. He is brought while a child to be confined in the camp. A searing beating

---

[1] **kite:** A type of bird of prey.

---

is given his body, an open wound inflicted on his eyebrows. His head is split open with a wound. He is laid down and he is beaten like papyrus. He is struck with torments. Come, [let me relate] to you his journey to Khor[2] and his marching upon the hills. His rations and his water are upon his shoulder like the load of an ass, while his neck has been made a backbone like that of an ass. The vertebrae of his back are broken, while he drinks of foul water. He stops work (only) to keep watch. He reaches the battle, and he is like a plucked fowl. He proceeds to return to Egypt, and he is like a stick which the worm has devoured. He is sick, prostration overtakes him. He is brought back upon an ass, his clothes taken away by theft, his henchman fled. Scribe Inena, turn back from the saying that the soldier's is more pleasant than the scribe's (profession).

---

[2] **Khor:** Syria.

Dialogue Between a Mesopotamian Schoolboy and an Adult (Eighteenth Century B.C.E.)

As they were in Egypt, Mesopotamian scribes were also conscious of their special status in society. Among the texts they had to copy to acquire their skills were some that described the life of students. The text translated here is formulated as a dialogue between an adult and a young student, who is proud of his accomplishments. The text is written in the Sumerian language, the oldest recorded language in Mesopotamia, and discusses aspects of its study. The young student probably spoke Akkadian at home and learned Sumerian as the language of culture, law, and administration.

ADULT: Young man, are you a student?
SCHOOLBOY: Yes, I am a student.
ADULT: If you are a student, do you know Sumerian?
SCHOOLBOY: Yes, I can speak Sumerian.
ADULT: You are so young; how can you express yourself so well?
SCHOOLBOY: I have listened many times to my master's explanations and can answer you.

ADULT: You can answer me, but what do you write?
SCHOOLBOY: If you examine what I write, you will see that I have to spend less than three months more in school. I have already recited and written the Sumerian and Akkadian words of the list called *a-a me-me*. I have written all the lines of the list of people's names called *Inanna-tesh* and of the word list called *lu* = *shu*, even the outdated ones. I can show the signs, their writing, and meaning; that is how I express myself.[1]
ADULT: Follow me!
SCHOOLBOY: I will not do anything too complicated for you, but if one assigns me the list *lu* = *shu* for my homework, I can already give the order of 600 lines. My time schedule at school is as follows: I have three days of vacation each month, and three festival days each month; so I spend twenty-four days per month in school. That is not a long time. In one day the master gives me four writing exercises, so that my writing skills do not disappear. From now on, I have to calculate the entries on balanced accounts. . . . I know to write perfectly and am skilled at everything. When my master shows me a sign, I can add several others from memory. After having been to school for the period foreseen, I will be informed about Sumerian, writing, the contents of tablets, and the calculation of balanced accounts. And I can speak Sumerian.
ADULT: But the meaning of Sumerian is not clear to you!
SCHOOLBOY: I want to write these tablets:
Tablets that measure grain up to 180,000 quarts; tablets that use weights from a few ounces to 20 pounds; marriage contracts; business arrangements — I can deal with heavy weights; sales of houses, fields, and slaves; securities with silver and field rental agreements; contracts for the cultivation of date palm groves; even adoption contracts; I can write all those.

---

[1] *a-a me-me, Inanna-tesh,* and *lu* = *shu* are the names of texts that Mesopotamian scribal students of the eighteenth century B.C.E. had to be able to write out early on in their training.

Translation by Marc Van De Mieroop.

Examining the Evidence

1. What does the Mesopotamian student claim to have already mastered?
2. According to these texts, why are scribes so important for the proper functioning of society?
3. According to these documents, why is the life of a scribe superior to that of other professions?

2.3 MARRIAGE AS EARLIEST INTERNATIONAL DIPLOMACY

Kadashman-Enlil of Babylon, *The King of Babylonia Complains He Cannot Get an Egyptian Princess as Wife* (1350 B.C.E.)

States do not exist in isolation, and although ancient royal inscriptions may focus on the kings' military exploits, in reality kings interacted with their equivalent colleagues in peaceful ways such as through diplomacy. Such relations are well verified in the eastern Mediterranean world of the second half of the second millennium B.C.E., when a group of large territorial states coexisted. To create friendly relations, the royal houses regularly arranged diplomatic marriages in which a princess was sent to the royal court abroad. Ideally, there was an exchange, but, as revealed in the letters translated in this document set, the Egyptians had a special attitude. The following letter was found in the archives of the Egyptian capital at the time, but a Babylonian king sent it and it was written in cuneiform and in the Akkadian language.

[*Moreove*]r, you, my brother, when I wrote [to you] about marrying your daughter, in accordance with your practice of not gi[ving] (a daughter), [wrote to me], saying, "From time immemorial no daughter of the king of Egy[pt] is given to anyone." Why *n*[*ot*]? You are a king; you d[o] as you please. Were you to give (a daughter), who would s[ay] anything? Since I was told of this message, I wrote as follows *t*[*o my brother*], saying, "[*Someone's*] grown daughters, beautiful women, must be available. Send me a beautiful woman as if she were [you]r daughter. Who is going to say, 'She is no daughter of the king!'?" But holding to your decision, you have not sent me anyone. Did not you yourself seek brotherhood and amity, and so wrote me about marriage that we might come closer to each other, and did [not] I, for my part, write you about marriage for this very same reason, i.e., brotherhood and amity, that we might come closer to each other? Why, then, did my brother not send me just one woman? Should I, perhaps, since you did not send me a woman, refuse you a woman, just as you did to me, and *n*[*ot send her*]? But my daughters being available, I will not refuse [*one*] to y[ou]. . . .

And as to the gold I wrote you about, send me *whatever i*[*s on hand*], (as) much (as possible), before your messenger [*comes*] to me, right now, in all haste, this summer, either in the month of Tammuz [June–July] or in the month of Ab [July–August], so I can finish the work that I am engaged on. If during this summer, in the months of Tammuz or Ab, you send the gold I wrote you about, I will give you my daughter. So please send me the gold you [*feel prompted t*]o. But if in the months of Tammuz or Ab you do not send me the gold and (with it) I do not finish the work I am engaged on, what would be the point of your being pleased to send me (gold)? Once I have finished the work I am engaged on, what need will I have of gold? Then you could send me 3,000 talents of gold, and I would not accept it. I would send it back to you, and I would not gi[ve] my daughter in marriage.

William L. Moran, ed. and trans., *The Amarna Letters* (Baltimore, MD: Johns Hopkins University Press, 1992), 8–9.

Puduhepa of Hatti, *The Queen of the Hittites Explains Why Her Daughter Has Not Yet Gone to Egypt* (c. 1260 B.C.E.)

In the second half of the second millennium B.C.E., Akkadian was the language of diplomacy. Consequently, even those from courts who did not speak Akkadian used that language to correspond with one another. The letter translated here is from the Queen of the Hittites to King Ramesses of Egypt and discusses the marriage between him and one of her daughters, a major event intended to seal the peace agreement between two states that had been at war not long before. Queen Puduhepa explains to her future son-in-law why she could not yet send her daughter to him.

Thus says Puduhepa, the Great Queen of Hatti, to Ramesses, the Great King, King of Egypt, my brother.

My brother wrote to me as follows: "When your messengers came to me and brought me my sister's greetings and gifts, I was happy." When I heard this, I was pleased. I, the wife of your brother [i.e., Puduhepa wife of the Hittite king Hattusili III], enjoy a full life. May my brother also enjoy a full life! Send me gold and let them have lapis lazuli inlays. Moreover, my lands enjoy a full life; may your lands also enjoy full life! I sent my brother greetings and gifts. May my brother also enjoy a full life!

My brother wrote as follows: "My sister wrote: 'I will give you a daughter,' but you have withheld her and you are now angry with me. Why did you not give her?" I did indeed withhold her, but you cannot complain. You must accept it, as I cannot give her to you at this time, my brother. Don't I know the treasury of Hatti as well as you do, my brother? It is a burned-out building, and whatever was left of it Urhi-Teshub[1] gave to the Great God. Since Urhi-Teshub is there, you can ask him if that is true or false. To whom should I compare the

daughter of heaven and earth whom I will give to my brother? Should I compare her to the daughter of Babylonia, or of Zulabi, or of Assyria? I cannot connect her in any way to them, because she is above them. Doesn't my brother own anything? Only when the son of the Sun god, the son of the Storm god and the Sea have nothing, will you have nothing. Do you want to enrich yourself at my expense, my brother? That is not worthy of your good name and lordliness! . . .

I, the Queen, have taken women from Babylonia and Amurru for myself, and did they not bring me respect from the people of Hatti? That is why I did it. I took foreigners, daughters of great kings, as my daughters-in-law. When later on messengers, a brother, or a sister would come in splendor to my daughter-in-law, was that not a source of pride for me? Was there no woman available in Hatti? Did I not do this for my good name?

Does my brother have no wife at all? Did he not make the wedding proposal thinking of his and my good name? Did he not make the proposal in the same way as the King of Babylonia did? Did the latter not take in marriage a daughter of the Great King, the King of Hatti, the mighty king? If you say: "The King of Babylonia is not a Great King," you do not know the rank of Babylonia. . . .

I know now that Egypt and Hatti will become a single country. Even if there is no treaty with Egypt now, I, the Queen, know that you will conclude one in consideration of my dignity. The goddess who placed me here never denied me anything and she will not deny me happiness: you will take my daughter in marriage as my son-in-law.

Examining the Evidence

1. What type of relationship do the correspondents in these letters claim to have?
2. Is marriage the only subject discussed in these letters?
3. What is Egypt's objection to a diplomatic marriage with the Babylonian king, and what ruse does the king suggest to overcome the objection?
4. What is Puduhepa's explanation for not having sent her daughter to Ramesses?

---

[1] **Urhi-Teshub:** King before Puduhepa's husband, Hattusili III. When Hattusili III removed him from the throne, Urhi-Teshub found refuge in Egypt.

Translation by Marc Van De Mieroop.

2.4   THE EGYPTIAN CONCERN WITH DEATH

Unas Pyramid Texts (c. 2345 B.C.E.)

Ancient Egypt is famous for its funerary monuments, and its pyramids and other tombs are widely known. The Egyptians also expressed their concerns with the afterlife in their writings, and throughout their history they composed inscriptions and texts on papyri to assist the deceased after death. At the end of the Old Kingdom, the inside walls of royal pyramids contained inscriptions with spells intended to help the king reach his place with the sun god Re in the afterlife. The Egyptians believed many challenges confronted the king's body, including attacks by dangerous animals. There was also the question of ascending into heaven, which could happen in numerous ways: being ferried in a boat, flying upward, and climbing a ladder, among others. The pyramid texts, as they are now called, are very diverse spells, often with numerous variations on how the king could proceed. They developed over centuries before they were written down and were never merged into a coherent whole. The spells quoted here are all from the pyramid of King Unas, who died around 2345 B.C.E.

Spell 217[1]

The king joins the sun-god

Re-Atum, this Unas comes to you,
A spirit indestructible
Who lays claim to the place of the four pillars!
Your son comes to you, this Unas comes to you,
May you cross the sky united in the dark,
May you rise in lightland, the place in which you
    shine!

---

[1] The utterance consists of four parts. In each, the king announces his arrival in the sky to the sun god and commands a certain god, associated with the four cardinal points, to broadcast his coming to the four sides of the universe. The symmetry of the composition is heightened by repetitions and relieved by variations. [Original note.]

Seth, Nephthys, go proclaim to Upper Egypt's gods
And their spirits:
"This Unas comes, a spirit indestructible,
If he wishes you to die, you will die,
If he wishes you to live, you will live!"
Re-Atum, this Unas comes to you,
A spirit indestructible
Who lays claim to the place of the four pillars!
Your son comes to you, this Unas comes to you,
May you cross the sky united in the dark,
May you rise in lightland, the place in which you
    shine!
Osiris, Isis, go proclaim to Lower Egypt's gods
And their spirits:
"This Unas comes, a spirit indestructible,
Like the morning star above Hapy,
Whom the water-spirits worship;
Whom he wishes to live will live,
Whom he wishes to die will die!"

Re-Atum, this Unas comes to you,
A spirit indestructible
Who lays claim to the place of the four pillars!
Your son comes to you, this Unas comes to you,
May you cross the sky united in the dark,
May you rise in lightland, the place in which you
    shine!
Thoth,[2] go proclaim to the gods of the west
And their spirits:
"This Unas comes, a spirit indestructible,
Decked above the neck as Anubis,
Lord of the western height,
He will count hearts, he will claim hearts,
Whom he wishes to live will live,
Whom he wishes to die will die!"

---

[2] **Thoth:** A deity in the form of an ibis who transports the king to the afterlife.

Re-Atum, this Unas comes to you,
A spirit indestructible
Who lays claim to the place of the four pillars!
Your son comes to you, this Unas comes to you,
May you cross the sky united in the dark,
May you rise in lightland, the place in which you
    shine!
Horus, go proclaim to the powers of the east And
    their spirits:
"This Unas comes, a spirit indestructible,
Whom he wishes to live will live,
Whom he wishes to die will die!"

Re-Atum, your son comes to you,
Unas comes to you,
Raise him to you, hold him in your arms,
He is your son, of your body, forever!

Spell 263

The king crosses over to the eastern sky
The sky's reed-floats are launched for Re,
That he may cross on them to lightland;
The sky's reed-floats are launched for Harakhty,
That Harakhty may cross on them to Re;
The sky's reed-floats are launched for Unas,
That he may cross on them to lightland, to Re;
The sky's reed-floats are launched for Unas
That he may cross on them to Harakhty, to Re.

It is well with Unas and his *ka*,[3]
Unas shall live with his *ka*,
His panther skin is on him,
His staff in his arm, his scepter in his hand.
He subjects to himself those who have gone there,
They bring him those four elder spirits,
The chiefs of the sidelock wearers,
Who stand on the eastern side of the sky
Leaning on their staffs,
That they may tell this Unas's good name to Re,
Announce this Unas to Nehebkau,[4]
and greet the entry of this Unas.
Flooded are the Fields of Rushes
That Unas may cross on the Winding Water:[5]

Ferried is this Unas to the eastern side of lightland,
Ferried is this Unas to the eastern side of sky,
His sister is Sothis,[6] his offspring the dawn.

Spell 270

The king summons the ferryman
Awake in peace, you of back-turned face,[7] in peace,
You who looks backward, in peace,
Sky's ferryman, in peace,
Nut's ferryman, in peace,
Ferryman of gods, in peace!
Unas has come to you
That you may ferry him in this boat in which you
    ferry the gods.
Unas has come to his side as a god comes to his side,
Unas has come to his shore as a god comes to his
    shore.
No one alive accuses Unas,
No dead accuses Unas;
No goose accuses Unas,
No ox accuses Unas.[8]
If you fail to ferry Unas,
He will leap and sit on the wing of Thoth,
Then he will ferry Unas to that side!

Spell 304

The king climbs to the sky on a ladder
Hail, daughter of Anubis, above the hatches of
    heaven,
Comrade of Thoth, above the ladder's rails,
Open Unas's path, let Unas pass!
Hail, Ostrich on the Winding Water's shore,
Open Unas's path, let Unas pass!
Hail, four-horned Bull of Re,
Your horn in the west, your horn in the east,
Your southern horn, your northern horn:
Bend your western horn for Unas, let Unas pass!
"Are you a pure westerner?"[9]

---

[3] **ka**: Like the spirit, which separates from the body after death.
[4] **Nehebkau**: A serpent-shaped god who guards Re.

[5] **Winding Water:** Waters surrounding the place that the dead king needs to reach.
[6] **Sothis:** The goddess who personified the star Sirius.
[7] The ferryman is said to look backward because he needs to look in both directions to steer his ship.
[8] No human or animal can accuse Unas of having done something wrong.

"I come from Hawk City."[10]
Hail, Field of Offerings,
Hail to the herbs within you!
"Welcome is the pure to me!"

[9] The bull asks the king whether he is pure enough to deserve an afterlife.
[10] **Hawk City:** The royal residence.

Examining the Evidence

1. How does Unas portray his relationship to the gods?
2. What are the physical characteristics of the world that Unas tries to reach?
3. The spells explore many ways in which Unas can reach his proper place in the hereafter. Give some examples.

CONTRASTING VIEWS

CAN HUMANS ATTAIN IMMORTALITY?

2.5 | *THE EPIC OF GILGAMESH* **(EIGHTEENTH OR SEVENTEENTH CENTURY** B.C.E.**)**

Although the Egyptians focused on attaining an afterlife that was filled with comfort, the Mesopotamians wondered whether real immortality was possible. In their opinion, as in that of most ancient peoples, the primary distinction between gods and humans was that the gods were immortal whereas humans had to die. In this passage from an early version of *The Epic of Gilgamesh*, the tale's hero laments his best friend and companion, Enkidu, whose death he refused to accept. The female tavern keeper to whom he speaks explains to him why death is unavoidable and recommends how he should live with this certainty.

"[My friend, whom I loved so deeply,]
who with me went through every danger
Enkidu, whom I loved so deeply,
Who with me went through every danger:

"he went to the doom of mortal men.
Weeping over him day and night,
I did not surrender his body for burial—
'Maybe my friend will rise at my cry!'—

"For seven days and seven nights,
until a maggot dropped from his nostril.
After he was gone I did not find life,
wandering like a trapper in the midst of
   the wild.

"O, tavern-keeper, I have looked on your face,
but I would not meet death, that I fear
   so much."

Said the tavern-keeper to him, to Gilgamesh:
"O Gilgamesh, where are you wandering?

"The life that you seek you never will find:
when the gods created mankind,
death they dispensed to mankind,
life they kept for themselves.

"But you, Gilgamesh, let your belly be full,
enjoy yourself always by day and by night!
Make merry each day,
dance and play day and night!

"Let your clothes be clean,
Let your head be washed, may you bathe in water!
Gaze on the child who holds your hand,
let your wife enjoy your repeated embrace!

"For such is the destiny [*of mortal men,*]"

Andrew George, trans., *The Epic of Gilgamesh: The Babylonian Epic Poem and Other Texts in Akkadian and Sumerian* (London: Penguin Classics, 2000, repr. 2003), 123–124.

(continued)

CONTRASTING VIEWS *(continued)*

THE EPIC OF GILGAMESH (SEVENTH CENTURY B.C.E.)

The Epic of Gilgamesh explored the possibility that a human could become immortal like the gods, but only Uta-napishti, the survivor of the mythological flood that wiped out all of humankind, did so and under very exceptional circumstances. A later version of the epic, excerpted here, indicates alternative ways to achieve immortality and begins with a poem of praise to Gilgamesh, explaining how he became famous and would be remembered forever. It suggests multiple ways in which such fame could be obtained and how Gilgamesh ensured that his name would survive in human memory.

He who saw the Deep, the country's foundation,
[who] knew . . . was wise in all matters!
[Gilgamesh, who] saw the Deep, the country's
    foundation,
[who] knew . . . , was wise in all matters!

[He] . . . everywhere . . .
and [*learnt*] of everything the sum of wisdom.
He saw what was secret, discovered what was hidden,
he brought back a tale of before the Deluge.

He came a far road, was weary, found peace,
and set all his labours on a tablet of stone.
He built the rampart of Uruk-the-Sheepfold,
of holy Eanna, the sacred storehouse.

See its wall like a strand of *wool*,
view its parapet that none could copy!
Take the stairway of a bygone era,
draw near to Eanna, seat of Ishtar the goddess,
that no later king could ever copy!
Climb Uruk's wall and walk back and forth!
Survey   its   foundations,   examine   the
    brickwork!
Were its bricks not fired in an oven?
Did the Seven Sages[1] not lay its foundations?

[A square mile is] city, [a square mile] date-grove, a
    square mile is
clay-pit, half a square mile the temple of Ishtar:
[three square miles] and a half is Uruk's expanse.

[*See*] the tablet-box of cedar,
[*release*] its clasp of bronze!
[*Lift*] the lid of its secret,
[*pick*] *up* the tablet of lapis lazuli and read out
the travails of Gilgamesh, all that he went through.
Surpassing all other kings, heroic in stature,
brave scion of Uruk, wild bull on the rampage!
Going at the fore he was the vanguard,
going at the rear, one his comrades could trust!

A mighty bank, protecting his warriors,
a violent flood-wave, smashing a stone wall!
Wild bull of Lugalbanda, Gilgamesh, the perfect in
    strength,
suckling of the august Wild Cow, the goddess Ninsun![2]

Gilgamesh the tall, magnificent and terrible,
who opened passes in the mountains,
who dug wells on the slopes of the uplands,
and crossed the ocean, the wide sea to the sunrise;

who scoured the world ever searching for life,
and reached through sheer force Uta-napishti the
    Distant;
who restored the cult-centres destroyed by the
    Deluge,
and set in place for the people the rites of the cosmos.

Who is there can rival his kingly standing?
and say like Gilgamesh, "It is I am the king"?
Gilgamesh was his name from the day he was born,
two-thirds of him god and one third human.

---

[1] *Seven Sages:* Mythical creatures who had given the elements of culture to humanity in primordial times.

[2] Lugalbanda and Ninsun are the parents of Gilgamesh.

Andrew George, trans., *The Epic of Gilgamesh: The Babylonian Epic Poem and Other Texts in Akkadian and Sumerian* (London: Penguin Classics, 2000), 1–2, lines 1–48.

2.6	SARGON OF ASSYRIA, THE KING BOASTS OF HIS BUILDING A NEW CAPITAL CITY (C. 710 B.C.E.)

The following passage, from King Sargon II of Assyria who ruled in the late seventh century B.C.E., also shows how a mortal man can find eternal fame: his body may not be immortal but his name is. Wherever Mesopotamian kings commissioned a building project, they made sure that future generations would know who had been responsible for sponsoring and building the project. They did this by inscribing the buildings that they erected with the details of their involvement and accomplishments. These inscriptions became very elaborate over time and were often copied numerous times so that they would survive for other generations to read. Sargon's text here is unique because it describes how he planned not just a single building, but an entire city.

The wise king, full of kind thoughts, who focused his mind on the resettlement of the abandoned countryside, the cultivation of lands left fallow, and the planting of orchards, who conceived the idea of raising a crop on slopes so steep that nothing had grown there since time immemorial, whose heart caused him to cultivate desolate areas which earlier kings had not known how to plow, in order to hear the work song, to cause the springs of the surrounding area to flow, to open ditches, and to make the water of abundance rise like the sea, above and below. The king, with open mind, sharp of eye, in everything the equal of the Master (Adapa[1]), who became great in wisdom and intelligence, and grew in understanding—to provide the wide land of Assyria with food to satisfaction and well-being, as befitting a king through the filling of their canals, to save [the people] from want and hunger, so that (even) the beggar will not . . . at the bringing of the wine, and so no interruption may occur in the offerings of the sick, so that the oil of abundance, which soothes men, does not become expensive in my land, and that sesame be bought at the (same) price as barley, to provide sumptuous offerings, fitting for the tables of god and king, the price of every article had its limit fixed, day and night I planned to build that city.

I ordered the building of a temple for the god Shamash, the highest judge of the great gods, who allows me to reach my goals.

About the place called Magganubba, which is located at the foot of Mount Musri near a well, and stands like a tower in the neighborhood of the city of Nineveh, none of the 350 rulers, who before me exercised kingship over Assyria and who one after the other ruled the subjects of the god Enlil, realized how excellent a place it was, nor had they thought of settling it or ordered to build a canal there.

With my encompassing understanding, which at the command of the god Lugalabzu, the lord of wisdom is filled with insight and ingenious plans, and with my sharp intellect, which the goddess Ninmenanna the creator of the gods made much greater than that of my predecessors, I was focused day and night on settling that city. I ordered its construction to be a sanctuary for the great gods as well as a palace as the seat of my kingship.

Faithful to my name, which the great gods bestowed on me, to preserve law and justice, help the powerless to keep their rights and protect the weak from injustice, I paid the price for the fields where the city would be built in accordance with the sale documents of their owners in silver or bronze, and in order to avoid unpleasantness I gave those who did not want silver for their field, an equivalent field wherever they wanted it.

I raised my hands in prayer to the gods Sigga and Lugaldingirra, the judges of humankind. In order to stay in the city with happy heart and with cheerfulness forever, I raised my hands to the goddess Shaushga, the fearful one of Nineveh.

The sincere speech from my mouth as well as the finest oil that I gave them pleased the gods, my lords, and they ordered me to build that city and dig the canal.

I trusted their unalterable command, mobilized my subjects in large numbers, and made them carry spades and baskets.

In the month of the rising sun, the month of the son of Daragal who makes decisions and gives signals, the shining one of heaven and earth, the hero of the gods, of the moon god Sin, the month that the gods Anu, Enlil, and Ea Nishiku have designated as the month of the god Kulla because it is good for the making of bricks and the building of cities and houses, in this month, on the feast day of the

[1] **Adapa:** One of the primordial beings who brought elements of civilization to humankind.

Translation by Marc Van De Mieroop.

(continued)

son of Bel, the wise one, that is, of the god Nabu the scribe who knows every subject and rules all the gods, I had the first brick made.

To Kulla, the divine lord of foundations and bricks, and Mushda, the divine architect of the god Enlil, I brought animal sacrifices and other offerings and I prayed.

In the month Abu, the month when the fire god rises to transform the still green meadows, and when one lays the first brick of a city or a house, I made it foundations and gave them strong brickwork. . . .

Subjects from all four directions, with foreign tongues and languages without harmony, inhabitants of mountains as well as lowlands, over all of whom the light of the god, the lord of everything guards, those whom I had subjected to my rule at the command of the god Assur, my lord, I made of one mind and made them reside in the city. Native Assyrians, who are skilled in their professions, I set over them as supervisors and leaders to make them do the work properly, and to make them fear god and king.

The gods who live in heaven, on earth and in this city, agreed with my command and recognized the building of the city as a place to grow old.

Whoever would alter the work of my hands, make my images unrecognizable, removes the wall reliefs I had sculpted or dissolves my statues, Assur, Adad, and all the gods who live here, will eradicate his name and offspring from the land and will make him sit at the feet of his enemies in chains.

COMPARING THE EVIDENCE

1. In what way is the tavern keeper's speech to Gilgamesh very different in its approach to life from the other two passages?
2. Where do the later version of *The Epic of Gilgamesh* and King Sargon agree about the possibility of gaining immortal fame?
3. According to the introduction to the seventh-century B.C.E. version of the epic, in what other ways did Gilgamesh attain immortality?
4. Compare how the gods are portrayed in these texts.

MAKING CONNECTIONS

1. The authors and people who appear in the written sources of the distant past are not from every level of society or profession. Discuss what types of individuals are made known to us through these documents.
2. Why do these works feature individuals from higher orders of society?
3. Gods feature prominently in the texts translated here. Discuss in what contexts they exist and what roles they assume.

Settlers and Migrants: The Creation of States in Asia, 5000–500 B.C.E.

It is not until the late second millennium B.C.E. that we find written materials from the cultures of South and East Asia. The late Shang dynasty in China (c. 1200–1050 B.C.E.) produced a large set of inscriptions on bones that is concerned with predictions of future events. In both China and South Asia, people also composed poems and sayings that often were recorded in writing many centuries later. Although the versions known to us may have been altered to appeal to a later audience when they were written down, they do provide insights into the lives of the people of the early Asian states.

3.1   UNDECIPHERED WRITING

Indus Valley Clay Tablet (2600–1900 B.C.E.)

Unfortunately, the script of the earliest literate culture of South Asia, the Indus Valley culture, is still undeciphered, and historians can use the written evidence only as additional examples of material culture. However, the remains still tell us much about the concerns of the people who created them. The object represented here was found at Mohenjo-Daro. It is a three-sided clay tablet, 1¾ inches long and 7/16 of an inch wide, decorated on all sides. Two sides contain imagery: a boat with birds perched on it and a crocodile with a fish in its mouth. The third side contains eight signs of the Indus Valley script.

Examining the Evidence

1. What sphere of human activity does the imagery on this object reflect?
2. Describe the signs of the Indus Valley script.
3. What might the function of this object have been?

Copyright J. M. Kenoyer/Harappa.com. Courtesy Department of Archaeology and Museums. Government of Pakistan.

3.2 SACRED KNOWLEDGE

Hymns from *The Rig Veda* (1500–900 B.C.E.)

The oldest literary compositions of India after the Indus Valley culture are the Vedas, a collection of hymns, prayers, and songs. They were at first created orally between 1500 and 900 B.C.E., and priests wrote them down, starting at around 600 B.C.E. We do not know the names of any of the authors, and scholars have very different opinions about when the Vedas were first composed. The Vedas contain elements of the earliest Indian culture, but these may have been adapted to later tastes when they were recorded in writing. *The Rig Veda* is a collection of hymns that concern many different subjects. We provide a small selection of them here that deals with creation (which in *The Hymn of Man* involved sacrificing the cosmic giant, Purusha, the primeval man), the horse sacrifice, and the goddess of the night.

Creation Hymn (10.129)

1. There was neither non-existence nor existence then; there was neither the realm of space nor the sky which is beyond. What stirred? Where? In whose protection? Was there water, bottomlessly deep?

2. There was neither death nor immortality then. There was no distinguishing sign of night nor of day.[1] That one breathed, windless, by its own impulse. Other than that there was nothing beyond.

3. Darkness was hidden by darkness in the beginning; with no distinguishing sign, all this was water. The life force that was covered with emptiness, that one arose through the power of heat.

4. Desire came upon that one in the beginning; that was the first seed of mind. Poets seeking in their heart with wisdom found the bond of existence in non-existence.

5. Their cord was extended across. Was there below? Was there above? There were seed-placers; there were powers. There was impulse beneath; there was giving-forth above.

6. Who really knows? Who will here proclaim it? Whence was it produced? Whence is this creation? The gods came afterwards, with the creation of this universe.[2] Who then knows whence it has arisen?

7. Whence this creation has arisen — perhaps it formed itself, or perhaps it did not — the one who looks down on it, in the highest heaven, only he knows — or perhaps he does not know.

Purusha-Sukta, or The Hymn of Man (10.90)

1. The Man has a thousand heads, a thousand eyes, a thousand feet. He pervaded the earth on all sides and extended beyond it as far as ten fingers.

2. It is the Man who is all this, whatever has been and whatever is to be. He is the ruler of immortality, when he grows beyond everything through food.

3. Such is his greatness, and the Man is yet more than this. All creatures are a quarter of him; three quarters are what is immortal in heaven.

4. With three quarters the Man rose upwards, and one quarter of him still remains here. From this[3] he spread out in all directions, into that which eats and that which does not eat.

5. From him Viraj[4] was born, and from Viraj came the Man. When he was born, he ranged beyond the earth behind and before.

6. When the gods spread the sacrifice with the Man as the offering, spring was the clarified butter, summer the fuel, autumn the oblation.

[1] There was no distinction between night and day.

[2] The gods cannot have been the source of creation, as they came after creation.

[3] That is, the quarter still remaining on earth.

[4] **Viraj:** The active female creative principle.

The Rig Veda: An Anthology, trans. Wendy Doniger O'Flaherty (Harmondsworth, UK: Penguin Books, 1981).

7. They anointed the Man, the sacrifice born at the beginning, upon the sacred grass. With him the gods, Sadhyas,[5] and sages sacrificed.

8. From that sacrifice in which everything was offered, the melted fat was collected, and he[6] made it into those beasts who live in the air, in the forest, and in villages.

9. From that sacrifice in which everything was offered, the verses and chants were born, the metres were born from it, and from it the formulas were born.

10. Horses were born from it, and those other animals that have two rows of teeth; cows were born from it, and from it goats and sheep were born.

11. When they divided the Man, into how many parts did they apportion him? What do they call his mouth, his two arms and thighs and feet?

12. His mouth became the Brahmin; his arms were made into the Warrior, his thighs the People, and from his feet the Servants were born.

13. The moon was born from his mind; from his eye the sun was born. Indra and Agni[7] came from his mouth, and from his vital breath the Wind was born.

14. From his navel the middle realm of space arose; from his head the sky evolved. From his two feet came the earth, and the quarters of the sky from his ear. Thus they[8] set the worlds in order.

15. There were seven enclosing-sticks[9] for him, and thrice seven fuel-sticks, when the gods, spreading the sacrifice, bound the Man as the sacrificial beast.

16. With the sacrifice the gods sacrificed to the sacrifice. These were the first ritual laws. These very powers reached the dome of the sky where dwell the Sadhyas, the ancient gods.

The Sacrifice of the Horse (1.162)

1. Mitra, Varuna, Aryaman the Active, Indra the ruler of the Rbhus,[10] and the Maruts[11] — let them not fail to heed us when we proclaim in the assembly the heroic deeds of the racehorse who was born of the gods.

2. When they lead the firmly grasped offering in front of the horse that is covered with cloths and heirlooms, the dappled goat goes bleating straight to the dear dwelling of Indra and Pushan.[12]

3. This goat for all the gods is led forward with the racehorse as the share for Pushan. When they lead forth the welcome offering with the charger, Tvastr[13] urges him on to great fame.

4. When, as the ritual law ordains, the men circle three times, leading the horse that is to be the oblation on the path to the gods, the goat who is the share for Pushan goes first, announcing the sacrifice to the gods.

5. The Invoker, the officiating priest, the atoner, the fire-kindler, the holder of the pressing-stones, the reciter, the priest who prays—fill your bellies with this well-prepared, well-sacrificed sacrifice.

6. The hewers of the sacrificial stake and those who carry it, and those who carve the knob for the horse's sacrificial stake, and those who gather together the things to cook the charger — let their approval encourage us.

7. The horse with his smooth back went forth into the fields of the gods, just when I made my prayer. The inspired sages exult in him. We have made him a welcome companion at the banquet of the gods.

8. The charger's rope and halter, the reins and bridle on his head, and even the grass that has been brought up to his mouth — let all of that stay with you[14] even among the gods.

9. Whatever of the horse's flesh the fly has eaten, or whatever stays stuck to the stake or the axe, or to the hands or nails of the slaughterer — let all of that stay with you even among the gods.

10. Whatever food remains in his stomach, sending forth gas, or whatever smell there is from his raw flesh — let the slaughterers make that well done; let them cook the sacrificial animal until he is perfectly cooked.

[5] **Sadhyas:** A class of demigods or saints.
[6] The Creator of Purusha.
[7] **Agni:** Fire god.
[8] The gods.
[9] Sticks around the fireplace.
[10] **Rbhus:** The craftsmen of the gods.
[11] **Maruts:** Storm gods, companions of Indra.
[12] **Pushan:** Charioteer of the sun.
[13] **Tvastr:** Artisan of the gods.
[14] Here the horse is directly addressed.

11. Whatever runs off your body when it has been placed on the spit and roasted by the fire, let it not lie there in the earth or on the grass, but let it be given to the gods who long for it.

12. Those[15] who see that the racehorse is cooked, who say, "It smells good! Take it away!", and who wait for the doling out of the flesh of the charger — let their approval encourage us.

13. The testing fork for the cauldron that cooks the flesh, the pots for pouring the broth, the cover of the bowls to keep it warm, the hooks, the dishes — all these attend the horse.

14. The place where he walks, where he rests, where he rolls, and the fetters on the horse's feet, and what he has drunk and the fodder he has eaten — let all of that stay with you even among the gods.

15. Let not the fire that reeks of smoke darken you, nor the red-hot cauldron split into pieces. The gods receive the horse who has been sacrificed, worshipped, consecrated, and sanctified with the cry of "Vasat!"[16]

16. The cloth that they spread beneath the horse, the upper covering, the golden trappings on him, the halter and the fetters on his feet — let these things that are his own bind the horse among the gods.

17. If someone riding you has struck you too hard with heel or whip when you shied, I make all these things well again for you with prayer, as they do with the oblation's ladle in sacrifices.

18. The axe cuts through the thirty-four ribs of the racehorse who is the companion of the gods. Keep the limbs undamaged and place them in the proper pattern. Cut them apart, calling out piece by piece.

19. One is the slaughterer of the horse of Tvastr; two restrain him. This is the rule. As many of your limbs as I set out, according to the rules, so many balls I offer into the fire.

20. Let not your dear soul burn you as you go away. Let not the axe do lasting harm to your body. Let no greedy, clumsy slaughterer hack in the wrong place and damage your limbs with his knife.

21. You do not really die through this, nor are you harmed. You go to the gods on paths pleasant to go on. The two bay stallions, the two roan mares[17] are now your chariot mates. The racehorse has been set in the donkey's yoke.

22. Let this racehorse bring us good cattle and good horses, male children and all-nourishing wealth. Let Aditi[18] make us free from sin. Let the horse with our offerings achieve sovereign power for us.

Night (10.127)

1. The goddess Night has drawn, near looking about on many sides with her eyes.[19] She has put on all her glories.

2. The immortal goddess has filled the wide space, the depths and the heights. She stems the tide of darkness with her light.

3. The goddess has drawn near, pushing aside her sister the twilight. Darkness, too, will give away.

4. As you came near to us today, we turned homeward to rest, as birds go to their home in a tree.

5. People who live in villages have gone home to rest, and animals with feet, and animals with wings, even the ever-searching hawks.

6. Ward off the she-wolf and the wolf; ward off the thief. O night full of waves, be easy for us to cross over.

7. Darkness — palpable, black, and painted — has come upon me. O Dawn, banish it like a debt.

8. I have driven this hymn to you as the herdsman drives cows. Choose and accept it, O Night, daughter of the sky, like a song of praise to a conqueror.

Examining the Evidence

1. Through various paradoxes, the first hymn describes conditions prior to creation. What are those paradoxes?
2. How does the second hymn portray the creation of humans? How does it justify the existing social order?

---

[15] The priests who see the horse.

[16] **"Vasat!":** Cry that is made when the offering is presented to the gods.

[17] Two bay stallions are the horses of Indra, the two roan (a solid coat color interspersed with white hairs) mares are the horses of the Maruts, and the donkey belongs to the twin sons of the sun.

[18] **Aditi:** The female principle of creation.

[19] The stars.

3. In early Indian society, the horse sacrifice was a royal prerogative. How does the third hymn portray the actions involved?

4. The imagery of the hymns derives from the lifestyle of the people who composed them. What lifestyle does the fourth hymn portray?

3.3 A VEDIC VIEW ON THE ROLE OF WOMEN

The Laws of Manu (c. 100 B.C.E.–200 C.E.)

The Laws of Manu, though written down in the first century B.C.E., was a product of India's Vedic age. Hindu tradition ascribes the laws to Manu, the legendary ancestor of humankind and a great sage, but the actual author or authors and the time of composition remain unknown. In this text, Manu reveals his laws through lectures to a group of ten seers who asked him to reveal the sacred laws of each of the four chief castes (*varna*) (Chapter 1, verse 2). The entire work contains twelve chapters, with a total of 2,694 statements. The extracts provided here concern the relationship between women and men.

Chapter III, 55–62

55. Women must be honoured and adorned by their fathers, brothers, husbands, and brothers-in-law, who desire (their own) welfare.

56. Where women are honoured, there the gods are pleased; but where they are not honoured, no sacred rite yields rewards.

57. Where the female relations live in grief, the family soon wholly perishes; but that family where they are not unhappy ever prospers.

58. The houses on which female relations, not being duly honoured, pronounce a curse, perish completely, as if destroyed by magic.

59. Hence men who seek (their own) welfare, should always honour women on holidays and festivals with (gifts of) ornaments, clothes, and (dainty) food.

60. In that family, where the husband is pleased with his wife and the wife with her husband, happiness will assuredly be lasting.

61. For if the wife is not radiant with beauty, she will not attract her husband; but if she has no attractions for him, no children will be born.

62. If the wife is radiant with beauty, the whole house is bright; but if she is destitute of beauty, all will appear dismal.

Chapter IX, 1–25

1. I will now propound the eternal laws for a husband and his wife who keep to the path of duty, whether they be united or separated.

2. Day and night woman must be kept in dependence by the males (of) their (families), and, if they attach themselves to sensual enjoyments, they must be kept under one's control.

3. Her father protects (her) in childhood, her husband protects (her) in youth, and her sons protect (her) in old age; a woman is never fit for independence.

4. Reprehensible is the father who gives not (his daughter in marriage) at the proper time; reprehensible is the husband who approaches not (his wife in due season), and reprehensible is the son who does not protect his mother after her husband has died.

5. Women must particularly be guarded against evil inclinations, however trifling (they may appear); for, if they are not guarded, they will bring sorrow on two families.

6. Considering that the highest duty of all castes, even weak husbands (must) strive to guard their wives.

7. He who carefully guards his wife, preserves (the purity of) his offspring, virtuous conduct, his family, himself, and his (means of acquiring) merit.

The Laws of Manu, trans. Georg Bühler (1886; repr., New York: Dover, 1969).

8. The husband, after conception by his wife, becomes an embryo and is born again of her; for that is the wifehood of a wife (gâyâ), that he is born (gâate) again by her.

9. As the male is to whom a wife cleaves,[1] even so is the son whom she brings forth; let him therefore carefully guard his wife, in order to keep his offspring pure.

10. No man can completely guard women by force; but they can be guarded by the employment of the (following) expedients:

11. Let the (husband) employ his (wife) in the collection and expenditure of his wealth, in keeping (everything) clean, in (the fulfillment of) religious duties, in the preparation of his food, and in looking after the household utensils.

12. Women, confined in the house under trustworthy and obedient servants, are not (well) guarded; but those who of their own accord keep guard over themselves, are well guarded.

13. Drinking (spirituous liquor), associating with wicked people, separation from the husband, rambling abroad, sleeping (at unseasonable hours), and dwelling in other men's houses, are the six causes of the ruin of women.

14. Women do not care for beauty, nor is their attention fixed on age; (thinking), "(It is enough that) he is a man," they give themselves to the handsome and to the ugly.

15. Through their passion for men, through their mutable temper, through their natural heartlessness, they become disloyal towards their husbands, however carefully they may be guarded in this (world).

16. Knowing their disposition, which the Lord of creatures laid in them at the creation, to be such, (every) man should most strenuously exert himself to guard them.

17. (When creating them) Manu allotted to women (a love of their) bed, (of their) seat and (of) ornament, impure desires, wrath, dishonesty, malice, and bad conduct.

18. For women no (sacramental) rite (is performed) with sacred texts, thus the law is settled; women (who are) destitute of strength and destitute of (the knowledge of) Vedic texts, (are as impure as) falsehood (itself), that is a fixed rule.

19. And to this effect many sacred texts are sung also in the Vedas, in order to (make) fully known the true disposition (of women); hear (now those texts which refer to) the expiation of their (sins).

20. "If my mother, going astray and unfaithful, conceived illicit desires, may my father keep that seed from me," that is the scriptural text.

21. If a woman thinks in her heart of anything that would pain her husband, the (above-mentioned text) is declared (to be a means for) completely removing such infidelity.

22. Whatever be the qualities of the man with whom a woman is united according to the law, such qualities even she assumes, like a river (united) with the ocean.

23. Akshamâlâ, a woman of the lowest birth, being united to Vasishtha and Sârangî (being united) to Mandapâla, became worthy of honour.[2]

24. These and other females of low birth have attained eminence in this world by the respective good qualities of their husbands.

25. Thus has been declared the ever pure popular usage (which regulates the relations) between husband and wife; hear (next) the laws concerning children which are the cause of happiness in this world and after death.

Examining the Evidence

1. According to Chapter III, how should male members of the household treat women?
2. What would you conclude about the status of women from reading this chapter alone?
3. What are a woman's duties according to *The Laws of Manu*, and (from reading only this chapter) what behavior should women avoid?

---

[1] **cleaves:** To adhere closely and to remain faithful.

[2] This refers to a story found in the *Mahabharata* ("Great Epic of the Bharata Dynasty").

3.4 THE EARLIEST EVIDENCE OF CHINESE WRITING

Oracle Bones (c. 1200–1050 B.C.E.)

The late Shang court (c. 1200–1050 B.C.E.) left behind some 150,000 oracle bone fragments, most of which were excavated in the cult center near modern-day Anyang. They were used to communicate with spiritual forces that could provide guidance on such things as how to behave, whether to make offerings to spirits of the deceased, or to go to war on a specific day. Most of the following examples are from the reign of the twenty-first king, Wu Ding (c. 1200–1181 B.C.E.), the period from which most bone inscriptions, covering the widest array of topics, are preserved. Many of the questions appear in pairs, both in the positive and negative form, and are placed in matching opposition on the bone.

Sacrifices and Rituals

[A] [Preface:] Divined: [Charge:] "[We] should offer to Xiang Jia, Father Geng, and Father Xin [the seventeenth, eighteenth, and nineteenth kings], one cow."

[B] [Preface:] Divined: [Charge:] "[We] should not offer to Xiang Jia, Father Geng, and Father Xin, one cow."

Mobilizations

[Preface:] Crack-making on *dingyou* [day 34], Que divined: [Charge:] "This season, the king raises five thousand men to campaign against the Tufang; he will receive assistance in this case." [Postface:] Third moon.

Military Campaigns

[A] Divined: "It should be Zhi Guo whom the king joins to attack the Bafang, [for if he does] Di[1] will [confer assistance] on us."

[B] "It should not be Zhi Guo whom the king joins to attack the Bafang [for if he does] Di may not [confer assistance] on us."

Meteorological Phenomena

[A] [Preface:] Crack-making on *bingshen* [day 33], Que divined: [Charge:] "On the coming *yisi* [day 42], [we] will perform the *you*-ritual to Xia Yi [the twelfth king]." [Prognostication:] The king read the cracks and said: "When [we] perform the *you*-ritual there will be occasion for calamities; there may be thunder." [Verification:] On *yisi* [day 42], [we] performed the *you*-ritual. At dawn it rained; at the beheading sacrifice it stopped raining; when the beheading sacrifice was all done, it likewise rained; when [we] displayed [the victims] and split them open, it suddenly cleared.

[B] [Verification:] In the night of *yisi* [day 42] there was thunder in the west.

Agriculture

[A] [Preface:] Crack-making on [*bing-*]*chen* [day 53], Que divined: [Charge:] "We will receive millet harvest."

[B] [Preface:] Crack-making on [*bing-*]*chen* [day 53], Que divined: [Charge:] "We may not receive millet harvest." (Postface:) Fourth moon.

[C] [Prognostication:] The king read the cracks and said: "Auspicious. We will receive this harvest."

Sickness

Divined: "There is a sick tooth; it is not Father Yi [the twentieth king, Wu Ding's father] who is harming [it]."

Childbirth

[A] [Preface:] Crack-making on *jiashen* [day 21], Que divined: [Charge:] "Lady Hao [a consort of Wu Ding] will give birth and it will be

---

[1] **Di:** The high god of the Shang.

David N. Keightley, "Shang Oracle-Bone Inscriptions," *Paleographic Sources of Early China*, ed. Edward L. Shaughnessy (Hong Kong: Chinese University Press, 1993).

good." [Prognostication:] The king read the cracks and said: "If it be on a *ding* day that she give birth, it will be good. If it be on a *geng* day that she give birth, it will be prolonged auspiciousness." [Verification:] [After] thirty-one days, on *jiayin* [day 51], she gave birth. It was not good. It was a girl.

[B] [Preface:] Crack-making on *jiashen* [day 21], Que divined: [Charge:] "Lady Hao will give birth and it may not be good." [Verification:] [After] thirty-one days, on *jiayin* [day 51], she gave birth. It really was not good. It was a girl.

Disaster, Distress, or Trouble

[A] Crack-making on *jiashen* [day 21], Zheng divined: "This rain will be disastrous for us."

[B] Divined: "This rain will not be disastrous for us."

Dreams

[A] Crack-making on *jichou* [day 26], Que divined: "The king's dream was due to Ancestor Yi."

[B] Divined: "The king's dream was not due to Ancestor Yi."

Settlement Building

[A] Crack-making on *renzi* [day 49], Zheng divined: "If we build a settlement, Di will obstruct [but] approve." Third moon.

[B] Crack-making on *guichou* [day 50], Zheng divined: "If we do not build a settlement, Di will approve."

Orders

Crack-making on [*jia*]*wu* [day 31], Bin divined: "It should be Lady Hao whom the king orders to campaign against the Yi."

Tribute Payments

[Marginal notation:] Wo brought in one thousand [shells]; Lady Jing [a consort of Wu Ding] ritually prepared forty of them. [Recorded by the diviner] Bin.

Divine Assistance or Approval

[A] Crack-making on *xinchou* [day 38], Que divined: "Di approves the king."

[B] Divined: "Di does not approve the king."

Requests to Ancestral or Nature Powers

Crack-making on *xinhai* [day 48], Gu divined: "In praying for harvest to Yue [a mountain spirit], [we] make a burnt offering of three small penned sheep [and] split open three cattle." Second moon.

The Night or the Day

[A] Crack-making on *renshen* [day 9], Shi divined: "This night there will be no disasters."

[B] Divined: "This night it will not rain." Ninth moon.

Hunting Expeditions and Excursions

On *renzi* [day 49] the king made cracks and divined: "[We] hunt at Zhi; going and coming back there will be no harm." [Prognostication:] The king read the cracks and said: "Prolonged auspiciousness." [Verification:] This was used. [We] caught forty-one foxes, eight *mi*-deer, one rhinoceros.

The Ten-Day Week

[A] On *guichou* [day 50], the king made cracks and divined: "In the [next] ten days, there will be no disasters." [Prognostication:] The king read the cracks and said: "Auspicious."

[B] On *guihai* [day 60], the king made cracks and divined: "In the [next] ten days, there will be no disasters." [Prognostication:] The king read the cracks and said: "Auspicious."

Examining the Evidence
1. Identify the various formats that the oracle bone inscriptions use.
2. What is the role of the king?
3. What is the role of Di?
4. What concerns do the oracle questions address?

3.5 LIFE IN EARLY CHINA

The Book of Songs (c. 1027–771 B.C.E.)

More than half of the 305 poems of *The Book of Songs* seem to have their origins in popular songs and reflect the concerns of ordinary people in the early Zhou period (1027–771 B.C.E.). Other songs are court poems that praise the founders of the Zhou dynasty; however, they also complain about the decay of royal power. The poems have fairly strict patterns in both rhyme and rhythm, they make great use of imagery, and they tend to be short. As one of the most revered of the Confucian classics, this collection of poems has been studied and memorized by scholars for centuries. They regarded the popular songs as good keys to understanding the troubles of the common people, and they often read them allegorically, for example, taking complaints against faithless lovers as protests against faithless rulers.

> Please, Zhongzi,
> Do not climb into our hamlet,
> Do not break our willow trees.
> It's not that I begrudge the willows,
> But I fear my father and mother.
> You I would embrace,
> But my parents' words —
> Those I dread.
>
> Please, Zhongzi,
> Do not leap over our wall,
> Do not break our mulberry trees.
> It's not that I begrudge the mulberries,
> But I fear my brothers.
> You I would embrace,
> But my brothers' words —
> Those I dread.
>
> Please, Zhongzi,
> Do not climb into our yard,
> Do not break our rosewood tree.
> It's not that I begrudge the rosewood,
> But I fear gossip.

> You I would embrace,
> But people's words —
> Those I dread.
>
> * * *
>
> In the seventh month the Fire star declines.
> In the ninth month we give out the clothes.
> In the days of the first, rushing winds.
> In the days of the second, bitter cold.
> Without coats and garments,
> How could we finish the year?
> In the days of the third, we plow.
> In the days of the fourth, we step out.
> Our wives and children
> Bring food to us in the southern field,
> And the inspector of the fields is pleased.
>
> In the seventh month the Fire star declines.
> In the ninth month we give out the clothes.
> Spring days are sunny
> And the oriole sings.
> The girls take their fine baskets,
> And walk down the little paths
> To collect the tender mulberry leaves.
> Spring days get longer,
> In groups they go to pick the Artemesia.
> A young girl is heart-sick,
> Waiting to go home with the lord's son.
>
> In the seventh month the Fire star declines.
> In the eighth month the rushes are ready.
> In the silkworm month, we prune the mulberry trees.
> We take axes and hatchet
> To cut off the far and high branches
> And make the small mulberry luxuriant.
> In the seventh month the shrike cries.
> In the eighth month we splice the thread,
> Both black and yellow.
> With red dye very bright
> We make a robe for the lord's son.

Patricia Buckley Ebrey, ed., *Chinese Civilization: A Sourcebook*, 2d ed. (New York: Free Press, 1993), 3–5.

In the fourth month the grasses mature.
In the fifth month the cicada sings.
In the eighth month the crops are gathered,
In the tenth month the leaves fall.
In the days of the first we hunt badgers.
We catch foxes and wildcats.
We make furs for the lord's son.
In the days of the second we assemble
To practice the military arts.
We keep for ourselves the young boars
And give to the lord the old ones.

In the fifth month the locusts move their legs.
In the sixth month the grasshoppers shake their
     wings.
In the seventh month, the insects are out in the
     meadows.
In the eighth month, they are under the roof.
In the ninth month, they are at the door.
In the tenth month, the crickets are under our beds.
We stop up the holes to smoke out the rats.
We seal the northern window and plaster shut the
     door.
Come, wife and children,
The new year is starting,
Let's move into this house.

In the sixth month we eat fruits and berries.
In the seventh month we cook vegetables and
     beans.
In the eighth month we pick dates.
In the tenth month we harvest rice.
We use it to make spring wine
As a tonic for long life.
In the seventh month we eat melons.
In the eighth month we split the gourds.
In the ninth month we harvest the hemp seed.
We gather herbs and firewood.
And we feed our farmworkers.

In the ninth month we make the garden into a
     threshing ground.
In the tenth month we bring in the harvest.
Millet of all varieties,
Rice and hemp, beans and wheat.
Oh, farmworkers,
The harvest is collected;
Come up to work in the house.

In the daytime you can gather grasses,
In the evening make them into rope.
Let us get quickly to the house.
Sowing grain starts again soon.

In the days of the second we cut the ice, ding-ding.
In the days of the third we take it to the ice house.
In the days of the fourth we get up early.
We make offerings of lamb and scallions.
In the ninth month the plants wither from the
     frost.
In the tenth month we clear the threshing ground.
We set out a feast with a pair of wine jars,
We slaughter lambs and sheep
And go up to the public hall.
Raising our cups of rhinoceros horn,
May you live forever!

* * *

We were harvesting
At the new field,
At the newly cleared acre,
When Fangshu arrived
With three thousand chariots
And a well-tested army.
Fangshu led them here,
Driving four dappled grey horses,
Such well-trained horses.
His chariot was red,
The canopy of bamboo mat, the quiver of fish skin.
He had breast plates with hooks and metal-
     rimmed reins.

We were harvesting
At the new field
In the central district
When Fangshu arrived
With his three thousand chariots
And emblazoned banners.
Fangshu led them here,
His wheel hubs wrapped, the yokes ornamented.
Eight bells tinkled on the bits.
He wore his official garb
With brilliant red knee-covers
And green pendants at his waist.

Swift flies the hawk,
Straight up to heaven.

Yet it stops here to roost.
Fangshu arrived
With three thousand chariots
And a well-tested army.
Fangshu led them here,
The musicians beating the drums.
He marshalled the army and lectured the troops.
Illustrious and faithful is Fangshu.
The drums sound,
And the troops move.

Foolish were you, tribes of Jing,
To make enemies of a great state.
Fangshu is an old man
Strong in his ability to plan.

Fangshu led them here,
Taking captives, capturing chiefs.
His war chariots rumble,
Rumble and crash,
Like thunder and lightning.
Illustrious and faithful is Fangshu.
He has already conquered the Xianyun
And now overawes the Jing tribes.

Examining the Evidence

1. What do the songs tell us about the lifestyles of the authors?
2. How do the songs address love?
3. What is the role of warfare in them?

MAKING CONNECTIONS

1. For almost all of the sources translated here, we do not know who composed them nor do we know at what time they were written. What do we know about the creative processes behind them?
2. The sources treat various aspects of society and life. What topics and themes do these documents share?
3. Several of the documents show direct interactions between humans and the gods. How are these interactions brought about, and what do they tell us about the nature of the divine?

CHAPTER 4

Empire and Resistance in the Mediterranean, 1550–330 B.C.E.

The ancient empires of North Africa and Southwest Asia left behind an abundance of documentation concerning many aspects of life. Military conquest was a major element in the formation of the empires and received much attention in official writings. However, the well-established imperial heartlands allowed for cultural developments and a flourishing of religious ideas (e.g., divination in Assyria). Because large territories were under the control of one political center, peoples and ideas traveled easily. Written sources describe the experiences of Nubians (people from the present-day Sudan) living in Egypt in the language and script from that northern neighbor, as well as the life of a farmer in early Greece in the newly developed Greek alphabetic script.

4.1 LIFE IN THE EGYPTIAN EMPIRE

Soldier Ahmose, *A Military Career in Egypt's New Kingdom* (c. 1550 B.C.E.)

Empires employed a large number of people. Administrators ran complex affairs over large territories to ensure that the imperial elite benefited from the subjected areas. The empires needed an army to conquer new regions and keep the conquered territories obedient. They also needed personnel to serve in the temples and palaces. Other groups were also involved in running the empire. These individuals were often from the empire's core, and they regularly benefited from the success of their masters. In New Kingdom Egypt, many officials, military men, and others who gained their livelihoods in the service of the empire were able to commission artists and scribes to create monuments and written works in their own honor, in which they described their careers. In this example, a military man who participated in the campaigns that created the Egyptian Empire narrates his accomplishments in the service of the king and how he was rewarded for them.

The Crew Commander Ahmose son of Abana, the justified; he says. I speak to you, all people. I let you know what favors came to me. I have been rewarded with gold seven times in the sight of the whole land, with male and female slaves as well. I have been endowed with very many fields. The name of the brave man is in that which he has done; it will not perish in the land forever.

He speaks as follows. I grew up in the town of Nekheb, my father being a soldier of the King of Upper and Lower Egypt, Seqenenre,[1] the justified. Baba, son of Reonet was his name. I became a soldier

in his stead on the ship "The Wild Bull" in the time of the Lord of the Two Lands, Nebpehtire,[2] the justified. I was a youth who had not married; I slept in. . . .

Expulsion of the Hyksos

Now when I had established a household,[3] I was taken to the ship "Northern," because I was brave. I followed the sovereign on foot when he rode about on his chariot. When the town of Avaris[4] was besieged, I fought bravely on foot in his majesty's presence. Thereupon I was appointed to the ship "Rising in Memphis." Then there was fighting on the water in "Pjedku" of Avaris. I made a seizure and carried off a hand.[5] When it was reported to the royal herald the gold of valor was given to me.

Then they fought again in this place; I again made a seizure there and carried off a hand. Then I was given the gold of valor once again.

Then there was fighting in Egypt to the south of this town, and I carried off a man as a living captive. I went down into the water—for he was captured on the city side—and crossed the water carrying him. When it was reported to the royal herald I was rewarded with gold once more. Then Avaris was despoiled, and I brought spoil from there: one man, three women; total, four persons. His majesty gave them to me as slaves.

Then Sharuhen[6] was besieged for three years. His majesty despoiled it and I brought spoil from

---

[1] **Seqenenre:** A king of the Seventeenth dynasty.

[2] **Nebpehtire:** The throne-name of Ahmose, the first king of the Eighteenth dynasty.
[3] That is, got married.
[4] **Avaris:** The capital of the Hyksos in the Nile Delta.
[5] He killed one enemy and cut off his hand as proof.
[6] **Sharuhen:** A town in the south of Palestine.

it: two women and a hand. Then the gold of valor was given me, and my captives were given to me as slaves.

Nubian Campaign of King Ahmose

Now when his majesty had slain the nomads of Asia, he sailed south to Khent-hen-nefer,[7] to destroy the Nubian Bowmen. His majesty made a great slaughter among them, and I brought spoil from there: two living men and three hands. Then I was rewarded with gold once again, and two female slaves were given to me. His majesty journeyed north, his heart rejoicing in valor and victory. He had conquered southerners, northerners.

Destruction of the Rebels Aata and Tetian

Then Aata came to the South.[8] His fate brought on his doom. The gods of Upper Egypt grasped him. He was found by his majesty at [a place called] Tent-taa. His majesty carried him off as a living captive, and all his people as booty. I brought two young warriors as captives from the ship of Aata. Then I was given five persons and portions of land amounting to five arurae[9] in my town. The same was done for the whole crew.

Then came that foe named Tetian.[10] He had gathered the malcontents to himself. His majesty slew him; his troop was wiped out. Then I was given three persons and five arurae of land in my town.

Nubian Campaign of King Amenhotep I

Then I conveyed King Djeserkare,[11] the justified, when he sailed south to Kush,[12] to enlarge the borders of Egypt. His majesty smote that Nubian Bowman in the midst of his army. They were

carried off in fetters, none missing, the fleeing destroyed as if they had never been. Now I was in the van of our troops and I fought really well. His majesty saw my valor. I carried off two hands and presented them to his majesty. Then his people and his cattle were pursued, and I carried off a living captive and presented him to his majesty.

I brought his majesty back to Egypt in two days from "Upper Well," and was rewarded with gold. I brought back two female slaves as booty, apart from those that I had presented to his majesty. Then they made me a "Warrior of the Ruler."

Nubian Campaign of King Thutmose I

Then I conveyed King Aakheperkare,[13] the justified, when he sailed south to Khent-hen-nefer, to crush rebellion throughout the lands, to repel the intruders from the desert region. I was brave in his presence in the bad water, in the towing of the ship over the cataract. Thereupon I was made crew commander.

Then his majesty [was informed that the Nubian] -----. At this his majesty became enraged like a leopard. His majesty shot, and his first arrow pierced the chest of that foe. Then those [enemies turned to flee], helpless before his Uraeus.[14] A slaughter was made among them; their dependents were carried off as living captives. His majesty journeyed north, all foreign lands in his grasp, and that wretched Nubian Bowman head downward at the bow of his majesty's ship "Falcon." They landed at Ipet-sut.[15]

Syrian Campaign of King Thutmose I

After this (his majesty) proceeded to Retjenu, to vent his wrath throughout the lands. When his majesty reached Nahrin,[16] his majesty found that foe marshalling troops. Then his majesty made a great slaughter of them. Countless were the living captives which his majesty brought back from his victories.

---

[7] **Khent-hen-nefer:** The northern part of Nubia, bordering Egypt.

[8] Aata seems to have been an enemy from farther south in Nubia.

[9] **arurae:** An Egyptian measure of area.

[10] **Tetian:** Believed to be an Egyptian rebel leader.

[11] **King Djeserkare:** King Amenhotep I.

[12] **Kush:** Nubia.

[13] **King Aakheperkare:** King Thutmose I.

[14] **Uraeus:** The image of the cobra snake on the royal crown.

[15] **Ipet-sut:** The city of Thebes.

[16] **Nahrin:** The area of northern Syria.

Now I was in the van of our troops, and his majesty saw my valor. I brought a chariot, its horse, and him who was on it as a living captive. When they were presented to his majesty, I was rewarded with gold once again.

I have grown old; I have reached old age. Favored as before, and loved [by my lord], I [rest] in the tomb that I myself made.

Examining the Evidence

1. Ahmose carved the inscription on the walls of his tomb. Why would he have done so?
2. What does Ahmose tell us about military events at the start of Egypt's New Kingdom?
3. How was Ahmose rewarded?
4. What is the role of the king in this inscription?

4.2   FOREIGN CONQUERERS IN EGYPT

King Piye, *The Nubian Conquest of Egypt* (727 B.C.E.)

In 727 B.C.E., King Piye of Nubia erected a large stone slab in the temple of Amun at Napata, on which he described his campaign through Egypt in the previous year against Egyptian rulers of the north. The text, recorded in the classical Egyptian language, portrays the Nubian king as being more Egyptian than the Egyptians. It depicts four local rulers submitting to Piye. One of the four presents the king with a horse, an animal for which Piye had special affection. Although a foreign king commissioned it, the inscription is a standard account of an Egyptian royal victor and is the longest such preserved account. In one particularly unusual passage, excerpted here, Piye reports on the lamentable condition of the stables in the city of Hermopolis, which he captured from King Namart. In the other passage, he describes his attack on Memphis, the northern capital of Egypt.

Piye Visits the Stables at Hermopolis

His majesty [Piye] proceeded to the house of [the Egyptian] King *Namart*. He went through all the rooms of the palace, his treasury and his storehouse. He (Namart) presented the royal wives and royal daughters to him. They saluted his majesty in the manner of women, while his majesty did not direct his gaze at them.

His majesty proceeded to the stable of the horses and the quarters of the foals. When he saw they had been [left] to hunger he said: "I swear, as the god Re loves me, as my nose is refreshed by life: that my horses were made to hunger pains me more than any other crime you committed in your recklessness! I would teach you to respect your neighbors. Do you not know god's shade is above me and does not let my action fail? Would that another, whoever he might be, had done it for me! I would not have to reprimand him for it. I was fashioned in the womb, created in the egg of the god! The seed of the god is in me! By his *ka*,[1] I act not without him; it is he who commands me to act!"

Then his goods were assigned to the treasury, and his granary to the endowment of the god Amun in Thebes. . . .

Piye Conquers Memphis

[His majesty proceeded to] Memphis. He sent to them, saying: "Do not close, do not fight, O home of the god Shu since the beginning! Let the entrant enter, the goer go; those who would leave shall not be hindered! I shall offer an oblation to the god Ptah and the gods of Memphis. I shall sacrifice to the god Sokar in Shetit. I shall see South-of-his-Wall. And I shall sail north in peace! - - - - - - [The people of]

[1] *ka*: The soul.

Ancient Egyptian Literature, Volume III: The Late Period by Miriam Lichtheim, pp. 73–76. Copyright © 1980 by the Regents of the University of California. Published by the University of California Press. Reproduced with permission of University of California Press–Books in the format Textbook via Copyright Clearance Center.

Memphis will be safe and sound; one will not weep over children. Look to the nomes[2] of the South! No one was slain there, except the rebels who had blasphemed god; the traitors were executed."

They closed their fort. They sent out troops against some of his majesty's troops, consisting of artisans, builders, and sailors [who had entered] the harbor of Memphis. And the Chief of Sais[3] arrived in Memphis by night to charge his soldiers, his sailors, all the best of his army, consisting of 8,000 men, charging them firmly:

"Look, Memphis is filled with troops of all the best of Lower Egypt, with barley, emmer, and all kinds of grain, the granaries overflowing; with weapons [of war] of all kinds. A rampart [surrounds it]. A great battlement has been built, a work of skilled craftsmanship. The river surrounds its east side; one cannot fight there. The stables here are filled with oxen; the storehouse is furnished with everything: silver, gold, copper, clothing, incense, honey, resin. I shall go to give gifts to the chiefs of Lower Egypt. I shall open their homes to them. I shall be - - -, [in a few] days I shall return." He mounted a horse (for) he did not trust his chariot, and he went north in fear of his majesty.

At dawn of the next day his majesty arrived at Memphis. When he had moored on its north, he found the water risen to the walls and ships moored at [the houses of] Memphis. His majesty saw that it was strong, the walls were high with new construction, and the battlements manned in strength. No way of attacking it was found. Every man of his majesty's army had his say about some plan of attack. Some said: "Let us blockade ---, for its troops are numerous." Others said: "Make a causeway to it, so that we raise the ground to its wall. Let us construct a siege tower, setting up masts and using sails as walls for it. You should divide it thus on each of its sides with ramparts and [a causeway] on its north, so as to raise the ground to its wall, so that we find a way for our feet."

Then his majesty raged against them like a panther, saying: "I swear, as Re loves me, as my father Amun favors me, . . . according to the command of Amun! This is what people say: ' - - - and the homes of the South opened to him from afar, though Amun

had not put (it) in their hearts, and they did not know what he had commanded. He (Amun) made him in order to show his might, to let his grandeur be seen.' I shall seize it like a cloudburst, for [Amen-Re] has commanded me!"

Then he sent his fleet and his troops to attack the harbor of Memphis. They brought him every ship, every ferry, every *shry*-boat, all the many ships that were moored in the harbor of Memphis, with the bow rope fastened to its houses. [There was not] a common soldier who wept among all the troops of his majesty. His majesty himself came to line up the many ships.

His majesty commanded his troops: "Forward against it! Mount the walls! Enter the houses over the river! When one of you enters the wall, no one shall stand in his vicinity, no troops shall repulse you! To pause is vile. We have sealed Upper Egypt; we shall bring Lower Egypt to port. We shall sit down in Balance-of-the Two-Lands [Memphis]!"

Then Memphis was seized as by a cloudburst. Many people were slain in it, or brought as captives to where his majesty was.

Now [when] it dawned on the next day his majesty sent people into it to protect the temples of god for him. The arm was raised over the holy of holies of the gods. Offerings were made to the Council (of the gods) of Memphis. Memphis was cleansed with natron[4] and incense. The priests were set in their places.

His majesty proceeded to the house of [Ptah]. His purification was performed in the robing room. There was performed for him every rite that is performed for a king when he enters the temple. A great offering was made to his father Ptah South-of-his-Wall of oxen, shorthorns, fowl, and all good things. Then his majesty went to his house.

Examining the Evidence

1. How does Piye present himself as a pious man?
2. Analyze the discussions between Piye and his men before the attack on Memphis. Why does Piye mention them?
3. Compare the representation of King Piye to that of his main opponent, the Chief of Sais.

---

[2] **nome:** An administrative district of Egypt.

[3] **Chief of Sais:** Piye's main opponent.

[4] **natron:** A type of salt used for cleansing in Egypt.

4.3 ASSYRIANS PREDICT THE FUTURE BY READING THE SIGNS OF THE GODS

Mesopotamian Omens (c. 650 B.C.E.)

Everyone would like to know what the future has in store for them, and many ancient people thought the gods were able to reveal that information. The Assyrians developed a massive literature to guide specialist diviners in reading the signs that gods left in every aspect of the world surrounding them. They formulated them as lists, first giving the appearance of a sign and then explaining what it meant for an individual or for the country. Tens of thousands of such cases are recorded on hundreds of cuneiform tablets, many of them collected in the library that King Assurbanipal created in his capital at Nineveh. Series of tablets combined specific ways in which to read the omens, for example, in the liver of a slaughtered sheep (extispicy) or in dreams. Here follows a small selection of different divinations.

Extispicy[1]

1. If there is a *Hal* sign[2] at the emplacement of "the well-being" the reign of Akkad[3] is over.

2. If the entire liver is anomalous—Omen of the king of Akkad regarding catastrophe.

3. Omen of Ibbi-Sin when Elam[4] reduced Ur to a ruin heap and rubble.

4. If the "rise of the head of the bird" is dark on the left and the right there will be *pitrustu*.[5]

5. When you make an extispicy and in a favorable result there is one *pitrustu* (the extispicy is) unfavorable; in an unfavorable result (the extispicy is) favorable).[6]

Behavior of the Sacrificial Sheep

6. If a sheep bites his right foot—raids of the enemy will be constant against my land.

Lecanomancy[7]

7. If (I throw oil (in)to water and) the oil divides itself into two—the sick person will die; for the campaign: the army will not return.

Anomalous Births[8]

8. If an anomaly has no right ear—the reign of the king will come to an end; his palace will be scattered; overthrow of the elders of the city; the king will have no advisors; the mood of the land will change; the herds of the land will decrease; you will make a promise to the enemy.

9. If an anomaly has no left ear—the god has heard the prayer of the king, the king will take the land of his enemy, the palace of the enemy will be scattered, the enemy will have no advisors, you will

---

[1] **Extispicy:** The examination of the entrails of animals, most often involving the liver of a sheep.

[2] *Hal* **sign:** A cuneiform sign formed with two horizontal wedges.

[3] This refers to the dynasty of King Sargon in the twenty-fourth century B.C.E. Omens such as these with references to historical events are rare.

[4] This refers to the end of the Ur III dynasty in the late twenty-first century B.C.E.

[5] *pitrustu*: A term with an unknown meaning but certainly negative.

[6] The *pitrustu* changes a positive into a negative omen and vice versa.

[7] **Lecanomancy:** The reading of omens by pouring oil on water.

[8] **Anomalous Births:** These omens are based on the discovery of newborn animals with physical deformities.

Translation from Ann Guinan in *The Context of Scripture*, ed. William W. Hallo. Vol. 1, *Canonical Compositions from the Biblical World* (Leiden: Brill, 1997), 423–426.

decrease the herd of the enemy, he will make a promise to you.

10. If an anomaly's right ear is cleft—that ox-fold will be scattered.

11. If an anomaly's left ear is cleft—that ox-fold will expand; the ox-fold of the enemy will be scattered.

12. If an anomaly has two ears on the left and none on the right—the enemy will take your border city, your adversary will prevail over you.

13. If an anomaly's horns are on the right—the prince will have auxiliary troops.

14. If an anomaly's horns are on the left—the enemy: the equivalent.

15. If a ram's horns protrude from its forehead—that ox-fold will be scattered.

Celestial Divination[9]

16. If there is an eclipse of the moon in the month Nisannu and it is red—prosperity for the people.

17. If Venus wears a black tiara (it means) Sa[turn(?)] stands in front of her.

If Venus wears a white tiara (it means) J[upiter] stands in front of her. . . .

If Venus wears a green tiara (it means) Mars stands in front of her.

If Venus wears a red tiara (it means) Mercury stands in front of her.

The Human Habitat

18. If a city lifts its head to the heaven—that city will be abandoned.

19. If a city's garbage pit is green—that city will be prosperous, variant: go to ruin.[10]

20. If there are many messengers in the city—dispersal [of the city.]

21. If a man repairs a moon-disk—his god wil[l always shepherd him] steadfastly.

22. If there are bearded women in a city—hardship will seize the land.

23. If in a man's house a dog is inscribed on the wall—worry [. . .]

24. If everything for a banquet in the temple is regularly provided—the house will have regular good fortune.

25. If a god enters a man's house for a banquet—constant uprising and contention will be constant for the man's house.

26. If syrup is seen in a house or on the walls of a house—the house will be devastated.

27. If the house makes the sound of a kettle-drum -[. . .]

28. If a man repairs a moon-disk—his god wil[l always shepherd him] steadfastly.

29. If a man repairs a sun-disk—his god wil[l always shepherd him] steadfastly.

30. If a king repairs (the statue) of the god—the god will [. . .].

31. If a man sees the body of a king—t[hat] man [. . .]

32. If there is black fungus in a man's house—there will be brisk trade in the man's house; the man's house will be rich.

33. If there is green and red fungus in a man's house—the master of the house will die, dispersal of the man's house. [. . .]

37. If a snake crosses from the right of a man to the left of a man—he will have a good name.

38. If a snake crosses from the left of a man to the right of a man—he will have a bad name.

39. If a white cat is seen in a man's house—(for) that land hardship will seize it.

If a black cat is seen in a man's house—that land will experience good fortune.

If a red cat is seen in a man's house—that land will be rich.

If a multicolored cat is seen in a man's house—that land will not prosper.

If a yellow cat is seen in a man's house—that land will have a year of good fortune.

40. If "mountain grass" is seen [in a fie]ld inside the city—the field will become fallow, that man will die.

41. If the linen curtain of a temple (in front of the cult statue) looks like a figure—those who have entered that temple will go out and never (re)enter the door. . . .

---

[9] **Celestial Divination:** Omen reading on the basis of signs in the sky.

[10] The writer acknowledges that the sources he used have two (contradictory) outcomes.

Dream Omens

56. [If] (he dreams) that a dog rips his [garment]—he will experience losses.

57. If a man (dreams) he kisses his penis—what he says will find acceptance; whatever he desires will not be withheld from him.

Physiognomic Omens

58. If a mole is very white—that man will become poor, very [. . .].

59. If a mole is very green—the same [. . .].

60. If a mole is very red—he will be ri[ch].

61. If his garment hangs down and is marked with white blemishes—garment of deprivations.

62. If the walls of a house are dotted with very white (spots)—the master of that house will die a death of violence.

63. If a man (while speaking) bites his lower lip—his word will find acceptance.

Examining the Evidence

1. What aspects of the world are consulted for divination in this selection?
2. The lists often include pairs of signs, such as something on the left and something on the right. How are the interpretations equally paired?
3. Identify other sequences listing variants of the same sign.

4.4   THE PERSIANS HONOR THE GOD AHURAMAZDA

Zoroaster, *Gathas* (date unknown)

The teachings of the prophet Zoroaster present one of the earliest monotheistic belief systems in world history. It is unknown when exactly he lived and modern scholars have made suggestions that range from 1700 to 500 B.C.E. The ancient Persians honored Zoroaster's god, Ahuramazda, in their inscriptions and seem to have used the teachings as the basis of their state religion, although they respected local religions throughout the empire. Like the hymns of *The Rig Veda* excerpted in Chapter 3, Zoroaster's sayings, or Gathas, were written down centuries after they were composed and integrated in a liturgical collection of the Yasna, one of the main divisions of the Avesta. Priests recited the Yasna, meaning "sacrifice," during the ceremony of the same name. We do not know whether the ancient Persians were familiar with these sayings in the form in which they are now preserved.

Yasna 30

1. (to the adherents). Yes, to those (of you) seeking, I shall speak of those things which are to be borne in mind—even by one who already knows—through both praise and worship for the very Wise Master of good thinking and for truth, which things are to be looked upon in joy throughout your days.

2. Listen with your ears to the best things. Reflect with a clear mind—man by man for himself—upon the two choices of decision, being aware to declare yourselves to Him before the great retribution.

3. Yes, there are two fundamental spirits, twins which are renowned to be in conflict. In thought and in word, in action, they are two: the good and the bad. And between these two, the beneficent have correctly chosen, not the maleficent.

4. Furthermore, when those two spirits first came together, they created life and death, and how, at the end, the worst existence shall be for the deceitful but the best thinking for the truthful person.

5. Of these two spirits, the deceitful one chose to bring to realization the worst things. (But) the very virtuous spirit, who is clothed in the hardest stones, chose the truth, and (so shall those) who shall satisfy the Wise Lord continuously with true actions.

S. Insler, *The Gathas of Zarathustra*. Vol. 1 of *Textes et Mémoires* (Téhéran: Bibliothèque Pahlavi, 1975; distributed by Brill), 33–35, 51–53.

6. The gods did not at all choose correctly between these two, since the deceptive one approached them as they were deliberating. Since they chose the worst thought, they then rushed into fury, with which they have afflicted the world and mankind.

7. But to this world He[1] came with the rule of good thinking and of truth, and (our) enduring piety gave body and breath (to it). He shall be here for the protection of these (faithful), just as He shall be the first (to do so) during the requitals with the molten iron.

8. (to the Wise Lord). And thus, when the punishment for these sinners shall come to pass, then, for Thee, Wise One, shall the rule of good thinking be at hand, in order to be announced to those, Lord, who shall deliver deceit into the hands of truth.

9. Therefore may we be those who shall heal this world! Wise One and ye other lords, be present to me with support and with truth, so that one shall become convinced even where his understanding shall be false.

10. For then shall descend the destruction of the prosperity of deceit, and there shall be yoked from the good dwelling place of good thinking the swiftest steeds, which shall race ahead unto the good fame of the Wise One and of truth.

11. (to the adherents). Men, when ye learn those commandments which the Wise One has posed, when ye learn (there is) both a way of easy access and one with no access, as well as long destruction for the deceitful but salvation for the truthful, then each one (of you) shall abide by (all) these commandments. Wish it so.

Yasna 33

1. (to the adherents). As in harmony with those things which are the laws of the foremost existence, the (final) judgment thus shall bring to realization the most just actions for the deceitful as well as for the truthful man, and for the person for whom falsity and honesty are held to be indifferent.

2. Therefore, who shall bring about what is bad for the deceitful one either by word or by thought, or with his hands, or who shall enlighten his guest in the good—all these shall bring success to His desire and be in the approval of the Wise Lord.

3. (to the Wise Lord). The person who is very good to a truthful man, be he allied by family, or a member of his community, or allied by clan, Lord, or be he someone who continues to serve the cow[2] with zeal, such a person shall be on the pasture of truth and good thinking.

4. Wise One, (it is) I who, through worship, shall turn away disobedience and bad thinking from Thee, and opposition from the family, and the nearest deceit of the community, and scorners from the clan, and the worst counselor[3] from the pasture of the cow.[4]

5. I who, at the stopping (of these), shall summon the all-greatest obedience for Thee, I shall attain for us here the long-lived rule of good thinking and the paths, straight in accord with truth, wherein the Wise Lord dwells.

6. The priest who is just in harmony with truth is the offspring from the best spirit. In consequence of this, he is allied with that (good) thinking by reason of which he has respected to bring to realization his pastoral duties. By reason of this very thinking, Wise Lord, I am eager for Thy sight and Thy counsel.

7. Come hither to me, ye best ones. Hither, both personally and boldly—Thou, Wise One, together with truth and good thinking—by reason of which I am to be famed before (every other) adherent. Let bright gifts and reverence (for all of you) be manifest amid us.

8. Take ye heed of these goals of mine, which I shall enact with good thinking: worship of all of you, Wise One, and words praiseworthy with truth. Your enduring worshipful offering has been established to be immortality and completeness.

9. Yes, for Thee, Wise One, let a person support with good thinking the very spirit of these two companions who increase truth through that happiness consisting of change. The association of these two has already arisen, under whom (all) souls are in harmony.

10. All those (beings) whose way of life is good for Thee—those who have been, and those who are, and those who shall be—give them a share in Thy approval, Wise One. (And) grow Thyself, in breath and body, through the rule of good thinking and of truth.

11. The Wise One who is the Mightiest Lord, and piety, and truth which prospers the creatures, and good thinking, and (good) rule listen to me, have mercy on me, when there is any requital.

12. Rise up to me, Lord. Along with Thy most virtuous spirit, Wise One, receive force through (our) piety, strength through (every) good requital, powerful might through truth, protection through (our) good thinking.

13. Lord of broad vision, disclose to me for support the safeguards of your rule, those which are the reward for good thinking. Reveal to me, by reason of my virtuous piety, those conceptions in harmony with truth.

14. For Zoroaster does give the breath of even his own person as a gift, in order that there be for the Wise One predominance of good thinking along with (predominance) of the action and the word allied with truth, that there be obedience and His (good) rule.

Examining the Evidence

1. Zoroaster's teachings stress the opposition between good and evil. How does he express that opposition? What other pairs parallel that of good and evil?
2. How does Yasna 30 describe the beginning of time?

---

[1] **He:** Ahuramazda, the Wise One.
[2] The good vision. [Original note.]
[3] The evil spirit. [Original note.]
[4] Symbol for the community of the faithful and the truthful. [Original note.]

4.5   DESCRIPTION OF A FARMER'S LIFE

Hesiod, *Works and Days* (c. 700 B.C.E.)

Hesiod (c. 700 B.C.E.), one of the earliest poets of ancient Greece, is best known for his poem entitled *Works and Days*. Markedly different from Homer's epics about the Trojan War and its aftermath, the poem considers the life of common people, the farmers of northern Greece. In the following excerpts, he gives advice on how to be a successful farmer, outlining the exact time of year when tasks should be performed and what type of help to use. Although Hesiod's subject matter is mundane, he expresses his thoughts in creative form through poetic verse.

Muses of Pieria[1] who give glory through song, come hither, tell of the god Zeus your father and chant his praise. Through him mortal men are famed or unfamed, sung or unsung alike, as great Zeus wills. For easily he makes strong, and easily he brings the strong man low; easily he humbles the proud and raises the obscure, and easily he straightens the crooked and blasts the proud,— Zeus who thunders aloft and has his dwelling most high.

Attend thou with eye and ear, and make judgements straight with righteousness. And I, Perses,[2] would tell of true things. . . .

For the gods keep hidden from men the means of life. Else you would easily do work enough in a day to supply you for a full year even without working; soon would you put away your rudder over the smoke, and the fields worked by ox and sturdy mule would run to waste. . . .

---

[1] **Pieria:** An area of northern Greece.

Reprinted by permission of the publisher and the Trustees of the Loeb Classical Library from *Hesiod*, Loeb Classical Library Volume 57, translated by Hugh G. Evelyn-White, pp. 3, 5, 33, 37, 39, 41, 47, 49, 53, 55. Cambridge, MA: Harvard University Press, 1914. Loeb Classical Library® is a registered trademark of the President and Fellows of Harvard College.

First of all, get a house, and a woman and an ox for the plough—a slave woman and not a wife, to follow the oxen as well—and make everything ready at home, so that you may not have to ask of another, and he refuse you, and so, because you are in lack, the season pass by and your work come to nothing. Do not put your work off till to-morrow and the day after; for a sluggish worker does not fill his barn, nor one who puts off his work: industry makes work go well, but a man who puts off work is always at hand-grips with ruin. . . .

Mark, when you hear the voice of the crane [mid-November] who cries year by year from the clouds above, for she give the signal for ploughing and shows the season of rainy winter; but she vexes the heart of the man who has no oxen. Then is the time to feed up your horned oxen in the byre; for it is easy to say: "Give me a yoke of oxen and a wagon," and it is easy to refuse: "I have work for my oxen." The man who is rich in fancy thinks his wagon as good as built already—the fool! He does not know that there are a hundred timbers to a wagon. Take care to lay these up beforehand at home.

So soon as the time for ploughing is proclaimed to men, then make haste, you and your slaves alike, in wet and in dry, to plough in the season for ploughing, and bestir yourself early in the morning so that your fields may be full. Plough in the spring; but fallow broken up in the summer will not belie your hopes. Sow fallow land when the soil is still getting light: fallow land is a defender from harm and a soother of children.

Pray to Zeus of the Earth and to pure goddess Demeter to make Demeter's holy grain sound and heavy, when first you begin ploughing, when you hold in your hand the end of the plough-tail and bring down your stick on the backs of the oxen as they draw on the pole-bar by the yoke-straps. Let a slave follow a little behind with a mattock and make trouble for the birds by hiding the seed; for good management is the best for mortal men as bad management is the worst. In this way your corn-ears will bow to the ground with fullness if the Olympian himself gives a good result at the last, and you will sweep the cobwebs from your bins and you will be glad, I ween [expect] as you take of your garnered substance. And so you will have plenty till you come to grey springtime,[3] and will not look wistfully to others, but another shall be in need of your help.

But if you plough the good ground at the solstice [December], you will reap sitting, grasping a thin crop in your hand, binding the sheaves awry, dust-covered, not glad at all; so you will bring all home in a basket and not many will admire you. Yet the will of Zeus who holds the aegis is different at different times; and it is hard for mortal men to tell it; for if you should plough late, you may find this remedy—when the cuckoo first calls [March] in the leaves of the oak and makes men glad all over the boundless earth, if Zeus should send rain on the third day and not cease until it rises neither above an ox's hoof nor falls short of it, then the late-plougher will vie with the early. Keep all this well in mind, and fail not to mark grey spring as it comes and the season of rain. . . .

While it is yet midsummer command your slaves: "It will not always be summer, build barns." . . .

Set your slaves to winnow Demeter's holy grain, when strong Orion first appears,[4] on a smooth threshing-floor in an airy place. Then measure it and store it in jars. And so soon as you have safely stored all your stuff indoors, I bid you put your bondman out of doors and look out for a servant-girl with no children;—for a servant with a child to nurse is troublesome. And look after the dog with jagged teeth; do not grudge him his food, or some time the Day-sleeper [a robber] may take your stuff. Bring in fodder and litter so as to have enough for your oxen and mules. After that, let your men rest their poor knees and unyoke your pair of oxen.

But when Orion and Sirius are come into mid-heaven, and rosy-fingered Dawn sees Arcturus,[5] then cut off all the grape-clusters, Perses, and bring them home. Show them to the sun ten days and ten nights: then cover them over for five, and on the sixth day draw off into vessels the gifts of joyful

---

[2] **Perses:** Hesiod's brother, whom he tries to guide toward an honest life.

[3] **grey springtime:** Spring is so described because the buds have not yet cast their iron-grey husks.

[4] **when strong Orion first appears:** The constellation Orion first appears in July.

[5] **Arcturus:** A star visible in the early morning in September.

Dionysus. But when the Pleiades and Hyades and strong Orion begin to set [end of October], then remember to plough in season: and so the completed year[6] will fitly pass beneath the earth. . . .

Bring home a wife to your house when you are of the right age, while you are not far short of thirty years nor much above; this is the right age for marriage. Let your wife have been grown up four years, and marry her in the fifth. Marry a maiden, so that you can teach her careful ways, and especially marry one who lives near you, but look well about you and see that your marriage will not be a joke to your neighbours. For a man wins nothing better than a good wife, and, again, nothing worse than a bad one, a greedy soul who roasts her man without fire, strong though he may be, and brings him to a raw old age.[7]

Examining the Evidence

1. Hesiod recommends that a farmer should be autonomous. How is this advice expressed in the excerpt?
2. What means does Hesiod use to indicate time? How does the text give a survey of the agricultural year?
3. What does the text tell us about the makeup of an early Greek household?
4. What does this work reveal about Greek society of the period? What values are expressed in the poem?

[6] **the completed year:** That is, the succession of stars that make up the full year.

[7] **raw old age:** An untimely, premature death.

CONTRASTING VIEWS

IS DEMOCRACY GOOD OR BAD?

4.6   THUCYDIDES, *THE PELOPONNESIAN WARS* (431 B.C.E.)

The idea of democracy is closely tied to classical Athens, where in the fifth century B.C.E. a system explicitly called *democratic* developed. Therefore, Athens is often held up as the birthplace of this type of political organization. One of the most eloquent praises of the democratic system is the oration of the politician Pericles (c. 495–429 B.C.E.) as quoted in Thucydides's *Peloponnesian Wars*. Pericles delivered the speech in 431 B.C.E. after the first year of war between Athens and Sparta (the Lacedaemonians) when he was asked to honor the soldiers killed in the conflict. He used the occasion, however, to contrast two political and social systems, Spartan autocracy and Athenian democracy, arguing that Athens' soldiers had died for a worthwhile cause.

During the same winter, in accordance with traditional custom, the funeral of those who first fell in this war was celebrated by the Athenians at the public charge. . . .

Over the first who were buried, Pericles was chosen to speak. At the fitting moment he advanced from the sepulcher to a lofty stage, which had been erected in order that he might be heard as far away as possible by the crowd, and spoke somewhat as follows: . . .

"I will speak of our ancestors first, for it is right and seemly that on such an occasion as this we should also render this honor to their memory. Men of the same stock, ever dwelling in this land, in successive generations to this very day, by their valor handed it down as a free land. They are worthy of praise, and still more are our fathers, who added to their inheritance, and after many a struggle bequeathed to us, their sons, the great empire we possess. . . . But before I praise the dead, I shall first proceed to show by what kind of practices we attained to our position, and under what kind of institutions and manner of life our empire became great. For I conceive that it would not be unsuited to the occasion that this should be told, and that this whole assembly of citizens and foreigners may profitably listen to it.

"Our institutions do not emulate the laws of others. We do not copy our neighbors: rather, we are an example to them. Our system is called a democracy, for it respects the majority and not the few; but while the law secures equality to all alike in their private disputes, the claim of excellence is also recognized; and when a citizen is in any way distinguished, he is generally preferred to the public service, not

Thucydides, *The Peloponnesian Wars*, trans. Benjamin Jowett (New York: Twayne, 1963), 65–72.

in rotation, but for merit. Nor again is there any bar in poverty and obscurity of rank to a man who can do the state some service. It is as free men that we conduct our public life, and in our daily occupations we avoid mutual suspicions; we are not angry with our neighbor if he does what he likes; we do not put on sour looks at him which, though harmless, are not pleasant. While we give no offense in our private intercourse, in our public acts we are prevented from doing wrong by fear; we respect the authorities and the laws, especially those which are ordained for the protection of the injured as well as those unwritten laws which bring upon the transgressor admitted dishonor.

"Furthermore, none have provided more relaxations for the spirit from toil; we have regular games and sacrifices throughout the year; our homes are furnished with elegance; and the delight which we daily feel in all these things banishes melancholy. Because of the greatness of our city, the fruits of the whole earth flow in upon us so that we enjoy the goods of other countries as freely as our own.

"Then, again, in military training we are superior to our adversaries, as I shall show. Our city is thrown open to the world, and we never expel a foreigner or prevent him from seeing or learning anything which, if not concealed, it might profit an enemy to see. We rely not so much upon preparations or stratagems, as upon our own courage in action. And in the matter of education, whereas from early youth they[1] are always undergoing laborious exercises which are to make them brave, we live at ease and yet are equally ready to face perils to which our strength is equal. And here is the evidence. The Lacedaemonians march against our land not by themselves, but with their allies: we invade a neighbor's country alone; and although our opponents are fighting for their homes and we are on a foreign soil, we seldom have any difficulty in overcoming them. . . .

"Nor is this the only cause for marveling at our city. We are lovers of beauty without extravagance and of learning without loss of vigor. Wealth we employ less for talk and ostentation than when there is a real use for it. To avow poverty with us is no disgrace: the true disgrace is in doing nothing to avoid it. The same persons attend at once to the concerns of their households and of the city, and men of diverse employments have a very fair idea of politics. If a man takes no interest in public affairs, we alone do not commend him as quiet but condemn him as useless; and if few of us are originators, we are all sound judges of a policy. In our opinion action does not suffer from discussion but, rather, from the want of that

instruction which is gained by discussion preparatory to the action required. For we have an exceptional gift of acting with audacity after calculating the prospects of our enterprises, whereas other men are bold from ignorance but hesitate upon reflection. But it would be right to esteem those men bravest in spirit who have the clearest understanding of the pains and pleasures of life and do not on that account shrink from danger. . . .

"This is why I have dwelt upon the greatness of Athens, showing you that we are contending for a higher prize than those who enjoy no like advantages, and establishing by manifest proof the merit of these men whom I am now commemorating. Their loftiest praise has been already spoken; for in descanting on the city, I have honored the qualities which earned renown for them and for men such as they. And of how few Hellenes can it be said as of them, that their deeds matched their fame! In my belief an end such as theirs proves a man's worth; it is at once its first revelation and final seal. For even those who come short in other ways may justly plead the valor with which they have fought for their country; they have blotted out evil with good, and their public services have outweighed the harm they have done in their private actions. . . . And when the moment for fighting came, they held it nobler to suffer death than to yield and save their lives; it was the report of dishonor from which they fled, but on the battlefield their feet stood fast; and while for a moment they were in the hands of fortune, at the height, less of terror than of glory, they departed. . . .

"To you who are the sons and brothers of the departed, I see that the struggle to emulate them will be arduous. For all men praise the dead; and, however preeminent your virtue may be, you would hardly be thought their equals, but somewhat inferior. The living have their rivals and detractors; but when a man is out of the way, the honor and good will which he receives is uncontested. And, if I am also to speak of womanly virtues to those of you who will now be widows, let me sum them up in one short admonition: 'Your glory will be great if you show no more than the infirmities of your nature, a glory that consists in being least the subjects of report among men, for good or evil.'

"I have spoken in obedience to the law, making use of such fitting words as I had. The tribute of deeds has been paid in part, for the dead have been honorably interred; it remains only that their children shall be maintained at the public charge until they are grown up: this is the solid prize with which, as with a garland, Athens crowns these men and those left behind after such contests. For where the rewards of virtue are greatest, there men do the greatest services to their cities. And now, when you have duly lamented, everyone his own dead, you may depart."

---

[1] **whereas** . . . **they:** Pericles talks here about the Lacedaemonians, that is, the Spartans who are at war with the Athenians.

(continued)

CONTRASTING VIEWS (*continued*)

4.7   PLATO, *THE REPUBLIC* (C. 380 B.C.E.)

Not all ancient thinkers, including those in Athens, thought that democracy was the ideal political system. Written around 380 B.C.E., Plato's *Republic* depicts the philosopher Socrates in conversation with various men about political institutions in the city. In his dialogue with someone called Adeimantus, Socrates (c. 470–399 B.C.E.) describes four types of constitution, each worse than the previous one. Earlier in the book, Socrates depicts the ideal city under the philosopher–king guided by true wisdom. Here he describes various stages of decline. He starts with rule by an oligarchy, whose members follow necessary inclinations. Such a city declines into the democratic one, ruled by people who obey any desire they may have. Democracy leads to tyranny, a lawless rule by someone who does whatever he wants.

SOCRATES: And so he lives on, yielding day by day to the desire at hand. Sometimes he drinks heavily while listening to the flute; at other times, he drinks only water and is on a diet; sometimes he goes in for physical training; at other times, he's idle and neglects everything; and sometimes he even occupies himself with what he takes to be philosophy. He often engages in politics, leaping up from his seat and saying and doing whatever comes into his mind. If he happens to admire soldiers, he's carried in that direction, if money-makers, in that one. There's neither order nor necessity in his life, but he calls it pleasant, free, and blessedly happy, and he follows it for as long as he lives.

ADEIMANTUS: You've perfectly described the life of a man who believes in legal equality.

SOCRATES: I also suppose that he's a complex man, full of all sorts of characters, fine and multicolored, just like the democratic city, and that many men and women might envy his life, since it contains the most models of constitutions and ways of living.

ADEIMANTUS: That's right.

SOCRATES: Then shall we set this man beside democracy as one who is rightly called democratic?

ADEIMANTUS: Let's do so.

SOCRATES: The finest constitution and the finest man remain for us to discuss, namely, tyranny and a tyrannical man.

ADEIMANTUS: They certainly do.

SOCRATES: Come, then, how does tyranny come into being? It's fairly clear that it evolves from democracy.

ADEIMANTUS: It is.

SOCRATES: And doesn't it evolve from democracy in much the same way that democracy does from oligarchy?

ADEIMANTUS: What way is that?

SOCRATES: The good that oligarchy puts before itself and because of which it is established is wealth, isn't it?

ADEIMANTUS: Yes.

SOCRATES: And its insatiable desire for wealth and its neglect of other things for the sake of money-making is what destroyed it, isn't it?

ADEIMANTUS: That's true.

SOCRATES: And isn't democracy's insatiable desire for what it defines as the good also what destroys it?

ADEIMANTUS: What do you think it defines as the good?

SOCRATES: Freedom: Surely you'd hear a democratic city say that this is the finest thing it has, so that as a result it is the only city worth living in for someone who is by nature free.

ADEIMANTUS: Yes, you often hear that.

SOCRATES: Then, as I was about to say, doesn't the insatiable desire for freedom and the neglect of other things change this constitution and put it in need of a dictatorship?

ADEIMANTUS: In what way?

SOCRATES: I suppose that, when a democratic city, athirst for freedom, happens to get bad cupbearers for its leaders, so that it gets drunk by drinking more than it should of the unmixed wine of freedom,[1] then, unless the rulers are very pliable and provide plenty of that freedom, they are punished by the city and accused of being accursed oligarchs.

ADEIMANTUS: Yes, that is what it does.

SOCRATES: It insults those who obey the rulers as willing slaves and good-for-nothings and praises and

---

[1] **unmixed wine of freedom:** The Greeks drank their wine mixed with water.

Plato, *Republic*, trans. G. M. A. Grube (Indianapolis: Hackett, 1992), 232–233.

honors, both in public and in private, rulers who behave like subjects and subjects who behave like rulers. And isn't it inevitable that freedom should go to all lengths in such a city?

ADEIMANTUS: Of course.

SOCRATES: It makes its way into private households and in the end breeds anarchy even among the animals.

ADEIMANTUS: What do you mean?

SOCRATES: I mean that a father accustoms himself to behave like a child and fear his sons, while the son behaves like a father, feeling neither shame nor fear in front of his parents, in order to be free. A resident alien or a foreign visitor is made equal to a citizen, and he is their equal.

ADEIMANTUS: Yes, that is what happens.

SOCRATES: It does. And so do other little things of the same sort. A teacher in such a community is afraid of his students and flatters them, while the students despise their teachers or tutors. And, in general, the young imitate their elders and compete with them in word and deed, while the old stoop to the level of the young and are full of play and pleasantry, imitating the young for fear of appearing disagreeable and authoritarian.

ADEIMANTUS: Absolutely.

SOCRATES: The utmost freedom for the majority is reached in such a city when bought slaves, both male and female, are no less free than those who bought them. And I almost forgot to mention the extent of the legal equality of men and women and of the freedom in the relations between them.

COMPARING THE EVIDENCE

1. Based on these excerpts, how would you characterize Pericles' and Socrates' attitudes toward freedom? Do they mean the same thing to both thinkers?

2. What do both texts tell us about the status of women in ancient Athenian society?

3. Compare how these works deal with the issue of wealth.

4. Why would Pericles disagree with Socrates' idea that democracy leads to tyranny?

MAKING CONNECTIONS

1. Several of the sources translated here mention contacts between people with different cultural backgrounds. How do the texts describe the differences between these people?

2. Almost all the people and actions described here have a connection to the state. Describe some of the relationships to state power.

3. Trace the role of the gods in these sources.

CHAPTER 5

Peoples and World Empires of Eurasia: 500 B.C.E.–500 C.E.

As was true of the ancient Greeks as suggested in Chapter 4, the period from 500 B.C.E. to 500 C.E. was one of great intellectual creativity throughout Eurasia as well, and many ideas formulated then became foundational for subsequent cultures. Included here is a small selection of the extensive writings from South Asia and China that reflect innovations in religious, political, and economic thought. Numerous great thinkers in both regions wrote down their ideas or had followers who recorded their sayings. Many of these texts became classics in the literatures of the regions and continue to be studied in modern times.

THE CONCEPT OF DHARMA IN HINDUISM, BUDDHISM, AND JAINISM

5.1 *THE BHAGAVAD GITA* (C. 300 B.C.E.– 300 C.E.)

Inserted into the massive epic *Mahabharata* ("Great Epic of the Bharata Dynasty"), the dialogue between Arjuna and his divine charioteer Krishna, the *Bhagavad Gita* ("Song of the Lord") contains guidelines on how to live a proper life within the system of Hinduism. It is uncertain when this very influential poem was composed; various scholars have suggested any date between 300 B.C.E. and 300 C.E. Set in the middle of a battle of cosmic scale, the poet stopped all action to allow the epic's hero to consider what he was about to do in killing others. His adviser told him to accept his place in a society where all individuals have a role to play, or duty, according to their status and caste. That duty is dharma.

The fourfold division of castes was created by me according to the apportionment of qualities and duties. . . .

The duties of Brahmans, Kshatriyas, and Vaisyas, and of Sudras, too, O terror of your foes! are distinguished according to the qualities born of nature. Tranquility, restraint of the senses, penance, purity, forgiveness, straightforwardness, also knowledge, experience, and belief (in a future world), this is the natural duty of Brahmans. Valor, glory, courage, dexterity, not slinking away from battle, gifts, exercise of lordly power, this is the natural duty of Kshatriyas. Agriculture, tending cattle, trade, (this) is the natural duty of Vaisyas, and the natural duty of Sudras, too, consists in service. (Every) man intent on his own respective duties obtains perfection. Listen, now, how one intent on one's own duty obtains perfection. Worshipping, by (the performance of) his own duty, him

from whom all things proceed, and by whom all this is permeated, a man obtains perfection. One's duty, though defective, is better than another's duty well performed. Performing the duty prescribed by nature, one does not incur sin. O son of Kunti,[1] one should not abandon a natural duty though tainted with evil; for all actions are enveloped by evil, as fire by smoke. One who is self-restrained, whose understanding is unattached everywhere, from whom affections have departed, obtains the supreme perfection of freedom from action by renunciation. Learn from me, only in brief, O son of Kunti, how one who has obtained perfection attains the Brahman, which is the highest culmination of knowledge. A man possessed of a pure understanding, controlling his self by courage, discarding sound and other objects of sense, casting off affection.

[1] **Kunti:** Arjuna's mother.

Kâshinâth Trimbak Telang, trans., *The Bhagavadgîtâ, with the Anatsugâtîya and the Anugîtâ*, vol. 8 of *The Sacred Books of the East*, ed. Max Müller (Oxford: Clarendon Press, 1882), 59, 126–127.

5.2 KING ASHOKA, *INSCRIPTIONS* (C. 260 B.C.E.)

Profoundly affected by the brutality of his conquest of the Kalinga region, the Mauryan king Ashoka of India (r. c. 265–238 B.C.E.; also given as c. 273–232 B.C.E.) renounced all violence and replaced military action with "conquest by dharma," that is, the principles of right life. To promote his new policy of nonviolence and religious tolerance, he commissioned the carving of inscriptions throughout his state in the various local dialects and languages. These works represent the oldest Indian writings after those of the Indus Valley culture. The text appears on rock façades and high stone pillars and contains a frank explanation of why the king abandoned his own old behavior and that of his predecessors in favor of tolerance. Although he did not intend to spread Buddhism, his beliefs were rooted in that new religion.

When the king, Beloved of the Gods and of Gracious Mien, had been consecrated eight years Kalinga was conquered, 150,000 people were deported, 100,000 were

killed, and many times that number died. But after the conquest of Kalinga, the Beloved of the Gods began to follow righteousness [dharma], to love righteousness, and to give

(continued)

CONTRASTING VIEWS (*continued*)

instruction in righteousness. Now the Beloved of the Gods regrets the conquest of Kalinga, for when an independent country is conquered people are killed, they die, or are deported, and that the Beloved of the Gods finds very painful and grievous. And this he finds even more grievous—that all the inhabitants—brahmans, ascetics, and other sectarians, and householders who are obedient to superiors, parents, and elders, who treat friends, acquaintances, companions, relatives, slaves, and servants with respect, and are firm in their faith—all suffer violence, murder, and separation from their loved ones. Even those who are fortunate enough not to have lost those near and dear to them are afflicted at the misfortunes of friends, acquaintances, companions, and relatives. The participation of all men in common suffering is grievous to the Beloved of the Gods. Moreover there is no land, except that of the Greeks, where groups of brahmans and ascetics are not found, or where men are not members of one sect or another. So now, even if the number of those killed and captured in the conquest of Kalinga had been a hundred or a thousand times less, it would be grievous to the Beloved of the Gods. The Beloved of the Gods will forgive as far as he can, and he even conciliates the forest tribes of his dominions; but he warns them that there is power even in the remorse of the Beloved of the Gods, and he tells them to reform, lest they be killed.

For all beings the Beloved of the Gods desires security, self-control, calm of mind, and gentleness. The Beloved of the Gods considers that the greatest victory is the victory of righteousness; and this he has won here [in India] and even five hundred leagues beyond his frontiers in the realm of the Greek king Antiochus, and beyond Antiochus among the four kings Ptolemy, Antigonus, Magas, and Alexander.[1] Even where the envoys of the Beloved of the Gods have not been sent men hear of the way in which he follows and teaches righteousness, and they too follow it and will follow it. Thus he achieves a universal conquest, and conquest always gives a feeling of pleasure; yet it is but a slight pleasure, for the Beloved of the Gods only looks on that which concerns the next life as of great importance.

I have had this inscription of righteousness engraved that all my sons and grandsons may not seek to gain new victories, that in whatever victories they may gain they may prefer forgiveness and light punishment, that they may consider the only [valid] victory the victory of righteousness, which is of value both in this world and the next, and that all their pleasure may be in righteousness.

[1] **Ptolemy . . . Alexander:** The kings of the Hellenistic Mediterranean world with whom he was in contact.

Ainslee T. Embree, ed. and trans., "The Thirteenth Rock Edict," in *Sources of Indian Tradition*, 2d ed., vol. 1 (New York: Columbia University Press, 1988), 142–143.

5.3   MAHAVIRA VARDHAMANA (ATTRIB.), *THE BOOK OF GOOD CONDUCT* (C. 540 B.C.E.–500 C.E.)

Jain ideas are contained in writings of various dates, and modern scholars assume that orally transmitted sayings and ideas attributed to Mahavira, whom tradition claims was born around 540 B.C.E., were only gradually put down in writing. The *Acaranga Sutra* or *Book of Good Conduct* is usually considered one of the oldest texts, though the exact date of its composition is unknown. This work contains guidelines on how to lead an ascetic lifestyle and urges a complete policy of nonviolence, or dharma.

Thus say all the perfect souls and blessed ones, whether past, present, or to come—thus they speak, thus they declare, thus they proclaim: All things breathing, all things existing, all things living, all beings whatever, should not be slain or treated with violence, or insulted, or tortured, or driven away.

This is the pure unchanging eternal law, which the wise ones who know the world have proclaimed, among the earnest and the non-earnest, among the loyal and the not-loyal, among those who have given up punishing others and those who have not done so, among those who are weak and those who are not, among those who delight in worldly ties and those who do not. This is the truth. So it is. Thus it is declared in this religion.

When he adopts this Law a man should never conceal or reject it. When he understands the Law he should grow indifferent to what he sees, and not act for worldly motives. . . .

What is here declared has been seen, heard, approved, and understood. Those who give way and indulge in pleasure will be born again and again. The heedless are outside [the hope of salvation]. But if you are mindful, day and night steadfastly striving, always with ready vision, in the end you will conquer.

COMPARING THE EVIDENCE

1. What does dharma mean for each of these three belief systems? What virtues are associated with it, and what rewards come with living according to such teachings?
2. Based on these documents, where do the Hindu, Buddhist, and Jain conceptions of dharma overlap, and where do they differ?
3. How does dharma support the social order?
4. Three literary genres are used to proclaim these ideas. Consider what you know about how these works were developed and recorded, and compare how the different written formats might have influenced how these teachings were received.

Ainslee T. Embree, ed. and trans., "The Book of Good Conduct," in *Sources of Indian Tradition,* 2d ed., vol. 1 (New York: Columbia University Press, 1988), 64–65.

5.4 THE POWER OF LOVE

Kalidasa, *Shakuntala* (c. 450 C.E.)

The most famous surviving Sanskrit drama is *Shakuntala* by Kalidasa (c. 390–470 C.E.), which tells of the love between a king and a hermit girl, Shakuntala, a story that appears in the *Mahabharata* epic. After the two meet accidentally and marry in secret, a curse placed on Shakuntala causes her husband not to recognize her until she can produce a ring he had given her but she had lost accidentally. In this scene from the beginning of the play, the king and Shakuntala have fallen passionately in love, although they have scarcely spoken to each other. Shakuntala reveals her feelings to her two friends, Anusuya and Priyamvada, while the king, hiding behind the bushes, listens. The two friends persuade Shakuntala to write a love letter to the king. The characters Kalidasa portrays in this and his other plays are men and women who stand out as virtuous and noble. He sets them up as aristocratic ideals to his audiences, who themselves were people living at court like the characters whose stories they followed.

(*Enter Shakuntala with her two friends.*)

THE TWO FRIENDS (*fanning her*): Do you feel better, dear, when we fan you with these lotus-leaves?

SHAKUNTALA (*wearily*): Oh, are you fanning me, my dear girls? (*The two friends look sorrowfully at each other.*)

KING: She is seriously ill. (*Doubtfully.*) Is it the heat, or is it as I hope? (*Decidedly.*) It must be so.

With salve upon her breast,
With loosened lotus-chain,
My darling, sore oppressed,
Is lovely in her pain.

Arthur W. Ryder, trans., *Kalidasa: Translations of Shakuntala, and Other Works* (London: J. M. Dent and Sons; New York: E. P. Dutton, 1914), 28–33.

Though love and summer heat
May work an equal woe,
No maiden seems so sweet
When summer lays her low.

PRIYAMVADA (*aside to Anusuya*): Anusuya, since she first saw the good king, she has been greatly troubled. I do not believe her fever has any other cause.

ANUSUYA: I suspect you are right. I am going to ask her. My dear, I must ask you something. You are in a high fever.

KING: It is too true.

Her lotus-chains that were as white
As moonbeams shining in the night,
Betray the fever's awful pain,
And fading, show a darker stain.

SHAKUNTALA (*half rising*): Well, say whatever you like.

ANUSUYA: Shakuntala dear, you have not told us what is going on in your mind. But I have heard old, romantic stories, and I can't help thinking that you are in a state like that of a lady in love. Please tell us what hurts you. We have to understand the disease before we can even try to cure it.

KING: Anusuya expresses my own thoughts.

SHAKUNTALA: It hurts me terribly. I can't tell you all at once.

PRIYAMVADA: Anusuya is right, dear. Why do you hide your trouble? You are wasting away every day. You are nothing but a beautiful shadow.

KING: Priyamvada is right. See!

Her cheeks grow thin; her breast and shoulders fail;
Her waist is weary and her face is pale:
She fades for love; oh, pitifully sweet!
As vine-leaves wither in the scorching heat.

SHAKUNTALA (*sighing*): I could not tell any one else. But I shall be a burden to you.

THE TWO FRIENDS: That is why we insist on knowing, dear. Grief must be shared to be endured.

KING:

To friends who share her joy and grief
She tells what sorrow laid her here;

She turned to look her love again
When first I saw her—yet I fear!

SHAKUNTALA: Ever since I saw the good king who protects the pious grove (*She stops and fidgets.*)

THE TWO FRIENDS: Go on, dear.

SHAKUNTALA: I love him, and it makes me feel like this.

THE TWO FRIENDS: Good, good! You have found a lover worthy of your devotion. But of course, a great river always runs into the sea.

KING (*joyfully*): I have heard what I longed to hear.

'Twas love that caused the burning pain;
'Tis love that eases it again;
As when, upon a sultry day,
Rain breaks, and washes grief away.

SHAKUNTALA: Then, if you think best, make the good king take pity upon me. If not, remember that I was.

KING: Her words end all doubt.

PRIYAMVADA (*aside to Anusuya*): Anusuya, she is far gone in love and cannot endure any delay.

ANUSUYA: Priyamvada, can you think of any scheme by which we could carry out her wishes quickly and secretly?

PRIYAMVADA: We must plan about the "secretly." The "quickly" is not hard.

ANUSUYA: How so?

PRIYAMVADA: Why, the good king shows his love for her in his tender glances, and he has been wasting away, as if he were losing sleep.

KING: It is quite true.

The hot tears, flowing down my cheek
All night on my supporting arm
And on its golden bracelet, seek
To stain the gems and do them harm,

The bracelet slipping o'er the scars
Upon the wasted arm, that show
My deeds in hunting and in wars,
All night is moving to and fro.

PRIYAMVADA (*reflecting*): Well, she must write him a love-letter. And I will hide it in a bunch of flowers and see that it gets into the king's hand as if it were a relic of the sacrifice.

ANUSUYA: It is a pretty plan, dear, and it pleases me. What does Shakuntala say?

SHAKUNTALA: I suppose I must obey orders.

PRIYAMVADA: Then compose a pretty little love-song, with a hint of yourself in it.

SHAKUNTALA: I'll try. But my heart trembles, for fear he will despise me.

KING:

Here stands the eager lover, and you pale
For fear lest he disdain a love so kind:
The seeker may find fortune, or may fail;
But how could fortune, seeking, fail to find?

And again:

The ardent lover comes, and yet you fear
Lest he disdain love's tribute, were it brought,
The hope of which has led his footsteps here–
Pearls need not seek, for they themselves are
sought.

THE TWO FRIENDS: You are too modest about your own charms. Would anybody put up a parasol to keep off the soothing autumn moonlight?

SHAKUNTALA (smiling): I suppose I shall have to obey orders. (She meditates.)

KING: It is only natural that I should forget to wink when I see my darling. For

One clinging eyebrow lifted,
As fitting words she seeks,
Her face reveals her passion
For me in glowing cheeks.

SHAKUNTALA: Well, I have thought out a little song. But I haven't anything to write with.

PRIYAMVADA: Here is a lotus-leaf, glossy as a parrot's breast. You can cut the letters in it with your nails.

SHAKUNTALA: Now listen, and tell me whether it makes sense.

THE TWO FRIENDS: Please.

SHAKUNTALA (reads):

I know not if I read your heart aright;
Why, pitiless, do you distress me so?
I only know that longing day and night
Tosses my restless body to and fro,
That yearns for you, the source of all its woe.

KING (advancing):

Though Love torments you, slender maid,
Yet he consumes me quite,
As daylight shuts night-blooming flowers
And slays the moon outright.

THE TWO FRIENDS (perceive the king and rise joyfully): Welcome to the wish that is fulfilled without delay. (Shakuntala tries to rise.)

KING: Do not try to rise, beautiful Shakuntala.

Your limbs from which the strength is fled,
That crush the blossoms of your bed
And bruise the lotus-leaves, may be
Pardoned a breach of courtesy. . . .

ANUSUYA: But, your Majesty, we hear that kings have many favorites. You must act in such a way that our friend may not become a cause of grief to her family.

KING: What more can I say?

Though many queens divide my court,
But two support the throne;[1]
Your friend will find a rival in
The sea-girt earth alone.

THE TWO FRIENDS: We are content. (Shakuntala betrays her joy.)

PRIYAMVADA (aside to Anusuya): Look, Anusuya! See how the dear girl's life is coming back moment by moment—, just like a peahen in summer when the first rainy breezes come.

SHAKUNTALA: You must please ask the king's pardon for the rude things we said when we were talking together.

THE TWO FRIENDS (smiling): Anybody who says it was rude, may ask his pardon. Nobody else feels guilty.

SHAKUNTALA: Your Majesty, pray forgive what we said when we did not know that you were present. I am afraid that we say a great many things behind a person's back.

KING (smiling):

Your fault is pardoned if I may
Relieve my weariness
By sitting on the flower-strewn couch
Your fevered members press.

PRIYAMVADA: But that will not be enough to satisfy him.

SHAKUNTALA (*feigning anger*): Stop! You are a rude girl. You make fun of me when I am in this condition.

ANUSUYA (*looking out of the arbour*): Priyamvada, there is a little fawn, looking all about him. He has probably lost his mother and is trying to find her. I am going to help him.

PRIYAMVADA: He is a frisky little fellow. You can't catch him alone. I'll go with you. (*They start to go.*)

SHAKUNTALA: I will not let you go and leave me alone.

THE TWO FRIENDS (*smiling*): You alone, when the king of the world is with you! (*Exeunt.*)

SHAKUNTALA: Are my friends gone?

Examining the Evidence

1. What does the passage say about true love and the usual marriages the king has already concluded?
2. What are the theatrical techniques Kalidasa uses to entertain his audience?
3. How does the author use aspects of nature to enhance the dramatic effect of his story?
4. How would the two young, innocent friends have known about love?

[1] The king was allowed to have many wives and concubines, mostly arranged for diplomatic reasons. He swears here that Shakuntala would be his preferred wife, equal to the earth itself.

5.5 ADVICE ON PROPER BEHAVIOR

Confucius, *Analects* (c. 479–100 B.C.E.)

Compiled probably by 100 B.C.E. in the form in which it is known today, Confucius's *Analects* document the Chinese philosopher's ideas about human nature, behavior, and the state. Confucius (551–479 B.C.E.) taught that proper conduct in all social interactions instilled in individuals a humaneness that emphasized benevolence and kindness. As did Indian thinkers around the same time, Confucius urged behavior that adhered to a moral code. The *Analects* became the most revered sacred text in the Confucian tradition. As one of the four ancient Confucian texts that were used as official subject matter for civil service examinations in China from 1313 to 1905 C.E., it had a long-lasting and decisive influence on later Chinese history.

Book I

1. The Master said, To learn and at due times to repeat what one has learnt, is that not after all a pleasure? That friends should come to one from afar, is this not after all delightful? To remain unsoured even though one's merits are unrecognized by others, is that not after all what is expected of a gentleman?

2. Master Yu[1] said, Those who in private life behave well towards their parents and elder brothers, in public life seldom show a disposition to resist the authority of their superiors. And as for such men starting a revolution, no instance of it has ever occurred. It is upon the trunk[2] that a gentleman works. When that is firmly set up, the Way grows. And surely proper behavior towards parents and elder brothers is the trunk of Goodness?

3. The Master said, "Clever talk and a pretentious manner" are seldom found in the Good.

4. Master Tseng said, Every day I examine myself on these three points: in acting on behalf of others, have I always been loyal to their interests? In intercourse with my friends, have I always been true to my word? Have I failed to repeat the precepts that have been handed down to me?

[1] **Master Yu:** One of Confucius's followers; we know from other sources that he was not a man of high social status.

[2] **It is upon the trunk:** What is fundamental.

Arthur Waley, trans., *The Analects of Confucius* (London: George Allen & Unwin, 1971), 83–84, 88–93, 102–103, 105–106.

5. The Master said, A country of a thousand war-chariots cannot be administered unless the ruler attends strictly to business, punctually observes his promises, is economical in expenditure, shows affection towards his subjects in general, and uses the labor of the peasantry only at the proper times of year.

6. The Master said, A young man's duty is to behave well to his parents at home and to his elders abroad, to be cautious in giving promises and punctual in keeping them, to have kindly feelings towards everyone, but seek the intimacy of the Good. If, when all that is done, he has any energy to spare, then let him study the polite arts. . . .

Book II

1. The Master said, He who rules by moral force is like the polestar, which remains in its place while all the lesser stars do homage to it.

2. The Master said, If out of the three hundred *Songs* I had to take one phrase to cover all my teaching, I would say "Let there be no evil in your thoughts."

3. The Master said, Govern the people by regulations, keep order among them by chastisements, and they will flee from you, and lose all self-respect. Govern them by moral force, keep order among them by ritual, and they will keep their self-respect and come to you of their own accord.

4. The Master said, At fifteen I set my heart upon learning. At thirty, I had planted my feet firm upon the ground. At forty, I no longer suffered from perplexities. At fifty, I knew what were the biddings of Heaven. At sixty, I heard them with docile ear. At seventy, I could follow the dictates of my own heart; for what I desired no longer overstepped the boundaries of right.

5. Meng I Tzu asked about the treatment of parents. The Master said, Never disobey! When Fan Ch'ih [a disciple] was driving his carriage for him, the Master said, Meng asked me about the treatment of parents and I said, Never disobey! Fan Ch'ih said, In what sense did you mean it? The Master said, While they are alive, serve them according to ritual. When they die, bury them according to ritual and sacrifice to them according to ritual.

6. Meng Wu Po asked about the treatment of parents. The Master said, Behave in such a way that your father and mother have no anxiety about you, except concerning your health.

7. Tzu-yu asked about the treatment of parents. The Master said, "Filial sons" nowadays are people who see to it that their parents get enough to eat. But even dogs and horses are cared for to that extent. If there is no feeling of respect, wherein lies the difference?

8. Tzu-hsia asked about the treatment of parents. The Master said, It is the demeanor that is difficult. Filial piety does not consist merely in young people undertaking the hard work, when anything has to be done, or serving their elders first with wine and food. It is something much more than that.

9. The Master said, I can talk to Yen Hui[3] a whole day without his ever differing from me. One would think he was stupid. But if I enquire into his private conduct when he is not with me I find that it fully demonstrates what I have taught him. No, Hui is by no means stupid.

10. The Master said, Look closely into his aims, observe the means by which he pursues them, discover what brings him content—and can the man's real worth remain hidden from you, can it remain hidden from you?

11. The Master said, He who by reanimating the Old can gain knowledge of the New is fit to be a teacher.

12. The Master said, A gentleman is not an implement.[4]

13. Tzu-kung asked about the true gentleman. The Master said, He does not preach what he practices till he has practiced what he preaches.

14. The Master said, A gentleman can see a question from all sides without bias. The small man is biased and can see a question only from one side.

15. The Master said, "He who learns but does not think, is lost." He who thinks but does not learn is in great danger.

16. The Master said, He who sets to work upon a different strand destroys the whole fabric.

[3] **Yen Hui:** Confucius's favorite.

[4] **implement:** Someone with specialized skills. A gentleman instead needs all-around moral qualifications.

17. The Master said, Yu, shall I teach you what knowledge is? When you know a thing, to recognize that you know it, and when you do not know a thing, to recognize that you do not know it. That is knowledge.

18. Tzu-chang was studying the *Song* Han-lu.[5] The Master said, Hear much, but maintain silence, as regards doubtful points and be cautious in speaking of the rest; then you will seldom get into trouble. See much, but ignore what it is dangerous to have seen, and be cautious in acting upon the rest; then you will seldom want to undo your acts. He who seldom gets into trouble about what he has said and seldom does anything that he afterwards wishes he had not done, will be sure incidentally to get his reward.

19. Duke Ai asked, What can I do in order to get the support of the common people? Master Kong replied, If you "raise up the straight and set them on top of the crooked," the commoners will support you. But if you raise the crooked and set them on top of the straight, the commoners will not support you.

20. Chi K'ang-tzu asked whether there were any form of encouragement by which he could induce the common people to be respectful and loyal. The Master said, Approach them with dignity, and they will respect you. Show piety towards your parents and kindness towards your children, and they will be loyal to you. Promote those who are worthy, train those who are incompetent; that is the best form of encouragement.

21. Someone, when talking to Master Kong, said, How is it that you are not in the public service? The Master said, The Book, says: "Be filial, only be filial and friendly towards your brothers, and you will be contributing to government." There are other sorts of service quite different from what you mean by "service."

22. The Master said, I do not see what use a man can be put to, whose word cannot be trusted. How can a wagon be made to go if it has no yoke-bar or a carriage, if it has no collar-bar?

23. Tzu-chang asked whether the state of things ten generations hence could be foretold. The Master said, We know in what ways the Yin modified ritual when they followed upon the Hsia.[6] We know in what ways the Zhou modified ritual when they followed upon the Yin. And hence we can foretell what the successors of Zhou will be like, even supposing they do not appear till a hundred generations from now.

24. The Master said, Just as to sacrifice to ancestors other than one's own is presumption, so to see what is right and not do it is cowardice.

Book IV

1. The Master said, It is Goodness that gives to a neighborhood its beauty. One who is free to choose, yet does not prefer to dwell among the Good—how can he be accorded the name of wise?

2. The Master said, Without Goodness a man
Cannot for long endure adversity,
Cannot for long enjoy prosperity.
The Good Man rests content with Goodness; he that is merely wise pursues Goodness in the belief that it pays to do so.

3, 4. Of the adage "Only a Good Man knows how to like people, knows how to dislike them," the Master said, He whose heart is in the smallest degree set upon Goodness will dislike no one.

5. Wealth and rank are what every man desires; but if they can only be retained to the detriment of the Way he professes, he must relinquish them. Poverty and obscurity are what every man detests; but if they can only be avoided to the detriment of the Way he professes, he must accept them. The gentleman who ever parts company with Goodness does not fulfill that name. Never for a moment does a gentleman quit the way of Goodness. He is never so harried but that he cleaves to this; never so tottering but that he cleaves to this. . . .

---

[5] *Song* **Han-lu:** From the *Book of Songs*.

[6] **Yin . . . Hsia:** Early dynasties before the Shang in Chinese tradition.

16. The Master said, A gentleman takes as much trouble to discover what is right as lesser men take to discover what will pay.

17. The Master said, In the presence of a good man, think all the time how you may learn to equal him. In the presence of a bad man, turn your gaze within!

18. The Master said, In serving his father and mother a man may gently remonstrate with them. But if he sees that he has failed to change their opinion, he should resume an attitude of deference and not thwart them; may feel discouraged, but not resentful.

19. The Master said, While father and mother are alive, a good son does not wander far afield; or if he does so, goes only where he has said he was going.

20. The Master said, If for the whole three years of mourning a son manages to carry on the household exactly as in his father's day, then he is a good son indeed.

21. The Master said, It is always better for a man to know the age of his parents. In the one case such knowledge will be a comfort to him; in the other, it will fill him with a salutary dread.

22. The Master said, In old days a man kept a hold on his words, fearing the disgrace that would ensue should he himself fail to keep pace with them.

23. The Master said, Those who err on the side of strictness are few indeed!

24. The Master said, A gentleman covets the reputation of being slow in word but prompt in deed.

Examining the Evidence

1. Why do you think "filial piety" (respect for parents and ancestors) plays such a primary role in Confucian philosophy? How is this devotion to be expressed? How does Confucius connect proper behavior toward one's family with proper government?
2. How should a ruler behave, and how should he treat his subjects?
3. What qualities should a gentleman possess?
4. Analyze the description of Confucius's own intellectual development in Book II. Why do you think he was able to "follow the dictates of [his] own heart" at age seventy?

5.6 GOVERNMENT MONOPOLIES

Huan Kuan, *The Debate on Salt and Iron* (81 B.C.E.)

Inspired by legalism, Emperor Wu (r. 141–87 B.C.E.) of the Han dynasty pursued activist policies to generate revenue to pay for his military campaigns: he manipulated coinage, confiscated the lands of nobles, sold offices and titles, and increased taxes. He also established government monopolies in the production of iron, salt, and liquor, enterprises that had previously been sources of great profit for private entrepreneurs. Large-scale grain dealing had also been a profitable business, which the government now took over under the name of equable marketing. Under this system, grain was to be bought where it was plentiful and inexpensive and either stored in granaries or transported to areas of scarcity. This procedure was supposed to eliminate speculation in grain, provide more constant prices, and bring profit to the government. Confucian scholars questioned the morality of these policies, and after Emperor Wu's death in 81 B.C.E., the new emperor invited them to argue their case with the chief minister. The passage here records the start of the debate.

Translation by Richard Von Glahn.

In 81 B.C.E. an imperial edict directed the chancellor and chief minister to confer with a group of wise and learned men about the people's hardships.

THE LEARNED MEN RESPONDED: We have heard that the Way of governing the people lies in guarding against frivolity and extravagance while enlarging morality and virtue, in suppressing the pursuit of base profit while opening the way for benevolence and duty. Only if the people are not exposed to the temptations of lucre can moral teachings thrive and the customs and habits of the people be improved.

Recently, salt and iron monopolies, a liquor excise tax, and a so-called "equitable marketing" system have been established throughout the realm which compete with the people for the profits of commerce. The native simplicity and magnanimity of the people has been dissipated, and instead they have become rude and greedy. For this reason few of the common folk stick to farming; rather, they flock to the secondary occupations. Now, when artifice flourishes, simplicity declines; when the secondary occupations prosper, farmers are impoverished. If the ruler devotes himself to the secondary occupations, the people become decadent; when he is devoted to the primary occupation, they remain simple. If the people are simple, their means will suffice for their needs; if they are extravagant, cold and hunger ensue.

We seek the abolition of the monopolies on salt, iron, and liquor and the system of equitable marketing so that the primary occupation will be encouraged and the people will be deterred from pursuing the secondary occupations. We benefit from increasing the rewards yielded by agriculture.

THE MINISTER: The Xiongnu have violated the truce and refuse to recognize the imperial authority of Han, frequently raiding and pillaging frontier settlements. Defending the realm places a great strain on the armies of the Central Kingdom, but if we take no action these forays and depredations will never cease. The late Emperor (i.e., Emperor Wu) felt sympathy for the long-suffering frontier settlers who live in fear of capture by these dogs (i.e, the Xiongnu). Therefore he built forts and signal beacon stations to provide a bulwark against foreign incursions. Since the revenues obtained from the frontier territories fell short, the Emperor instituted the salt and iron monopolies, the liquor levy, and the equitable-marketing system. By accumulating stocks of goods and increasing revenues he defrayed the costs of frontier defense.

Now our critics wish to abolish these measures. They would deplete the treasuries and storehouses in the capital, and deprive our frontier troops of the funds they need to ensure our protection. The soldiers manning the forts and guarding the Great Wall would perish from hunger and cold, since there is no other way to supply them. What benefit would come from abolition of these measures?

THE LEARNED MEN: Confucius observed: "The ruler of a state or the head of a household fears not scarcity but inequity; he fears not poverty but discontent" (Analects XIII.16). For this reason the Son of Heaven does not speak of plenty and scarcity, the noble lords do not speak of profit and deficit, nor do the ministers of state speak of gain or loss. Instill benevolence and duty in order to transform the people through suasion rather than coercion, and expand moral conduct in order to express concern for their welfare. Then the neighboring peoples will meekly defer to the emperor's authority and even distant kingdoms will gladly submit to his rule. Thus the skillful conqueror need not engage in battle; the skillful warrior has no need of soldiers; and the skillful general need not array his troops in battle formation.

If the ruler conducts himself properly in the ancestral temple and the court, he need only make a bold show of force and then bring home his troops. The king who practices benevolent government has no peer on earth. What need has he to expend funds?

THE MINISTER: The Xiongnu are savage and cunning. They brazenly storm through the frontier passes and encroach upon the territory of the Central Kingdom, attacking and killing provincial officials and frontier officers. Their incorrigibly lawless and refractory behavior has long deserved fitting punishment. Your Majesty graciously takes pity on the financial exigencies of the multitude and cannot bear to expose Your officers and soldiers on the field of battle. Still, we are dedicated to girding ourselves in battle-dress and taking up arms to drive the Xiongnu back beyond the northern border.

I again assert that doing away with the salt and iron monopolies and equitable marketing system would gravely diminish resources for defense and compromise military strategy. I cannot endorse a proposal that so sorely neglects frontier defense.

THE LEARNED MEN: The ancients honored government by virtue and discredited the use of arms. Confucius said, "When distant subjects are refuse to submit, then the ruler must attract them by enhancing his refinement and virtue, and once they have arrived he makes them content" (Analects XVI.1). At present, moral teachings have been discarded in favor of relying on military force. Troops are raised for campaigns and garrisons are manned for defense. The lengthy campaigns expose our soldiers on the frontier to privation and hardship, while the ceaseless transportation of provisions burdens our people at home. The establishment of the salt and iron monopolies was intended to be a temporary expediency, not a permanent policy. Thus it behooves us to abolish them.

THE MINISTER: The ancient founders of our realm laid the groundwork for both the primary and secondary occupations to facilitate exchange between producers and consumers, providing marketplaces so that all could obtain the goods they desired. Noble and commoner mingled together in the market, where every kind of commodity was gathered in one place. The farmer, the merchant, and the artisan could each satisfy his needs by exchanging what he had for what he wanted. The Book of Changes says, "Facilitate exchange so that the people will not be overworked." Thus, without artisans the farmers will lack tools, and without merchants neither luxuries nor staples will be available. If farmers lack tools, grain is not planted, and when luxuries and staples are unavailable, both the state and the people will be impoverished. Now, the salt and iron monopolies and the equitable marketing system are intended to circulate accumulations of wealth and adjust the supply of and demand for goods. Surely it would be unwise to abolish them.

THE LEARNED MEN: Guide the people with virtue, and they will be inspired by magnanimity; entice the people with profit, and they will sink into depravity. Depraved habits will cause the people to turn their backs on duty in pursuit of self-interest. Soon the common folk will throng the thoroughfares and marketplaces. When Laozi[1] said, "A poor country will appear to have a surplus," he was not speaking of a surfeit of material wealth. When wants and desires multiply the people become restless. For this reason the true king promotes the primary occupation and discourages trade and crafts. He restrains the people through ritual and duty. Wishing to ensure a sufficiency of grain and goods, he makes certain that in the marketplaces merchants do not trade in worthless goods and artisans do not make shoddy tools.

The purpose of merchants is to circulate goods, and the purpose of artisans is to furnish tools. These matters are not the primary concern of government.

THE MINISTER: Guanzi[2] is reported to have said, "If a country possesses fertile land and yet its people are underfed, the reason is that there are not enough tools. If a country possesses rich natural resources in its mountains and seas and yet the people remain poor, the reason is that there are not enough merchants and artisans."

Crimson lacquer and pennant feathers from Sichuan and Shaanxi; leather goods, bone, and

---

[1] **Laozi:** The author of the *Classic of Integrity and the Way*.

[2] **Guanzi:** A text written by Guan Zhong, a seventh-century B.C.E. minister who was famous for his economic policies.

ivory from Hunan and Hubei; cedar, catalpa, bamboo, and thatch from south of the Yangzi River; fish, salt, felt, and furs from the northeast; silk yarn, linen, and hemp cloth from Shandong and Henan—all are necessary to nourish us in life or provide for us in death. We depend on artisans for their production and merchants for their distribution. Therefore the ancient sages built boats to cross rivers and domesticated cattle and horses to cross mountains and plains. By traveling to distant lands and exploring remote places they were able to trade a multitude of goods for the benefit of the people.

Thus, the late Emperor appointed Iron Commissioners to meet the needs of farmers, and initiated the equitable marketing system to assure an adequate supply of goods for the people. The bulk of the population looks to the salt and iron monopolies and the equitable marketing system as the sources for the goods they require. Abolishing them would cause hardship.

THE LEARNED MEN: The ancients, when levying taxes on the people, only requisitioned goods the people were skilled at producing and never demanded goods that the people knew not how to make. Farmers contributed their harvest, and women weavers the fruits of their skill. Now the government ignores what the people have and exacts what they lack. The common folk must sell their products cheaply to satisfy the demands of the ruler. Recently, some of the commanderies and fiefdoms ordered the people to produce linen and wool. Having imposed this burden on the people, the local officials then sold them the cloth they needed to submit as tax payments. The officials requisitioned not only the renowned fine silks of Qi and Tao and the broadcloth of Shu and Han, but even the ordinary cloth people make. These heinous officials then could sell these textiles at whatever price they dictated. The farmers suffered twice over and women weavers were doubly taxed. Where is the "equity" in this marketing system?

Government officials swarm into the marketplaces to corner the supply of goods. With the supply of goods cornered, prices soar and merchants profit from speculation. Buying on their own account, officials resort to all kinds of trickery and intimidation. Powerful officials and wealthy merchants are able to hoard commodities in expectation of future demand. Quick traders and unscrupulous officials buy low and sell high. Where is the "balance" in this standard?

The equitable marketing system of antiquity aimed at facilitating the submission of tribute while ensuring that the tax burden is shared equally among the people. It surely was not intended to involve the government in the exchange of goods for the sake of profit.

Examining the Evidence

1. Examine the arguments of both sides of the debate. Why do the learned men call for the abolition of the monopolies? According to the minister, what would happen if these policies were abolished?
2. How do the learned men use writings of intellectuals like Confucius, Laozi, and others to support their case?
3. Is there a connection between government interference in the economy and corruption?
4. What aspects of the debate remind you of today's political culture?

5.7 WHAT LAW TO OBEY: HUMAN OR DIVINE?

Sophocles, *Antigone* (c. 441 B.C.E.)

The ancient Greeks often receive praise for their focus on the human mind and the power of rational thought, and their philosophers deserve credit for their attempts to explain human and natural phenomena without relying on the workings of the gods. This did not mean, however, that the divine was without meaning to them; the issue of human versus divine law was a complicated one. In Sophocles' (c. 496–406 B.C.E.) tragedy *Antigone*, the king of Thebes, Creon, prohibited the burial of Polyneices, the brother of Antigone and Ismene, who had attacked the city under its previous ruler, Eteocles, another brother. Antigone took the lead in disobeying the order, and when a guard caught her, he took her to Creon. The ensuing discussion centers on the confrontation between human and divine law.

GUARD: It was like this: when we got back again
  struck with those dreadful threatenings of yours,
  we swept away the dust that hid the corpse.
  We stripped it back to slimy nakedness.
  And then we sat to windward on the hill
  so as to dodge the smell.
  We poked each other up with growling threats
  if anyone was careless of his work.
  For some time this went on, till it was noon.
  The sun was high and hot. Then from the earth
  up rose a dusty whirlwind to the sky,
  filling the plain, smearing the forest-leaves,
  clogging the upper air. We shut our eyes,
  sat and endured the plague the gods had sent.
  So the storm left us after a long time.
  We saw the girl. She cried the sharp and shrill
  cry of a bitter bird which sees the nest
  bare where the young birds lay.
  So this same girl, seeing the body stripped,
  cried with great groanings, cried a dreadful curse
  upon the people who had done the deed.
  Soon in her hands she brought the thirsty dust,

and holding high a pitcher of wrought bronze
  she poured the three libations for the dead.
  We saw this and surged down. We trapped her fast;
  and she was calm. We taxed her with the deeds
  both past and present. Nothing was denied.
  And I was glad, and yet I took it hard.
  One's own escape from trouble makes one glad;
  but bringing friends to trouble is hard grief
  Still, I care less for all these second thoughts
  than for the fact that I myself am safe.
CREON: You there, whose head is drooping to the ground,
  do you admit this, or deny you did it?
ANTIGONE: I say I did it and I don't deny it.
CREON (*to the guard*): Take yourself off wherever you wish to go free of a heavy charge.
CREON (*to Antigone*): You—tell me not at length but in a word.
  You knew the order not to do this thing?
ANTIGONE: I knew, of course I knew. The word was plain.
CREON: And still you dared to overstep these laws?
ANTIGONE: For me it was not Zeus who made that order.
  Nor did that justice who lives with the gods below
  mark out such laws to hold among mankind.
  Nor did I think your orders were so strong
  that you, a mortal man, could over-run
  the gods' unwritten and unfailing laws.
  Not now, nor yesterday's, they always live,
  and no one knows their origin in time.
  So not through fear of any man's proud spirit
  would I be likely to neglect these laws,
  draw on myself the gods' sure punishment.
  I knew that I must die; how could I not?
  even without your warning. If I die
  before my time, I say it is a gain.

Sophocles, *Antigone*, trans. Elizabeth Wyckoff, in *Sophocles I*, ed. David Greene and Richard Lattimore, *The Complete Greek Tragedies* (Chicago: University of Chicago Press, 1954), 172–177.

Who lives in sorrows many as are mine
how shall he not be glad to gain his death?
And so, for me to meet this fate, no grief.
But if I left that corpse, my mother's son,
dead and unburied I'd have cause to grieve
as now I grieve not.
And if you think my acts are foolishness
the foolishness may be in a fool's eye.

CHORUS: The girl is bitter. She's her father's child.
She cannot yield to trouble; nor could he.[1]

CREON: These rigid spirits are the first to fall.
The strongest iron, hardened in the fire,
most often ends in scraps and shatterings.
Small curbs bring raging horses back to terms.
Slave to his neighbor, who can think of pride?
This girl was expert in her insolence
when she broke bounds beyond established
law.
Once she had done it, insolence the second,
to boast her doing, and to laugh in it.
I am no man and she the man instead
if she can have this conquest without pain.
She is my sister's child,[2] but were she child
of closer kin than any at my hearth,
she and her sister should not so escape
their death and doom. I charge Ismene too.
She shared the planning of this burial.
Call her outside. I saw her in the house,
maddened, no longer mistress of herself.
The sly intent betrays itself sometimes
before the secret plotters work their wrong.
I hate it too when someone caught in crime
then wants to make it seem a lovely thing.

ANTIGONE: Do you want more than my arrest and
death?

CREON: No more than that. For that is all I need.

ANTIGONE: Why are you waiting? Nothing that you say
fits with my thought. I pray it never will.
Nor will you ever like to hear my words.
And yet what greater glory could I find
than giving my own brother funeral?
All these would say that they approved my act

did fear not mute them.
(A king is fortunate in many ways,
and most, that he can act and speak at will.)

CREON: None of these others see the case this way.

ANTIGONE: They see, and do not say. You have them
cowed.

CREON: And you are not ashamed to think alone?

ANTIGONE: No, I am not ashamed. When was it shame
to serve the children of my mother's womb?

CREON: It was not your brother who died against
him, then?

ANTIGONE: Full brother, on both sides, my parents'
child.

CREON: Your act of grace, in his regard, is crime.

ANTIGONE: The corpse below would never say it was.

CREON: When you honor him and the criminal just
alike?

ANTIGONE: It was a brother, not a slave, who died.

CREON: Died to destroy this land the other guarded.

ANTIGONE: Death yearns for equal law for all the
dead.

CREON: Not that the good and bad draw equal
shares.

ANTIGONE: Who knows that this is holiness below?

CREON: Never the enemy, even in death, a friend.

ANTIGONE: I cannot share in hatred, but in love.

CREON: Then go down there, if you must love, and
love
the dead. No woman rules me while I live.

Examining the Evidence

1. How does Antigone justify her disobedience?

2. Consider the issue of gender in this passage. How does Creon feel about being challenged by a woman?

3. Creon believes that anyone would agree with him. How does Antigone counter that?

4. Greek tragedies did not use action on stage but focused on the beauty of language. How does Sophocles here inform the audience of the events that led to the confrontation between Creon and Antigone?

5. What does this excerpt suggest about the Greek ideal of individual agency? What role does this play in the conflict between Antigone and Creon?

---

[1] **She . . . nor could he:** Antigone was the daughter of Oedipus, whose stubbornness led to his downfall in Sophocles' tragedy *Oedipus the King.*

[2] **She is my sister's child:** Antigone and Ismene's mother Jocasta was Creon's sister.

MAKING CONNECTIONS

1. In what ways does Confucius's philosophy in the *Analects* (Document 5.5) emerge in the "Debate on Salt and Iron" (Document 5.6)?
2. Compare the advice in the three documents on dharma (Documents 5.1–5.3) to the teachings in Confucius's *Analects*. What shared values can you trace across these belief systems? Do you see any points of contrast?
3. Many of the sources included in this chapter contain words of wisdom and advice; in what literary formats are the ideas communicated? How do the different formats affect how the message is conveyed?
4. What is the importance of debate in these texts?
5. How important is the role of an individual master or leader in the various teachings?

CHAPTER 6

The Unification of Western Eurasia, 500 B.C.E.–500 C.E.

Like the societies of India and China discussed in Chapter 5, the period from 500 B.C.E. to 500 C.E. was also one of great cultural advancement and much literary productivity in western Eurasia. An enormous amount of Roman writings covered numerous aspects of life, ranging from practical subjects such as politics, law, and engineering to more contemplative elements. Once the Romans had absorbed ancient Greek cultural traditions, they elaborated on many of its intellectual and artistic innovations. Poets such as Virgil followed Homer's example when writing about Rome, and historians such as Livy adopted the techniques of Thucydides. Many religious thinkers at the start of the Common Era used the written word to merge ideas from religious texts with those of ancient philosophy. The production and spread of these works profited to a great extent from the success of the empire. Emperors and other wealthy Romans supported authors and thinkers, and the wide geographical range of the empire guaranteed that their ideas could reach a vast audience both in the empire and beyond.

6.1 THE DECLINE OF ROMAN MORAL VALUES

Livy, *Roman Women Protest Against the Oppian Law* (c. 20 B.C.E.)

In 195 B.C.E., the upper-class women of Rome started a protest against the Oppian law, which had been passed during the Second Punic War (218–201 B.C.E.) to reduce friction between rich and poor. The law restricted the amount of luxuries that women could display in public and the use of carriages, but the new generation of rich women considered these restrictions no longer acceptable. They pressured male magistrates to change the law, which most of them were willing to do. However, the conservative consul Cato objected to overturning the law; his speech is reproduced in the *Early History of Rome*, written by the Roman historian Livy between the late first century B.C.E. and the early first century C.E.

The crowd of women grew larger day by day; for they were now coming in from the towns and rural districts. Soon they dared even to approach and appeal to the consuls, the praetors [magistrates], and the other officials, but one consul, at least, they found adamant, Marcus Porcius Cato, who spoke thus in favor of the law whose appeal was being urged.

"If each of us, citizens, had determined to assert his rights and dignity as a husband with respect to his own spouse, we should have less trouble with the sex as a whole; as it is, our liberty, destroyed at home by female violence, even here in the Forum crushed and trodden underfoot, and because we have not kept them individually under control, we dread them collectively. For my part, I thought it a fairy-tale and a piece of fiction that on a certain island all the men were destroyed, root and branch, a conspiracy of women; but from no class is there not the greatest danger if you permit them meetings and gatherings and secret consultations. And I can scarcely decide in my own mind whether the act itself or the precedent it sets is worse; the act concerns us consuls and other magistrates; the example, citizens, rather concerns you. For whether the proposal which is laid before you is in the public interest or not is a question for you who are soon to cast your votes; but this female madness, whether it is spontaneous or due to your instigation, Marcus Fundanius and Lucius Valerius, but which beyond question brings discredit upon the magistrates — I do not know, I say, whether this madness is more shameful for you, tribunes, or for the consuls: for you, if you have brought these women here to support tribunicial seditions; for us, if we must accept laws given us by a secession of women, as formerly by a secession of plebeians.

"For myself, I could not conceal my blushes a while ago when I had to make my way to the Forum through a crowd of women. Had not respect for the dignity and modesty of some individuals among them rather than of the sex as a whole kept me silent, lest they should seem to have been rebuked by a consul, I should have said, 'What sort of practice is this, of running out into the streets and blocking the roads and speaking to other women's husbands? Could you not have made the same requests, each of your own husband, at home? Or are you more attractive outside and to other women's husbands than to your own? And yet, not even at home, if modesty would keep matrons within the limits of their proper rights, did it become you to concern yourselves with the question of what laws should be adopted in this place or repealed.' Our ancestors permitted no woman to conduct even personal business without a guardian to intervene in her behalf; they wished them to be under the control of fathers, brothers, husbands; we (Heaven help us!)

allow them now even to interfere in public affairs, yes, and to visit the Forum and our informal and formal sessions. What else are they doing now on the streets and at the corners except urging the bill of the tribunes and voting for the repeal of the law? Give loose rein to their uncontrollable nature and to this untamed creature and expect that they will themselves set bounds to their license; unless you act, this is the least of the things enjoined upon women by custom or law and to which they submit with a feeling of injustice. It is complete liberty or, rather, if we wish to speak the truth, complete license that they desire.

"If they win in this, what will they not attempt? Review all the laws with which your forefathers restrained their license and made them subject to their husbands; even with all these bonds you can scarcely control them. What of this? If you suffer them to seize these bonds one by one and wrench themselves free and finally to be placed on a parity with their husbands, do you think that you will be able to endure them? The moment they begin to be your equals, they will be your superiors. But, by Hercules, they object to the passage of any new law against them, they complain not of law but of wrongs done them; what they want, rather, is that you repeal this law which you have approved and ratified and which in the trial and experience of so many years you found good: in other words, that by abolishing this one law you weaken the force of all the rest. . . .

What pretext, respectable even to mention, is now given for this insurrection of the women? 'That we may glitter with gold and purple,' says one, 'that we may ride in carriages on holidays and ordinary days, that we may be borne through the city as if in triumph over the conquered and vanquished law and over the votes which we have captured and wrested from you; that there may be no limits to our spending and our luxury.'

"You have often heard me complaining of the women and often of the men, both private citizens and magistrates even, and lamenting that the state is suffering from those two opposing evils, avarice and luxury, which have been the destruction of every great empire. The better and the happier becomes the fortune of our commonwealth day by day and the greater the empire grows — and already we have crossed into Greece and Asia, places filled with all the allurements of vice, and we are handling the treasures of kings — the more I fear that these things will capture us rather than we them. Tokens of danger, believe me, were those statues which were brought to this city from Syracuse.[1] Altogether too many people do I hear praising the baubles of Corinth and Athens and laughing at the fictile antefixes of our Roman gods.[2] I prefer that these gods be propitious to us, and I trust that they will be if we allow them to remain in their own dwellings. In the memory of our forefathers Pyrrhus,[3] through his agent Cineas, tried to corrupt with gifts the minds of our men and women as well. Not yet had the Oppian law been passed to curb female extravagance, yet not one woman took his gifts. What do you think was the reason? The same thing which caused our ancestors to pass no law on the subject: there was no extravagance to be restrained. As it is necessary that diseases be known before their cures, so passions are born before the laws which keep them within bounds. What provoked the Licinian law[4] about the five hundred iugera except the uncontrolled desire of joining field to field? What brought about the Cincian law[5] except that the plebeians had already begun to be vassals and tributaries to the senate? And so it is not strange that no Oppian or any other law was needed to limit female extravagance at the time when they spurned gifts of gold and purple voluntarily offered to them. If it were today that Cineas were going about the city with those presents he would have found women standing in the streets to receive them. And for some desires I can find no

---

[1] **statues . . . from Syracuse:** Cato refers to Greek statues brought to Rome after the capture of Syracuse in 212 B.C.E., which changed Roman taste in art.

[2] **antefixes . . . gods:** Clay ornaments that were placed on early Roman temples, seemingly considered old-fashioned at this time.

[3] **Pyrrhus:** A Hellenistic Greek king who attacked Rome in the early third century.

[4] **Licinian law:** A law that limited the amount of public land that an individual could own.

[5] **Cincian law:** A law that forbade advocates to charge fees for their services.

reason or explanation. For though it may perhaps cause some natural shame or even anger that what is denied to you is permitted to another, yet, when the dress of all is made alike, what is there which any of you fears will not be conspicuous in herself? The worst kind of shame, I tell you, is that derived from stinginess or poverty; but the law takes from you the chance of either, since you do not have what it is not allowed you to have. 'It is just this equality that I will not put up with,' says yonder rich woman. 'Why do I not stand out conspicuous by reason of gold and purple? Why does the poverty of other women lie concealed under cover of this law, that it may seem that, had it been legal, they would have owned what it is not in their power to own?' Do you wish, citizens, to start a race like this among your wives, so that the rich shall want to own what no other woman can have and the poor, lest they be despised for their poverty, shall spend beyond their means? Once let these women begin to be ashamed of what they should not be ashamed, and they will not be ashamed of what they ought. She who can buy from her own purse will buy; she who cannot will beg her husband. Poor wretch that husband, both he who yields and he who yields not, since what he will not himself give he will see given by another man. Now they publicly address other women's husbands, and, what is more serious, they beg for a law and votes, and

from sundry men they get what they ask. In matters affecting yourself, your property, your children, you, Sir, can be importuned; once the law has ceased to set a limit to your wife's expenditures you will never set it yourself. Do not think, citizens, that the situation which existed before the law was passed will ever return. It is safer for a criminal to go unaccused than to be acquitted; and luxury, left undisturbed, would have been more endurable then than it will be now, when it has been, like a wild beast, first rendered angry by its very fetters and then let loose. My opinion is that the Oppian law should on no account be repealed; whatever is your decision, I pray that all the gods may prosper it."

Examining the Evidence

1. How does Cato connect the women's demands to other social pressures in Rome?
2. What objections does he have against the women's behavior?
3. What does Cato tell us about the status of women in both public and private life in early Rome?
4. Is Cato critical only of women in this excerpt?
5. How does Cato explain the origins of specific laws?
6. How does Cato connect the influx of wealth from the empire to moral decay?

6.2 A GLORIFICATION OF EMPEROR AUGUSTUS

Virgil, *The Aeneid* (19 B.C.E.)

Augustus (r. 31 B.C.E.–14 C.E.) was a vigorous sponsor of the arts, and scholars regard his reign as the golden age of Roman art, architecture, and literature. Under Augustus, Rome was transformed into a city with majestic marble buildings and statuary. Although the emperor and his friends generously supported poets and writers, their support was not entirely selfless. In return for their

support, the artists glorified Augustus as the savior of Rome, bringing peace and prosperity. One author who benefited from the emperor's generosity was Virgil, whose epic about Rome's legendary foundation, *The Aeneid*, glorifies Augustus, who for the characters in his poem is a man of the distant future. In one passage, the poet describes the shield that the divine blacksmith Vulcan (also known as Mulciber) made for the hero Aeneas. On the shield are representations of the history

Virgil, *The Aeneid*, trans. Robert Fitzgerald (New York: Vintage, 1983), 253–256.

of the city of Rome, including famous characters such as Romulus and Remus. The final event it depicts is the battle of Actium in 31 B.C.E., in which Augustus defeated Marc Antony (Marcus Antonius) and Cleopatra, and it also portrays Caesar Augustus's triumph after his victory. This victory is represented as the culmination of Rome's glorious history.

> Mid-shield,
> The pictured sea flowed surging, all of gold,
> As whitecaps foamed on the blue waves, and
> dolphins
> Shining in silver round and round the scene
> Propelled themselves with flukes and cut through
> billows.
> Vivid in the center were the bronze-beaked
> Ships and the fight at sea off Actium.
> Here you could see Leucata[1] all alive
> With ships maneuvering, sea glowing gold,
> Augustus Caesar leading into battle
> Italians, with both senators and people,
> Household gods and great gods: there he stood
> High on the stem, and from his blessed brow
> Twin flames gushed upward, while his crest revealed
> His father's star. Apart from him, Agrippa,[2]
> Favored by winds and gods, led ships in column,
> A towering figure, wearing on his brows
> The coronet[3] adorned with warships' beaks,
> Highest distinction for command at sea.
> Then came Antonius with barbaric wealth
> And a diversity of arms, victorious
> From races of the Dawnlands[4] and Red Sea,
> Leading the power of the East, of Egypt,
> Even of distant Bactra of the steppes.
> And in his wake the Egyptian consort came
> So shamefully. The ships all kept together
> Racing ahead, the water torn by oar-strokes,
> Torn by the triple beaks, in spume and foam.
> All made for the open sea. You might believe
> The Cyclades[5] uprooted were afloat
> Or mountains running against mountain heights
> When seamen in those hulks pressed the attack
> Upon the other turreted ships. They hurled
> Broadsides of burning flax on flying steel,
> And fresh blood reddened Neptune's fields.
> The queen
> Amidst the battle called her flotilla on

> With a sistrum's beat, a frenzy out of Egypt,
> Never turning her head as yet to see
> Twin snakes of death behind, while monster forms
> Of gods of every race, and the dog-god
> Anubis barking, held their weapons up
> Against our Neptune, Venus, and Minerva.
> Mars, engraved in steel, raged in the fight
> As from high air the dire Furies came
> With Discord, taking joy in a torn robe,
> And on her heels, with bloody scourge, Bellona.[6]
>
> Overlooking it all, Actian Apollo[7]
> Began to pull his bow. Wild at this sight,
> All Egypt, Indians, Arabians, all
> Sabaeans put about in flight, and she,
> The queen, appeared crying for winds to shift
> just as she hauled up sail and slackened sheets.
> The Lord of Fire had portrayed her there,
> Amid the slaughter, pallid with death to come,
> Then borne by waves and wind from the northwest,
> While the great length of mourning Nile
> awaited her
> With open bays, calling the conquered home
> To his blue bosom and his hidden streams.
> But Caesar then in triple triumph rode
> Within the walls of Rome, making immortal
> Offerings to the gods of Italy—
> Three hundred princely shrines throughout the city.
> There were the streets, humming with festal joy
> And games and cheers, an altar to every shrine,
> To every one a mothers' choir, and bullocks
> Knifed before the altars strewed the ground.
> The man himself, enthroned before the
> snow-white
> Threshold of sunny Phoebus, viewed the gifts
> The nations of the earth made, and he fitted them
> To the tall portals. Conquered races passed
> In long procession, varied in languages
> As in their dress and arms. Here Mulciber,

---

[1] **Leucata:** A promontory near Actium in Greece.

[2] **Agrippa:** The son-in-law and close friend of Augustus.

[3] **coronet:** A small crown.

[4] **Dawnlands:** Eastern countries.

[5] **Cyclades:** Islands to the east of Greece.

[6] **Bellona:** A goddess of war.

[7] **Actian Apollo:** At Actium was a temple to the god Apollo.

Divine smith, had portrayed the Nomad tribes
And Afri with ungirdled flowing robes,
Here Leleges and Carians,[8] and here
Gelonians[9] with quivers. Here Euphrates,
Milder in his floods now, there Morini,[10]
Northernmost of men; here bull-horned Rhine,
And there the still unconquered Scythian Dahae;
Here, vexed at being bridged, the rough Araxes.[11]
All these images on Vulcan's shield,
His mother's gift, were wonders to Aeneas.

Knowing nothing of the events themselves,
He felt joy in their pictures, taking up
Upon his shoulder all the destined acts
And fame of his descendants.

Examining the Evidence

1. Although the battle of Actium was a contest between two Roman generals (Octavian and Antony), the passage describes it as a clash of cultures. What cultures clash here, and how are they in opposition to each other?
2. How does the passage suggest that Augustus became ruler of the universe?
3. How does the poet connect the natural world to human actions?

[8] **Leleges and Carians:** Two peoples from Anatolia.
[9] **Gelonians:** A people of Scythia.
[10] **Morini:** A people of northern Gaul.
[11] **Araxes:** A river in Central Asia.

6.3 MERGING BIBLICAL AND ROMAN IDEAS

Augustine, *City of God* (413–426 C.E.)

In the early centuries of the Common Era, thinkers with training in classical philosophy used their skills to give an intellectual foundation to the new religious ideas of Christianity. Central in this process was the North African bishop Augustine (354–430 C.E.). Augustine left behind numerous writings, most notably his account of his conversion to the new faith, *Confessions*, and *City of God*, which he wrote in installments from 413 to 426 C.E. to defend Christians against the accusation that they caused the sack of Rome in 410. Here Augustine contrasts the origin and development of two cities, the city of God and the earthly city. He exposed biblical text to a reading inspired by classical philosophical traditions, which enabled him to formulate Christian thought as a rational system rooted in Platonic ideals. Augustine's work was widely read in western Europe in the Middle Ages and thereby greatly influenced later Roman Catholic and Protestant thought.

Book XIV.28: The Nature of the Two Cities

What we see, then, is that two societies have issued from two kinds of love. Worldly society has flowered from a selfish love which dared to despise even God, whereas the communion of saints is rooted in a love of God that is ready to trample on the self. In a word, this latter relies on the Lord, whereas the other boasts that it can get along by itself. The city of man seeks the praise of men, whereas the height of glory for the other is to hear God in the witness of conscience. The one lifts up its head in its own boasting; the other says to God: "Thou art my glory, thou liftest up my head."

In the city of the world both the rulers themselves and the people they dominate are dominated by the lust for domination; whereas in the City of God all citizens serve one another in charity, whether they serve by the responsibilities of office or by duties of obedience. The one city loves its

Patrick V. Reid, *The Middle Ages Through the Reformation*, vol. 2, *Readings in Western Religious Thought* (Mahwah, NJ: Paulist Press, 1995), 29–31.

leaders as symbols of its own strength; the other says to its God, "I love thee, O Lord, my strength" (Psalms 17:2). Hence, even the wise men in the city of man live according to man, and their only goal has been the goods of their bodies or of the mind or of both; though some of them have reached a knowledge of God, "they did not glorify him as God or give thanks but became vain in their reasonings, and their senseless minds have been darkened. For while professing to be wise" (that is to say, while glorying in their own wisdom, under the domination of pride), "they have become fools, and they have changed the glory of the incorruptible God for an image made like to corruptible man and to birds and four-footed beasts and creeping things" (meaning that they either led their people, or imitate them, in adoring idols shaped like these things), "and they worshipped and served the creatures rather than the Creator who is blessed forever" (Romans 1:21–25). In the City of God, on the contrary, there is no merely human wisdom, but there is a piety which worships the true God as He should be worshipped and has as its goal that reward of all holiness whether in the society of saints on earth or in that of angels of heaven, which is "that God may be all" (1 Corinthians 15:28).

Book XV.1: The Founder of the Earthly City Was Cain, a Murderer

Now, the first man born of the two parents of the human race was Cain. He belonged to the city of man. The next born was Abel, and he was of the City of God. Notice here a parallel between the individual man and the whole race. We all experience as individuals what the Apostle[1] says: "It is not the spiritual that comes first, but the physical, and then the spiritual" (1 Corinthians 15:46). The fact is that every individual springs from a condemned stock, and because of Adam, must be first cankered and carnal, only later to become sound and spiritual by the process of rebirth in Christ. So, too, with the human race as a whole, as soon as human birth and death began the historical course of the two cities, the first to be born was a citizen of this world and

only later came the one who was an alien in the city of men but at home in the City of God, a man predestined by grace and elected by grace. By grace an alien on earth, by grace he was a citizen of heaven. In and of himself, he springs from the common clay, all of which was under condemnation from the beginning, but which God held in His hands like a potter, to borrow the metaphor which the Apostle so wisely and deliberately uses. For, God could make "from the same mass one vessel for honorable, another for ignoble use" (Romans 9:21). The first vessel to be made was "for ignoble use." Only later was there a vessel for honorable use. And as with the race, so, as I have said, with the individual. First comes the clay that is only fit to be thrown away, with which we must begin, but in which we need not remain. Afterwards comes what is fit for use, that into which we can be gradually molded and in which, when molded, we may remain. This does not mean that every one who is wicked is to become good, but that no one becomes good who was not once wicked. What is true is that the sooner a man makes a change in himself for the better the sooner he has a right to be called what he has become. The second name hides the first.

Now, it is recorded of Cain that he built a city, while Abel, as though he were merely a pilgrim on earth, built none. For, the true City of the saints is in heaven, though here on earth it produces citizens in whom it wanders as on a pilgrimage through time looking for the Kingdom of eternity. When that day comes it will gather together all those who, rising in their bodies, shall have that kingdom given to them in which, along with their Prince, the King of Eternity, they shall reign for ever and ever.

Book XV.5: The Fratricidal Act of the Founder of the Earthly City and the Corresponding Crime of the Founder of Rome

Now, the city of man was first founded by a fratricide who was moved by envy to kill his brother, a man who, in his pilgrimage on earth, was a citizen of the City of God. It need not surprise us, then, that long afterwards, in the founding of that city which was to dominate so many peoples and become the capital of

---

[1] **the Apostle:** A reference to Paul, whose letters are quoted.

that earthly city with which I am dealing, the copy, so to speak, corresponded to the original — to what the Greeks call the archetype. For, in both cases, we have the same crime. As one of the poets puts it: "With brother's blood the earliest walls were wet" (Lucan, *Pharsalia* 1.95).[2] For Rome began, as Roman history records, when Remus was killed by Romulus, his brother. However, in this case, both men were citizens of the earthly city. It was the ambition of both of them to have the honor of founding the Roman republic, but that was an honor that could not be shared; it had to belong to one or the other. For, no one who had a passion to glory in domination could be fully the master if his power were diminished by a living co-regent. One of the two wanted to have the whole of the sovereignty; therefore, his associate was removed. Without the crime, his position would have had less power, but more prestige. However, the crime made everything worse than before.

In the case of the brothers Cain and Abel, there was no rivalry in any cupidity for the things of earth, nor was there any envy or temptation to murder arising from a fear of losing the sovereignty if both were ruling together. In this case, Abel had no ambition for domination in the city that his brother was building. The root of the trouble was that diabolical envy which moves evil men to hate those who are good for no other reason than that they are good. Unlike material possessions, goodness is not diminished when it is shared, either momentarily or permanently, with others, but expands and, in fact the more heartily each of the lovers of goodness enjoys the possession the more does goodness grow. What is more, goodness is not merely a possession that no one can maintain who is unwilling to share it, but it is one that increases the more its possessor loves to share it.

What, then, is revealed in the quarrel between Remus and Romulus is the way in which the city of man is divided against itself, whereas, in the case of Cain and Abel, what we see is the enmity between the two cities, the city of man and the City of God. Thus, we have two wars, that of the wicked at war with the wicked and that of the wicked at war with the good. For, of course, once the good are perfectly good, there can be no war between them. This much is true, however, that while a good man is still on the way to perfection one part of him can be at war with another of his parts; because of this rebellious element, two good men can be at war with each other. The fact is that in every one "the flesh lusts against the spirit, and the spirit against the flesh" (Galatians 5:17).

The spiritual longing of one good man can be at war with the fleshly passion of another just as fleshly passion in one man can resist spiritual tendencies in another. And the war here is much like that between good and wicked men. So, too, a good deal like the war of the wicked against the wicked is the rivalry of fleshly desires in two good men, and this will continue until grace wins the ultimate victory of soundness over sickness in both of them.

Examining the Evidence
1. Explain how Augustine contrasts the city of god to the city of man.
2. In what ways does his focus on the city as an institution fit within the Greek tradition of political thought?
3. How does Augustine use the Bible as a foundation for his arguments?
4. How does he use Roman history as a foundation for his arguments?

---

[2] **Lucan, *Pharsalia* 1.95:** A reference to a history of the civil war between Julius Caesar and Pompey, written by the Roman poet Lucan in the first century B.C.E.

6.4 ROME MEETS THE EAST

The Story of Queen Zenobia (c. 395 C.E.)

The Roman Empire suffered a period of decline in the third century C.E., with weak emperors and internal economic problems. Some eastern states took advantage of the empire's weakness to expand their regional influence and power. One such state was centered on the Syrian oasis city of Palmyra, where King Odaenathus and his wife, Zenobia, established an empire that was so large that it even included Egypt. When the king died, his wife assumed control of the government. In 274 C.E., the Romans finally managed to defeat her and brought her as a prisoner to Rome. The Romans found her a remarkable figure, both because of her engagement in what Romans considered to be men's activities and because she embodied the stereotype of the exotic East. The description of the queen included here appears in a history of various Roman emperors from 117 to 284 C.E., the product of six authors (probably from the late fourth century) known as the Writers of Augustan History.

N ow all shame is exhausted, for in the weakened state of the commonwealth things came to such a pass that, while Gallienus[1] conducted himself in the most evil fashion, even women ruled most excellently. For, in fact, even a foreigner, Zenobia by name, about whom much has already been said, boasting herself to be of the family of the Cleopatras and the Ptolemies, proceeded upon the death of her husband Odaenathus to cast about her shoulders the imperial mantle; and arrayed in the robes of Dido and even assuming the diadem, she held the imperial power in the name of her sons Herennianus and Timolaus, ruling longer than could be endured from one of the female sex. For this proud woman performed the functions of a monarch both while Gallienus was ruling and afterwards when Claudius[2] was busied with the war against the Goths, and in the end could scarcely be conquered by Aurelian[3] himself under whom she was led in triumph and submitted to the sway of Rome.

There is still in existence a letter of Aurelian's which bears testimony concerning this woman, then in captivity. For when some found fault with him, because he, the bravest of men, had led a woman in triumph, as though she were a general, he sent a letter to the senate and the Roman people, defending himself by the following justification: "I have heard, Conscript fathers, that men are reproaching me for having performed an unmanly deed in leading Zenobia in triumph. But in truth those very persons who find fault with me now would accord me praise in abundance, did they but know what manner of woman she is, how wise in counsels, how steadfast in plans, how firm toward the soldiers, how generous when necessity calls, and how stern when discipline demands. I might even say that it was her doing that Odaenathus defeated the Persians and, after putting Sapor[4] to flight, advanced all the way to Ctesiphon.[5] I might add thereto that such was the fear that this woman inspired in the peoples of the East and also the Egyptians that neither Arabs nor Saracens nor Armenians ever moved against her. Nor would I have spared her life, had I not known that she did a great service to the Roman state when she preserved the imperial power in the East for herself, or for her children. Therefore let those whom nothing pleases keep the venom of their own tongues to themselves. For if it is not suitable to vanquish a woman

[1] **Gallienus:** Roman emperor from 253 to 268 C.E.

[2] **Claudius:** Emperor from 268 to 270 C.E.

[3] **Aurelian:** Emperor from 270 to 275 C.E.

[4] **Sapor:** The Sasanid king Shapur I.

[5] **Ctesiphon:** A Sasanid royal city in Mesopotamia.

Reprinted by permission of the publishers and the Trustees of the Loeb Classical Library from *Scriptores Historiae Augustae: Volume III*, Loeb Classical Library Volume 263, translated by David Magie, pp. 135, 137, 139, 141, 143. Cambridge, MA: Harvard University Press, 1932. Loeb Classical Library® is a registered trademark of the President and Fellows of Harvard College.

and lead her in triumph, what are they saying of Gallienus, in contempt of whom she ruled the empire well? What of the Deified Claudius, that revered and honored leader? For he, because he was busied with his campaigns against the Goths, suffered her, or so it is said, to hold the imperial power, doing it of purpose and wisely, in order that he himself, while she kept guard over the eastern frontier of the empire, might the more safely complete what he had taken in hand." This speech shows what opinion Aurelian held concerning Zenobia.

Such was her continence, it is said, that she would not know even her own husband save for the purpose of conception. For when once she had lain with him, she would refrain until the time of menstruation to see if she were pregnant; if not, she would again grant him an opportunity of begetting children. She lived in regal pomp. It was rather in the manner of the Persians that she received worship and in the manner of the Persian kings that she banqueted; but it was in the manner of a Roman emperor that she came forth to public assemblies, wearing a helmet and girt with a purple fillet, which had gems hanging from the lower edge, while its center was fastened with the jewel called cochlis,[6] used instead of the brooch worn by women, and her arms were frequently bare. Her face was dark and of a swarthy hue, her eyes were black and powerful beyond the usual wont, her spirit divinely great, and her beauty incredible. So white were her teeth that many thought that she had pearls in place of teeth. Her voice was clear and like that of a man. Her sternness, when necessity demanded, was that of a tyrant, her clemency when her sense of right called for it, that of a good emperor. Generous with prudence, she conserved her treasures beyond the wont of women. She made use of a carriage, and rarely of a woman's coach, but more often she rode a horse; it is said, moreover, that frequently she walked with her foot-soldiers for three or four miles. She hunted with the eagerness of a Spaniard. She often drank with her generals, though at other times she refrained, and she drank, too, with the Persians and the Armenians, but only for the purpose of getting the better of them. At her banquets she used vessels of gold and jewels, and she even used those that had been Cleopatra's.

As servants she had eunuchs of advanced age and but very few maidens. She ordered her sons to talk Latin, so that, in fact, they spoke Greek but rarely and with difficulty. She herself was not wholly conversant with the Latin tongue, but nevertheless, mastering her timidity she would speak it; Egyptian, on the other hand, she spoke very well. In the history of Alexandria and the Orient she was so well versed that she even composed an epitome [summary], so it is said; Roman history, however, she read in Greek.

When Aurelian had taken her prisoner, he caused her to be led into his presence and then addressed her thus: "Why is it, Zenobia, that you dared to show insolence to the emperors of Rome?" To this she replied, it is said: "You, I know, are an emperor indeed, for you win victories, but Gallienus and Aureolus and the others I never regarded as emperors. Believing Victoria to be a woman like me, I desired to become a partner in the royal power, should the supply of lands permit." And so she was led in triumph with such magnificence that the Roman people had never seen a more splendid parade. For, in the first place, she was adorned with gems so huge that she labored under the weight of her ornaments; for it is said that this woman, courageous though she was, halted very frequently, saying that she could not endure the load of her gems. Furthermore, her feet were bound with shackles of gold and her hands with golden fetters, and even on her neck she wore a chain of gold, the weight of which was borne by a Persian buffoon [court jester]. Her life was granted her by Aurelian, and they say that thereafter she lived with her children in the manner of a Roman matron on an estate that had been presented to her at Tibur, which even to this day is still called Zenobia, not far from the palace of Hadrian or from that place which bears the name of Concha.

Examining the Evidence

1. How, in the author's estimation, does Zenobia compare to Roman emperors of the third century C.E.? How does her depiction reinforce the image of Roman decline?
2. How does Zenobia confuse gender roles, and how does Aurelian address this issue?
3. How does Zenobia's description reinforce the stereotypes of the exotic East?

---

[6] **cochlis:** A large precious stone found in Arabia.

6.5 RELIGIOUS DEBATES IN THE EARLY CENTURIES C.E.

Mani, *The Three Great Founders* (c. 250 C.E.)

Many new religions developed in the modern Middle East in the first centuries C.E., often sharing crucial concepts and building on older religions from the region and adjacent areas. Among those new religions, the teachings of Mani (c. 250 C.E.) were very popular. He acknowledged his debt to Judaism, Christianity, Zoroastrianism, and Buddhism but saw his ideas as superior. Manicheanism became persecuted in the Roman Empire and in the Middle East, but its ideas are accessible to us from a variety of writings in various languages, often presented as statements that Mani himself made. The passage reproduced here derives from a collection of manuscripts discovered in Egypt, dating to around 400 C.E. and written in the Christian Coptic language. Here, the teacher discusses the relationship of his ideas to those of Jesus, Zoroaster, and the Buddha.

From the Introduction

My beloved ones: At the time that Jesus trod . . . the land of the west . . . He proclaimed his hope . . . his disciples . . . which Jesus uttered . . . after him they wrote . . . his parables . . . and the signs and wonders . . . they wrote a book concerning his . . .

The Apostle of Light, the glorious Illuminator[1] . . . he came to Persia, to Hystaspes the king[2] . . . he chose disciples, righteous men of truth . . . he proclaimed his hope in Persia. But . . . Zoroaster too did not write books. Rather, his disciples who came after him, they remembered; they wrote . . . that they read today . . .

[1] **The glorious Illuminator:** Zoroaster.
[2] **Hystaspes the king:** According to Zoroastrian tradition a Persian ruler, Hystaspes, was the patron of the prophet.

Again, for his part, when Buddha came . . . about him, for he too proclaimed his hope and great wisdom. He chose his churches, and perfected his churches. He unveiled to them his hope. And yet he too did not write his wisdom in books. His disciples who came after him are the ones who remembered something of the wisdom that they had heard from Buddha. They wrote it in scriptures.

From Chapter 1

The advent of Jesus the Christ, our Master. He came . . . in a spiritual (form), in a body . . . as I have told you about him. I . . . him; for he came without a body, and, as his apostles have preached concerning him, he received a servant's form, an appearance as of men. He came below. He manifested in the world in the sect of the Jews. He chose his Twelve and his Seventy-two. He did the will of his Father who had sent him into the world.

Afterwards, the Evil One awoke envy in the sect of the Jews. Satan entered into Judas the Iscariot, one among the Twelve of Jesus. He accused him before the sect of the Jews with his kiss. He gave him over into the hands of the Jews, and the cohort of the soldiers. The Jews themselves took hold of the Son of God. They passed judgment upon him in their lawlessness, in their assembly. They condemned him in their iniquity, though he had not sinned. They lifted him up on the wood of the Cross. They crucified him with some robbers on the Cross.

They brought him down from the Cross. They placed him in the grave; and after three days he arose from among the dead. He came towards his disciples, and was visible to them. He laid upon them a power. He breathed into them his Holy Spirit. He sent them out through the whole world, that they would preach the Greatness. Yet he himself rose up to the heights. . . .

Andrew Welburn, *Mani, the Angel and the Column of Glory: An Anthology of Manichaean Texts* (Edinburgh: Floris Books, 1998), 210–212.

. . . while the Apostles stood in the world, Paul the Apostle reinforced them. He also came forth. He preached . . . He gave power to the Apostles. He made them strong . . . the Church of the Savior . . . he preached a . . . he too went up and rested in . . .

After Paul the Apostle, little by little and day after day all mankind began to stumble. They left righteousness behind them, and the path which is narrow and difficult. They preferred to go on the path which is broad.

At this same time also, in the Last Church, a righteous man of truth appeared,[3] belonging to the Kingdom. . . . they cared for the Church of our Master according to their capacity, and they too were raised up to the Land of Light. After those ones again, little by little, the Church perished. The world remained behind without a Church — as a tree will be picked and the fruits of it taken away, and it remains behind without fruit.

When the Church of the Savior was raised to the heights [i.e., no longer on earth] my Apostolate began, which you asked me about. From that time on was sent the Paraclete,[4] the Spirit of Truth: the one who has come to you in this last generation. Just as the Savior said: I go, but I will send you the Paraclete. When the Paraclete comes he can upbraid the world concerning sin, and he can speak with you on behalf of righteousness and about judgment, concerning the sinners who believe me not . . . he can speak with you . . . and he can speak with you and preach . . . that . . . the one who will honor me and . . . and he gives to you.

Hegemonius, *The Deeds of Archelaos* (c. 350 c.e.)

The early Christian church fathers did not appreciate competing religious teachings such as those of Mani and published treatises to counter them. Among the attacks is a work by an otherwise unknown

---

[3] **a righteous man . . . appeared:** This must refer to one of the preachers of the early centuries c.e. that the Gnostics considered important.

[4] **Paraclete:** The title refers to Mani and literally means "the one who brings comfort."

Hegemonius, now preserved only in Latin but originally written in Greek, called *Acta Archelai*, or the *Deeds of Archelaos*. It contains a debate between the Christian bishop Archelaos and Mani, which Archelaos is said to have won. In it, Archelaos summarizes his opponent's ideas on creation so as to make them less appealing to Christians.

Summary of the sacrilegious teachings of Mani:

If you wish to become acquainted with Mani's belief, then hear it from me in a brief summary. He reveres two unbegotten, eternal gods original from their own nature, of whom the one is the adversary of the other. He introduces the one as good, the other as evil. To the one he gives the name light, to the other darkness, and he says that the soul which is in man is part of light, whereas the body belongs to darkness and is a creation of matter.

He says that a mixture or confusion of them came about in the following way, comparing the two gods with the following illustration. Like two kings fighting each other, who have been enemies from the beginning and each of whom respectively has his own territory, darkness by coincidence rose up out of its limits and attacked light.

However, when the good Father noticed that darkness had penetrated his land, he caused to emanate from himself a power, the so-called Mother of Life and from this emanated the First Man (and) the five elements. These are wind, light, water, fire, and air.

And when he had put on these as battle armor, he descended and fought with darkness. The rulers of darkness then went over to a counterattack and ate of his armor, which is the soul.

Then the First Man down below was pressed very hard by darkness, and if the Father had not heard his prayer and sent out another power, which emanated from him, that is the so-called Living Spirit, and if this latter had not descended and stretched out his right hand, leading the First Man out of darkness, then he would long ago have risked being held fast. So from then on he left the soul down there.

Iain Gardner and Samuel N. C. Lieu, eds., *Manichaean Texts from the Roman Empire* (Cambridge, UK: Cambridge University Press, 2004), 182–183.

It is for this reason that the Manicheans shake each other by the right hand when they meet, as a sign that they are saved from darkness. For, he says, all the sects are in the darkness. Then the Living Spirit created the world, put on three other powers, descended, brought up the rulers and crucified them in the firmament, which is their body, the sphere.

Examining the Evidence

1. According to Mani, what distinguishes Manicheanism from other religions?
2. How does he acknowledge earlier religious thinkers? Does he respect them?
3. What is the essence of the Christian attack on Manicheanism as described by Hegemonius?

MAKING CONNECTIONS

1. The Roman world presents a culmination of developments in ancient Eurasian history, building on ideas that originated in earlier periods. What inspirations can you identify in the sources in this chapter?
2. How do the documents in this chapter deal with issues of tradition and change?
3. Although Rome was a world empire that spread a uniform culture over a vast area, there still is tension visible between East and West. How is this tension reflected in these documents?
4. What do the descriptions of the women protesters (Document 6.1) and the account of Zenobia (Document 6.4) reveal about Roman views on the role of women in society?

CHAPTER 7

Reading the Unwritten Record: Peoples of Africa, the Americas, and the Pacific Islands, 3000 B.C.E.–500 C.E.

In Chapters 2 through 6, we have concentrated on written works as sources of insight. However, most of the inhabitants of the ancient world did not write, and in this chapter we look at some of their cultures through a variety of alternative sources. These include not only visual remains of the cultures themselves, but also descriptions from foreign travelers and later records of ancient stories. Although these sources provide insight into these societies, they were, of course, colored by the perspectives of those who reported on these cultures or recorded their ideas in writing. The written word is of crucial importance for the historian who seeks to study the ancient past, but we also must consider how conscious some of the ancient writers were about the value of what they left behind.

7.1
AN EARLY ETHNOGRAPHIC DESCRIPTION OF SUB-SAHARAN AFRICA

Ibn Battuta, *Travels* (1353–1355 C.E.)

Throughout world history, people have traveled and observed cultures foreign to their own, which they described after they returned home. Such descriptions, when written down and preserved, can provide modern historians insights that are difficult to obtain otherwise, as they often comment on aspects of life not elucidated in official records. One of the greatest early travelers of premodern history was Ibn Battuta (1304–1368/9 or 1377), who was born in the area of modern-day Morocco. A pilgrimage to Mecca in his early twenties inspired him to travel as far as possible, and he crisscrossed Asia and East Africa, even reaching Beijing in China. After Ibn Battuta returned home, the local sultan asked him to visit the kingdom of Mali in West Africa. The description of those travels provides us with the earliest explicit account of life in sub-Saharan Africa. Toward the end of his life he dictated his memoirs.

When I decided to make the journey to Málli [the city of Mali], which is reached in twenty-four days from Iwalatan[1] if the traveler pushes on rapidly, I hired a guide from the Massufa (for there is no necessity to travel in a company on account of the safety of that road), and set out with three of my companions. On the way there are many trees, and these trees are of great age and girth; a whole caravan may shelter in the shade of one of them. There are trees which have neither branches nor leaves, yet the shade cast by their trunks is sufficient to shelter a man. Some of these trees are rotted in the interior and the rainwater collects in them, so that they serve as wells and the people drink of the water inside them. In others there are bees and honey, which is collected by the people. I was surprised to find inside one tree, by

which I passed, a man, a weaver, who had set up his loom in it and was actually weaving.

A traveler in this country carries no provisions, whether plain food or seasonings, and neither gold nor silver. He takes nothing but pieces of salt and glass ornaments, which the people call beads, and some aromatic goods. When he comes to a village the womenfolk of the blacks bring out millet, milk, chickens, pulped lotus fruit, rice, *fúni* (a grain resembling mustard seed, from which *kuskusu* [couscous] and gruel are made), and pounded haricot beans. The traveler buys what of these he wants, but their rice causes sickness to whites when it is eaten, and the *fúni* is preferable to it. . . .

I saw a crocodile in this part of the Nile,[2] close to the bank; it looked just like a small boat. One day I went down to the river to satisfy a need, and lo, one of the blacks came and stood between me and the river. I was amazed at such lack of manners and decency on his part, and spoke of it to someone or other. [That person] answered. "His purpose in doing that was solely to protect you from the crocodile, by placing himself between you and it." . . .

Thus I reached the city of Málli, the capital of the king of the blacks. I stopped at the cemetery and went to the quarter occupied by the whites, where I asked for Muhammad ibn al-Faqíh. I found that he had hired a house for me and went there. His son-in-law brought me candles and food, and next day Ibn al-Faqíh himself came to visit me, with other prominent residents. I met the qádi [judge] of Málli, ʿAbd ar-Rahman, who came to see me; he is a negro, a pilgrim, and a man of fine character. I met also the interpreter Dugha, who is one of the principal men among the blacks. All these persons sent me hospitality-gifts of food and treated me with the utmost

---

[1] **Iwalatan:** Walata, an oasis town in southeast Mauritania.

[2] **in this part of the Nile:** Actually, the Niger River.

Ibn Battuta, *Travels in Asia and Africa, 1325–1354*, trans. and ed. H. A. R. Gibb (London: George Routledge & Sons, 1939), 321–324, 326–331.

generosity — may God reward them for their kindnesses! Ten days after our arrival we ate a gruel made of a root resembling colocasia, which is preferred by them to all other dishes. We all fell ill — there were six of us — and one of our number died. I for my part went to the morning prayer and fainted there. I asked a certain Egyptian for a loosening remedy and he gave me a thing called *baydar*, made of vegetable roots, which he mixed with aniseed and sugar, and stirred in water. I drank it off and vomited what I had eaten, together with a large quantity of bile. God preserved me from death but I was ill for two months.

The sultan of Málli is Mansá Sulaymán, *mansá* meaning sultan, and Sulaymán being his proper name. . . .

On certain days the sultan holds audiences in the palace yard, where there is a platform under a tree, with three steps; this they call the *pempi*. It is carpeted with silk and has cushions placed on it. [Over it] is raised the umbrella, which is a sort of pavilion made of silk, surmounted by a bird in gold, about the size of a falcon. The sultan comes out of a door in a corner of the palace, carrying a bow in his hand and a quiver on his back. On his head he has a golden skull-cap, bound with a gold band which has narrow ends shaped like knives, more than a span in length. His usual dress is a velvety red tunic, made of the European fabrics called *mutanfas*. The sultan is preceded by his musicians, who carry gold and silver guimbris,[3] and behind him come three hundred armed slaves. He walks in a leisurely fashion, affecting a very slow movement, and even stops from time to time. On reaching the *pempi* he stops and looks round the assembly, then ascends it in the sedate manner of a preacher ascending a mosque-pulpit. As he takes his seat the drums, trumpets, and bugles are sounded. Three slaves go out at a run to summon the sovereign's deputy and the military commanders, who enter and sit down. Two saddled and bridled horses are brought, along with two goats, which they hold to serve as a protection against the evil eye. Dugha stands at the gate and the rest of the people remain in the street, under the trees.

The negroes are of all people the most submissive to their king and the most abject in their behavior before him. They swear by his name, saying *Mansá*

Sulaymán ki.[4] If he summons any of them while he is holding an audience in his pavilion, the person summoned takes off his clothes and puts on worn garments, removes his turban and dons a dirty skull-cap, and enters with his garments and trousers raised knee-high. He goes forward in an attitude of humility and dejection and knocks the ground hard with his elbows, then stands with bowed head and bent back listening to what he says. If anyone addresses the king and receives a reply from him, he uncovers his back and throws dust over his head and back, for all the world like a bather splashing himself with water. . . .

I was at Málli during the two festivals of the sacrifice and the fast-breaking. On these days the sultan takes his seat on the *pempi* after the midafternoon prayer. The armor-bearers bring in magnificent arms — quivers of gold and silver, swords ornamented with gold and with golden scabbards, gold and silver lances, and crystal maces. At his head stand four amirs driving off the flies, having in their hands silver ornaments resembling saddle-stirrups. The commanders, qádi and preacher sit in their usual places. The interpreter Dugha comes with his four wives and his slave-girls, who are about a hundred in number. They are wearing beautiful robes, and on their heads they have gold and silver fillets, with gold and silver balls attached. A chair is placed for Dugha to sit on. He plays on an instrument made of reeds, with some small calabashes at its lower end, and chants a poem in praise of the sultan, recalling his battles and deeds of valor. The women and girls sing along with him and play with bows. Accompanying them are about thirty youths, wearing red woolen tunics and white skull-caps; each of them has his drum slung from his shoulder and beats it. Afterwards come his boy pupils who play and turn wheels in the air, like the natives of Sind. They show a marvelous nimbleness and agility in these exercises and play most cleverly with swords. Dugha also makes a fine play with the sword. Thereupon the sultan orders a gift to be presented to Dugha and he is given a purse containing two hundred *mithqáls* of gold dust and is informed of the contents of the purse before all the people. The commanders rise and twang their bows in thanks to the sultan. The next day each

---

[3] **guimbris:** Two-stringed guitars.

[4] ***Mansá Sulaymán ki:*** In Mande, "the emperor Sulayman has commanded."

one of them gives Dugha a gift, every man according to his rank. Every Friday after the *'asr* prayer, Dugha carries out a similar ceremony to this that we have described.

On feast-days after Dugha has finished his display, the poets come in. Each of them is inside a figure resembling a thrush, made of feathers, and provided with a wooden head with a red beak, to look like a thrush's head. They stand in front of the sultan in this ridiculous make-up and recite their poems. I was told that their poetry is a kind of sermonizing in which they say to the sultan: "This *pempi* which you occupy was that whereon sat this king and that king, and such and such were this one's noble actions and such and such the other's. So do you too do good deeds whose memory will outlive you." After that the chief of the poets mounts the steps of the *pempi* and lays his head on the sultan's lap, then climbs to the top of the *pempi* and lays his head first on the sultan's right shoulder and then on his left, speaking all the while in their tongue, and finally he comes down again. I was told that this practice is a very old custom amongst them, prior to the introduction of Islam, and that they have kept it up. . . .

The negroes possess some admirable qualities. They are seldom unjust, and have a greater abhorrence of injustice than any other people. Their sultan shows no mercy to anyone who is guilty of the least act of it. There is complete security in their country. Neither traveler nor inhabitant in it has anything to fear from robbers or men of violence. They do not confiscate the property of any white man who dies in their country, even if it be uncounted wealth. On the contrary, they give it into the charge of some trustworthy person among the whites, until the rightful heir takes possession of it. They are careful to observe the hours of prayer, and assiduous in attending them in congregations, and in bringing up their children to them. On Fridays, if a man does not go early to the mosque, he cannot find a corner to pray in, on account of the crowd. It is a custom of theirs to send each man his boy [to the mosque] with his prayer-mat; the boy spreads it out for his master in a place befitting him [and remains on it] until he comes to the mosque. Their prayer-mats are made of the leaves of a tree resembling a date-palm, but without fruit.

Another of their good qualities is their habit of wearing clean white garments on Fridays. Even if a man has nothing but an old worn shirt, he washes it and cleans it, and wears it to the Friday service. Yet another is their zeal for learning the Qur'an by heart. They put their children in chains if they show any backwardness in memorizing it, and they are not set free until they have it by heart. I visited the qádi in his house on the day of the festival. His children were chained up, so I said to him, "Will you not let them loose?" He replied, "I shall not do so until they learn the Qur'an by heart." The date of my arrival at Málli was 14th Jumada I, 53 [June 28, 1352] and of my departure from it 22nd Muharram of the year 54 [February 27, 1353].

Examining the Evidence

1. Travelers' accounts tend to focus on specific aspects of the regions visited; on what elements does Ibn Battuta focus here?
2. How do Ibn Battuta's own cultural traditions affect the way he talks about the people and customs of Mali?
3. How useful is a description of this type for study of ancient African history?

7.2   WEAVING AS VISUAL EXPRESSION

The Paracas Mantle (c. 100–300 C.E.)

People do not express ideas solely in writing. They also convey them in visual works like paintings and sculptures. When studying prehistoric cultures, historians often turn to such sources to find clues concerning their beliefs and values. In many South American cultures, textile weaving was very elaborate and intricate, providing vivid visual imagery that reflects the mythology of the people. The following example of a textile comes from the

Detail of *Mantle, known as The Paracas Textile, Fragments.* Culture: Nasca Early Intermediate Period, 100–300 C.E. Cotton, camelid fiber textile: 58¼ × 24½ in. support: 67¼ × 33¼ in. *Brooklyn Museum 38.121* John Thomas Underwood Memorial Fund.

Detail of image: "Paracas Textile brochure." 1991. Printed material, 12 × 22 in. (31 × 56 cm). Brooklyn Museum Libraries (NK8839.1_B79). Drawings and text by Lois Martin.

south-central Peruvian peninsula of Paracas, a region famed for its weaving. It is part of a woven cloak, whose central panel contains thirty-two images of a head that represents a mythical creature that Andean scholars call the Oculate Being because of its large eyes. The textile's border consists of ninety figures—plants and animals, mythological creatures, and costumed individuals—that are sewn onto and extend beyond the band of flowers that encircles the textile. Outline drawings of three of the border figures are also shown above. Scholars interpret the border figures as a microcosm of life on Peru's south coast, with a particular focus on agriculture, because many of the images illustrate native flora and fauna as

well as cultivated plants. The order in which the figures repeat has led some scholars to conclude that the textile is a lunar calendar.

Examining the Evidence

1. What does the textile tell us about the importance of weaving in this culture?
2. From a twenty-first-century vantage point, how reliably can we interpret the images on the textile?
3. What may have been the function of the cloak?

7.3 TALES OF ANDEAN ORIGINS

Huarochiri Manuscript (c. 1600 C.E.)

The Spanish conquerors of Latin America in the fifteenth and sixteenth centuries C.E. brought with them missionaries who showed interest in the religions of the indigenous populations and recorded stories that had previously only been preserved orally. These included very ancient tales that reflect ideas that were in existence many centuries before the Conquest. We must read these accounts with much caution as the prejudices of the Christian recorders altered them; moreover, in the

centuries before they were written down, they were exposed to numerous influences often unknown to us. The most important account of the pre-Columbian beliefs of the people of the Andes is written on the *Huarochiri Manuscript*, recording stories of the Checas tribes in the region of Huarochiri in modern-day Peru. These tribes were integrated into the Inca Empire before the sixteenth-century C.E. Spanish Conquest, but the tales preserve earlier ideas in Quechua, South America's indigenous language. The manuscript renders the tale in Quechua but also contains annotations in Spanish.

Kenneth Mills and William B. Taylor, eds., *Colonial Spanish America: A Documentary History* (Wilmington, DE: SR Books, 1998), 7–11.

Preface

If the ancestors of the people called Indians had known writing in earlier times, then the lives they lived would not have faded from view until now.

As the mighty past of the Spanish Vira Cocha[1] is visible until now so, too, would theirs be.

But since things are as they are, and since nothing has been written until now,

I set forth here the lives of the ancestors of the Huaro Cheri people, who all descend from one forefather:

What faith they held, how they live up until now those things and more;

Village by village it will be written down: how they lived from their dawning age onward.

Chapter 1: How the Idols of Old Were, and How They Warred Among Themselves, and How the Natives Existed at That Time

In very ancient times, there were huacas[2] named Yana Namca and Tuta Namca.

Later on another huaca named Huallallo Caruincho defeated them.

After he defeated them, he ordered the people to bear two children and no more.

He would eat one of them himself.

The parents would raise the other, whichever one was loved best.

Although people did die in those times, they came back to life on the fifth day exactly.

And as for their foodstuffs, they ripened exactly five days after being planted.

These villages and all the others like them were full of Yunca.[3]

[margin, in Quechua: full of Yunca]

When a great number of people had filled the land, they lived really miserably, scratching and digging the rock faces and ledges to make terraced fields.

These fields, some small, others large, are still visible today on all the rocky heights.

And all the birds of that age were perfectly beautiful, parrots and toucans all yellow and red.

Later, at the time when another huaca named Paria Caca appeared, these beings and all their works were cast out to the hot Anti lands by Paria Caca's actions.

Further on we'll speak of Paria Caca's emergence and of his victories.

Also, as we know there was another huaca named Cuni Raya.

Regarding him, we're not sure whether he existed before Paria Caca or maybe after him.

[margin, in Spanish: Find out whether he says that it isn't known if he was before or after Caruincho or Paria Caca.]

However, Cuni Raya's essential nature almost matches Vira Cocha's. For when people worshipped this huaca, they would invoke him, saying,

Cuni Raya Vira Cocha,
You who animate mankind,
Who charge the world with being,
All things are yours!
Yours the fields and yours the people.

And so, long ago, when beginning anything difficult, the ancients, even though they couldn't see Vira Cocha, used to throw coca leaves to the ground, talk to him, and worship him before all others, saying,

Help me remember how,
Help me work it out,
Cuni Raya Vira Cocha!

And the master weaver would worship and call on him whenever it was hard for him to weave,

For that reason, we'll write first about this huaca and about his life, and later on about Paria Caca.

---

[1] **Vira Cocha:** The creator god in Andean culture. The author uses this name to refer to the Christian god so that it will be clear to an Andean audience.

[2] **huaca:** A divine ancestor of the ancient past.

[3] **Yunca:** The name of a group of inhabitants of the Andes.

Chapter 2: How Cuni Raya Vira Cocha Acted in His Own Age. The Life of Cuni Raya Vira Cocha. How Caui Llaca Gave Birth to His Child, and What Followed

[margin, crossed out, in Spanish: Note that it isn't known whether this was before or after Caruincho.]

A long, long time ago, Cuni Raya Vira Cocha used to go around posing as a miserably poor and friendless man, with his cloak and tunic all ripped and tattered. Some people who didn't recognize him for who he was yelled, "You poor lousy wretch!"

Yet it was this man who fashioned all the villages. Just by speaking he made the fields, and finished the terraces with walls of fine masonry. As for the irrigation canals, he channeled them out from their sources just by tossing down the flower of a reed called pupuna.

After that, he went around performing all kinds of wonders, putting some of the local huacas to shame with his cleverness.

Once there was a female huaca named Caui Llaca.

Caui Llaca had always remained a virgin. Since she was very beautiful, every one of the huacas and villcas[4] longed for her. "I've got to sleep with her!" they thought. But she never consented.

Once this woman, who had never allowed any male to fondle her, was weaving beneath a lúcuma tree.

Cuni Raya, in his cleverness, turned himself into a bird and climbed into the lúcuma.

He put his semen into a fruit that had ripened there and dropped it next to the woman.

The woman swallowed it down delightedly.

Thus she got pregnant even though she remained untouched by man.

In her ninth month, virgin though she was, she gave birth just as other women give birth.

And so, too, for one year she nursed her child at her breast, wondering, "Whose child could this be?"

In the fullness of the year, when the youngster was crawling around on all fours, she summoned all the huacas and villcas to find out who was the child's father.

When the huacas heard the message, they were overjoyed, and they all came dressed in their best clothes, each saying to himself, "It's me!" "It's me she'll love!"

This gathering took place at Anchi Cocha, where the woman lived.

[margin, in Spanish: The gathering was in Anchi Cocha.]

When all the huacas and villcas had taken their seats there, that woman addressed them:

"Behold, gentlemen and lords. Acknowledge this child. Which of you made me pregnant?" One by one she asked each of them:

"Was it you?"

"Was it you?"

But nobody answered, "The child is mine."

The one called Cuni Raya Vira Cocha had taken his seat at the edge of the gathering. Since he looked like a friendless beggar sitting there, and since so many handsome men were present, she spurned him and didn't question him.

She thought, "How could my baby possibly be the child of that beggar?"

Since no one had said, "The child is mine," she first warned the huacas, "If the baby is yours, it'll crawl up to you," and then addressed the child:

"Go, identify your father yourself!"

The child began at one end of the group and crawled along on all fours without climbing up on anyone, until reaching the other end, where its father sat.

On reaching him, the baby instantly brightened up and climbed onto its father's knee.

When its mother saw this, she got all indignant: "Atatay,[5] what a disgrace! How could I have given birth to the child of a beggar like that?" she said. And taking along only her child, she headed straight for the ocean.

And then, while all the local huacas stood in awe, Cuni Raya Vira Cocha put on his golden garment.

---

[4] **villcas:** A demigod-like human.

[5] **Atatay:** Quechua for "ouch."

He started to chase her at once, thinking to himself, "She'll be overcome by sudden desire for me." "Sister Caui Llaca!" he called after her. "Here, look at me! Now I'm really beautiful!" he said, and he stood there making his garment glitter.

Caui Llaca didn't even turn her face back to him. "Because I've given birth to the child of such a ruffian, such a mangy beggar, I'll just disappear into the ocean," she said. She headed straight out into the deep sea near Pacha Camac, out there where even now two stones that clearly look like people stand.

And when she arrived at what is today her dwelling, she turned to stone.

Yet Cuni Raya Vira Cocha thought, "She'll see me anyway, she'll come to look at me!" He followed her at a distance, shouting and calling out to her over and over.

First, he met up with a condor.

"Brother, where did you run into that woman?" he asked him.

"Right near here. Soon you'll find her," replied the condor.

Cuni Raya Vira Cocha spoke to him and said,

"You'll live a long life. You alone will eat any dead animal from the wild mountain slopes, both guanacos and vicuñas,[6] of any kind and in any number. And if anybody should kill you, he'll die himself, too."

Farther on, he met up with a skunk.

"Sister, where did you meet that woman?" he asked. "You'll never find her now. She's gone way far away," replied the skunk.

When she said this, he cursed her very hatefully, saying, 'As for you, because of what you've just told me, you'll never go around in the daytime. You'll only walk at night, stinking disgustingly. People will be revolted by you."

Next he met up with a puma. "She just passed this way. She's still nearby. You'll soon reach her," the puma told him. Cuni Raya Vira Cocha spoke to him, saying, 'You'll be well loved. You'll eat llamas, especially the llamas of people who bear guilt. Although people may kill you,

they'll wear you on their heads during a great festival and set you to dancing. And then when they bring you out annually, they'll sacrifice a llama first and then set you to dancing."

Then he met up with a fox. "She's already gone way far away. You'll never find her now," that fox told him. When the fox said this, he replied, "As for you, even when you skulk around keeping your distance, people will thoroughly despise you and say, 'That fox is a sneak thief.' When they kill you, they'll just carelessly throw you away, and your skin, too." . . .

And so he traveled on. Whenever he met anyone who gave him good news, he conferred on him good fortune. But he went along viciously cursing those who gave him bad news. When he reached the seashore, [crossed out in original manuscript: he went straight over it. Today people say, "He was headed for Castile," but in the old days people said, "He went to another land."] he turned back toward Pacha Camac.

He arrived at the place where Pacha Camac's two daughters lived, guarded by a snake.

Just before this, the two girls' mother had gone into the deep sea to visit Caui Llaca. Her name was Urpay Huachac.

While Urpay Huachac was away, Cuni Raya Vira Vocha seduced one girl, her older daughter.

When he sought to sleep with the other sister, she turned into a dove and darted away. That's why her mother's name means "Gives Birth to Doves."

At that time there wasn't a single fish in the ocean.

Only Urpay Huachac used to breed them, at her home, in a small pond. It was these fish, all of them, that Cuni Raya angrily scattered into the ocean, saying,

"For what did she go off and visit Caui Llaca, the woman of the ocean depths?"

Ever since then, fish have filled the sea.

Then Cuni Raya Vira Cocha fled along the seashore.

When Urpay Huachac's daughters told her how he'd seduced them, she got furious and chased him. As she followed him, calling him again and again, he waited for her and said, "Yes?"

"Cuni, I'm just going to remove your lice," she said, and she picked them off.

---

[6] **guanacos and vicuñas:** Llama-like animals.

While she picked his lice, she caused a huge abyss
   to open up next to him, thinking to herself,
   "I'll knock Cuni Raya down into it."
But Cuni Raya in his cleverness realized this; just
   by saying, "Sister, I've got to go off for a
   moment to relieve myself," he made his get-
   away to these villages.
He traveled around this area for a long, long time,
   tricking lots of local huacas and people, too.

[marginal note, in Spanish, crossed out: n.b. This
   huaca's end will be told below.]

Examining the Evidence

1. How does the beginning of the text compare
   the Spanish Christians' use of writing and the
   Andean people's oral tradition?
2. How does the story depict the succession of
   huacas?
3. How does the story explain human attitudes
   toward specific animals?

7.4 WOMEN AND WRITING IN ANCIENT CHINA

Ban Zhao, *Lessons for Women* (c. 100 C.E.)

Few people in the ancient world knew how to read and
write, and women especially were rarely educated in
these skills. But there are notable exceptions in all cultures, including the Chinese Ban Zhao (c. 45–120 C.E.). As
the daughter of a highly cultured family, she was not only
literate but was so well trained as a historian that the
emperor asked her to finish her father's work, *The History
of the Former Han Dynasty*, and gave her access to the
imperial archives. Her work, *Lessons for Women*, gives
some autobiographical information and aims to provide
guidance to her daughters, whom she feels she has insuf-
ficiently prepared for married life. Here follow some passages, which later Chinese authors used to justify the
inferior role of women in society.

Introduction

I, the unworthy writer, am unsophisticated, unen-
lightened, and by nature unintelligent, but I am fortunate both to have received not a little favor from my
scholarly father, and to have had a cultured mother
and instructresses upon whom to rely for a literary
education as well as for training in good manners.
More than forty years have passed since at the age of
fourteen I took up the dustpan and the broom in the
Cao family.[1] During this time with trembling heart
I feared constantly that I might disgrace my parents,
and that I might multiply difficulties for both the
women and the men of my husband's family. Day and
night I was distressed in heart, but I labored without
confessing weariness. Now and hereafter, however, I
know how to escape from such fears.

Being careless, and by nature stupid, I taught and
trained my children without system. Consequently
I fear that my son Gu may bring disgrace upon the
Imperial Dynasty by whose Holy Grace he has un-
precedentedly received the extraordinary privilege
of wearing the Gold and the Purple, a privilege for
the attainment of which by my son, I a humble subject never even hoped. Nevertheless, now that he is
a man and able to plan his own life, I need not again
have concern for him. But I do grieve that you, my
daughters, just now at the age for marriage, have
not at this time had gradual training and advice;
that you still have not learned the proper customs

---

[1] **the Cao family:** The family into which she married.

Introduction from Nancy Lee Swann, *Pan Chao: Foremost Woman Scholar of China; First Century A.D.* (New York: Russell & Russell,
1968), 82–83.

for married women. I fear that by failure in good manners in other families you will humiliate both your ancestors and your clan. I am now seriously ill, life is uncertain. As I have thought of you all in so untrained a state, I have been uneasy many a time for you. At hours of leisure I have composed in seven chapters these instructions under the title, "Lessons for Women." In order that you may have something wherewith to benefit your persons, I wish every one of you, my daughters, each to write out a copy for yourself.

From this time on every one of you strive to practice these lessons.

Chapter I: Humility

In ancient times, on the third day after a girl was born, people placed her at the base of the bed, gave her a pot shard to play with and made a sacrifice to announce her birth. She was put below the bed to show that she was lowly and weak and should concentrate on humbling herself before others. Playing with a shard showed that she should get accustomed to hard work and concentrate on being diligent. Announcing her birth to the ancestors showed that she should focus on continuing the sacrifices. These three customs convey the unchanging path for women and the ritual traditions.

Humility means yielding and acting respectful, putting others first and oneself last, never mentioning one's own good deeds or denying one's own faults, enduring insults and bearing with mistreatment, all with due trepidation. Industriousness means going to bed late, getting up early, never shirking work morning or night, never refusing to take on domestic work, and completing everything that needs to be done neatly and carefully. Continuing the sacrifices means serving one's husband-master with appropriate demeanor, keeping oneself clean and pure, never joking or laughing, and preparing pure wine and food to offer to the ancestors.

There has never been a woman who had these three traits and yet ruined her reputation or fell into disgrace. If a woman loses these three traits, she will have no name to preserve and will not be able to avoid shame. . . .

Chapter V: Devotion

According to the rites, a man is obligated to take a second wife but nothing is written about a woman marrying twice. Hence the saying, "A husband is one's Heaven: one cannot flee Heaven; one cannot leave a husband." Heaven punishes those whose actions offend the spirits; a husband looks down on a wife who violates the rites and proprieties. Thus the *Model for Women* says, "To please one man is her goal; to displease one man ends her goal." It follows from this that a woman must seek her husband's love — not through such means as flattery, flirting, or false intimacy, but rather through devotion.

Devotion and proper demeanor entail propriety and purity, hearing nothing licentious, seeing nothing depraved, doing nothing likely to draw notice when outside the home; never neglecting one's appearance when at home; never gathering in groups or watching at the doorway. By contrast, those incapable of devotion and proper demeanor are careless in their actions, look at and listen to whatever they like, let their hair get messy when at home, put on an act of delicacy when away, speak of things they should not mention, and watch what they should not see.

Examining the Evidence

1. How does Ban Zhao portray herself and her own learning?
2. How does she connect her own writing to the position of women in the Chinese society of her day?
3. What can you gather from this passage about the position of women in Chinese society at the time?

Chapters I and V from Patricia Buckley Ebrey, ed., *Chinese Civilization: A Sourcebook*, 2d ed. (New York: Free Press, 1993), 75–76.

7.5   THE POWER OF WRITING

Horace, *Odes* (23 B.C.E.)

When we study people of the past, we are often amazed at the monuments and buildings they left behind, made with tools and technologies that seem primitive compared to those available to us today. Ancient monuments like the great pyramids of Egypt, the tomb of the first Chinese emperor Shi Huangdi, the Roman Colosseum, and many others continue to impress us today. The works of innumerable people, they call to our attention those who commissioned them. But many individual creators were also responsible for the sources of our histories, and chief among these creators were writers. We feel close to them because in the words they left behind we hear their personal voices. The people of the ancient world were not unaware of the legacy of their works, and a number of texts have been produced that compare the work of writers to monuments made of stone and metal. The poem quoted here, written by the Roman author Horace (65 B.C.E.–8 B.C.E.), appeared at the end of three books of short poems called *Odes*.

> I've made a monument to outlast bronze,
> Rise higher than the pyramid of a king;
> No gnawing rain, no north wind's violence,
> Or countless ranks of years and the fleeing
> Of time could e'er this monument erase.
> I shall not all die; some great part of me
> Will escape Death's goddess. With posthumous
>   praise,
> I'll freshly grow, be renewed constantly,
> So long as priest with silent priestess shall
> Climb upward to the Roman Capitol.
> I shall be famed where Aufidus'[1] torrents roar
> and where waterless Daunus reigned as king
> Of rustic folk.[2] Humble, I rose to power,

[1] **Aufidus:** A river in southern Italy.
[2] **where . . . rustic folk:** Central Italy.

> And I became the first of men to sing
> Aoelian song transposed to Italian measures.[3]
> Let my merits afford you supreme pleasures;
> Grant me the Delphic laurel willingly,
> And crown my head with it, Melpomene.[4]

Anonymous, *A Eulogy to Dead Authors* (c. 1200 B.C.E.)

Long after the start of Egyptian culture and its development of script, at the height of Egypt's political power in the New Kingdom, ancient Egyptian writers were well aware of how their works survived over time and could outlive monumental buildings and certainly human beings. Rather than praising their own works, as Horace did, they mentioned authors of Egypt's past whom they depicted as sages whose wisdom was preserved through the ages. We know when some of the people named had lived, such as Imhotep, who was the architect of Djoser's pyramid built some 1500 years before this text was written. That accomplishment, however, was less important in the eyes of the writer quoted here than his written work.

> But, should you do these things, you are wise in
>   writings,
> As for those scribes and sages
> from the time which came after the gods
> — those who would foresee what was to come,
>   which happened —
> their names endure for eternity,
> although they are gone, although they completed
>   their lifetimes and all their people are
>   forgotten.
>
> They did not make pyramids of bronze,
>   with stelae of iron.

[3] **And I became . . . Italian measures:** That is, the speaker was the first to use a certain Greek poetic form in Latin.
[4] **Melpomene:** The Muse of tragedy.

Stuart Lyons, *Horace's Odes and the Mystery of Do-Re-Mi* (Oxford: Aris & Phillips, 2007), 174.

R. B. Parkinson, *Voices from Ancient Egypt: An Anthology of Middle Kingdom Writings* (Norman: University of Oklahoma Press, 1991), 149–150.

They recognized not how heirs last as children,
with [offspring] pronouncing their names;
they made for themselves heirs
as writings and the Teachings they made.

They appointed [for themselves] the book as
    the lector-priest,
the writing board as Beloved-Son,
the Teachings as their pyramids,
the pen as their baby,
the stone-surface as wife.
From the great to the small
are given to be his children:
the scribe, he is their head.

Doors and mansions were made: they have fallen,
their funerary priests leaving,
while their stelae are covered with earth,
their chambers forgotten.
(Yet) their names are (still) pronounced over
    their rolls
which they made, from when they were.
Howgoodisthememoryofthemandwhattheymade—
for the bounds of eternity!

Be a scribe! Put it in your heart,
that your name shall exist like theirs!
The roll is more excellent than the carved stela,
than the enclosure which is established.
These act as chapels and pyramids
in the heart of him who pronounces their names.
Surely a name in mankind's mouth
is efficacious in the necropolis!

A man has perished: his corpse is dust,
and his people have passed from the land;
it is a book which makes him remembered
in the mouth of a speaker.

More excellent is a [papyrus] roll than a built house,
than a chapel in the west.
It is better than an established villa,
than a stela in a temple.

Is there any here like Hordedef?
Is there another like Imhotep?
There is none among our people like Neferti,
or Khety their chief.
I shall make you know the name of Ptahemdje-
    huty and Khakheperresonbe.
Is there another like Ptahhotep,
or likewise, Kaires?[1]

These sages, who foretold what comes—
what came from their mouths happened—
one benefits from the lines
written in their books.
To them the offspring of others are given,
to be heirs as if their own children.
They hid from the masses their magic,
which is read from their Teachings.
Departing life has made their names forgotten;
it is the writings which make them remembered.

Examining the Evidence

1. To what other remains do both Horace and the Egyptian author compare the written word?
2. What other ways of being remembered are mentioned in these excerpts?
3. Writing surpasses not only the boundaries of time but also the boundaries of space. How does Horace express that idea?

---

[1] **Is there another like . . . Kaires:** These are names of earlier Egyptians who were considered sages and the authors of literary works.

MAKING CONNECTIONS

1. In the Preface of Document 7.3, the Spanish author states, "If the ancestors of the people called Indians had known writing in earlier times, then the lives they lived would not have faded from view until now." Do you agree with this statement, and how does the selection of documents presented here contribute to your answer?
2. Historians are sometimes called time travelers. How do the documents presented here support this metaphor?
3. Do you agree with the idea Horace and the Egyptians expressed that writings can make you immortal? Explain.

The Formation of Regional Societies, 500–1450 C.E.

CHAPTER 8

The Worlds of Christianity and Islam, 400–1000

The rapid spread of Christianity and Islam inevitably provoked conflicts with existing religious traditions and the established social hierarchy. In contrast to religious traditions that focused on worship of the gods to obtain worldly blessings, both Christianity and Islam emphasized scrupulous spiritual discipline and otherworldly reward. This emphasis on personal morality required new role models, such as the ones we encounter in the biography of Saint Eligius, the anecdotes recorded by the Muslim jurist al-Muhassin, or the life story of the prophet Muhammad. In addition, the relationship between secular rulers and religious authority was fraught with tension. Although Byzantine emperors, German kings, and Islamic caliphs all professed their religious devotion and portrayed themselves as defenders of the true faith, their actions did not always conform to the doctrines of their chosen creed. Even religious leaders held sharply different views about the proper forms of worship, as the controversy over the veneration of icons within the Byzantine Christian church shows.

8.1 THE MAKING OF A CHRISTIAN SAINT

Dado, *The Life of Saint Eligius* (c. 660–686)

The Life of Eligius, compiled by his friend Dado, bishop of Rouen, is typical of the hagiographies written to confirm the Christian God's active presence in the world. Born near the city of Limoges in southern France, Eligius (588–660) was a talented goldsmith who traveled to Paris and gained the patronage of the Frankish king Clothar II (r. 613–629) and his successors. His wealth and fame aroused envy, but Eligius lived an austere and pious life. Eligius, we are told, repeatedly emptied his purse to purchase the freedom of slaves brought to Paris for sale. He also lavished his charity on religious institutions, building a monastery near Limoges and a nunnery in Paris. In 658, he was elected bishop of Noyon in Flanders. By this time, Eligius had acquired a reputation for miracle working and prophetic powers. After his death, his tomb at Noyon also won fame for its miraculous powers, attracting numerous pilgrims.

Eligius was born and nurtured in the true faith and imbued by his parents with the Catholic Christian religion. When he had passed the years of boyhood, he entered adolescence with industry and took up whatever work suitable to his age came to his hand and completed it with wonderful aptitude. When his father saw that his son was so skillful, he apprenticed him to an honorable man, Abbo, a proven goldsmith who at that time performed the public office of fiscal moneyer in the city of Limoges. Soon he was fully trained in the uses of this office and began to be honored with praise among the dwellers and neighbors in the lord. For he acted with dovelike simplicity lest he bring pain to anyone, and he had the wisdom of the serpent lest he fall into traps set by others. He was worthy both in having his skills and in his easy and pure speech. Often he entered into the meetings of the church giving gold to whomever was there reciting the sacred scripture. . . .

Afterwards . . . he left his native land and his parents and went to the soil of the Franks. Only a few days passed before he came to the notice of a certain royal treasurer named Bobo, an honest and mild man, who committed him to his patronage and put him to work under his tuition. . . .

After a while, a certain cause brought him to the notice of King Clothar of the Franks. For that king wanted a seat urbanely made with gold and gems but no one could be found in his palace who could do the work as he conceived it. But when the aforesaid royal treasurer had satisfied himself of Eligius's skill, he began to investigate whether he might complete the work as it was planned. . . . Then the king most readily gave him a great weight of gold which he in turn gave to Eligius. Having taken it, he began the work immediately and with diligence speedily completed it. . . . The king began to marvel and praise such elegant work and ordered that the craftsman be paid in a manner worthy of his labor. . . . From this of course, the goldsmith rose and his work was always most wonderfully done with the most learned skill, and he began to find increased favor in the king's eyes. . . .

When he reached the age of virility, desiring to show himself a vessel sanctified to God and fearing that some sin might stain his breast, he confessed his adolescent deeds to the priest. Imposing severe penances with mortifications on himself, he began to resist the flesh with the fires of the spirit in labors following the apostle, vigils, fasts, chastity, in much patience and unfeigned love. . . . His fasts made him pale and his body withered with thirst but always his mind thirsted more sharply with love of the eternal fatherland. . . . The more he humiliated himself, the humbler he became and so much more did he profit. As much as he sorrowed, so much he was forgiven and as much as he humbly afflicted himself, so much did he deserve to be raised on high by God. . . .

Dado of Rouen, *Vita S. Eligius*, ed. Levinson, MGH SS Mer. 4, 669–742. Translated by Jo Ann McNamara.

He grew more in vigils, in fasts, and in charity. For the king's use, he made many utensils from gold and gems. . . . Sitting at the work, he propped open a book before his eyes so that even while laboring he might receive divine mandates. Thus he performed double offices, his hands to the uses of man and his mind bound to divine use. . . .

Among other things, he acquired a villa in the neighborhood of Limoges called Solignac. . . . There in that place, first the most powerful man of God built a monastery. Then having constituted an abbot, he freed many of his domestic slaves to the number of a hundred from different provinces and added fifty monks with enough land to support them abundantly. He lavished so much love and devotion on the place that whatever he had, whatever the king gave him, whatever he could buy, whatever he was paid in gratuities by the powerful, he sent to that place. There you would see loaded carts, vessels for every use of both copper and wood, vestments and lectuaries and linens and volumes of sacred scripture and all things needful for the use of a monastery in such profusion that it kindled the envy of many depraved great folk. . . .

He began to raise in his own house . . . [in Paris], which he had received as a gift from the king in that same city, a domicile of virgins of Christ. After long and sweaty labor, he constructed a monastery worthy of holy virgins. There, constituting the strict discipline of the rule, he gathered thirty girls from diverse tribes, some from among his own [maidservants] and other more noble matrons of the Franks. He appointed an abbess fitting to God, a girl named Aurea, daughter of Maurinus and Quiria. He assigned land with high revenue and turned it over from all his property. From hither and thither you could see deliveries of everything necessary or useful for a monastery, vessels and vestments, sacred books, and other ornaments. . . .

Eligius once served the eternal king of all princes, Christ, in the palace under secular habit. He remained in this way from the middle of Clothar's time as king of the Franks, through the whole time of the famous prince Dagobert and his son Clovis and even to the beginning of the reign of the junior Clothar. But in those days the simoniac [sale of church offices] heresy cruelly pullulated [sprouted]

in the cities and even to the borders of the Frankish kingdom and most of the time the unhappy Queen Brunhilde violated the Catholic faith with this contagion even to the time of King Dagobert. The holy men Eligius and Ouen, in common council with other Catholic men, warned the prince and his optimates [nobles] that this death dealing virus must swiftly be eliminated from the body of Christ which is the universal church. Their pious petition had its effect and they freely obtained what they had requested devoutly. Thus a single counsel was pleasing to all, accepted in the Holy Spirit and by royal order, that no one who had paid a price should be admitted to sacerdotal offices. . . .

And in that spirit they chose Eligius for the merits of his sanctity and good works, now radiating light, for the holy sacerdotal office. He was to preside over Noyon after Acharius, the antistes [bishop] of that town, had died in the turning of his years. . . . So the unwilling goldsmith was tonsured [ordained] and constituted guardian of the towns . . . of Vermandois which includes the metropolis, Tournai, which was once a royal city, and Noyon and Ghent and Coutrai of Flanders. . . .

With the care of a solicitous pastor, he cast his eye over the towns committed to him and their surroundings. But in Flanders and Antwerp, Frisians and Suevi and other barbarians coming from the seacoasts or distant lands not yet broken by the plow, received him with hostile spirits and adverse minds. Yet a little later after he gradually began to insinuate the word of God among them by the grace of Christ, the greater part made truce and the barbarian people left their idols and converted, becoming subject to the true God and Christ. Thus like a light shining from heaven or the rays of the sun breaking through, he illuminated every barbarian land. . . .

In those days, after Eligius had borne all the burdens and labors of this world with equanimity, transacted all the administration of this temporary life, after so many works of mercy, after sweet examples, after freeing an innumerable flock of prisoners, after binding a copious multitude of monks and virgins to God in communities, after distributing an immense heap of his substance in alms, after the accumulated merits of dispensation of money to the believing faithful, he became elderly. Having passed seventy years of age full of good works, he felt his body approaching dissolution. . . . Ever more certain that divine providence was bringing his death, he ordered all his servants and ministers to be gathered whom he had governed for a long, fleeting time. And he began to pass his last days publicly as he had always done, preaching to them always to keep peace with one another, considering themselves their brothers' keepers in charity, bound by the chains of love and unity. . . . Now, as I began to say, when the blessed man lay in his last illness and his infirmity had continued for five or six days, he pretended that he could go on as always, walking about supported by a staff. Nor would he abandon the works of God, seeking good to the exhaustion of his strength, so that he retained even to the end what he had borne under the yoke through the long space of his life. All night long, with prayers and vigils he forced his weakening limbs to serve his spirit. Keeping in mind the memory of future bliss, he awaited the road to his desire with great joy. Meanwhile, on the Calends of December,[1] when he felt the day of his completed salvation approaching, he gathered all his servants and disciples whom he was leaving as orphans, not in spirit but in body, and exhorted them [missing text] . . . and this said, among these words he emitted his spirit. And suddenly at the first hour of the night a blinding brightness was seen,

shining like a great beacon from that house and among the wondering watchers a fiery orb taking on the shape of the cross scattered the density of the clouds with its swift course to penetrate the heavens on high. So in this manner his holy soul was liberated from the pressure of the abject flesh which encased it and flew joyfully to its author. After long wandering here, to the rejoicing of heaven, the weeping of earth, and the applause of the angels, it arose at last rejoicing to its ancient estate. So all the love that the blessed man had among the people was clearly demonstrated in his death. Hardly had he exhaled his spirit and rendered the soul he owed to Christ than, as the messengers ran, weeping resounded through the whole town to heaven and all the streets were suddenly filled with noise and in the city everyone mourned this death as a common disaster. What more? When the composed body was carried to the church on its bier [coffin], as is customary, the people came for vigil, keeping watch in turns, the clergy with hymns and the people lamenting through the night.

Examining the Evidence

1. According to Dado's account, what cardinal virtues did Eligius exemplify throughout his lifetime?
2. Why was Eligius, at the time still a layperson, chosen to be bishop of Noyon?
3. In what ways did Eligius's life serve as a model of a proper Christian life?

---

[1] **Calends of December:** The calends was the first day of the month in the Roman calendar.

8.2 THE PASTORAL MISSION

Pope Gregory the Great, *Letters* (591–597)

Pope Gregory I (590–604) transformed the organization of the Latin Christian church and its sense of mission. Born into one of Rome's leading aristocratic families,

Gregory had embarked on a promising political career before retiring from public life after his father's death in 576 to become a monk. His political experience and his reputation for asceticism (self-denial) contributed to his election as pope in 590. Gregory supervised his church by carrying on a vigorous correspondence with clergy

John R. C. Martyn, trans., *The Letters of Gregory the Great,* vol. 1 (Toronto: Pontifical Institute of Mediaeval Studies, 2004), 175, 212, 292–293, 472–473, 501, 503–504.

and prominent laity; nearly 700 of his letters survive. The roots of Christianity in Europe were still fragile at this time. Despite the conversion of the Frankish king Clovis to Latin Christianity a century earlier, pre-Christian beliefs and practices persisted among the Gauls, and the practice of simony (the sale of clerical offices) was rampant. In numerous letters to the Frankish queen Brunhilde—one of which is included at the end of this document—Gregory sought to enlist her aid in the cause of reforming the Gallic church.

To Felix, Bishop of Siponto (July 591)

It has come to our attention that the church of Canusium [modern Cannes, in France] is so destitute of the office of priesthood that the dying cannot receive penitence there, nor infants baptism. Most disturbed by the importance of something so holy and necessary, we order your Beloved to go and visit the above mentioned church, supported by the authority of this injunction, and you should ordain two parish priests at least, but only those whom you have seen as worthy of such an office through the holiness of their life and gravity of their morals, and men subject in no way to the rules of canon law, so that Canusium is provided with the worthy safeguard of a sacred church.

To John, Bishop of Squillace (July 592)

The care of a pastoral office requires us to appoint their own bishops to establish churches deprived of them, who should govern the Lord's flock with pastoral concern. For that reason we have thought it necessary to appoint you, John, bishop of the city of Alessio [in northern Italy] captured by the enemy [the Slavs], as incardinate priest in the church of Squillace, so that you both carry out the care of souls once you accept it, by looking forward to the coming judgment, and although you have been driven out of your church by the enemy threat, you should govern another church which is without a pastor. But do so in such a way that if your city happens to be freed from the enemy and restored to its former state, with the Lord's protection, you should return to the church in which you were first consecrated. . . .

But we order you never to ordain anyone illegally, and do not permit anyone to take on holy orders who is a bigamist, or one whose wife was not a virgin, or an illiterate person, or one infected in any part of his body, or a penitent, or a person bound to a court [seeking to evade the law by joining the Church] or to any state of servitude. But if you should discover any men of this sort, please do not dare to promote them. On no account accept Africans indiscriminately, nor unknown strangers, who want to be ordained. For some of the Africans are in fact Manicheans [a sect following the teachings of Mani, an Iranian, which combined elements of Zoroastrianism, Buddhism, and Christianity], others re-baptized [considered a heretical practice], and most foreigners in fact, even when established in the minor orders, have often been proved to have had pretensions of higher honors. We also advise your Fraternity to pay careful attention to the souls entrusted to you, and to turn them more to the profits of the soul rather than to the comforts of the present life. Be diligent in conserving and disposing the property of the church, so that the future judge, when he has come to give his judgment, may approve the fact that you have carried out the office of priest undertaken by you in a worthy manner.

To Janarius, Bishop of Caligari (September 593)

Pastoral zeal itself certainly ought to have inspired you sufficiently to protect the flock which you have taken on, profitably and providently, even without our help, and to preserve that flock with diligent circumspection from the cunning deceptions of its enemies. But because we have found that your Beloved also needs a letter with our authority to augment your firmness, it was necessary for us to strengthen your hesitant mind for the exertion of religious vigor, with an exhortation of fraternal love.

For indeed it has come to our attention that you are taking inadequate care over the convents situated in Sardinia. And, although it had been prudently arranged by your predecessors that certain approved men from the clergy should take care of them by attending to their needs, this has now been totally neglected. The result is that women principally dedicated to God are themselves compelled to go on their own to the public officials for their taxes and other duties, and are forced to run about through the villages and farms and to engage themselves inadequately in men's business, to supplement their income. Let your Fraternity remove this evil with an easy correction. Carefully select one man, proven in his way of life and morals, whose age and rank leave him open to no suspicion of evil. With the fear of God, this man should be able to attend the convents themselves, so that the nuns are no longer allowed to wander outside their venerable abodes, contrary to the rule, for any reasons whether private or public. . . .

Yet if any of them, through the earlier freedom, or through an evil custom of impunity, has either been seduced in the past or will be dragged down into the abyss of adultery in the future, we want her to suffer the severity of appropriate punishment, and then be consigned to another stricter convent of virgins, to do penance. There let her improve herself with prayers and fasting and penitence, and let her provide a fearful example to others of a stricter discipline. But the man who is found in some wicked act with women of this sort must be deprived of communion, if he is a layman. If he is a cleric, he must also be removed from his office and be confined to a monastery, to bewail his failures in self-control for evermore. . . .

To Gregoria, Lady-in-Waiting to the Empress (June 597)

I have received the letters I wanted from your Sweetness, in which you have been keen to accuse yourself in every way over a multitude of sins. But I know that you love almighty God fervently, and I trust in his mercy that this sentence proceeding from the mouth of Truth, and originally said about a certain holy woman [Mary Magdalene], also applies to you: "Her many sins have been forgiven, because she has shown great love." . . .

But as for what your Sweetness has added in your letters, that you are going to pester me, until I write that it has been revealed to me that your sins have been forgiven, you have demanded something both difficult and also fruitless. Difficult, indeed, because

I am not worthy of having anything revealed to me, but useless, because you should not become secure about your sins, except when, in the very last day of your life, when you will no longer have any power at all to bewail those same sins. Until that day comes, ever suspicious and ever fearful, you ought to be afraid of your sins, and wash them daily with your tears. . . .

To Brunhilde, Queen of the Franks (September 597)

You show in a praiseworthy manner with what great solidarity the mind of your Excellency has been strengthened by your fear of almighty God, among other good deeds that you do, most of all in your love of his priests. And we receive great joy over your Christianity, because you are keen to increase with honors those whom you truly love, venerating them as servants of Christ.

For it is proper for you, most excellent daughter, it is proper for you to be such a person that you could be subject to the Ruler. For in him, you confirm the rule of your power also over subject peoples, whereby you subject the neck of your mind to the fear of our almighty Lord, and in the way in which you submit yourself to the service of our Creator, in that way you bind your subjects to you in more devoted servitude. . . .

So that this care may be fruitful for you before the eyes of our Creator, let the concern of your Christianity diligently keep watch, and do not allow anyone who is under your rule to be promoted to Holy Orders through gifts of money, or through the patronage of any persons, or through the right of a near relationship. Rather, a man should only be elected to the rank of bishop or to any other Holy Order, if he has been shown worthy of it by his way of life and morality. Otherwise, if the honor of the priesthood is for sale, which we hope is not so, then simoniacal heresy, which first appeared in the Church and was condemned by the vote of the Fathers, may rise up in those districts, and weaken the strength (Heaven forbid!) of your kingdom. For it is an extremely serious crime, indescribably so, to sell the Holy Spirit who redeemed the World.

But take note of this also. Because the outstanding preacher totally forbids a novice from being appointed to the office of priesthood, as you know, do not allow anyone from the laity to be consecrated as a bishop. For what sort of master will he be, who has never been a pupil? Or what sort of leader for the Lord's flock, who has not been subject to the discipline of the shepherd? If, therefore, someone's way of life was such that he deserved to be promoted to this rank, first he ought to serve as a minister of the Church, so that, through the practice of long experience, he may see what he should imitate and learn what he should teach, in case the newness of his conversion might perhaps bear the burden of rule, and a chance of ruin might arise from his premature promotion. . . .

Furthermore, be keen to recall those whom the error of the schismatics dissociates from the unity of the Church to a harmonious unity, which will be added to your reward. For so far they have been wrapped up in the blindness of their ignorance for no other reason than to escape the discipline of the Church, and to have the freedom to live sinfully, as they want to do. . . .

We also exhort you equally to restrain the rest of your subjects also, beneath a moderating discipline, so that they might not offer sacrifices to idols, or continue to worship trees or to make sacrilegious offerings over the heads of animals. For we have learnt that many of the Christians flock to the churches, but, terrible to relate, they do not give up the worship of demons. But since these things are thoroughly displeasing to our God, and because he does not own minds that are divided, ensure that they should be banned profitably from these unlawful practices, in case (Heaven forbid!) the sacrament of holy baptism might not save them, but punish them. And so, if you learn that some are violent, some adulterous, and some are thieves, or they practice other wicked acts, hasten to please God over their correction, so that through you he may not bring in the scourge of faithless races, that has been aroused to punish many nations, as we see.

Examining the Evidence

1. In Gregory's view, what were the chief deficiencies of the Christian clergy?
2. What did Gregory regard as the main responsibilities of the bishops?
3. What does Gregory's letter to Brunhilde reveal about the role of secular rulers in the administration of the Christian church?

8.3 THE TYRANNICAL RULE OF JUSTINIAN AND THEODORA

Procopius, *The Secret History* (c. 550 – c. 560)

The Byzantine emperor Justinian I (r. 527–565) harbored grand ambitions to restore the Roman Empire to its former glory. He raised great armies to conquer Italy and North Africa, and built an extensive network of walls and forts to defend against the Slavs and nomad invasions. Justinian also envisioned himself as the defender of the Orthodox Christian Church against heresy. However, his ruthless lust for power caused many to brand him a tyrant. *The Secret History*, written by the contemporary historian Procopius (c. 500–565), is a scathing indictment of Justinian's misrule and of his notorious empress Theodora, an actress and courtesan Justinian had plucked out of Constantinople's demimonde. Procopius's book remained hidden until after both he and the emperor had died.

Procopius, *The Secret History*, trans. G. A. Williamson (London: Penguin Books, 1966), 76–80, 96–98, 166–171.

In build [Justinian] was neither tall nor unusually short, but of normal height; not at all skinny but rather plump, with a round face that was not unattractive; it retained its healthy color even after a two-day fast. . . . Such then was his outward appearance; his character was beyond my powers of accurate description. For he was both prone to evil-doing and easily led astray—both knave and fool, to use a common phrase. . . .

This emperor was dissembling, crafty, hypocritical, secretive by temperament, two-faced; a clever fellow with a marvelous ability to conceal his real opinion, and able to shed tears, not from any joy or sorrow, but employing them artfully when required in accordance with the immediate need, lying all the time; not carelessly, however, but confirming his undertakings both with his signature and with the most fearsome oaths, even when dealing with his own subjects. But he promptly disregarded both agreements and solemn pledges, like the most contemptible slaves, who by fear of the tortures hanging over them are driven to confess misdeeds they have denied on oath. A treacherous friend and an inexorable enemy, he was passionately devoted to murder and plunder; quarrelsome and subversive in the extreme; easily led astray into evil ways but refusing every suggestion that he should follow the right path; quick to devise vile schemes and to carry them out; and with an instinctive aversion to the mere mention of anything good. . . .

When people are confident of the future they find their present troubles more tolerable and easier to bear; but when they are subjected to violence by the State authorities they are naturally more distressed by the wrongs they have suffered, and fall into utter despair through the hopelessness of expecting justice. Justinian betrayed his subjects not only because he absolutely refused to uphold the victims of wrong, but because he was perfectly prepared to set himself up as the recognized champion of the partisans; for he lavished great sums of money on these young men and kept many of them in his entourage, actually promoting some to magistracies and other official positions.

Such then was the state of affairs in Byzantium and everywhere else. For like any other disease the infection that began in the capital rapidly spread all over the Roman Empire. The Emperor took no notice at all of what was going on, since he was a man incapable of perception, although he was invariably an eyewitness of all that happened in the hippodromes [stadiums for chariot and horse racing]. For he was extremely simple, with no more sense than a donkey, ready to follow anyone who pulls the rein, waving its ears all the time. . . .

Throughout the Roman Empire there are many unorthodox beliefs generally known as heresies—Montanism, Sabbatarianism, and numerous others which continually lead men into doctrinal error. All the adherents of these were ordered to renounce their former beliefs under threat of many penalties for disobedience, above all the withdrawal of the right to bequeath their possessions to their children or relations. The churches of these heretics, as they are called, especially those who professed the doctrine of Arius, possessed unheard-of riches. Neither the whole Senate nor any other very large body in the Roman State could compete with them in wealth with these churches. They possessed treasure of gold and silver, and ornaments covered with precious stones, beyond description and beyond counting, houses and villages in great numbers, and many acres of land in all quarters of the world, and every other kind of wealth that exists and is named anywhere on earth, since none of the long line of emperors had ever interfered with them. A great number of people, even though they held orthodox beliefs, depended upon them at all times for their livelihood, justifying themselves on the ground that they were merely following their regular occupations. So by first of all confiscating the property of these churches the Emperor Justinian suddenly robbed them of all they possessed. The result was that from that moment most of the men were deprived of their own means of support. An army of officials was at once sent out in all directions to force everyone they met to renounce his ancestral beliefs. In the eyes of country people such a suggestion was blasphemous; so they resolved one and all to stand their ground against the men who made this demand. Many in consequence perished at the hands of the soldiers; many even put an end to their own lives, being foolish enough to think this the godliest course; and the great majority abandoned the land of their birth and went into banishment. . . . The result was that the whole Roman Empire was one great scene of slaughter and banishment.

A similar law being next passed in respect of the Samaritans, tumultuous disorders descended upon Palestine. All who lived in my own Caesarea [on the Palestinian coast] and the other cities, thinking it silly to endure any sort of distress for the sake of a nonsensical dogma, discarded their old names and called themselves Christians, maintaining by this presence to shake off the danger threatened by the law. Those among them who were at all prudent and reasonable were quite agreeable to remaining loyal to their new faith; but the majority, apparently feeling indignant that in defiance of their wishes they were being compelled by this law to abandon the beliefs they had inherited, very soon defected to the Manichees and "Polytheists." But the peasants at a mass meeting resolved as one man to take up arms against the Emperor, putting forward as the emperor of their own choice a bandit named Julian, son of Savarus. They joined battle with the soldiers and held out for some time, but in the end they lost the fight and were cut to pieces, together with their leader. It is said that a hundred thousand men lost their lives in this engagement, and the most fertile land in the world was left with no one to till it. For the owners of these acres, Christians one and all, this business had disastrous consequences, for though the land was yielding them no profit at all they were compelled to pay to the Emperor in perpetuity annual taxes on a crippling scale, since these demands were pressed relentlessly.

Next he turned the persecutions against the "Greeks" [pagans], torturing their bodies and looting their property. Many of these decided to assume for appearance's sake the name of Christian in order to avert the immediate threat; but it was not long before they were for the most part caught at their libations and sacrifices and other unholy rites. . . .

When this couple of monarchs had put almost all commodities in the hands of the "monopolies," all the time relentlessly choking the life out of would-be customers, and only the clothiers' shops were free from their clutches, they contrived a scheme for disposing of these as well. The manufactures of silken garments had for many generations been a staple industry of Beirut and Tyre, two cities of Phoenicia. The merchants who handled these and the skilled and semi-skilled workmen who produced them had lived there from time immemorial, and their wares were carried from there into every land. When Justinian was on the throne, those engaged in this business in Byzantium and the other cities began to charge a higher price for dress materials of this kind, justifying themselves on the ground that they were now having to pay the Persians more for it than in the past, and that it was no longer possible to avoid paying the ten per cent duty on imports.

The Emperor gave everyone to understand that he was highly displeased at this, and published a law debarring anyone from charging more than £16 for twelve ounces of this material. The penalty fixed for anyone who broke the law was to forfeit all his property. The reaction of the public was to condemn this legislation as impracticable and quite impossible. For how could the importers who had bought the material at a higher price be expected to sell it to their customers at a lower? The result was that they were no longer prepared to spend their energies in this traffic, and proceeded to dispose of their remaining stocks by selling under the counter, presumably to some of the men about town who enjoyed parading in such finery however much it might deplete their finances, or felt it incumbent on them to do so. But when the Empress as a result of certain whispers became aware of what was going on, she did not stop to investigate the rumors, but immediately stripped the owners of all their stocks, fining them £15,000 in gold into the bargain. . . .

The importers who hitherto had been occupied with this trade in Byzantium and all the other cities, whether operating on the sea or the land, naturally had to endure the hardships resulting from these operations. And in the cities referred to almost the whole population suddenly found themselves beggars. Mechanics and handicraftsmen were inevitably compelled to struggle against starvation, and many in consequence abandoned the community to which they belonged and fled to the land of Persia. Year after year the whole profit from this trade came into the hands of one man, the Treasurer, who as we have said was good enough to hand a portion of his receipts from this source to the Emperor, but secured the bulk for himself and grew rich at the cost of public misery. . . .

Again, [Justinian] caused doctors and teachers of gentlemen's sons to go short of the elementary necessities of life. For the free rations which earlier emperors ordered to be issued to members of these professions Justinian took away altogether. Moreover, the whole of the revenues which all the municipalities had raised locally for communal purposes and for entertainments he took over and shamelessly pooled with the revenues of the central government. From then on doctors and teachers counted for nothing; no one was now in a position to plan any public building projects; no lamps were lit in the streets of the cities; and there was nothing else to make life pleasant for the citizens. Theaters, hippodromes, and circuses were almost all shut—the very places where his wife had been born and brought up, and had received her early training. Later on he gave orders that all these places of entertainment should be closed down in Byzantium, to save the Treasury from having to finance the payments hitherto made to the people—so numerous that I cannot estimate their numbers—who depended on them for a living. Both in private and in public there was grief and dejection, as if yet another visitation from heaven had struck them, and all laughter had gone out of life. People discussed no subject whatsoever, whether they were at home or meeting each other in the forum or passing a few moments in the churches other than calamities and miseries and a shoal of unexampled misfortunes. Such was the state of affairs in the cities. . . .

Now I have said enough, I think, to make clear how this destroyer has swallowed up all the funds of the State, and has stripped all members of the Senate, both individually and collectively, of their possessions. I think too that I have given an adequate description of the way in which by employing blackmail he succeeded in getting a grip on all others who were believed to be wealthy, thereby stripping them of their property—soldiers, servants of all the ministers, Palace Guards, farmers, landowners and freeholders, professional pleaders; and again, importers, shipowners and merchant seamen, mechanics, artisans, and retail traders, and those who make their living from the activities of the theater; and yet again, pretty well all the others who are indirectly affected by the damage done to these.

Examining the Evidence

1. Of Justinian's many vices, which did Procopius portray as the most harmful to proper government?
2. Did Procopius agree with Justinian's views on the dangers posed by heretics?
3. What were the economic consequences of Justinian's rule?

THE DEBATE OVER DIVINE IMAGES IN BYZANTINE CHRISTIANITY

8.4 JOHN OF DAMASCUS, FROM *ON HOLY IMAGES* (c. 730)

In 726, the Byzantine emperor Leo III (r. 717–741) decreed that all images of Jesus, the Virgin Mary, and the saints must be removed from churches and public monuments. Leo III's decision aroused intense opposition. One of the most vociferous defenders of holy images was John of Damascus, a monk attached to a monastery near Jerusalem. John sharply rebuked the emperor for interfering in matters of church doctrine, but he also developed a set of sophisticated arguments in defense of the veneration of icons. John carefully distinguishes between *latreia*, the worship that is due to God alone, and the use of images as representations to help Christians comprehend the nature of the divine, which is otherwise invisible to mortals.

Deno John Geanakoplos, *Byzantium: Church, Society, and Civilization Seen Through Contemporary Eyes* (Chicago: University of Chicago Press, 1984), 153–154.

For the invisible things of God since the creation of the world are made visible through images. We see images in creation which remind us faintly of God, as when, for instance, we speak of the holy and adorable Trinity, imaged by the sun, or light, or burning rays, or by a running fountain, or a full river, or by the mind, speech, or the spirit within us, or by a rose tree, or a sprouting flower, or a sweet fragrance.

Again, an image is expressive of something in the future, mystically shadowing forth what is to happen. For instance, the ark represents the image of Our Lady, Mother of God; so does the staff and the earthen jar. The serpent brings before us Him who vanquished on the cross the bite of the original serpent; the sea, water, and the cloud the grace of baptism.

Again, things which have taken place are expressed by images for the remembrance either of a wonder, or an honor, or dishonor, or good or evil, to help those who look upon it in after times that we may avoid evils and imitate goodness. It is of two kinds, the written image in books, as when God had the law inscribed on tablets, and when He enjoined that the lives of holy men should be recorded and sensible memorials be preserved in remembrance; as, for instance, the earthen jar and the staff in the ark. So now we preserve in writing the images and the good deeds of the past. Either, therefore, take away images altogether and be out of harmony with God who made these regulations, or receive them with the language and in the manner which befits them. In speaking of the manner let us go into the question of worship.

Worship is the symbol of veneration and honor. Let us understand that there are different degrees of worship. First of all the worship of *latreia*, which we show to God, who alone by nature is worthy of worship. Then, for the sake of God who is worshipful by nature, we honor His saints and servants, as Joshua and Daniel worshiped an angel, and David His holy places, when he says, "Let us go to the place where his feet have stood." Again, in His tabernacles, as when all the people of Israel adored in the tent, and standing round the temple in Jerusalem, fixing their gaze upon it from all sides, and worshiping from that day to this, or in the rulers established by Him, as Jacob rendered homage to Esau, his elder brother, and to Pharaoh, the divinely established ruler. Joseph was worshiped by his brothers, I am aware that worship was based on honor, as in the case of Abraham and the sons of Emmor. Either, then, do away with worship, or receive it altogether according to its proper measure. . . .

Of old, God the incorporeal and uncircumscribed was never depicted. Now, however, when God is seen clothed in flesh, and conversing with men, I make an image of the God whom I see. I do not worship matter, I worship the God of matter, who became matter for my sake, and deigned to inhabit matter, who worked out my salvation through matter. I will not cease from honoring that matter which works my salvation. I venerate it, though not as God. How could God be born out of lifeless things? And if God's body is God by union, it is immutable. The nature of God remains the same as before, the flesh created in time is quickened by a logical and reasoning soul. I honor all matter besides, and venerate it. Through it, filled, as it were, with a divine power and grace, my salvation has come to me. Was not the thrice happy and thrice blessed wood of the Cross matter? Was not the sacred and holy mountain of Calvary matter? What of the life-giving rock, the Holy Sepulchre, the source of our resurrection: was it not matter? Is not the most holy book of the Gospels matter? Is not the blessed table matter which gives us the Bread of Life? Are not the gold and silver matter out of which crosses and altar-plate and chalices are made? And before all these things, is not the body and blood of our Lord matter? Either do away with the veneration and worship due to all these things, or submit to the tradition of the Church in the worship of images, honoring God and His friends, and following in this the grace of the Holy Spirit.

8.5 | THE COUNCIL OF 754 CONDEMNS ICONS

In 754, Emperor Constantine V (r. 741–775) convened a council of bishops, held at Hieria near Constantinople, to ratify the iconoclast position as formal church doctrine. The council stigmatized the defenders of icons by associating them with Nestorius and others deemed heretics for trying to separate the divine nature of Jesus from his human nature. The council's statement also reveals the continued fear of pagan forms of worship. The Hieria council decreed that images should be destroyed and declared an anathema (excommunication) against John of Damascus. In 787, however, the Second Nicene Council overturned the Hieria council and restored images to churches. Subsequently, the use of icons in devotion became a prominent feature of Byzantine Christianity.

Philip Schaff and Henry Wace, eds., *The Seven Ecumenical Councils of the Undivided Church*, vol. 14 of *A Select Library of Nicene and Post-Nicene Fathers of the Christian Church* (New York: Scribner's, 1900), 543–544.

(continued)

CONTRASTING VIEWS (*continued*)

Satan misguided men, so that they worshiped the creature instead of the Creator. The Mosaic law[1] and the prophets cooperated to undo this ruin; but in order to save mankind thoroughly, God sent his own Son, who turned us away from error and the worshiping of icons, and taught us the worshiping of God in spirit and in truth. As messengers of his saving doctrine, he left us his Apostles and disciples, and these adorned the Church, his Bride, with his glorious doctrines. This ornament of the Church the holy Fathers and the six Ecumenical Councils have preserved inviolate. But the before-mentioned demiurgos [one who works to cause evil] of wickedness could not endure the sight of this adornment, and gradually brought back idolatry under the appearance of Christianity. As then Christ armed his Apostles against the ancient idolatry with the power of the Holy Spirit, and sent them out into all the world, so has he awakened against the new idolatry his servants our faithful Emperors, and endowed them with the same wisdom of the Holy Spirit. Impelled by the Holy Spirit they could no longer be witness of the Church being laid waste by the deception of demons, and summoned the sanctified assembly of the God-beloved bishops, that they might institute at a synod a scriptural examination into the deceitful coloring of the pictures which draws down the spirit of man from the lofty adoration [*latreia*] of God to the low and material adoration of the creature, and that they, under divine guidance, might express their view of the subject. . . .

After we had carefully examined their decrees [the decrees of earlier church councils] under the guidance of the Holy Spirit, we found that the unlawful art of painting living creatures blasphemed the fundamental doctrine of our salvation—namely, the Incarnation of Christ—and contradicted the six holy synods. These condemned Nestorius because he divided the one Son and Word of God into two sons, and on the other side, Arius, Dioscorus, Eutyches, and Severus [were also condemned by preceding ecumenical councils] because they maintained a mingling of the two natures of the one Christ.

Wherefore we thought it right, to show forth with all accuracy, in our present definition the error of such as make and venerate these, for it is the unanimous doctrine of all the holy Fathers and of the six Ecumenical Synods, that no one may imagine any kind of separation of mingling in opposition to the unsearchable, unspeakable, and incomprehensible union of the two natures in the one hypostasis or person. What avails, then, the folly of the painter, who from sinful love of gain depicts that which should not be depicted—that is, with his polluted hands he tries to fashion that which should only be believed in the heart and confessed with the mouth? He makes an image and calls it Christ. The name *Christ* signifies *God and Man*. Consequently, it is an image of God and man, and consequently, he has in his foolish mind, in his representation of the created flesh, depicted the Godhead which cannot be represented, and thus mingled what should not be mingled. Thus he is guilty of a double blasphemy—the one in making an image of the Godhead, and the other by mingling the Godhead and manhood. Those fall into the same blasphemy who venerate the image, and the same woe rests upon both, because they err with Arius, Dioscorus, and Eutyches, and with the heresy of the Acephali.[2] When, however, they are blamed for undertaking to depict the divine nature of Christ, which should not be depicted, they take refuge in the excuse: We represent only the flesh of Christ which we have seen and handled. But that is a Nestorian error.[3] For it should be considered that the flesh was also the flesh of God the Word, without any separation, perfectly assumed by the divine nature and made wholly divine. How could it now be separated and represented apart? . . .

The only admissible figure of the humanity of Christ, however, is bread and wine in the holy Supper. This and no other form, this and no other type, has he chosen to represent his incarnation. Bread he ordered to be brought, but not a representation of the human form, so that idolatry might not arise. And as the body of Christ is made divine, so also this figure of the body of Christ, the bread, is made divine by the descent of the Holy Spirit; it becomes the divine body of Christ by the mediation of the priest who, separating the oblation [the Eucharist sacrament] from that which is common, sanctifies it.

[1] **Mosaic law:** The laws Moses delivered to the Israelites.

[2] **Arius . . . heresy of the Acephali:** Arius, Dioscorus, and Eutyches were Christian theologians whose views on the nature of Christ were condemned as heresy by official church councils in the fourth and fifth centuries. The Acephali were followers of Eutyches who refused to accept the authority of the Christian church's leadership.

[3] **Nestorian error:** Nestorius, archbishop of Constantinople, was condemned as a heretic by the Council of Ephesus in 431 for his insistence on Christ's human nature.

The evil custom of assigning names to the images does not come down from Christ and the Apostles and the holy Fathers; nor have these left behind them any prayer by which an image should be hallowed or made anything else than ordinary matter.

If, however, some say, we might be right in regard to the images of Christ, on account of the mysterious union of the two natures, but it is not right for us to forbid also the images of the altogether spotless and ever-glorious Mother of God, of the prophets, apostles, and martyrs, who were men and did not consist of two natures; we may reply first of all: If those fall away, there is no longer need of these. But

we will also consider what may be said against these in particular. Christianity has rejected the *whole* of heathenism, and not merely heathen sacrifices, but also the heathen worship of images. The Saints live on eternally with God, although they have died. If anyone thinks to call them back again to life by a dead art, discovered by the heathen, he makes himself guilty of blasphemy. Who dares attempt with heathenish art to paint the Mother of God, who is exalted above all heavens and the Saints? It is not permitted to Christians, who have the hope of resurrection, to imitate the customs of demon-worshippers, and to insult the Saints, who shine in so great glory, by common dead matter.

8.6 JOHN OF JERUSALEM ON THE ORIGINS OF THE ICONOCLASM MOVEMENT (787)

In 787, the Second Nicene Council restored the veneration of icons as an appropriate form of Christian piety. The council also made Muslims and Jews, who were regarded as the enemies of Christians, the scapegoats for the misbegotten iconoclasm campaign. In a report to the council, John of Jerusalem accused the Umayyad caliph Yazid II (r. 720–724) of initiating the destruction of holy images in Christian churches. John also identified a mysterious Jewish "wizard" and a wayward bishop, Constantine of Nacolia, as the real instigators of the iconoclasm campaign. Most historians question the reliability of John's testimony; certainly there is no reference in Arabic sources to an iconoclasm edict issued by Yazid II. Regardless of its historical accuracy, however, John's accusation became a fixture of the Byzantine Empire's official history of the iconoclasm episode.

Patriarch Tarasius said, "It will now be right for us to hear our brother and beloved lord John, legate of the Apostolic Thrones of the East; for he has with him a writing which will explain how the subversion of images began."

The Holy Council said, "We should like much, my lord, to hear about this." . . .

[John spoke:] "I, unworthy and humblest of all, wish to lay before this, your Holy and Sacred Council, in all truth, how, when, and whence this most vile and God-detested heresy of the detractors of Christianity had its beginning; and, being anxious to use what brevity I can, I have decided to read to you from a written document, so that no element of truth should escape me." . . .

John proceeded: "On [the caliph Umar's] death, [Yazid II (r. 720–724)], a man of frivolous and unstable turn of mind, succeeded him. There lived a certain man at Tiberias, a ringleader of the lawless Jews, a magician and fortuneteller, an instrument of soul-destroying demons, whose name was Tessarakontapechys, a bitter enemy of

the Church of God. On learning of the frivolity of the ruler Yazid, this most-wicked Jew approached him and attempted to utter prophecies . . . saying, 'You will remain thirty years in this your kingship if you follow my advice.' That foolish tyrant, yearning for a long life (for he was self indulgent and dissolute), answered: 'Whatever you say, I am ready to do, and, if I attain my desire, I will repay you with highest honors.' Then the Jewish magician said to him, 'Order immediately, without any delay or postponement, that an encyclical letter be issued throughout your empire to the effect that every representational painting, whether on tablets or in wall mosaics, on sacred vessels or on altar coverings, and all such objects as are found in Christian churches, be destroyed and thoroughly abolished, nay also representations of all kings that adorn and embellish the market places of cities.' And moved by satanic wickedness, the false prophet added: 'every likeness,' contriving thereby to make unsuspected his hostility against us.

"The Iconoclastic Edict of the Caliph Yazid II, A.D. 721," by A.A. Vasiliev, pp. 28–30. © 1956 Dumbarton Oaks Research Library and Collection, Trustees of Harvard University. Originally printed in *Dumbarton Oaks Papers 9*.

(continued)

CONTRASTING VIEWS (*continued*)

"The wretched tyrant, yielding most readily to this advice, sent officials and destroyed the holy icons and all other representations in every province under his rule, and, because of the Jewish magician, thus ruthlessly robbed the churches of God under his sway of all ornaments, before the evil came into this land. As the God-loving Christians fled, lest they should have to overthrow the holy images with their own hands, the emirs who were sent for this purpose pressed into service abominable Jews and wretched Arabs; and thus they burned the venerable icons, and either smeared or scraped the ecclesiastical buildings.

"On hearing this, the pseudo-bishop [Constantine] of Nacolia and his followers imitated the lawless Jews and impious Arabs, outraging the churches of God. . . . When, after doing this, the Caliph [Yazid] died, no more than two and a half years later, and went into the everlasting fire, the images were restored to their original position and

honor. His son Walid, filled with indignation, ordered the magician to be ignominiously put to death for his father's murder, as just punishment for his false prophecy."

COMPARING THE EVIDENCE

1. Why did the iconoclasts deem the veneration of icons to be blasphemy?
2. Why did the question of the divine nature of Jesus Christ become a central issue in the iconoclasm controversy?
3. Both sides of the iconoclasm controversy accused the other of heresy. How did they differ in what they meant by *heresy*?
4. In what ways is John of Jerusalem's blaming Muslims and Jews for the earlier ban on icons an attempt to ignore the church's own anti-icon edict of the Council of 754?

8.7 MUHAMMAD BEGINS HIS PUBLIC PREACHING

Muhammad ibn Ishaq, *The Life of the Messenger of God* (Eighth Century)

After receiving his first revelations circa 610, Muhammad mostly confined his religious instruction to family members. In 613, however, he received a revelation commanding him to propagate Islam publicly. Muhammad's message quickly won converts, especially among Mecca's humble population. The growing popularity of Muhammad's teachings aroused opposition from the Quraysh, Mecca's ruling tribe, of which Muhammad himself was a member. After failing to dissuade Muhammad from his preaching, the Quraysh launched a campaign of vilification against him. In 622, Muhammad was forced to flee to Medina, where he received a more favorable reception. The following account of Muhammad's conflict with the Quraysh leaders is taken from an early biography

of Muhammad composed by the Baghdad scholar Muhammad ibn Ishaq (d. 761 or 767) and later revised by other scholars.

People began to accept Islam, both men and women, in large numbers until the fame of it was spread throughout Mecca, and it began to be talked about. Then God commanded His apostle to declare the truth of what he had received and to make known His commands to men and to call them to Him. Three years elapsed from the time that the apostle concealed his state until God commanded him to publish his religion, according to the information which has reached me. Then God said, "Proclaim what you have been ordered and turn aside from the polytheists." And again, "Warn thy family, thy nearest relations, and lower thy wing to the followers who follow thee." . . .

A. Guillaume, trans. and ed., *The Life of Muhammad: A Translation of Ishaq's Sirat Rasul Allah* (Oxford: Oxford University Press, 1955), 117–119, 130, 133–135.

When the apostle openly displayed Islam as God ordered him his people did not withdraw or turn against him, so far as I have heard, until he spoke disparagingly of their gods. When he did that they took great offense and resolved unanimously to treat him as an enemy, except those whom God had protected by Islam from such evil, but they were a despised minority. Abu Talib his uncle treated the apostle kindly and protected him, the latter continuing to obey God's commands, nothing turning him back. When Quraysh saw that he would not yield to them and withdrew from them and insulted their gods and that his uncle treated him kindly and stood up in his defense and would not give him up to them, some of their leading men went to Abu Talib. . . . They said, "O Abu Talib, your nephew has cursed our gods, insulted our religion, mocked our way of life and accused our forefathers of error; either you must stop him or you must let us get at him, for you yourself are in the same position to him and we will rid you of him." He gave them a conciliatory reply and a soft answer and they went away. . . . Abu Talib was deeply distressed at the breach with his people and their enmity but he could not desert the apostle and give him up to them. . . .

After hearing these words from the Quraysh, Abu Talib sent for his nephew and told him what his people had said. "Spare me and yourself," he said. "Do not put on me a burden greater than I can bear." The apostle thought that his uncle had the idea of abandoning and betraying him, and that he was going to lose his help and support. He answered, "O my uncle, by God, if they put the sun in my right hand and the moon in my left on the condition that I abandoned this course, until God has made it victorious, or I perish therein, I would not abandon it." Then the apostle broke into tears, and got up. As he turned away his uncle called him and said, "Come back, my nephew," and when he came back, he said, "Go and say what you please, for by God I will never give you up on any account." . . .

When the Quraysh became distressed by the trouble caused by the enmity between them and the apostle and those of their people who accepted his teaching, they stirred up against him foolish men who called him a liar, insulted him, and accused him of being a poet, a sorcerer, a diviner, and of

being possessed. However, the apostle continued to proclaim, concealing nothing, and exciting their dislike by condemning their religion, forsaking their idols, and leaving them to their unbelief. . . .

Islam began to spread in Mecca among men and women of the tribes of the Quraysh, though Quraysh were imprisoning and seducing as many of the Muslims as they could. . . . The leading men of every clan of Quraysh . . . decided to send for Muhammad and to negotiate and argue with him so that they could not be held to blame on his account in the future. When they sent for him the apostle came quickly because he thought that what he had said to them had made an impression, for he was most zealous for their welfare, and their wicked way of life pained him. When he came and sat down with them, they explained that they had sent for him in order that they could talk together. No Arab had ever treated his tribe as Muhammad had treated them, and they repeated the charges which have been mentioned on several occasions. If it was money he wanted, they would make him the richest of all; if it was honor, he should be their prince; if it was sovereignty, they would make him king; if it was a spirit which had gotten possession of him, then they would exhaust their means in finding medicine to cure him. The apostle replied that he had no such intention. He sought not money, nor honor, nor sovereignty, but God had sent him as an apostle, and revealed a book to him, and commanded him to become an announcer and a warner. He had brought them the messages of his Lord, and given them good advice. If they took it then they would have a portion in this world and the next; if they rejected it, he could only patiently await the issue until God decided between them, or words to that effect.

"Well, Muhammad," they said, "if you won't accept any of our propositions, you know that no people are more short of land and water, and live a harder life than we, so ask your Lord, who has sent you, to remove for us these mountains which shut us in, and to straighten out our country for us, and to open up in it rivers like those of Syria and Iraq, and to resurrect for us our forefathers, and let there be among those that are resurrected for us Qusayy b. Kilab, for he was a true sheikh, so that we may ask them whether what you say is true or false. If they say you are speaking the truth, and you do what we have asked you, we will believe in you, and we shall know what your position with God is, and that He has actually sent you as an apostle as you say."

He replied that he had not been sent to them with such an object. He had conveyed to them God's message, and they could either accept it with advantage, or reject it and await God's judgment. They said that if he would not do that for them, let him do something for himself. Ask God to send an angel with him to confirm what he said and to contradict them; to make him gardens and castles, and treasures of gold and silver to satisfy his obvious wants. He stood in the streets as they did, and he sought a livelihood as they did. If he could do this, they would recognize his merit and position with God, if he were an apostle as he claimed to be. He replied that he would not do it, and would not ask for such things, for he was not sent to do so, and he repeated what he said before. They said, "Then let the heavens be dropped on us in pieces, as you assert that your Lord could do if He wished, for we will not believe you unless you do so." The apostle replied that this was a matter for God; if He wanted to do it with them, He would do it. They said, "Did not your Lord know

that we would sit with you, and ask you these questions, so that He might come to you and instruct you how to answer us, and tell you what He was going to do with us, if we did not receive your message? Information has reached us that you are taught by this fellow in al-Yamama, called al-Rahman, and by God we will never believe in the Rahman. Our conscience is clear. By God, we will not leave you and our treatment of you, until either we destroy you or you destroy us." . . .

When they said this the apostle got up and left them . . . and went to his family, sad and grieving, because his hope that they had called him to accept his preaching was vain, and because of their estrangement from him.

Examining the Evidence

1. What was the principal objection of the Quraysh leaders to Muhammad's preaching?
2. In what ways did Muhammad pose a threat to the established social order in Mecca?
3. What do the tests proposed by the Quraysh leaders reveal about their conception of the relationship between human beings and the divine?

8.8 THE CALIPH RELIEVES AN HONORABLE JURIST OF HIS DEBTS

al-Muhassin, *The Table-Talk of a Mesopotamian Judge* (Tenth Century)

Al-Muhassin (940–994) spent his career serving as *qadi* (chief judge) in various towns of Mesopotamia (modern Iraq). In the preface to this work, he announces his intention to record stories that he had heard in conversations with numerous learned men over a period of twenty years. He wrote his book, he tells us, "to provide the intelligent person . . . such matter as will train him for this

world and the next, teach him the consequences of well-doing and ill-doing, how actions must ultimately turn out, how a republic should be administered, and what mistakes he should avoid." The following anecdote is set in the time of the caliph Ma'mun (r. 813–833), a figure al-Muhassin held in high esteem.

I was told by my father on the authority of the hero of the story, by a chain of tradition which he gave, that Abu Hassan Ziyadi was one of the leading jurists of our [Hanafi] school, and a disciple of Abu Yusuf,

D. S. Margoliouth, trans., *The Table-Talk of a Mesopotamian Judge* (London: Royal Asiatic Society, 1922), 230–234.

and further a traditionalist. He at one time held a judgeship, but was afterwards out of employment, and became very poor. He frequented a mosque which was opposite his dwelling, where he gave opinions, taught law, led prayer, and repeated traditions [*hadith*]. Each day his financial difficulties increased while his efforts at obtaining employment or allowance were unsuccessful. One day when he had exhausted all his funds, sold all his property, he was visited by a man from Khurasan [in Central Asia], who was in Baghdad at the time when people were leaving the city for Mecca. The man said to him, "I am about to start on pilgrimage, and here are 10,000 dirhams [silver coins] which I have upon me; take them as a deposit, and if I return from the pilgrimage restore it to me, whereas if the others return but I do not, then know that I have met my end, and it is a gift to you which you may use without scruple." "So," said Abu Hassan, "I took the deposit home, and told the story to my wife. She observed that we were in great straits and that I had better make use of the money at once, pay my debts, and buy comforts, since perhaps God would make the money mine ultimately, and I should only have anticipated the enjoyment of it. I declined to do this, but the whole day and night she kept urging me and finally I assented. So the next day I broke the seal of the purse, paid my debt, purchased stores and comfort for my home, and clothes for her, myself, and my daughters. For all these purposes I had spent some 5,000 dirhams.

"After some three or four days as I turned round after prayer, I saw the man from Khurasan behind me. When I saw him, I was overwhelmed with confusion, and asked him what had happened. He said that he had abandoned his journey to Mecca, and wished to stay in Baghdad; please then, he said, return me the deposit. I said, 'I cannot do it this moment, come to me tomorrow morning.' He departed, and I too started homeward, but scarcely had the strength to walk the distance between the mosque and my house; and I fainted when I got inside. My household collected and when I was conscious they asked me what had befallen me. I said to them, 'You induced me to use the money of that man from Khurasan, and he has just come back and is demanding it. What am I to do? I shall be disgraced and my reputation will be gone. I shall

disappear from among men, be imprisoned and die of hardship.' They howled and so did I, and when the prayer of sunset was to be said, I was unable to go out to the mosque, as also when it was time for evening prayer. So I prayed at home, and said, 'This is a matter which God only could set right, and with Him only can I take refuge.' So I renewed my purification and put my feet close together in the sanctuary praying, weeping, and supplicating, until I had finished the *Qur'an*.

"Dawn was near breaking and I had had no sleep. I said to my people, 'The man will soon be coming to the mosque, and what am I to do?' They told me that they did not know. I ordered my people to saddle a mule which I had and rode, saying to them, 'I am now going to ride, I know not whither, and I shall not return to you; for though I were to perish I have not the face to speak to the man from Khurasan. If he demands the money of you and threatens you with trouble, give him the remains of the money and tell him the truth; but if you can put him off, leave me with my credit unimpaired and perhaps I may return with deliverance or some scheme for dealing with him.'

"So I rode forth not knowing my destination, without lantern or slave, leaving the mule's rein upon its neck. It brought me to the bridge, which I crossed to the eastern side [of the Tigris River]. I did not dismount but let it take me to the Taq Gate, whence it turned into the great road which leads to the Caliph's Palace. Midway we came into a great procession with lights and people coming from the direction of the Palace. I thought I had best get out of the way in order not to be jostled by their horses, so I drew the rein with the intention of going up one of the side streets. They shouted to me, and when I stopped asked me who I was. 'A jurist,' I replied. They then seized me, and when I resisted, the head of the party came and said, 'Who are you, God have mercy on you? No harm will befall you if you tell the truth.' I replied that I was a jurist and a judge. 'What is your name?' he asked. 'Abu Hassan Ziyadi,' I replied. At this he cried out, 'God is Great!' repeatedly, and bade me answer the call of the Commander of the Faithful [the caliph].

"So I went along with him until I was brought before Ma'mun, who asked me who I was. I said, 'A jurist and judge known as the Ziyadite. . . .'

"'What,' he asked, 'is your patronymic?'

"'Abu Hassan,' I replied.

"'Tell me,' he said, 'what has befallen you, for the Prophet would not let me sleep yesterday on your account. He came to me once in the beginning of the night and again in the middle, saying, "Assist Abu Hassan the Ziyadite." I woke up, but not knowing you I forgot to ask about you; but just now he came to me and said, "Assist Abu Hassan the Ziyadite," and I did not venture to go to sleep again, but have kept awake since then, and have dispatched people on both sides of the city to find you.'

"So I told him the truth, concealing nothing, saying that I was a man who had served Rashid as judge in a certain region under Abu Yusuf, but after his death I had been cashiered and my allowances stopped, and I had been continuously unemployed and in straits, and then this had occurred with the man from Khurasan. We both burst into tears, and he said, 'We are God's and to Him do we return. Bring me 5,000 dirhams!' They brought them and he bade me take them and replace with them those which I had spent. Then he ordered another 10,000 to be brought, and bade me take them and use them for the settlement of my affairs, and the purchase of comforts. Then he ordered 30,000 more to be brought and bade me use them for the outfit and the marriage of my daughters. 'And,' he said, 'on the next festival day present yourself before us in black that we may appoint you to a post and assign you an allowance.' I praised God, thanked Him, invoked the prayers on the Prophet and blessings on the Commander of the Faithful and went home laden with the money.

"When I got there the sun had not yet risen, and the people were waiting for me to come out and lead prayer, and were vexed at my procrastination. Dismounting, I led them in prayer and when I had pronounced the blessing I saw the man from Khurasan. Taking him into my house I produced the remains of his money, and he remarked that the seal had been tampered with. I said, 'Take this, which is what remains of your money, for I have been using it.' Then, pointing to the money that I had brought, I said, 'Take the balance.' He asked me to explain what had occurred, and when I told him the story he was deeply affected, and vowed that he would take nothing. I adjured him, but he said, 'No, I will not take it nor take into my possession any of these people's property.'

"So I began to think about my daughters, their marriage and their outfit, and ordered the purchase of a black uniform, a horse and a slave, and went to Ma'mun on the festival day, was received, saluted, and was placed with the judges. He produced a deed of investiture from beneath the oratory which he handed to me, telling me that he appointed me judge of the western side. 'This,' he said, 'is my deed of investiture, and fear God; I have ordered a certain sum to be paid to you as allowance every month.'"

Abu Hassan continued to occupy this office through the days of Ma'mun.

Examining the Evidence

1. Why did the man from Khurasan refuse to take back his money from Abu Hassan?

2. What does this story tell us about the position of the *qadi* in Islamic society?

3. Al-Muhassin's stories, set in the recent past, were intended to provide lessons for his contemporaries in the present day. What message did al-Muhassin seek to convey in this story?

MAKING CONNECTIONS

1. To what extent did Christians and Muslims share similar conceptions of personal virtue and how to lead a proper life?

2. Compare the relationship between religious and political authorities as seen in the letters of Pope Gregory with that between the emperor and the church in the Byzantine world. How did they differ?

3. How and why did Christian and Muslim attitudes toward miracles differ?

4. In what ways did the position and duties of the judge in Islamic society vary from the role of the Christian clergy?

CHAPTER 9

Religion and Cross-Cultural Exchange in Asia, 400–1000

The period 450–1000 marked the heyday of the overland Silk Roads of Central Asia. The rise of the first nomadic empires and the expansion of East–West trade spurred an unprecedented circulation of people and ideas throughout Asia. The most spectacular example of cross-cultural exchange in this era was the spread of Buddhism from its homeland in India to Central and Southeast Asia, China, and finally Korea and Japan. In India itself, however, Buddhism was eclipsed by the reinvigoration of ancient beliefs and practices in the form now known as Hinduism. However, this was also an age of political instability and strife. Monarchs and aristocrats—both in the ancient centers of civilization such as India and China and in recently established states in Southeast Asia, the Korean peninsula, and the Japanese islands—were compelled to devise new strategies to secure their power, wealth, and social status. These elites often were the first to embrace foreign ideas and innovations.

9.1 TRAVELS OF THE BUDDHIST PILGRIM XUANZANG IN SOGDIA AND AFGHANISTAN

Huili, *The Life of Xuanzang* (688)

Troubled by the profusion of competing Buddhist schools and doctrines, the Chinese monk Xuanzang (602–664) set out for India in 629 to learn the true meaning of the Buddha's teachings. He spent many years in India, visiting holy sites, lecturing before local rulers, and debating with theologians and philosophers. The following selections from the biography of Xuanzang by his disciple Huili describe Xuanzang's travels to Samarkand, the capital of the Sogdian kingdom, and Afghanistan. Both the Hinayana and Mahayana traditions of Buddhism flourished in Afghanistan. The Hinayana (or Theravada) tradition emphasized achieving enlightenment through one's own efforts by joining a monastic order and devoting oneself to study, prayer, and religious practices. Mahayana Buddhists, in contrast, believed in the existence of many buddhas and bodhisattvas who acted as divine saviors and aided the faithful in their quest for enlightenment.

[After] traveling for more than 500 *li* [6 *li* = 1 mile], [the Master] reached the country of Samarkand. The king and the people did not believe in Buddhism but worshipped fire [referring to the fire altar, the ritual centerpiece of the Zoroastrian religion of Iran]. There were two monastery buildings but no monks lived in them. If a guest monk attempted to stay in them, the native people would drive him out with fire.

When the Master first arrived, the king treated him with arrogance. After staying for one night, the Master preached on the law of cause and effect among men and heavenly beings, and told the king about the merits and advantages of praising and worshipping the Buddha. The king was impressed. He begged to observe the precepts. Then he respected the Master.

Two of the Master's attending monks went to worship the Buddha in the monasteries and were driven out by the native people with fire. The novices reported to the king, who on hearing it ordered the arrest of the men who had tried to burn them. The king had the arrested men brought before him, and after assembling the people, ordered that the hands of the prisoners be cut off.

With a mind of kindness, the Master could not bear to see them mutilated and rescued them. Thereupon the king ordered that they be thrashed severely, and driven out of the city. After which the king and people believed in Buddhism and a great meeting was held to ordain some people, who afterwards lived in the monasteries.

Wherever the Master went, he corrected those who were wrong and enlightened those who lacked knowledge just as stated above.

Once more proceeding on his way he went towards the west. . . .

* * *

From Balika [modern Balkh, in northern Afghanistan] going south, the Master and [his companion] Prajnakara arrived in the country of Gachi together and entered the Great Snow Mountains [the Hindu Kush] in the southeast. After traveling for more than 600 *li*, they came out of the territory of Tukhara and entered the country of Bamiyan [in Afghanistan]. Bamiyan was 2,000 *li* from east to west and was situated in the Snow Mountains. The roads were more dangerous and harder to travel than among the Ice Mountains or in the deserts. Thick clouds and flying snow never ceased for a moment, and at the worst places the snow accumulated for scores of feet. Song You [an ancient Chinese poet] had said that the way to the West was

Monk Huili, *The Life of Hsuan-Tsang: The Tripitaka-Master of the Great Tzu En Monastery*, trans. Li Yung-hsi (Beijing: Chinese Buddhist Printing Association, 1959), 40–47, 52–57.

so difficult that one had to pass for a thousand *li* through a land of ice with flying snow, and this was the place which he had referred to. Who would travel in this place at the risk of his life except those who had the intention of acquiring the supreme Law for the benefit of all beings? . . .

The Master made slow progress but finally reached the capital of Bamiyan. Here were some ten monasteries, with several thousand monks, who studied the teachings of the Hinayana Lokattaravadinah School. The king of the Bamiyan came to receive him and invited him to his palace, and entertained him there for several days. In the capital were two monks of the Mahasamghika School, Aryadasa and Aryasena, both well versed in the theories of the Dharamalaksana School. On seeing the Master they were surprised to know that there should be such a monk as the Master in a country as distant as China. With great courtesy they accompanied him to all the holy places.

On a hill to the northeast of the royal city was an image made of stone, 150 feet high. To the east of the image stood a monastery, and to the east of the monastery a standing image of the Sakyamuni Buddha, made of bronze, 100 feet high. In the monastery was a recumbent image of the Buddha, in the posture of entering nirvana, 1,000 feet in length. All these images were made in a stately and beautiful manner.

Departing, he went southeast for more than 200 *li*, crossed the Great Snow Mountains, and reached a small valley, where in a monastery was a Buddha's tooth-relic. There was also a tooth of a *pratyeka-buddha* [one who achieves enlightenment through his own efforts] who lived . . . [eons ago], five inches long and less than four inches wide; a tooth of a Golden Wheel King, three inches long and two inches wide; an iron eating bowl of Sanakavasa [an Indian merchant who gave up his wealth to become a Buddhist monk] . . . ; and his deep red . . . [monk's robe]. This man had worn this robe during five hundred lives in his past and he was always born with it. Later it had become a religious robe and the story was related in detail in a book.

Traveling for fifteen days the Master came out of Bamiyan, but he encountered a snowstorm in which he lost his way for two days. At the Small Sandy Peak, he met some hunters who showed him the way. After crossing the Black Mountain, he reached the domain of Kapisa [near Kabul, the capital of modern Afghanistan]. This country was more than 4,000 *li* in circuit and it bordered on the Snow Mountain in the north. The king, being a *kshatriya* [a member of the warrior caste], was a powerful man of great ability and he ruled over more than ten countries.

When the Master approached the capital, the king and the monks came out of the city to welcome him. The city contained more than 100 monasteries, and the monks vied with one another in inviting him to stay. One Hinayana monastery was known by the name of Salaka. According to tradition it was built at the time when a prince of the emperor of China was sent to Kapisa as a hostage. The monks of this monastery said, "Our monastery was built by the son of the emperor of China, and now as you have come from that land, you should stay in our monastery first."

Seeing their sincerity, and as his companion, Prajnakara, was a Hinayana monk who did not desire to live in a Mahayana monastery, the Master accepted their invitation.

When the hostage prince built this monastery, he buried a vast amount of valuables under the feet of the great deity in the south of the eastern gate of the Buddha Hall, for the purpose of defraying the cost of future repairs. Out of gratitude the monks had painted the figure of the hostage prince in frescoes everywhere in the monastery, and they performed religious services for his benefit at the beginning and end of each rainy season. This had been done generation after generation without cessation till the present time.

An evil king who was covetous and cruel lately had intended to seize the treasure of the monks. He ordered his men to dig under the feet of the deity, but the earth quaked and the figure of a parrot on the top of the deity flapped its wings and screamed in alarm when it saw the men digging. The king and his soldiers fell down unconscious, and finally they went away in fear.

In the monastery a stupa [a shrine containing Buddhist relics] had become dilapidated, and the monks wished to take out the treasure in order to repair it. But the earth quaked with a roar and nobody dared venture near it. When the Master arrived, the monks assembled and told him about the event. He and the monks went to the deity and prayed to him with the burning of incense, saying, "When the hostage prince stored up this treasure, he intended it to be used for meritorious deeds. It is now time to bring it out for use. I wish you would discern our true mind and relax your sense of responsibility. With your permission, I will open up the treasure and find out the exact amount before I hand it over to the authorities and request them to repair the stupa without any waste of money. Being a divine deity, you may understand our mind."

Saying so the Master asked the people to dig the ground, and they did so without any trouble. Having dug for seven or eight feet, they unearthed a large bronze vessel containing several hundred catties of gold and many lustrous pearls. The monks were delighted and they all praised the Master.

The Master stayed in this monastery for the summer retirement. The king despised the arts, but he believed in Mahayana Buddhism and liked to listen to preaching. So he invited the Master and the reverend teacher Prajnakara to hold a discussion meeting in a Mahayana monastery. Three learned teachers, Manojnaghosa of the Mahayana school, Aryavarman of the Sarvastivadin school, and Gunabhadra of the Mahisasaka school, all were religious teachers but they were not learned in both the Mahayana and the Hinayana teachings. Though

well versed in the theories of one school, they did not know much about the doctrines of the other. The Master alone knew the teachings of all schools and could answer all questions according to the theories of the different schools. Because of this, the people respected him for his learning.

The discussion meeting lasted for five days and then the people dispersed. The king was highly pleased and he separately presented five rolls of pure silk to the Master as a special honor.

After having spent the summer season in the Salaka Monastery, the reverend teacher Prajnakara was again invited by the king of Tukhara to return to that country, and so the Master parted company with him.

Traveling toward the east for more than 600 *li*, he crossed the Black Mountain and entered the territory of North India.

Examining the Evidence

1. Who was the principal audience for Xuanzang's preaching during his travels in Central Asia?
2. What were the main forms of Buddhist worship practiced in Central Asia at this time?
3. According to Huili, how did Xuanzang demonstrate his superior mastery of Buddhism?

9.2 IBN FADLAN'S TRAVELS AMONG THE TURKS AND KHAZARS

Ibn Fadlan, *Journey to Russia* (921–922)

In the early tenth century, the king of the Bulghars—Turkish nomads living in the steppes of southern Russia—appealed to the Abbasid caliph seeking support to free himself from the overlordship of the Khazars. The Khazar khans (a Turkish term for a ruler) ruled over a mixed

population of Christians, Muslims, Jews, and pagan nomads. Though few in number, Jews had gained control of the khanate through the institution of dual kingship, in which the secondary ruler ("Khagan Bih" in Ibn Fadlan's account) controlled the actual operations of government. In 921, the caliph Al-Muqtadir dispatched Ibn Fadlan as an envoy to the Bulghar king (referred to in this document as the "king of the Saqaliba"). The mission ended in

Richard N. Frye, trans., *Ibn Fadlan's Journey to Russia: A Tenth-Century Traveler from Baghdad to the Volga River* (Princeton, NJ: Markus Wiener, 2005), 33, 35, 54–55, 61–62, 75–77.

failure, but Ibn Fadlan's record of his journey contains rare firsthand observations about the livelihood, customs, and political institutions of the nomadic peoples of the Russian steppe.

We reached a Turkish tribe, which are called Oghuz. They are nomads and have houses of felt. They stay for a time in one place and then travel on. One sees their dwellings placed here and there according to nomad custom. Although they lead a hard existence they are like asses gone astray. They have no religious bonds with God, nor do they have recourse to reason. They never pray, rather do they call their headmen lords. . . . Their undertakings are based upon counsel solely among themselves; when they come to an agreement on a matter and have decided to put it through, there comes one of the lowest and basest of them and disrupts their decision. . . .

Their marriage customs are as follows: one of them asks for the hand of a female of another's family, whether his daughter or his sister or any other one of those over whom he has power, against so and so many garments from Khwarazm [in the Caucasus region]. When he pays it he brings her home. The marriage price often consists of camels, pack animals, or other things; and no one can take a wife until he has fulfilled the obligation on which he has come to an understanding with those who have power over her in regard to him. If, however, he has met it, then he comes with[out] any ado, enters the abode where she is, [and] takes her in the presence of her father, mother, and brothers; these do not prevent him. If a man dies who has a wife and children, then the eldest of his sons takes her to wife if she is not his mother. . . .

* * *

[Speaking of the Bulghar Turks:] Most of what they eat is millet and horsemeat, although wheat and barley are plentiful. Everyone who grows something takes it for himself, the king having no claim to it. However, they render to him every year a sable skin from each household. When the king orders a raiding party to make a foray against a country, and booty is taken, he along with them is due a share. It is incumbent on anyone who holds a wedding feast, or invites a guest to a banquet, that the king

receives a portion commensurate with the size of the feast, as well as a bowl of honey drink, and some bad wheat. It is bad because their soil is black and putrid. They have no places for the storage of their food. Consequently, they dig wells in the ground and put the food in them. After a few days it begins to turn, becomes malodorous, and cannot be made use of.

They have neither olive oil, nor sesame oil, nor cooking oil of any kind. They use instead of these oils fish oil, and everything that they use reeks of fish oil. They make a soup from barley, which they feed to both the female and male slaves. Sometimes they cook the barley with meat. The masters eat the meat while the barley is fed to the slave girls, unless it be the head of a goat, in which case the slave girls are fed meat. . . .

All of them live in tents, but the tent of the king is extremely large, holding up to a thousand persons and more. It is spread with Armenian carpets, and in the center of it the king has a throne covered with Greek brocade.

Among their customs is the fact that when a male child is born to the son of a certain man, his grandfather and not his father takes him, saying: "I have more right to raise him until he reaches the state of manhood than his own father." When a man dies among them, his brother rather than his son becomes his heir. I informed the king that this was unlawful, and explained the principles of inheritance according to Muslim law until he understood them. . . .

The women do not cry over the dead man; rather it is the men among them who weep over him. They come on the day in which he dies and stand at the door of his tent. They then give vent to the most disgusting and uncanny wailing. These are the freeborn men. When their crying is done, slaves arrive carrying braided strands of leather. They do not cease to cry and to beat their sides and the uncovered parts of their bodies with those thongs until there appears on their bodies something similar to welts caused by whip strokes. They inevitably raise a standard at the door of the dead man's tent. They bring his weapons and place them around his grave. They do not stop crying for two years. When the two years have passed, they haul down the standard and cut their hair. The relatives of the dead man issue an invitation to a meal, which is a sign indicating that they are coming out of mourning, and if he happens to have had a wife, she remarries. This is so if he happens to be one of their chiefs. As regards the common people, they perform only some of those rites for their dead.

There is imposed on the king of the Saqaliba a tribute that he pays to the king of the Khazars, namely a sable skin for each household in his kingdom. When a ship from the country of the Khazars arrives in the country of the Saqaliba, the king rides out, takes stock of what is on board, and takes a tenth of the entire merchandise. When the Rus, or the members of some other races, come with slaves, the king has the right to choose for himself one out of every ten head.

The son of the king of the Saqaliba is held as a hostage at the court of the king of the Khazars. The king of the Khazars had learned of the beauty of the daughter of the king of the Saqaliba, and sent an emissary asking for her hand in marriage. The king of the Saqaliba protested and refused his request. Whereupon the king of the Khazars sent troops and seized her by force, although he was a Jew and she was a Muslim, and she died at his court. He then sent an emissary asking for the hand of another of his daughters. As soon as the king of the Saqaliba learned of this he acted without delay and married her off to the king of the Eskel, who was subject to him, out of fear that the king of the Khazars might seize her by force, as he had done with her sister. What induced the king of the Saqaliba to write and ask the Caliph to build a fortress for him was the fear of the king of the Khazars. . . .

* * *

The king of the Khazars is called Khaqan [khan], and he only appears in public promenading once every four months. He is called the Great Khaqan and his viceroy is called Khaqan Bih. It is the latter that leads and controls the armed forces, conducts affairs of the kingdom, appears before the people, and leads raids [on enemies]. It is to him that the neighboring kings submit. Every day he humbly goes to the Great Khaqan, showing humility and deference. He does not go into his presence except barefoot and carrying firewood in his arms. When

he greets him [the ruler] he kindles the fire in front of him, and when he has finished lighting the fire with the firewood, he sits with the king at this right side of the throne. . . . A custom of the king is that he does not sit and receive people in audience, nor does he speak to them, nor does anyone other than those mentioned enter his presence. Powers of appointments and dismissals, and of imposing punishments, as well as the management of the affairs of state, all are the responsibility of the Khaqan Bih.

It is the custom that when the great king dies a large house is built for him, in which are twenty excavated rooms, in each of which a sepulcher is dug. And stone is carved such that it is shaped like the firmament, and placed in the house, and stones are crushed until they become like powders and spread on the floor. Below the building is a larger river flowing, and they channel the river over that tomb so, as they say, that the devil cannot reach it, nor any person, nor any worms or serpents. When he is buried the company that buried him are beheaded, so it is not known where his grave is in those rooms. They call his grave heaven, and they say, verily he has entered heaven. And each of the rooms is covered with brocade and gold weave.

A custom of the king of the Khazars is that he has twenty-five wives, each of whom is a daughter of a neighboring king. He takes her voluntarily or by force. He has sixty concubines for his bed, each of whom is of surpassing beauty. Every one of them, free women and concubines, is placed in a separate palace; each has a cupola covered with teak, and each surrounded by a large pavilion. Each woman has a eunuch who keeps her in seclusion. . . .

When the king dispatches an army group, they do not turn their backs for any reason. If they are defeated, every one of them who returns is put to death. When his leaders and viceroy are put to flight, he brings them before him with their wives and children, and gives the latter as gifts to others in their presence while they are viewing it. He does the same with their horses, goods, weapons, and houses. Sometimes he cuts each of them in two pieces and exposes [them] on a gibbet [gallows]. Sometimes he hangs them by their necks from trees, or if he is well disposed toward them he makes them stable servants.

The king of the Khazars has a large city on the river Itil [Volga River], which is situated on both sides of the river. On one side are Muslims, while the king and his companions are on the other. Over the Muslims is a servant of the king called Khaz [khan?], who is himself a Muslim. Legal decisions concerning Muslims living in the land of the Khazars, and the Muslims who visit them in their trading activities, are referred to this Muslim servant. He alone looks into their affairs, and no one else acts as a judge among them. . . .

The Khazars and their king are all Jews. The Saqaliba, and all those neighboring them, give obedience to the king. He speaks to them as to slaves, and they show him fealty (loyalty).

Examining the Evidence

1. According to Ibn Fadlan, what features of nomadic social life and customs violated Islamic religious principles?
2. What were the principal sources of wealth among the steppe nomads whom Ibn Fadlan encountered?
3. In your view, did Ibn Fadlan regard the political and social order of the nomads as just? Why or why not?

9.3 INSTRUCTIONS FOR MY SONS

Yan Zhitui, *Family Instructions of the Yan Clan* (589)

Yan Zhitui (531–591) was descended from an aristocratic family of scholar–officials who traced their ancestry back to the Han dynasty. Yan's career reflected the chaotic political world of sixth-century China. He served as an adviser to Emperor Yuan (r. 552–554) of the Liang dynasty, but after the Turks captured and killed the emperor, Yan became a prisoner of war. Yan escaped two years later, but he was forced to remain in exile at Ye, capital of the "barbarian" Northern Qi dynasty (550–577), where he was welcomed as a distinguished man of letters. Two years before his death, Yan completed the *Family Instructions of the Yan Clan*, in which he advised his sons on how to ensure the family's survival in such turbulent times through prudent management of family affairs.

Teaching Children

Those of the highest intelligence will succeed without teaching; those of great stupidity even if taught will amount to nothing; those of medium ability will be ignorant unless taught. The ancient sage-kings had rules for pre-natal training. In the third month of pregnancy the queen was moved from her living quarters to a secluded place where sly glances would not be seen nor disturbing sounds heard, and where the tone of music and the flavor of food were controlled by the ritual codes. These rules were written on jade tablets and kept in a golden box. After the child was born, royal tutors conversant with filial piety, benevolence, ritual propriety, and righteousness guided and trained him.

The common people cannot follow such ways. But as soon as a baby can recognize facial expressions and understand approval and disapproval, training in doing what is told and halting when so ordered should begin. For several years, punishment with the bamboo rod should be avoided. Parental strictness and dignity mingled with tenderness will usually lead boys and girls to a feeling of respect and carefulness and so arouse filial piety. I have noticed in this generation that where there is merely love without training this result is never achieved. Children eat, drink, speak, and act as they please. Instead of needed prohibitions they receive praise; instead of urgent reprimands they receive smiles.

Yen Chih-T'ui, *Family Instructions for the Yen Clan*, trans. Teng Ssu-Yu (Leiden, The Netherlands: Brill, 1968), 3, 9–10, 16–20, 52–54.

Even when children are old enough to learn, such treatment is still regarded as the proper method. Only after the child has formed proud and arrogant habits do the parents begin to discipline him. But whipping the child even to death will not lead him to repentance, while the growing anger of the parents only increases his resentment. After he grows up such a child in the end becomes nothing but a scoundrel. Confucius was right in saying, "What is acquired in babyhood is like original nature; what has been formed into habits is equal to instinct." A common proverb says, "Train a wife from first arrival; teach a son in his babyhood." How true such sayings are! . . .

Brothers

Upon the arrival of humankind in the world, there ensued conjugal relationships. The conjugal relationship led in turn to the parental relationship, and the parental was followed by the fraternal. Within the family, these three are the intimate relationships. The degrees of kinship all develop from these three. Therefore, those who regard human relationships as important must necessarily be trustworthy with brothers who share the same blood inheritance and the same vital spirit. In infancy, they are led by their parents' left or right hand and cling to their parents' front or back garments. They eat at the same table and wear the clothes handed down from one to another. In school they have the same tasks and in their walks they take the same direction. Even though sometimes quarrelsome and disorderly, brothers still cannot help loving each other. When grown, each marries a wife and begets children. They cannot avoid a little coolness even when there is true affection between them. Sisters-in-law, compared with brothers, are more distantly related. If such distantly connected persons are used to measure intimate affection, it would be like placing a round cover over a square base — it cannot be made to fit. This predicament can be avoided only by deep-seated brotherly affection that others cannot alter.

After the death of their parents, brothers should regard each other as bonded together like an object is to its shadow, or a sound to its echo. They should love the body bequeathed by their deceased parents and have sympathy with the vital spirit that is part of their own. Who else except brothers can share these common elements? The relationship between elder and younger brothers differs from that between other persons. To expect too much easily causes hatred; close intimacy is apt to produce resentment. Take living in a house as an example. When there is a hole, stop it up; or a crack, plaster it; there will then be no danger of ruin. If one is careless about sparrows and mice and defenseless against wind and rain, walls collapse, pillars are undermined and the house cannot be saved. Servants and concubines are like sparrows and mice; wives and sons are like wind and rain — how terrible! . . .

Household Management

Manners and breeding are transmitted from the upper to the lower classes, and bequeathed by the elder generations to their posterity. So if a father is not kind, a son will not be filial; if an elder brother is not cordial, the younger brother will not be respectful; if a husband is unjust, his wife will not be obedient. When a father is kind but the son refractory, when an elder brother is cordial but the younger becomes arrogant, when a husband is just yet his wife is cruel, then indeed they are evil people who must be controlled with punishments. Teaching and guidance will not change them. . . .

Confucius said, "Extravagance leads to ostentation, and frugality to shabbiness. I would rather be shabby than ostentatious." On another occasion he said, "Even with a man as gifted as the Duke of Zhou, if he was proud and miserly, then the rest of his qualities are not worthy of admiration." That is to say, a man may be thrifty but he should not be stingy. Thrift means strict economy in offering presents; stinginess means showing no pity for those in poverty and urgent need. Nowadays those able to give alms are extravagant; those of frugal nature are stingy. It is proper to give alms without extravagance, and to be frugal without being stingy.

The livelihood of the people depends on farming, which supplies them with food, and silkworms and fiber crops, which provide them with clothing. A plenitude of fruits and vegetables from the orchard and garden, delicacies of pork and fowl from the pen and coop, beams and rafters for the house, tools and implements, fuel and candles, all these come from what is sown and grown. Thus, he who is steadfast in husbandry will find all of his needs met from the produce of his own land, except for salt. Nowadays it is commonplace in the north that people provide for their own food and clothing by personal thrift and economical expenditure. In the south, by contrast, unrestrained extravagance holds sway. . . .

A wife who is placed in charge of household provisions should use wine, food, and clothing only as the ceremonial rules stipulate. Just as women should never be allowed to participate in affairs of state, so too within the family they must not meddle in the affairs of others. If they are wise, talented, and versed in the ancient and modern writings, they ought to help their husbands by making up for their husbands' deficiencies. Yet no hen should herald the dawn, lest misfortune arise.

In the region around Nanjing [the capital of the Southern Dynasties] women engaged little in social intercourse. Even families related by marriage might for ten years or so have no contact except for expressions of intimacy and goodwill through the exchange of messengers and presents. But in the city of Ye it was the custom for women to handle all family business, to demand justice and straighten out legal disputes, to make social calls and curry favor with the powerful. They flooded the streets with their carriages, filled the government offices with their fancy dresses, begged official posts for their sons, and made complaints about the injustices done to their husbands. These customs perhaps were handed down from the Tuoba rulers of the Northern Wei.

In the south, the people, though usually poor, still were concerned about outward appearance to such a degree that their carriages and attire had to be neat even though their wives, children, and household suffered from hunger and cold. Most people north of the Yellow River let their wives handle domestic affairs. To these ladies, satin and silk, gold and jade were indispensable. Yet lean horses and decrepit servants were good enough for service. Husband and wife sometimes could address each other by "thee" and "thou." . . .

It is common for women to dote on a son-in-law and maltreat a daughter-in-law. Doting on a son-in-law gives rise to hatred from brothers. Maltreating

a daughter-in-law elicits slander from sisters. A woman, whether married or not, brings trouble to her household; but really it is the mother who causes it. Hence a proverb states, "Bickering forever at the dinner table by a mother-in-law." That is her recompense. With such difficulties common in family life, should we not be very cautious? . . .

To Encourage Study

No child of the scholar-official class fails to receive an education after attaining a few years of age. Those who are especially adept master the *Book of Rites* and the *Chronicles of Zuo*, while those of modest ability at least manage to read the *Book of Odes* and the *Analects*. Upon reaching the age of capping[1] and marriage, by which time their bodies and habits are fully formed, a double effort is needed in instruction and guidance to take advantage of their faculties. Ambitious and determined youths should be trained and encouraged to ensure they attain their proper station in life. Those without firm resolve henceforth will sink to the level of commoners.

Every man born into society should have a profession: farmers plan for plowing and sowing, merchants deal with goods and prices, workmen apply their energies to making excellent and useful objects, artists ponder their skills and subjects, scholars plumb the wisdom of classical books. I have often seen so-called scholars who felt it disgraceful to associate with farmers and merchants, or to exert themselves like a workman or an artist. In archery they are incapable of shooting through a coat of mail, and in writing they are competent only for signing their own names. Satiated with feasting, intoxicated by drink, loafing without proper work, they thus waste their days and end their years. Sometimes, by inheriting noble rank from their family, they obtain a lowly position in government and become smugly self-satisfied, entirely neglecting study. In matters of great fortune or misfortune and deliberations of possible success or failure, they sit with foolish looks and wide-opened mouths as if sitting in a cloud or fog. At public and private gatherings, when the conversation turns to ancient history or

---

[1] **capping:** A ceremony signifying eligibility for marriage, usually at 19 years of age for men.

a poetry competition is held, they silently hang their heads, yawning and stretching, unable to say or do anything. The learned bystanders would like to sink into the ground for them. Why do they refuse to spend a few years in diligent study so that they might avoid enduring a lifetime of shame and disgrace? . . .

Those who possess learning and skill can settle down anywhere. In these disordered times I have seen many prisoners of war who, though low-bred for a hundred generations, have become teachers through knowledge and study of the *Analects* and the *Book of Filial Piety*. Others, though they had a noble heritage dating back a thousand years, became mere farmers or stable grooms because they were unable to read and write. Seeing such reversals in fortune, how can you not exert yourselves? Whoever can keep steadily at work on a few hundred volumes ultimately will not remain a commoner.

Examining the Evidence

1. Why did Yan Zhitui consider education of vital importance in preserving the family's welfare?
2. What did Yan Zhitui regard as the greatest threats to the survival and welfare of the family?
3. In Yan's view, what were the virtues and vices of northerners (foreigners) and southerners (Chinese)?

CONTRASTING VIEWS

THE RECEPTION OF BUDDHISM IN EAST ASIA

9.4 YAN ZHITUI, *A CONFUCIAN SCHOLAR'S DEDICATION TO BUDDHISM* (589)

We have already encountered Yan Zhitui's *Family Instructions of the Yan Clan* (see Document 9.3) in which Yan strongly urged his sons to remain steadfast in their studies and to achieve mastery of the Confucian classics. Yet, like many of his contemporaries among the Chinese aristocracy, Yan also professed devotion to Buddhism, which he embraced without any sense of contradiction with his deeply cherished belief in Confucian norms and traditional values. In the following excerpts, also from *Family Instructions*, Yan addressed some of the principal arguments raised against both Buddhist doctrines and the Buddhist clergy.

It is traditional in our family to turn our hearts (to Buddhism), you should not neglect it. Its profound theories are fully explained in the *sūtras* (basic discourses) and *abhidharmas* (treatises by later masters). I cannot again briefly praise and narrate them here. Nevertheless, fearing that you are not yet firm in your faith, I therefore repeat my little advice and persuasion. . . .

The two religions, the Inner (Buddhism) and the Outer (Confucianism), are, however, fundamentally the same. Gradually they became very different from each other in depth and shallowness. At the entrance to the Inner scriptures there are five prohibitions which correspond to the humanity, justice, propriety, wisdom, and sincerity of the Outer scriptures. Humanity corresponds to the prohibition against taking life. Justice corresponds to the prohibition against stealing. Propriety corresponds to the prohibition against depravity. Wisdom corresponds to the prohibition against lust, and sincerity corresponds to the prohibition against falsehood. As for hunting and fighting, feasting and punishment, the original characteristics of the people cannot be eradicated all at once, but should be restrained from excess. To turn to the Duke of Zhou and Confucius and reject Buddhism is foolish indeed!

The common slanderers (against Buddhism) usually make five points; first, they regard things beyond this world and the boundlessness of divine transformations as absurd and unreliable; secondly, they regard good luck or bad, disaster or happiness, since these sometimes are not in line with retribution, as deceitful and cheating; third, they regard the conduct and acts of monks and nuns, since many of them are insincere and impure, as immoral and hypocritical; fourth, they regard the waste of money and

Yen Chih-T'ui, *Family Instructions for the Yen Clan*, trans. Teng Ssu-Yu (Leiden, The Netherlands: Brill, 1968), 137–140, 142–148.

treasure, and loss in taxes and labor services as harmful to the state; fifth, even though there is a causality which commands retribution, they wonder how the painful exertions of the man of today can benefit the man of a future generation; thus he is an atypical man. Let me now explain these points as follows.

In explanation of the first point . . .

All human beliefs depend only on eyes and ears; whatever is outside that which is not seen and heard is to be doubted. . . .

People living amid mountains do not believe that there are fish as large as a tree—people dwelling on the seashore do not believe that there are trees as large as fish. . . . When western barbarians saw brocade, they did not believe that the material came from a worm that eats leaves and spins silk. Formerly when I was south of the Yangtze I did not believe there were tents that could shelter a thousand persons; when I came north of the Yellow River, I found there were people who did not believe there were ships that could carry twenty thousand piculs. These are all practical examples. . . .

In explaining the second point, . . . [s]ometimes, because people's devotion and faith are not sufficiently earnest and the causality of karma has not yet been effected, it appears that the time of fulfillment has been deferred or delayed; but eventually the due retribution will be received. Good or evil acts bring disastrous or fortunate consequences. The Nine Schools and the Hundred Philosophers all agree upon this theory. Are the Buddhist scriptures alone to be held as untrue and unreliable? . . . If, when you see those who do good occasionally suffering a disastrous result or those doing evil sometimes rewarded with good fortune, you complain and consider the Buddhist doctrine to be a lie and a cheat; then the theory of emperors Yao and Shun may be said to be false, and the Duke of Zhou and Confucius are also untrue. What then would you like to believe and rely upon as the guide of your life?

To explain the third point, I say that from the creation of the universe, the bad people have been numerous and the good ones few. By what means can we urge them all to be devoted and pure? Seeing an eminent good monk with high conduct, people leave him unmentioned; if ordinary monks imbued with vulgar habits are seen, slander and defamation immediately arise. When a student is not diligent, is it his teacher's fault? How does the study of *sūtras* and discipline texts by ordinary monks differ from studying the *Book of Odes* and the

Book of Rites by secular students? If one takes the teaching of the *Odes* and *Rites* as a standard in judging courtiers and ministers, few will be found with perfect conduct; if one takes the prohibitions from the *sūtras* and discipline texts to check those who have given up their families (i.e. monks), can we blame them that none is faultless? Moreover, officials lacking good conduct still seek for higher salaries and posts; why should monks who have broken the prohibitions be ashamed to receive presents and supplies? Their conduct undoubtedly violates the prohibition, yet once they have put on the monk's robe they are living in the monastery, where every year if we count the number of days they devote to fasting, preaching and chanting, they are much more (lit. like mountain and sea) pious than the white-clothes people (laymen).

To explain the fourth point, I would say that Buddhism has many avenues of approach. To give up one's family (by entering a monastery) is only one of them. If you can really cherish faith and filial piety, act with humanity and charity, then like Xuda (Sudatta) and Liushui (Jalavāhana), it is not necessary to shave the beard and hair. How could one demand that all the land be exhausted to build monasteries or all the people be registered as monks and nuns? (That this happens) is all due to the inability of the government to restrain illegal monasteries from obstructing the people's farm work and idle monks from decreasing national taxation. . . . A faithful minister who dies for his lord will disregard his parents; a filial son who brings peace to his family will forget his nation. Each has its virtue. There were Confucianists who did not bow to king or noble but loftily carried out their own way; there were hermits who gave up a kingship or resigned from a prime ministership to retire from the world into mountainous forests. Can we make the matter of taxation a basis for condemning them as guilty? . . .

To explain the fifth point, I would say that though the body dies, the soul is still preserved. When a man is alive in the world, it seems inappropriate to look for future existence; but after death the relation to former existence resembles that of old age to youth or morning to night. There are not a few cases in society where souls have appeared in dreams, descending upon the body of concubines or inspiring a wife or maid to ask for food or request a blessing. Nowadays people, if poor, humble, sick or sorrowful, without exception blame themselves for not cultivating virtuous deeds in a former life. From this point of view, how can one not prepare for a good place in the

(continued)

future life? . . . If you, my sons, want to plan worldly affairs and establish families, and cannot leave your wives and sons to become monks, you should nevertheless cultivate your pious conduct, observe the precepts and pay attention to chanting and reading the scriptures in order to provide a passage to your future stage of existence. The opportunity for human life is difficult to get; do not pass it in vain!

9.5   HAN YU, *MEMORIAL ON THE BONE OF THE BUDDHA* (819)

Han Yu (786–824), a renowned poet and writer, was one of the forefathers of the reinvention of the Confucian tradition known as Neo-Confucianism. Han saw himself waging a lonely battle, defending the essential moral values of Chinese civilization against the corruption of foreign influences, especially Buddhism. In 819, the Tang emperor Xianzong (r. 805–820) ordered that a holy relic—a finger bone of the Buddha—be put on public display in the capital. Han wrote a scathing denunciation of the emperor's action, prompting the emperor to banish him to the farthest southern frontier of the empire.

Your servant begs leave to say that Buddhism is no more than a cult of the barbarian peoples which spread to China in the time of the Later Han. It did not exist here in ancient times. . . . When Emperor Gaozu [founder of the Tang dynasty] received the throne from the House of Sui, he deliberated upon the suppression of Buddhism. But at that time the various officials, being of small worth and knowledge, were unable fully to comprehend the ways of the ancient kings and the exigencies of past and present, and so could not implement the wisdom of the emperor and rescue the age from corruption. Thus the matter came to naught, to your servant's constant regret.

Now Your Majesty, wise in the arts of peace and war, unparalleled in divine glory from countless ages past, upon your accession prohibited men and women from taking Buddhist orders and forbade the erection of temples and monasteries, and your servant believed that at Your Majesty's hand the will of Gaozu would be carried out. Even if the suppression of Buddhism should be as yet impossible, your servant hardly thought that Your Majesty would encourage it and on the contrary cause it to spread. Yet now your servant hears that Your Majesty has ordered the community of monks to go to Fengxiang to greet the bone of Buddha, that Your Majesty will ascend a tower to watch as it is brought into the palace, and that the various temples have been commanded to welcome and worship it in turn. Though your servant is abundantly ignorant, he understands that Your Majesty is not so misled by Buddhism as to honor it thus in hopes of receiving some blessing or reward, but only that, the year being one of plenty and the people joyful, Your Majesty would accord with the hearts of the multitude in setting forth for the officials and citizens of the capital some curious show and toy for their amusement. How could it be, indeed, that with such sagely wisdom Your Majesty should in truth give credence to these affairs? But the common people are ignorant and dull, easily misled and hard to enlighten, and should they see their emperor do these things, they might say that Your Majesty was serving Buddhism with a true heart. "The Son of Heaven is a great Sage," they would cry, "and yet he reverences and believes with all his heart! How should we, the common people, then begrudge our bodies and our lives?" Then would they set about singeing their heads and scorching their fingers, binding together in groups of ten and a hundred, doffing their common clothes and scattering their money, from morning to evening urging each other on lest one be slow, till old and young alike had abandoned their occupations to follow Buddhism. If this is not checked and the bone is carried from one temple to another, there will be those who will cut off their arms and mutilate their flesh in offering to the Buddha. Then will our old ways be corrupted, our customs violated, and the tale will spread to make us the mockery of the world. This is no trifling matter!

Now Buddha was a man of the barbarians who did not speak the language of China and wore clothes of a different

Wm. Theodore de Bary, Wing-tsit Chan, and Burton Watson, eds., *Sources of Chinese Tradition* (New York: Columbia University Press, 1960), 427–429.

fashion. His sayings did not concern the ways of our ancient kings, nor did his manner of dress conform to their laws. He understood neither the duties that bind sovereign and subject, nor the affections of father and son. If he were still alive today and came to our court by order of his ruler, Your Majesty might condescend to receive him, but it would amount to no more than one audience in the Xuanzheng Hall, a banquet by the Office for Receiving Guests, the presentation of a suit of clothes, and he would then be escorted to the borders of the nation, dismissed, and not allowed to delude the masses. How then, when he has long been dead, could his rotten bones, the foul and unlucky remains of his body, be rightly admitted to the palace? Confucius said, "Respect ghosts and spirits, but keep them at a distance!" So when the princes of ancient times went to pay their condolences at a funeral within the state, they sent exorcists in advance with peach wands to drive out evil, and only then would they advance. Now without reason Your Majesty has caused this loathsome thing to be brought in and would personally go to view it. No exorcists have been sent ahead, no peach wands employed. The host of officials has not spoken out against this wrong, and the censors have failed to note its impropriety. Your servant is deeply shamed and begs that this bone be given to the proper authorities to be cast into fire and water, that this evil may be rooted out, the world freed from its error, and later generations spared this delusion. Then may all men know how the acts of their wise sovereign transcend the commonplace a thousand-fold. Would this not be glorious? Would it not be joyful?

Should the Buddha indeed have the supernatural power to send down curses and calamities, may they fall only upon the person of your servant, who calls upon High Heaven to witness that he does not regret his words. With all gratitude and sincerity your servant presents this memorial for consideration, being filled with respect and awe.

9.6   THE CHRONICLE OF JAPAN (NIHONGI) (720)

First introduced to Japan from Korea in 552, Buddhism received a mixed reception from Japan's ruling clans. Soga no Umako, head of the powerful Soga family, championed the adoption of Buddhism, but his rivals objected to worship of a foreign faith. After gaining official endorsement from Empress Suiko (r. 593–628) and her regent, Prince Shōtoku (573–621), Buddhism quickly won favor among the aristocratic elite. The following records of the introduction of Buddhism are taken from the *Chronicle of Japan (Nihongi)*, an official history of Japan since the time of creation that was compiled at the Japanese imperial court circa 720.

552, Winter, 10th Month

King Seong (r. 523–554) of the Korean kingdom of Paekche dispatched Nuri Sachi of the Ji clan and other retainers to Japan. They offered as tribute a gold and copper statue of Sakyamuni Buddha, ritual banners and canopies, and several volumes of sutras [scriptures] and commentaries. In a separate declaration, King Seong praised the merit of propagating and worshipping the dharma [Buddhist teachings], stating, "This dharma is superior to all others. It is difficult to understand and difficult to attain. Neither the Duke of Zhou nor Confucius was able to comprehend it. This dharma can produce immeasurable, limitless karmic merit, leading to the attainment of supreme wisdom. It is like a person who has a wish-fulfilling gem whose every desire is granted. The jewel of this wonderful dharma is also like this. Every prayer is answered and not a need goes unfulfilled. Moreover, from distant India all the way to China this teaching has been followed and upheld. There is no one who does not revere it. Accordingly, I, King Seong, your vassal, have humbly dispatched my retainer, Nuri Sachi, to the Imperial Kingdom of Japan to transmit and propagate this teaching. . . ."

That very day the emperor heard this declaration and leapt with joy. He declared to the Korean envoys, "From ancient times to the present we have not heard of such a fine dharma as this. Nevertheless, we cannot ourselves decide whether to accept this teaching." Thereupon the emperor inquired of his assembled officials, "The Buddha presented to us from the country to our west has a face of extreme solemnity. We have never known such a thing before. Should we worship it or not?"

William E. Deal, trans., "Buddhism and the State in Early Japan," in *Buddhism in Practice*, ed. Donald S. Lopez (Princeton, NJ: Princeton University Press, 1995), 218–220, 223–224; and W. G. Aston, trans., *Nihongi: Chronicles of Japan from the Earliest Times to A.D. 697* (London: Kegan Paul, 1896), 126.

(continued)

CONTRASTING VIEWS (*continued*)

Soga no Iname humbly responded: "The many countries to the west all worship this Buddha. Is it only Yamato [Japan] that will reject this teaching?"

Mononobe no Okoshi and Nakatomi no Kamako together humbly responded: "The rulers of our country have always worshipped throughout the four seasons the 180 deities of heaven and earth. If they now change this and worship the deity of a foreign country, we fear that the deities of our country will become angry."

The emperor declared, "I grant to Soga no Iname the worship of this Buddha in order to test its efficacy."

Soga no Iname knelt down and received the statue. With great joy, he enshrined it in his home at Owarida and devotedly performed the rituals of a world renouncer [i.e., someone who has taken monastic vows]. He also purified his home at Mukuhara and made it into a temple.

Later, an epidemic afflicted the country and cut short the lives of many people. With the passing of time, more and more people died of this incurable disease. Mononobe no Okoshi and Nakatomi no Kamako together humbly addressed the emperor: "Previously, the counsel we offered went unheeded. As a result, this epidemic has occurred. Now, before it is too late, this situation must be rectified. Throw away the statue of the Buddha at once and diligently seek future blessings."

The emperor responded: "We will do as you have counseled."

The emperor's officials took the Buddha statue and threw it into the waters of the Naniwa canal. They then set fire to the temple in which it was enshrined and burned it to the ground. At this time, although the winds were calm and the sky cloudless, suddenly a fire broke out in the great hall of the Imperial Palace. . . .

584, Autumn, 9th Month

Minister Kabuka returned from the Korean kingdom of Paekche, bringing with him a stone statue of Maitreya Buddha. Minister Saeki also returned with a Buddhist statue. The same year, Soga no Umako [son of Soga no Iname] requested these two statues. He then dispatched . . . [several persons named] to seek out and bring back practitioners of the dharma. It was only in Harima Province that they discovered a former Korean monk who had returned to lay life by the name of Eben. Soga no Umako made him his dharma teacher and allowed Shima, the daughter of Shimedachito, to become a nun. She was eleven years old and took the Buddhist name Zenshin.

Two of Zenshin's disciples also became nuns: Toyome, Ayahito no Yabo's daughter, who took the Buddhist name Zenzō, and Ishime, Nishikori no Tsubu's daughter, who took the Buddhist name Ezen. Umako, in accord with the Buddha's dharma, reverenced the three nuns. . . .

602, Winter, 10th Month

A Paekche monk named Kwallŭk arrived and presented by way of tribute books on calendar-making, astronomy, and [geomancy[1]], and also books on the art of invisibility and magic. At this time three or four pupils were selected and made to study under Kwallŭk. . . .

623, Spring, 4th Month, 3rd Day

A monk took an axe and struck his grandfather. When Empress Suiko learned of this, she summoned the Great Minister, Soga no Umako, and issued the following imperial edict: "A world renouncer should earnestly take refuge in the Three Treasures [the Buddha, his law, and the clergy] and fully uphold the rules of monastic conduct. How can one, without repentance, easily commit evil acts in violation of the precepts? Now I have heard that there is a monk who struck his grandfather. Therefore, gather together all of the monks and nuns of the various temples and question them. If what I have heard is true, serious punishment must be meted out."

Accordingly, the monks and nuns of the various temples were assembled and questioned. The monk who had violated the precepts, as well as the other monks and nuns, were about to be punished. At this time the monk Kwallŭk from the Korean kingdom of Paekche presented a memorial to the empress, saying: "The Buddha's dharma came from India to China, and three hundred years later, China transmitted it to Paekche. A mere hundred years after this King Seong heard of the wisdom of the Emperor Kimmei and offered in tribute a statue of the Buddha and sutras. Since then, not even one hundred years have passed, so that at this time the monks and nuns have not yet learned the monastic precepts and easily violate them. As a result, the monks and nuns are afraid because they do not know what is right. I respectfully request that the monks and nuns who have not violated the precepts be pardoned and not punished. This would be an act of great merit." Thereupon the empress granted his request.

---

[1]**geomancy:** Divination based on the physical features of a site.

13th Day

The following edict was issued: "Even followers of the way violate the Buddha's law. How then can the laity be instructed? Therefore, from this time forward, we will appoint superintendents who shall oversee the monks and nuns."

17th Day

The monk Kwallŭk was appointed Superintendent of the Clergy and Kuratsukuri no Tokushaku his auxiliary. The same day, Azumi no Muraji was appointed Head of the Buddhist Law.

Autumn, 9th Month, 3rd Day

There was a review of the temples, and the monks and nuns. The reason temples were built, and the reasons why the monks and nuns entered the Buddhist path, as well as the year, month, and day of their entry, were recorded in detail. At this time there were 46 temples, 816 monks, and 569 nuns; in total, 1,385 people.

645, 8th Month, 8th Day

A messenger was dispatched to the Great Temple. Gathering the monks and nuns together, he pronounced an imperial edict: "In the 13th year of the reign of King Kimmei, King Seong of the Korean kingdom of Paekche offered the Buddha's dharma in tribute to Japan. At this time the ministers were united in their desire not to accept it. Only Soga no Iname placed faith in the Buddhist dharma. Thus the emperor decreed to Soga no Iname that he would be allowed to revere the dharma. In the reign of Emperor Bidatsu [r. 572–585], Soga no Umako, out of respect for the deeds of his father, deeply revered the Buddha's dharma. However, some ministers did not place faith in the dharma and tried to destroy it completely. Emperor Bidatsu issued an edict to Soga no Umako decreeing that he should revere the Buddha's dharma. In the reign of Empress Suiko, Soga no Umako constructed sixteen-foot embroidered and copper images of the Buddha on her behalf. He extolled the Buddha's teaching and revered the monks and nuns. We now wish to reiterate our desire to revere the Buddha's true teaching and to shine widely the light of this great dharma. Therefore we appoint the following priests as dharma teachers: the Korean dharma masters Poknyang, Hyeun, Syangan, Nyŏngun, and Hyechi, and the temple heads Sōmin, Dōto, Erin, and Emyō. We separately appoint dharma teacher Emyō the head priest of the Kudara Temple. These dharma teachers will thoroughly instruct the monastic community and lead them in the practice of the Buddha's teaching so the Buddha's dharma is properly followed. From the emperor to the managerial class, we will all assist in the building of temples. We will now appoint temple head priests and lay administrators. Temples will be visited to determine the actual situation pertaining to monks and nuns, their servants, and their rice fields. All findings will be presented to the emperor."

COMPARING THE EVIDENCE

1. What features of Buddhist teachings appear to have been most difficult for the Chinese to accept?
2. To what extent was Buddhism seen as a threat to native religious traditions and values in China and Japan?
3. Why was the Buddhist clergy often regarded with suspicion?
4. What reasons motivated rulers in China, Japan, and Korea to patronize the Buddhist faith and clergy?

9.7 CONDUCT OF THE WELL-BRED TOWNSMAN

Vatsyayana, *Kama Sutra* (c. 400)

Hinduism advocates an approach to life that balances obligations to family and society with the individual's quest of release from mortal existence (*moksha*). The place of *kama*, or the pursuit of pleasure, in Hinduism reflects the great importance attached to the role of the married householder. The *Kama Sutra*, written by Vatsyayana (c. 400), enumerates for the ideal householder—the well-bred townsman—the correct ways of

Alain Danielou, trans., *The Complete Kama Sutra* (Rochester, VT: Park Street Press, 1994), 15, 25–26, 28–29, 31, 41, 57–59, 61–62, 65–66, 71–73, 277–280, 282, 284.

enjoying pleasure and preventing its degeneration into self-indulgence. Vatsyayana also sets down rules of behavior for women, including wives, concubines, and lovers. *Note*: In this translation Vatsyayana's text appears in roman type; the italicized text is taken from a thirteenth-century commentary.

Praised be the three aims of life: virtue [*dharma*], prosperity [*artha*], and love [*kama*], which are the subject of this work.

There are four social functions in this world, namely the priest's, the warrior's, the merchant's, and the artisan's, as well as the four stages of life, that of the student, the married man, withdrawal into the forest, and the mendicant monk. For Brahmans and others, so long as they are heads of a family, the search for spiritual realization is not practicable, and the aims of life are limited to three. The advocates of eroticism consider that love, given its results, is the most important inasmuch as virtue and prosperity both depend on it and without it they would not exist. . . .

During the one hundred years of his life, a man must pursue the three aims successively, without one being prejudicial to another.

Childhood must be dedicated to acquiring knowledge.

Eroticism predominates in adulthood.

Old age must be dedicated to the practice of virtue and spiritual pursuit [*moksha*]. . . .

Celibacy is recommended during the period of study, for the acquiring of knowledge. . . .

Artha signifies material goods, wealth. *Artha* consists of acquiring and increasing — within the limits of dharma — knowledge, land, gold, cattle, patrimony, crockery, furniture, friends, clothing, etc. . . .

Kama signifies the mental inclination toward the pleasures of touch, sight, taste, and smell, to the extent that the practitioner derives satisfaction from it. . . .

The relative importance and value of things must be taken into account. Money is more important than love, social success more important than success in love, and virtue is more important than success and fortune.

Money is the basis of royal power. Life's journey is based on it. It is the means of realizing the three aims of life, even in the case of prostitutes. . . .

Effort does not bring riches. Rites and regular work bring nothing, but fortune comes by chance, without logic. Fortune depends on destiny. Since it is without logic, effort serves no purpose. It follows its whim. It appears unexpectedly. This is why the texts that explain the means to acquire it are useless.

Everything in this world depends on destiny. . . .

Having completed his studies and acquired the means of livelihood by gifts received, conquest, trade, and work, or else by inheritance, or both; and having married, the well-bred townsman must settle down in a refined manner.

In order to establish himself, a Brahman acquires assets through gifts; a noble (kshatriya) by arms and conquest; a merchant by trade; a worker by hard work and service. The way of life recommended by Vatsyayana is not for the penniless and applies to all four castes.

He must establish himself in a big city, a town, or even a large village, near the mountains, where a decent number of persons of good society are living. He may also, for a time, go journeying.

He must build himself a house with two separate apartments, on a site near water, with trees and a garden and a separate place of work.

The antechamber, outside the private apartments, must be vast, pleasant, with a wide divan in the center covered with a white cloth. Close to this great bed, another similar one shall be placed, for the games of love.

A well-bred townsman gets up very early in the morning, performs his natural functions, and cleans his teeth. Having carefully washed his face, he rubs it with ointment and marks the sacred signs on his brow, using sandalwood. He dyes his hair, using wax and lacquer, while looking at himself in a mirror. Then, having eaten some betel, he places a necklace of scented flowers around his neck, after which he begins his daily routine.

He must bathe every day, have a massage every two days, soap himself every three days. . . .

Two main meals should be taken each day, in the morning and in the evening before nightfall. . . .

In the evening, at nightfall, receptions are organized with music, dancing, singing, and instruments. When the guests are gathered, the master of the house, splendidly dressed, enters the reception hall, located on one side of the entrance courtyard.

Receptions were organized for seasonal festivities or events, for concerts or entertainments, for drinking parties, witticisms, or for strolls in the garden.

Events mostly include pilgrimages to visit sanctuaries where people gather and, related to these, receptions taking place among the various social groups, at which theatrical entertainments are prevalent. In the afternoon, gatherings take place for amusement and for drinking, at which are found those that drink and those that do not. Such gatherings mainly take place in the gardens. . . .

Every fortnight or every month, on the proper days, it is a duty to gather at the sanctuary of the goddess Sarasvati.

The proper days depend on the phases of the moon. The fourth day is dedicated to Ganapati, the fifth to Sarasvati, patron of dancing and music, the eighth to Shiva. The townspeople come to an agreement to organize dance spectacles at one another's house, each fifth day of the lunar calendar, in order to worship the goddess. . . .

Whatever the divinity worshipped, strangers must be welcomed according to the possibilities and the festival rules.

When a reception takes place in the house of a courtesan or in the house of a gentleman, the company of friends or comrades must be chosen for their common culture, intelligence, fortune, age, and character. This makes for pleasant conversation with the courtesans.

When gatherings take place to discuss matters of literature and art, talented celebrities are honored and uninvited artists welcomed respectfully. . . .

An intelligent and well-born man, expert in the arts, who has dissipated his wealth and broken off with his family, but is esteemed in the houses of the courtesans and in the fashionable circles and lives at their expense is known as a gigolo.

Having squandered his fortune on pleasure during his youth, he now finds himself destitute, although he comes of a good family. He is of the place and not from outside. If he has a wife, he may not leave the country due to this bond. For a living he works as a pithamarda, *a man of all work, but, due to his qualities and his education, he is still a man of the world. He is intelligent and cultivated and attends receptions* *as a sponger. For other resources, he stays with the courtesans, living at their expense, despite the ill-will of their menfolk. Since he lives parasitically on them, he is called a gigolo. . . .*

If he does not know the tricks, he is a plaything, an object of amusement, but if he inspires confidence, he becomes a companion and amusing confidant, while continuing sometimes to play the clown.

Employed as a secretary, he busies himself with the appointments and breaches between courtesans and citizens.

He is considered a second-class citizen. His qualities are to understand the right time and place for meetings or breaches.

He utilizes beggar women, shaven-headed nuns expert in the arts, women of irregular life, or old whores, to arrange appointments.

If one lives in a village, one must surround oneself with people of one's own milieu, intelligent, willing to be amused, active, well mannered, and respecting the castes. Receptions must be organized, since people amuse themselves when they are together. In business, one must treat one's employees with kindness, even when faced with their failings. Such is the behavior of the well-brought-up man. His dependents must be respectful but, during festivals and journeys, as also in business, one must be courteous and aid each other reciprocally.

At gatherings, an educated man should not speak solely in Sanskrit or solely in the language of the people.

A prudent man will not attend meetings where there are enemies, spies, or criminals.

The wise predict a sure success for a man of wit with moderate behavior, who plays only reasonable games.

* * *

The only wife is totally trusting, considering her husband a god and completely devoted to him.

She takes responsibility for the household, and so on.

She attends to cleaning the clothes, tidying the rooms, flower arrangements, cleaning the floor, being attractive to look at, performing the three daily rites of offering to the gods and of worshipping them at their domestic shrine. . . .

The wife must behave suitably to her husband's elderly parents, servants, his sisters, and their husbands.

On carefully prepared ground, she must sow aromatic plants and vegetables, and plant sugarcane in clumps, mustard, cumin, asafetida, cinnamon, fennel, and small cardamoms. . . .

She must keep beggars out of the way, also wandering Buddhist or Jain monks, women of bad reputation, mountebanks, and magicians. . . .

Sending the servants away, she bows at her husband's feet.

Even when alone with her master, she never shows herself without her jewels.

In the case of his making excessive or useless expenditures, she scolds him when they are alone.

She must ask her husband's permission to attend marriage ceremonies with her girlfriends, or to go to receptions or temples. Otherwise she will be suspected of improper behavior.

It is only with his approval that she takes part in games.

She must go to sleep after him and awaken before him. . . .

If her husband behaves badly she must show her displeasure, without exaggerating her reproaches. . . .

She must never speak to anyone about what she possesses, or of what she knows about her husband.

In comparison with women of the same age, she should excel them by her accomplishments in the kitchen and her behavior.

She must regulate her spending by calculating her annual income.

A good wife should always take care to make butter with leftover milk; prepare molasses with sugarcane and oil with colza, etc.; spin cotton and make cloth with the thread; stow away pieces of string, cord, thread, or bark; check stores of wheat and rice; supervise the servants; set aside the rice water, wheat bran, and burnt charcoal for reuse; take care of the domestic animals, the sheep, chickens, quails, parrots, mynahs, nightingales, and peacocks; and each day make account of entries and expenses. . . .

She does not go to visit her own family, except in case of sickness or for religious festivals, and always accompanied by someone of her husband's family as witness to the purity of her trip. She must not absent herself for long. She must never go out without being accompanied.

Examining the Evidence

1. What virtues should the well-bred townsman possess?
2. Why did Vatsyayana believe that residing in a town was necessary for the proper pursuit of pleasure and the cultivation of virtue?
3. In what ways do the *Kama Sutra*'s rules of social conduct for men and women reflect different conceptions of male and female virtues and vices?

9.8   SCENES FROM EIGHTH-CENTURY JAVA

Borobodur Monument, Central Java (c. 760–820)

The Sailendra rulers of central Java constructed the great monument of Borobodur as a testament to their devotion to Mahayana Buddhism. The monument rises in pyramid fashion, forming ten concentric terraces with a bell-shaped stupa, a Buddhist shrine used as a repository for relics, at its summit. The terraces are adorned with more than 1,400 carved reliefs depicting episodes from the

Mahayana scriptures. The carvings imitate the sculptural style then prevalent in India, but most of the stonecutting was performed by local villagers working in teams who may have donated their labor as an act of religious merit. On the lower levels of the Borobodur monument are 720 panels illustrating episodes from the lives of the Buddha and other heroic figures in Buddhist literature. One series of panels narrates the story of the virtuous king Rudrayana and his evil son. Rudrayana, a devout Buddhist, abdicated his throne to take up a monastic life.

Julio Etchart/ullstein bild via Getty Images

On the right side of the panel shown on page 139, Hiru travels by ship to his new home. Above, the ship's passengers are greeted by a man and his wife, who offer food to the refugees.

But Rudrayana's son, Sikhandin, became a tyrant. After Rudrayana chastised him, Sikhandin had his father murdered. The minister Hiru, who had sought to reform Sikhandin, gathered up the kingdom's Buddhist treasures and fled to another country across the sea, where he founded a new city.

Examining the Evidence

1. What were the distinctive features of the nautical technology used in Southeast Asian seas at this time?

2. What can the depiction of the dress, posture, and arrangement of these figures tell us about the social ideals and conceptions of male and female beauty in Javanese society?
3. In what ways does the architecture of the house in the background represent an adaptation to the tropical climate of Southeast Asia?

MAKING CONNECTIONS

1. In what ways do the accounts of Xuanzang and Ibn Fadlan differ in their depiction of Central Asia as foreign and exotic?
2. Compare the ideal qualities of the head of the household depicted in Yan Zhitui's *Family Instructions* and the *Kama Sutra*. To what extent do they overlap?
3. Explain how the Buddhist icons described by Xuanzang, the "bone of the Buddha" described by Han Yu, and the Borobodur monument illustrate different ways to inspire faith in Buddhist teachings.
4. Compare the social roles performed by women encountered in this chapter, including Yan Zhitui's family manual, the *Kama Sutra*, the Japanese court chronicle, and the Borobodur monument. To what extent do they agree on the place of women in the family and society? In what ways do they disagree?

CHAPTER 10

Societies and Networks in the Americas and the Pacific, 300–1200

With a few exceptions such as the Maya, the societies examined in this chapter were not literate and thus have left no written documents recording their history. Scholars must rely on other types of sources—such as archaeological and artifactual evidence, written accounts by outsiders, and oral traditions passed down through many generations to recent times—to recover their histories. In Mesoamerica and the Andean region, a rich abundance of stone monuments, painted pottery, and decorated textiles has been preserved that can be read as historical "texts"; in the Maya case, figurative illustrations and written texts often are combined, as in the inscription from the Temple of the Tree of Yellow Corn. Although the artifactual evidence for the Pueblo peoples of the American Southwest is much more limited, oral traditions provide important testimony about their past. The material culture of Hawaii and other Pacific islands consisted chiefly of perishable objects such as wood, fibers, and feathers that readily disintegrated in the tropical climate. Here, too, historians must draw inferences from later artifacts and oral traditions.

10.1 A MAYA SCULPTED TABLET

Inscription of the Temple of the Tree of Yellow Corn (690)

In Maya belief, the movements of the sun, the moon, and the planets determined the outcomes of human actions. Therefore, the Maya took great care to record precisely the dates of important events by compiling calendars that spanned hundreds of years. Maya rulers used these calendars to ensure that major undertakings in the present—such as the coronation of kings and military campaigns—coincided with auspicious events in the past. The Temple of the Tree of Yellow Corn was built in 690 to commemorate the ascension of Sun-Eyed Snake Jaguar (r. 684–702) as the ruler of the Maya city-state of Palenque. The sculpted tablet placed in the temple's back wall combines textual and pictorial elements to illustrate Sun-Eyed Snake Jaguar's destiny to become an "Egret Lord," or ruler of Palenque ("Cloudy Center").

The tablet's central image is the Tree of Yellow Corn. Sun-Eyed Snake Jaguar is shown twice: as a seven-year-old boy on the right, and as an adult at left. The boy stands on a conch shell that symbolizes the gateway to the underworld, while the adult ruler stands on the split skull of a monster identified as First Corn Tassel Mountain. It was from this split skull that Maya heroes retrieved corn and other plants hidden in an earlier age. The adult figure holds an image of Young Mirror Scepter, a guardian spirit associated with the planet Saturn.

The accompanying inscriptions flanking the tablet (not included in the tablet shown below) describe celestial events that occurred on the night the temple was dedicated. The right-hand inscription begins with the celestial conjunction of the moon and the three planets on the night of July 21, 690. Two days later Sun-Eyed Snake Jaguar summoned the ghost of Lady Cormorant, his paternal grandmother (r. 612–615), and received paper blotted with sacrificial blood from her. The blood-stained paper signified the transmission of lordship from one ruler to the next.

The narrative then shifts to earlier events in Sun-Eyed Snake Jaguar's life—his birth on May 21, 635, and his succession as ruler on January 8, 684—before returning to the celestial conjunction on his coronation. The text also describes the appearance of Venus—whose guardian spirit is the god One Lord, one of the Hero Twins—in the eastern morning sky.

Inscription (included in illustration from previous page)

On 8 Foot 3 Song, the white paper was presented to him, to Sun-Eyed Snake Jaguar. He renovated the temple of Quetzal Jaguar, Lord at Cloudy Center.

Here in the sanctuary of the home of spirits is the ballplayer with the segmented guardian spirit, Sun-Eyed Snake Jaguar, lord who makes offerings for the Egrets.

When he entered the tree, he joined the first among all sprouts, One Lord.[1] The Red Snake was lying face down together with Akan,[2] unseen, when he received the mirror scepter—

this flower of the lord who saw 5 score stones[3], Sun-Eyed Corn Tassel Shield,[4] lord who offers shells for the Egrets.

---

[1] **One Lord:** Hun Ahau, the elder of the Hero Twins who in Maya mythology defeated the lords of the underworld. Subsequently, Hun Ahau ascended into the sky as the planet Venus, and his brother as the sun.

[2] **Akan:** A star god associated with alcoholic beverages.

[3] **stone:** Dates were measured in "stones" and "days."

[4] **Sun-Eyed Corn Tassel Shield:** Father of Sun-Eyed Snake Jaguar.

Left Inscription (not included in tablet)

Wind counts the drumbeats, counts the scores
    of stones:

After one bundle of stones,
Eighteen score stones,
Five single stones,
Four score days,
And no single days,
The date was One Lord
13 Turtle, the headband was worn by the eighth
    lord of the night,
And 10 days ago the fifth in a series of moons had
    arrived.
White Foot is the birth name of the new
Month of a score and ten days. 19
And 14 score days ago, on 1 Portal
7 Green, had come the standing
Of the mirror scepter where the sun goes in,
And then the third one was born
In the new sky, the scepter personified;
The third giver of blessings to arise
Young Mirror Scepter (Saturn).
After 1 score of stones, 14 single stones,
And 14 score and no single days
Came the arrival of Young
Mirror Scepter at invisibility.
And then, after 2 bundles of stones had been
    completed,

On 2 Lord 3 Spirit,
His spirit was summoned
By the Lady of Split Place, Cormorant
Lady who makes offerings for the invisible.
It happened on First Corn Tassel
Mountain, White Flower, near
The Temple of the Tree of Yellow Corn, on 1 Lord
13 Turtle. After 7 bundles of stones
7 score stones, 7 single stones,
And 3 score and 16 days,

Right Inscription (not included in tablet)

On 2 Honey 14 Cluster,
Came the delay, the capture
Of one of the divine triplets:[5] the mirror
Of Sun Jaguar, Mirror Scepter.
On the day 3 Earth
15 Cluster, the one who turned around
In the Sun-Eyed Quetzal Jaguar Temple,
Inside the home of those who fast
Was Sun-Eyed Snake Jaguar, lord who offers ev-
    erything for the Egrets.
On the third day, he summoned the ghost

---

[5] **divine triplets:** The planets visible in the western sky that
evening.

Of the namesake of the lady of the sky,[6] a wise
woman,
By letting his blood. She handed over the white
paper
Of her spirit to Sun-Eyed Snake Jaguar,
Lord who makes offerings for the Egrets. It hap-
pened where the river
Is channeled by the cave. At the cave
Of Sixth Sky[7] were three fierce Thunderbolts
And the lady who offers gems for the Four Hun-
dred. 4 and 6 score days
9 single stones, and 2 score stones
After he was born, the white paper was handed
over
To the one with the segmented guardian spirit,
Sun-Eyed Snake Jaguar, lord who makes offerings
for the Egrets,
On 8 Foot 3 Song.
6 and 11 score days and 6 stones
After he was seated in kingship
Came the delay, the capture
Of the divine triplets, Corn Silk [Mars],

Mirror Scepter [Saturn], and Sun-Eyed Lord of the
Shield [Jupiter].
The Thunderbolt star guardian with Akan the
Destroyer
Was One Lord. This was experienced
By Sun-Eyed Snake Jaguar. In 4 and 12 days
And 1 stone will come
8 Lord 8 Sign, marking the 13th score of stones,
Coming after the event of 2 Honey, when he went
into seclusion,
When Sun-Eyed Snake Jaguar, lord who makes
offerings for the Egrets, was alone.

Examining the Evidence

1. What does the positioning of the ruler's
images on this sculpted tablet suggest about
the role the Maya rulers played in the struggle
between the forces of life and death?
2. In this inscription, the gods are associated
with celestial bodies on one hand and plants
and animals on the other. What do these associations tell us about the Maya ideas of
divine power and its relationship to human
society?
3. What does the Maya obsession with timing
present-day actions with events in the past tell
us about their conception of history?

[6] **namesake . . . sky:** Lady Cormorant.
[7] **Sixth Sky:** The part of the heavens corresponding to the constellation Scorpio.

<table>
<tr><td>**10.2**</td><td># ORIGINS OF THE HUMAN RACE IN MAYA MYTHOLOGY</td></tr>
</table>

Popol Vuh: The Sacred Book of the Maya (c. mid-1500s)

One version of the Maya legends of creation has been preserved in the *Popol Vuh* ("Book of Council"), composed in the mid-sixteenth century by descendants of the lords of the Quiché kingdom. Although written down long after the passing of the Maya classical age, many of the *Popol Vuh* stories can be identified in sculptures and painted pottery from the classical era.

The *Popol Vuh* begins by relating how the gods of the primordial sea—Framer, Shaper, and so on—and the primordial heavens—Heart of Sky, Heart of Earth, and so on—formed the earth and its creatures. The gods' first experiments to create human beings failed, however. Finally, the diviner Xmucane—portrayed as an elderly woman—succeeded in fashioning humans from corn (maize) and water. The first four men created by the gods—Balam Quitze, Balam Acab, Mahucutah,

Allen J. Christenson, trans., *Popol Vuh: The Sacred Book of the Quiché Maya People* (Norman: University of Oklahoma Press, 2007), 180–196.

and Iqui Balam—were the founders of the principal Quiché lineages.

The Creation of Humanity

THIS, then, is the beginning of the conception of humanity, when that which would become the flesh of mankind was sought. Then spoke they who are called She Who Has Borne Children and He Who Has Begotten Sons, the Framer and the Shaper, Sovereign and Quetzal Serpent:

"The dawn approaches, and our work is not successfully completed. A provider and a sustainer have yet to appear—a child of light, a son of light. Humanity has yet to appear to populate the face of the earth," they said.

Thus they gathered together and joined their thoughts in the darkness, in the night. They searched and they sifted. Here they thought and they pondered. Their thoughts came forth bright and clear. They discovered and established that which would become the flesh of humanity. This took place just a little before the appearance of the sun, moon, and stars above the heads of the Framer and the Shaper.

The Discovery of Maize

IT was from within the places called Paxil and Cayala that the yellow ears of ripe maize and the white ears of ripe maize came.

THESE were the names of the animals that obtained their food—fox and coyote, parakeet and raven. Four, then, were the animals that revealed to them the yellow ears of maize and the white ears of maize. They came from Paxil and pointed out the path to get there.

Thus was found the food that would become the flesh of the newly framed and shaped people. Water was their blood. It became the blood of humanity. The ears of maize entered into their flesh by means of She Who Has Borne Children and He Who Has Begotten Sons.

Thus they rejoiced over the discovery of that excellent mountain that was filled with delicious things, crowded with yellow ears of maize and white ears of maize. It was crowded as well with pataxte[1] and chocolate, with countless zapotes and anonas, with jocotes and nances, with matasanos

and honey.[2] From within the places called Paxil and Cayala came the sweetest foods in the citadel. All the small foods and great foods were there, along with the small and great cultivated fields. The path was thus revealed by the animals.

The yellow ears of maize and the white ears of maize were then ground fine with nine grindings by Xmucane. Food entered their flesh, along with water to give them strength. Thus was created the fatness of their arms. The yellowness of humanity came to be when they were made by they who are called She Who Has Borne Children and He Who Has Begotten Sons, by Sovereign and Quetzal Serpent.

Thus their frame and shape were given expression by our first Mother and our first Father. Their flesh was merely yellow ears of maize and white ears of maize. Mere food were the legs and arms of humanity, of our first fathers. And so there were four who were made, and mere food was their flesh.

The First Four Men

THESE are the names of the first people who were framed and shaped: the first person was Balam Quitze, the second was Balam Acab, the third was Mahucutah, and the fourth was Iqui Balam. These, then, were the names of our first mothers and fathers.

The Miraculous Vision of the First Men

IT is said that they were merely given frame and shape. They had no mother. They had no father. They were merely lone men, as we would say. No woman gave them birth. Nor were they begotten by the Framer or the Shaper, by She Who Has Borne Children or He Who Has Begotten Sons. Their frame and shape were merely brought about by the miraculous power and the spirit essence of the Framer and the Shaper, of She Who Has Borne Children and He Who Has Begotten Sons, of Sovereign and Quetzal Serpent.

---

[1] **pataxte:** A type of cacao tree. The Maya made chocolate from the seeds of both cacao and pataxte.

[2] Zapote (also written as *sapote*), anona, jocote, nance, and matasanos are all varieties of tropical fruits.

Thus their countenances appeared like people. People they came to be. They were able to speak and converse. They were able to look and listen. They were able to walk and hold things with their hands. They were excellent and chosen people. Their faces were manly in appearance. They had their breath, therefore they became. They were able to see as well, for straightaway their vision came to them.

Perfect was their sight, and perfect was their knowledge of everything beneath the sky. If they gazed about them, looking intently, they beheld that which was in the sky and that which was upon the earth. Instantly they were able to behold everything. They did not have to walk to see all that existed beneath the sky. They merely saw it from wherever they were. Thus their knowledge became full. Their vision passed beyond the trees and the rocks, beyond the lakes and the seas, beyond the mountains and the valleys. Truly they were very esteemed people, these Balam Quitze, Balam Acab, Mahucutah, and Iqui Balam.

The Gratitude of the First Men

THEN the Framer and the Shaper asked them: "What is the nature of your existence? Do you know it? Do you not look and listen? Are not your speech and your walk good? Behold now, therefore, and see that which is beneath the sky. Are not the mountains clear? Do you not see the valleys? Try it then," they were told.

Thus their vision of everything beneath the sky was completed, and they gave thanks to the Framer and the Shaper:

"Truly we thank you doubly, triply that we were created, that we were given our mouths and our faces. We are able to speak and to listen. We are able to ponder and to move about. We know much, for we have learned that which is far and near. We have seen the great and the small, all that exists in the sky and on the earth. We thank you, therefore, that we were created, that we were given frame and shape. We became because of you, our Grandmother, and you, our Grandfather," they said when they gave thanks for their frame and shape.

Their knowledge of everything that they saw was complete—the four corners and the four sides, that which is within the sky and that which is within the earth.

But this did not sound good to the Framer and the Shaper:

"It is not good what they have said, they that we have framed and shaped. They said, 'We have learned everything, great and small.'"

The Displeasure of the Gods

THUS their knowledge was taken back by She Who Has Borne Children and He Who Has Begotten Sons:

"What now can be done to them so that their vision reaches only nearby, so that only a little of the face of the earth can be seen by them? For it is not good what they say. Is not their existence merely framed, merely shaped? It is a mistake that they have become like gods.

"But if they do not multiply or are increased, when will the first planting be? When will it dawn? If they do not increase, when will it be so? Therefore we will merely undo them a little now. That is what is wanted, because it is not good what we have found out. Their works will merely be equated with ours. Their knowledge will extend to the furthest reaches, and they will see everything."

Thus spoke Heart of Sky and Huracan, Youngest Thunderbolt and Sudden Thunderbolt, Sovereign and Quetzal Serpent, She Who Has Borne Children and He Who Has Begotten Sons, Xpiyacoc and Xmucane, the Framer and the Shaper, as they are called. Thus they remade the essence of that which they had framed and shaped.

The Creation of the Mothers of the Quiché Nation

THEIR eyes were merely blurred by Heart of Sky. They were blinded like breath upon the face of a mirror. Thus their eyes were blinded. They could see only nearby; things were clear to them only where they were. Thus their knowledge was lost. The wisdom of the first four people was lost there at their foundation, at their beginning. Thus were the framing and the shaping of our first grandfathers and fathers by Heart of Sky and Heart of Earth.

Then their companions, their wives, also came to be. It was the gods alone who conceived them as well. As if it were in their sleep they received them.

The women were truly beautiful who were with Balam Quitze, Balam Acab, Mahucutah, and Iqui Balam. Thus when the men were brought to life, their wives truly came to be as well. At once their hearts rejoiced because of their mates.

These, then, are the names of their wives: Cahapaluna was the name of the wife of Balam Quitze. Chomiha was the name of the wife of Balam Acab. Tzununiha was the name of the wife of Mahucutah. Caquixaha was the name of the wife of Iqui Balam. These, therefore, were the names of their wives, they who came to be our rulers. These were they who multiplied the nations both small and great.

This, therefore, was our foundation, we the Quiché people. There were many who came to be bloodletters and sacrificers. There are no longer merely four now, but four were the mothers of the Quiché people. Each of the people had different names when they multiplied there in the East. Truly these became the names of the people—Sovereign, Ballplayer, Masker, and Sun Lord. These are the titles of the people. It was there in the East that they multiplied.

The beginning of the Tamub and the Ilocab[3] (the Quiché ancestors) is known. As one they came from there in the East.

Balam Quitze was the grandfather, the father of nine great houses of the Cavecs. Balam Acab was the grandfather, the father of nine great houses of the Nihaibs. Mahucutah was the grandfather, the father of four great houses of Ahau Quichés. Thus there were three divisions of lineages that existed. The names of their grandfathers and their fathers were not forgotten—they who multiplied and proliferated there in the East.

The Tamub and the Ilocab came as well, along with the thirteen allied nations, the thirteen houses: The Rabinals, the Cakchiquels, and the Ah Tziquinahas; as well as the Zacahs and the Lamacs, the Cumatz and the Tuhalhas, the Uchabahas and the Ah Chumilahas, along with the Ah Quibahas and the Ah Batenahas, the Acul Vinacs and the Balamihas, the Can Chahels and the Balam Colobs.

Of these we shall speak only of the nations that became great among the allied nations. They who became great we shall declare. There were many others that came out of the citadel after them, each one of them a division. We have not written their names, but they also multiplied there in the East. Many people arrived in darkness in the days of their increase, for the sun was yet to be born. There was no light in the days of their increase. They were all as one, crowded together as they walked there in the East. There was no one to provide for their sustenance. They would merely lift up their faces to the sky, for they did not know where to go.

This they did for a long time there among the magueys; among the black people and the white people, the people of many appearances and many tongues. They were destitute in their existence at the edge of the sky's foundation. And there were mountain people. They were hidden, and without homes. Only among the small mountains and the great mountains did they go. It is as if they were lacking in direction, as they used to say. It is said that in those days they quarreled with the mountain people.

There they looked for the coming forth of the sun, when they had one common language. They did not yet call upon wood or stone (images of the gods). They remembered the word of the Framer and the Shaper, of Heart of Sky and Heart of Earth, it was said. They would merely plead for their heartening, their sowing and their dawning. These were people of esteemed words, of esteem, of honor, and of respect. They would lift up their faces to the sky as they pleaded for their daughters and their sons:

"Alas, you, Framer, and you, Shaper: Behold us! Hear us! Do not abandon us. Do not allow us to be overthrown. You are the god in the sky and on the earth, you, Heart of Sky, Heart of Earth. May our sign, our word, be given for as long as there is sun and light. Then may it be sown, may it dawn. May there be true life-giving roads and pathways. Give us steadfast light that our nation be made steadfast. May the light be favorable that our nation may be favored. May our lives be favored so that all creation may be favored as well. Give

---

[3] **The beginning of . . . Ilocab:** At the time of the composition of the *Popol Vuh*, the Quiché peoples were divided into three main groups: the ruling Nima Quiché, who were subdivided into the Cavec, Nihaib, and Ahau Quiché subgroups mentioned in the next paragraph; the Tamub; and the Ilocab.

this to us, you, Huracan, Youngest Thunderbolt, and Sudden Thunderbolt, Youngest Nanavac and Sudden Nanavac, Falcon and Hunahpu, Sovereign and Quetzal Serpent, She Who Has Borne Children and He Who Has Begotten Sons, Xpiyacoc and Xmucane, Grandmother of Day and Grandmother of Light. Then may it be sown. Then may it dawn," they said.

Then they fasted and cried out in prayer. They fixed their eyes firmly on their dawn, looking there to the East. They watched closely for the Morning Star [Venus], the Great Star that gives its light at the birth of the sun. They looked to the womb of the sky and the womb of the earth, to the pathways of framed and shaped people.

Then spoke Balam Quitze, Balam Acab, Mahucutah, and Iqui Balam:

"We shall surely await the dawn," they said.

They were great sages and wise men, bloodletters and honorers, as they are called. There did not exist then wood or stone to watch over our first mothers and fathers. They were therefore weary in their hearts as they awaited the dawn.

There were many nations then, there with the Yaqui people, the bloodletters and sacrificers.

"Let us go and search, to look for one who may protect us. We may find one before whom we may speak. For here we only feign existence and there is not a guardian for us," said therefore Balam Quitze, Balam Acab, Mahucutah, and Iqui Balam.

They heard news of a citadel and there they went.

Examining the Evidence

1. Why did the gods regret granting humanity the gift of knowledge?
2. In what sense were humans indebted to the gods? How must that debt be paid?
3. What implications did the creation of women have for the evolution of human society?

10.3 PEOPLES AND CUSTOMS OF THE LAKE TITICACA REGION

Pedro de Cieza de León, *Crónica del Peru* (1553)

Pedro de Cieza de León (1520–1554) left Spain for the Americas in 1534 at the age of fourteen, shortly after the Spanish Conquest of Peru. In 1546, Cieza accompanied a military expedition sent to subdue renegade conquistadors in Peru. This mission took him on a two-year journey through the lands along the "royal road" of the Incas, running down the spine of the Andes mountain range. Cieza claimed that he was named a royal chronicler, although no record of such an appointment has survived. After further travels in Peru to gather information for his history of the Incas, he submitted his *Crónica del Peru* to the colonial authorities in Lima in 1550. In the following passages on the Colla, Aymara-speaking inhabitants of the Andean highlands, Cieza provides the earliest description of the ruins of Tiwanaku, which he rightly recognized as being far more ancient than the Incas.

The Collas

The region of the Collas [around Lake Titicaca] is the largest of all Peru, and in my opinion the most thickly settled. . . . To the east lie the mountains of the Andes, to the west the promontories of the snow-capped sierras and their flanks, which descend to the Southern Sea. Aside from the territories occupied by their settlements and fields, there are great unsettled regions full of wild flocks [of llamas and alpacas]. The lands of the Colla are all level, and through them run many rivers of good water. In these

---

Harriet de Onis, trans., *The Incas of Pedro de Cieza de León*, ed. Victor Wolfgang von Hagen (Norman: University of Oklahoma Press, 1976), 270–271, 273–274, 276, 282–284.

plains there are beautiful broad meadows always thick with grass, and part of the time very green, though in summer they turn brown as in Spain. The winter begins, as I have written, in October and lasts until April. The days and nights are of almost equal length, and this is the coldest region of all Peru, aside from the high snow-capped sierras, because of its elevation. The fact of the matter is that if this land of the Colla were a low-lying valley like that of Jauja or Chuquiabo, where corn could be raised, it would be considered one of the best and richest of much of these Indies. It is very difficult to walk against the wind in these plains of the Colla; when there is no wind and the sun shines, it is a real pleasure to see these beautiful and thickly settled meadows. But as it is so cold, corn cannot grow nor any kind of tree; on the contrary, none of the many fruits produced in the other valleys can be raised here. The villages of the natives are close together, the houses one beside the other, not very large, all of stone, with roofs of thatch, which they all use instead of tile.

In olden times this region of the Collas was thickly settled, and there were large villages close together. Around them the Indians have their fields where they plant their crops. Their principal article of food is potatoes, which are like truffles, as I have stated before in this relation, and they dry them in the sun and keep them from one harvest to the other. They call these dried potatoes *chuño*, and among them they are highly esteemed and valued, for they have no irrigation system, as in many other parts of this kingdom, to water their fields. On the contrary, if there is a shortage of rainfall for their crops, they would go hungry if it were not for these dried potatoes. Many Spaniards became rich and went back to Spain prosperous just by selling this *chuño* in the mines of Potosí. They have another article of food called *oca*, which is also useful, but even more so is a cereal they grow known as *quinoa*, which is small like rice. When it is a good year, all the inhabitants of Colla live happy and satisfied; but if it is a dry year and there is a shortage of rain, they undergo great hardships. . . .

They all agree that their forefathers lived with little order before the Incas ruled them, and that on the heights of the mountains they had their fortified settlements, from which they went forth to make war. . . . The headmen always go accompanied by a large retinue, and when they travel, they are borne in a litter and treated with the greatest respect by all these Indians. In the wasteland and secret places they have their *huacas*, or temples, where they pay homage to their gods, employing their vain superstitions, and those selected for this purpose converse with the devil in their shrines. The most extraordinary thing to be seen here in the Colla is, in my opinion, the graves of the dead. When I went through, I stopped to set down what seemed to me the most noteworthy things about the Indians. And truly it amazes me to think how little store the living set by having large, fine houses, and the care with which they adorned the graves where they were to be buried, as though this constituted their entire happiness. Thus, all through the meadows and plains around the settlements were the tombs of these Indians, built like little four-sided towers, some of stone only, some of stone and earth, some wide, others narrow, according to their means or taste. Some of the roofs were covered with straw, others with large stone slabs, and it seems to me that the door of these tombs faced the rising sun. . . .

As these people set such importance by burying their dead as I have described in the preceding chapter, after the funeral the women and servants who were left cut off their hair and dressed themselves in their poorest clothes, with little attention to their person. And aside from this, to make their grief more apparent, they put hempen ropes about their heads, and spent a year in continual mourning if the deceased was a headman, kindling no fire in the house where he had died for several days. Misled by the devil like all the others, God so permitting, with his false arts he created in them the illusion that they saw certain of those who had died walking about their fields, adorned and dressed as they had been laid in the grave. And further to honor their dead, these Indians observed, and still do, anniversary celebrations, on which occasions they take certain plants and animals and kill them beside the grave, and burn the tallow of llamas. And when they have done this, they pour jugs of their liquor into the grave, and with this they conclude this blind, vain superstition. As this nation of the Collas was so large, in olden times they had great temples and religious rites, venerating those who were their priests and talked with the devil. And they observed their feasts at the time of the digging the potatoes, which is their principal food, killing of their animals for the necessary sacrifices. . . .

Tiwanaku

Tiahuanacu [Tiwanaku] is not a very large town, but it is famous for its great buildings which, without question, are a remarkable thing to behold. Near the main dwellings is a man-made hill, built on great stone foundations. Beyond this hill there are two stone idols of human size and shape, with the features beautifully carved, so much so that they seem the work of great artists or masters. They are so large that they seem small giants, and they are wearing long robes, different from the attire of the natives of these provinces. They seem to have an ornament on their heads. Close by these stone statues there is another building, whose antiquity and this people's lack of writing is the reason there is no knowledge of who the people that built these great foundations and strongholds were, or how much time has gone by since then, for at present all one sees is a finely built wall which must have been constructed many ages ago. Some of the stones are very worn and wasted, and there are others so large that one wonders how human hands could have brought them to where they now stand. Many of these stones are carved in different ways, and some of them are in the form of human bodies, and these must have been their idols. Along the wall there are many underground hollows and cavities. In another spot farther to the west there are other still greater antiquities, for there are many large gates with jambs, threshold, and door all of a single stone. What struck me most when I was observing and setting down these things was that from these huge gateways other still

larger stones project on which they were set, some of which were as much as thirty feet wide, fifteen or more long, and six thick, and this and the door, jamb, and threshold were one single stone, which was a tremendous thing. When one considers the work, I cannot understand or fathom what kind of instruments or tools were used to work them, for it is evident that before these huge stones were dressed and brought to perfection, they must have been much larger to have been left as we see them. One can see that these buildings were never completed, for all there is of them are these great gateways and other stones of incredible size, some of them which I saw, cut and prepared to go into the building. A great stone idol, which they probably worshipped, stands a short distance away in a small recess. It is even said that beside this idol a quantity of gold was found, and around this shrine there were a number of other stones, large and small, dressed and carved like those already mentioned. . . .

In conclusion, I would say I consider this the oldest antiquity in all of Peru. It is believed that long before the Incas reigned, long before, certain of these buildings existed, and I have heard Indians say that the Incas built their great edifices of Cuzco along the lines of the wall to be seen in this place.

Examining the Evidence

1. Did Cieza regard the high plains around Lake Titicaca as an economically prosperous region? Why or why not?
2. What can Cieza's remarks tell us about the cultural and religious values of the peoples inhabiting the Andean highlands?
3. Does Cieza's description suggest that the inhabitants of the Lake Titicaca region descended from the builders of Tiwanaku? Why or why not?

10.4 ZUNI ORAL TRADITIONS ON THE ORIGINS AND DISPERSAL OF THE CLANS

Frank Hamilton Cushing, *The Mythic World of the Zuni* (1891–1892)

The Zuni are one of the Pueblo peoples inhabiting the southwestern deserts of the United States. Like Chaco Canyon, eighty miles to the north, Zuni Pueblo enjoyed its greatest prosperity during the mild and wet centuries from 1100 to 1300. During this period, the Zuni participated in far-flung trade and cultural networks spanning the entire American Southwest. Zuni oral traditions describe the origins and migrations of the Zuni people, culminating with their arrival at Zuni Pueblo, "the middle place," in present-day New Mexico. These narratives have been preserved in the form of chants or prayers recited during religious ceremonies. The versions of the Zuni oral traditions reproduced here were recorded by Frank Hamilton Cushing, who, beginning in 1879, spent four years carrying out an ethnographic survey of the Zuni on behalf of the Smithsonian Institution. Cushing's versions take the form of poetic renditions rather than verbatim translations.

Birth of the Twins

Deep in the lowermost womb, in the stygian cave-world of Anosin Tehuli, the place of first formation, the seed of men and creatures took shape, multiplying in kind and increasing until the space was overfilled. Unfinished beings were everywhere, crawling like reptiles over one another in the filth and darkness of the first world until, like the swollen egg case of some insect, it threatened to burst. So thickly crowded together that they trod upon one another, they lived in mud burrows and ate grass seeds as they slowly grew wiser and more man-like until many sought to escape.

Long and deeply the Sun Father took counsel with himself over the problem of the living creatures as they clamored ever more loudly below, before he came to a decision. Casting his glance about the Great Waters beneath, he searched until he spied a bubble capped with foam floating near the Earth Mother. With a single ray he impregnated it as it nestled there. Nurtured by the Earth Mother's warmth and the soft gentle rain, the cap of foam grew and brought forth twin boys, the Beloved Twain Who Descended, two brothers, one preceding, the other following, like voice and echo, the elder Ko'wituma, the younger Wats'usi.

To these children the Sun Father imparted much of this sacred knowledge, giving them devices to better perform their duties. In recognition of their origin and close ties to the Earth Mother and himself he gave each a cap patterned after the original cap of foam. With the great cloud bows and flint-tipped arrows he armed the Twins. For protection, he gave each the fog-making shield of netting spun from floating clouds and the wind-driven spray that would both hide and defend. Then, as a man gives control of his work to his two hands, the Sun Father gave his sons dominion or fathership over all men and creatures.

Well instructed by the Sun Father, they lifted him with their great cloud bows into the vault of the zenith so the earth might become warm and thus more fit for their children, men and creatures alike. Then seated upon their shields, the Twin Gods floated swiftly westward seeking the best place to enter the dark netherworld. Grasping their flint-tipped thunderbolts, they selected a place and cleft the land, penetrating to its depths; still seated upon their shields they sank into the blackness of the first Underworld [to release humanity into the world of light].

Frank Hamilton Cushing, *The Mythic World of the Zuni*, ed. Barton Wright (Albuquerque: University of New Mexico Press, 1988), 9–10, 17–18, 21–22, 25–26.

The Daylight World

At long last the Two led forth the nations of men and the groups of creatures into the great upper world of the Sun, Tek'ohaian Ulahnane, the Daylight World. The men and creatures that emerged were more like one another than they are now, for our fathers were black like the caves they came from, with cold and scaly skins like other mud creatures. Their eyes bulged and blinked constantly like those of the owl. Their ears were bat-like and their feet and hands were webbed as those of the ones who walk in wet soft places. All had tails which became longer with age. They crouched and crawled like lizards and toads and moved bent over with the uncertain steps of infants fearful of falling or stumbling in the dim light. Hence it was that the Twins brought forth Mankind late at night so they might be more easily accommodated.

As the great star of morning, Moyachun Thlanna [Venus], rose and its light struck their eyes they thought it was like the Sun Father, for it burned their weak vision. But it was only the Elder of the Bright Ones who, with his shield of flame, heralded the arrival of the Sun Father.

When the Sun Father did appear, low in the east rising from the Great Waters, they were blinded by his glory and flung themselves on the ground, wallowing in the dirt and covering their eyes with bare arms and hands as they cried out in anguish. Yet like the moth that goes back to the flame even though burned, they looked again and again.

Before long they grew accustomed to the light and rising up, saw the great world they had entered. When they arose and no longer stayed bent and crouched they saw each other as naked. Rushing about they covered themselves with girdles of bark or rushes and wove plaited sandals of yucca fiber for their sore feet.

It was then that men grew to know things and were instructed by what they saw, becoming wiser and more able to receive the words of the Twin Gods, of elder brothers, fathers, and priests. For in each world there had been those who found and cherished things given by the gods, gifts of unknown purpose or function. But in the light of the Sun Father, all became clear. The first and most perfect of these men, Yana-uluha, brought up water from the Inner Ocean and seeds of growing things as well as other objects of great power.

The Winter and Summer People

The first wise man, Yana-uluha, came carrying a staff which appeared now in the daylight to be covered with many plumes of striking color—yellow, blue green, red, white, black, and variegated. Attached to the staff were sea shells and other potent things brought from the Underworld. When the people saw this beautiful staff and heard the song-like tinkle of the sacred shells, they stretched forth their hands toward it and cried out like children asking questions.

Yana-uluha, having been made wise by the masters of life or god beings, replied, "It is a staff to test the hearts and understandings of the children." Balancing it in his hand he struck it on a hard place and blew upon it. Instantly amid the plumes there appeared four round things, the seeds of moving creatures, eggs. Two of these were blue like the sky or turquoise and the other two were a dun red like the flesh of the Earth Mother. Again the people cried out in wonder, asking many questions.

Then Yana-uluha said, "These are the seeds of living things. From two shall emerge beautiful things with plumage colored like the leaves and shoots of summer plants. Where they fly you must follow, for where they are it will be everlasting summer. You will know neither pain nor toil but will always have fertile fields of food. From the other pair shall come ugly beings, uncolored, black, or piebald. Where they fly you must follow. There winter will contend with the summer. You will work hard in the fields and your offspring will compete with those of the birds for the fruit of your labors."

With scarcely a thought, the strongest and hastiest people rushed to take the beautiful blue eggs, leaving the other two for those who cautiously waited. The hasty ones carried the turquoise eggs gently to the warm sands below a cliff and guarded them there, speculating as they waited on the beauty the eggs must contain. At last small beaks emerged through cracks in the shells. Those who had chosen them plied the unseen hatchlings with morsels of their own food to give them strength, thus building the appetites of the little birds for the food of men. But when at last these birds hatched they were black with white bandings, for they were the magpie and the raven, who flew away croaking and mocking our fathers.

The eggs taken by the patient ones who had waited became gorgeous macaws and parrots that Yana-uluha wafted to the far southland with a toss of his wand. As father, yet child, of the macaw, he chose the symbol and the name for himself and for those who had waited. The macaw and the kindred of the macaw became the Mulakwe, while those who had chosen the magpie and raven became the Ka'kakwe, the Raven People.

Thus were the people divided into the People of Winter and the People of Summer. Those who chose the raven were many, forceful and strong. Those who chose the macaw were fewer in number, less lusty, more deliberate in nature. Their father, Yana-uluha, being wise, readily saw the ways of the Father and partaking of the Sun's breath, Yana-uluha became among men as the Sun Father is to the little moons of the sky. He became Speaker to the Sun Father, keeper and giver of precious things and commandments, the first Sun Priest. He and his sisters became the seed of all priests of the midmost clan, the Master of the House of Houses.

The Origins of Clans and Societies

Gathering the first Priest Fathers in council, the Beloved Twins met with them to select and name groups of men and the kinds of creatures and things. They decided that the Summer People belonged to the south where it was warm, and to the producing Earth Mother. The Winter People were made the children of the north and the quickening Sky Father.

In each of these groups were people who liked one thing or another and understood it better than all others so that was selected for their name. Among the Summer People those who loved the sun became the Sun People, others who loved the water became the Frog, Turtle, or Toad clans. Still others who knew

seeds became the First-Growing Grass or Tobacco People. Because the Badger liked the warm southern slopes and lived among the dry roots used for fire he and the ones who understood him became a part of the Summer People rather than being with the North People and the other animals. The Winter People according to their natures, talents, and inclinations became the Bear, the Coyote, and the Deer People. Others became the Turkey, the Crane, or the Grouse clans.

In this way the people were divided into clans, brothers and sisters who may not marry and who will cherish each other's offspring as their own. From each of these clans a headman was selected for instruction by the gods and the Father of the House of Houses, and was breathed upon by them. In this way these men became Masters of Secrets and the Keepers of Sacred Things. The Badger people were given the great shell whose core has an affinity for fire just as the Earth Mother is sensitive to earthquakes. Thus the younger and elder Badger clan heads became the Keepers of the Shell and Wardens of Fire. The Winter People were given seed substances for hail, snow, and new soil, the Water Peoples were given the seed of water, and to the still others, the germ of corn or tobacco was given. . . .

In the beginning there were only four societies: the Shiwanakwe or priesthood of the Priest People; the Saniakiakwe, the priesthood of the Hunters who were from the Coyote, Eagle, and Deer clans and were keepers of the germ of game; the Achiakiakwe or Great Knife People who were the makers and defenders of pathways for the people; and the Newekwe, keepers of magic medicines and knowledge, who were invincible against evil.

Examining the Evidence

1. According to this Zuni oral tradition account, what was the most important gift the gods bestowed on humans?
2. How did Zuni oral narratives explain the division of the world into different clans and peoples?
3. How and why did the People of Summer and the People of Winter differ from each other?

10.5 IMAGES OF DIVINE POWER

Hawaiian Gods of Agriculture and War (Late Eighteenth–Early Nineteenth Centuries)

In the eyes of the Polynesian peoples, the gods were powerful but unpredictable, equally responsible for life-giving rains and bountiful harvests as well as destructive storms and typhoons. Since the gods could be either beneficent or malevolent, the same images or icons might be used to represent different aspects of divine power. Hawaiian chiefs assumed the attributes of various gods on different ritual occasions.

The four principal gods of Hawaiian religion each had their special domain of activity: Kanaloa (the sea), Kane (forests), Ku (warfare), and Lono (agriculture). Temple compounds—known as *heiau*—for offering sacrifices to the gods proliferated across the Hawaiian Islands after 1400. In the seventeenth century, *heiau* began to divide into two distinct types: community shrines for offering thanksgiving to the gods and war temples where chiefs conducted divination rituals before undertaking military campaigns.

The arrival of the British explorer Captain James Cook in 1768 dramatically changed the balance of power in Hawaii. After Kamehameha I (c. 1758–1819), the paramount chief of the island of Hawaii, conquered the other islands and created a single Hawaiian kingdom in 1810, he converted all of the major temples into war temples dedicated to his patron deity, Kukailimoku (Ku, Snatcher of Lands).

Our knowledge of Polynesian societies before contact with the West is hindered not only by the lack of written records, but also by the limited archaeological remains. Even the most sacred treasures—chiefs' regalia, temples, and images of the gods—were made of perishable materials such as wood, fibers, and feathers. Historians must rely on more recent artifacts and oral traditions passed down over many generations to reconstruct the history of the Pacific islands.

The first image dates from the time of Cook's voyages. The feathered head—fashioned from honeycreeper feathers attached to a basket frame—probably was the most prevalent type of god image in the pre-contact era. The open mouth and protruding chin were regarded as a gesture of scorn and disrespect in Polynesian culture, and thus suggest the fearsome qualities associated with Ku. However, on appropriate festival occasions, the same icon may have been used to represent Lono.

The colossal (nearly 9 feet tall) wooden effigy in the second image undoubtedly represents Kamehameha I's patron deity, Kukailimoku. Although this image—with its more pronounced "mouth of disrespect"—clearly epitomizes the martial aspect of Ku, it also combines elements associated with Lono: the animal head above the nose is either a pig or dog, both sacrificial animals used in offerings to Lono. This statue may be one of the figures shown in the illustration of the dismantling of a *heiau* drawn by a member of a French expedition to Hawaii in 1819 (the third image in the set). The engraving depicts an oracle tower, an offering platform (with pig skeleton), and twelve large wooden figures within the enclosed temple precinct.

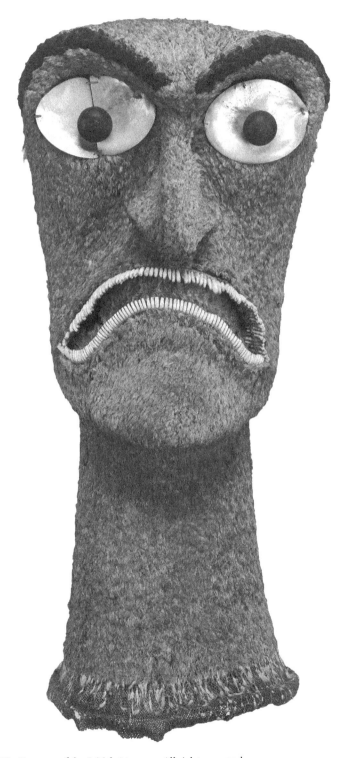

Sandwich Islands: View of the Morai of the King, at Kayakakoua on the Island of Owhyhi, from "Voyage Autour du Monde sur les Corvettes de L'Uranie 1817–1829," engraved by Lejeune, published 1825 after a work by Jacques Etienne Victor Arago (1790–1855). Private Collection/Bridgeman Images.

Examining the Evidence

1. How does the construction of these figures reflect the natural environment of the Hawaiian Islands?
2. What do these figures tell us about the self-image of Hawaiian chiefs?
3. What does the shift from the feathered head to the wooden effigy suggest about changes in the nature of chiefly authority after contact with the West?

MAKING CONNECTIONS

1. What features do the origin myths of the Maya and the Zuni peoples have in common? Do they depict the relationship between gods and humans in similar terms?
2. Based on their images of gods and rulers, did the Maya and the Hawaiians share similar ideas about the nature of divine power and human authority?
3. Is the conception of divine authority conveyed by the Inscription of the Temple of the Tree of Yellow Corn consistent with the image of the gods portrayed in the *Popol Vuh*'s narrative of the origins of the human race? Why or why not?
4. How did the relationship between rulers and subjects differ in the societies examined in the documents included in this chapter?

CHAPTER 11

The Rise of Commerce in Eurasia and Africa, 900–1300

Prolonged economic growth, widespread prosperity, and far-flung maritime commercial exchange across Eurasia and Africa were the most striking features of the period 900–1300 in world history. Agricultural improvement, the spread of new crops and farming techniques, and advances in the organization and management of business enterprises spearheaded these dramatic economic changes. Entrepreneurial merchants banded together in partnerships, guilds, and alliances, pooling resources, sharing risks, and forming commercial networks that spanned vast distances. Markets filled with staple goods as well as exotic luxuries from distant lands. The rise of commerce also fostered spectacular urban growth. The increasingly commercial character of cities attracted large numbers of immigrants seeking to earn a living in this ever more money-conscious world. Cities also became crossroads of culture where peoples of many lands mingled. Political and religious authorities struggled to impose their vision of social order on these restless, heterogeneous, and fiercely competitive urban populations.

11.1   GUIDELINES FOR ESTATE MANAGEMENT

[Robert Grosseteste?], *The Rules* (c. 1240)

The Rules has been attributed to Robert Grosseteste (c. 1175–1253), a leading scholastic philosopher and former chancellor of Oxford University. *The Rules* was originally written in French, the language of the business world as well as high society in England at that time. Grosseteste, appointed bishop of Lincoln in 1235, addressed the book to the recently widowed Countess of Lincoln as guidance on the administration of her large and far-flung landholdings. *The Rules* contain specialized knowledge of accounting and advice about collecting rents and marketing grain that a clergyman and scholar such as Grosseteste was unlikely to possess. Most likely the text was written by someone with more practical business experience. The book also was translated into Latin—perhaps by Grosseteste himself—for the benefit of clergy in need of professional advice.

> Here begin the rules, which Robert Grosseteste
>   the good bishop of Lincoln
> made for the Countess of Lincoln, on how to
>   guard and govern lands and household.
> He who will keep to the rules will live well and
>   comfortably off his demesne[1]
> and keep himself and his people.

The first rule teaches how lord or lady shall know for each manor all the lands by their parcels, all the rents, customs, usages, bond services, franchises, fees, and holdings.

With regard to those of your lands which are not part of your demesne manors, begin by having the King's writ bought so that an inquiry can be made on each manor, on oath by twelve free men, into all the lands by their parcels, all the rents, customs,

usages, bond services, franchises, your fees, and your holdings. And this ought to be inquired into carefully and in a lawful manner by the most loyal and the most knowledgeable among the freemen and the villeins[2] and it ought then to be enrolled clearly in such a way that your chief steward has one and you another full roll and each bailiff has that portion which pertains to his bailiwick. And if plaintiffs come to you about injuries done them or demands made on them you yourself ought to study your rolls concerning that manor and answer them accordingly and so have justice maintained.

The second rule teaches how you may know, by common inquiry, what movables and immovables are on each manor.

Afterwards arrange without delay that a just inquest is held and all your demesne manors in England are enrolled on another roll, distinctly; each by itself and as soon as possible: how many plows you have in each place small or large, and how many you can have; how many acres of arable land, how many of meadow; how much pasture for sheep, how much for cows and so for all kinds of beasts and in definite numbers; and how much you have in movables at the time in each place in form of live-stock. And keep this roll by you and often study the first roll and this one also so that you can find out quickly what you ought to do. All your manorial servants ought to be on fixed payment and after August all your granges [barns] ought to be closed.

The third rule teaches the reasoning which the lord or lady ought to put to their chief steward in the presence of some of their good friends.

[1] **demesne:** All of the land directly managed by a lord and farmed by his serfs, in contrast to lands rented out to free tenants.

[2] **villeins:** Serfs legally bound to the land they worked and under the judicial authority of their masters. Villeins cultivated the demesne lands.

Dorothea Oschinsky, *Walter of Henley and Other Treatises on Estate Management and Accounting* (Oxford: Clarendon Press, 1971), 389, 391, 393, 395, 397, 399.

When the aforesaid rolls and inquests have been made and as soon as you are able, so as not to impede the work of your people, call your chief steward and in the presence of persons whom you trust speak to him thus:

Good sir, you see plainly that I have had these inquests and enrollments made to shed light on my rights and to know more certainly the state of affairs of my people and of my lands and to be able to decide henceforth what to do and what not to do with my property. I now beg of you—as the man to whom I have entrusted all that is in my ward and government—and strictly command you that you keep my rights, franchise, and my real property whole and undamaged and that you recall, as far as it is in your power, anything that through the negligence or wrongdoing of others is suppressed or infringed upon; and that you increase and faithfully guard, in an honest and correct manner, my personal property and my stock; and that you arrange for the income from my lands, rents, and property to be sent without fraud and disloyal reduction to me personally and to my wardrobe so that it may be spent according to my directions in such a way that God and my honor are served and any profit enhanced through my own foresight and that of you and of my other friends. On the other hand I firmly command that neither you nor any of your bailiffs under you molest, hurt, or ruin any of my tenants rich or poor in any way through tyrannical demands or fear or accusations or through the receipts of presents or gifts. And if they are in any of the aforesaid ways harmed, hurt, or ruined I wish you to ascertain the facts by formal inquiry wherever this can be done, when you make your round, and that you have the matter appropriately amended and redressed.

The fourth rule teaches how lord or lady can examine their demesne estate, i.e., how he or she can live throughout the year off their demesne lands.

In two ways you can, by estimation, ascertain your position. In this way: command emphatically that in each place, when the corn [grain] is brought in, the twentieth sheaf of each kind of corn is thrown aside as it enters the grange and is threshed and measured by itself; and based on this measure you can estimate all the other corn in the grange. And when this is being done I advise you to send to the best manors among your lands those men from your household in whom you have the greatest trust so that they be present at harvest time when the corn is brought in and there supervise this operation. And if this does not please you, use this method: Command your steward that he arranges for knowledgeable and loyal men to estimate every year at Michaelmas[3] all the stacks, within and without the grange, of each kind of corn; how many quarters[4] there ought to be, and how many quarters in seed-corn and in liveries of corn to servants the soil will take back. And the sum of what there is and what will be left after the seed-corn and the liveries to the servants have been deducted write down and base on it the consumption of your household in bread and ale.

Here you will see how many quarters of corn you will be likely to use weekly in livery [allowance for domestic use] of bread and how many in alms; that is, if you spend two quarters daily that will be fourteen quarters weekly, and seven hundred and twenty-eight quarters in one year. And if, to increase your alms, you spend two and a half quarters daily, that will come to seventeen and one-half quarter in the week and nine hundred and ten quarters in one year. And when you have deducted this sum from the total amount of your corn then you may subtract the amount for ale according to the customary weekly amount used for the brewing in your household. And then be careful with the amount which will remain for sale.

And with the moneys from your corn, from your rents, and from the profits from the pleas in your courts and from your stock take the expenditure for your kitchen and your wines, for your wardrobe and the wages for your servants, and also increase your stock. But on all manors be certain that your corn is not sold out of season or without necessity; that is to say, if your rents and your other profits are sufficient for the expenses of your chamber, wines, and kitchen, then leave your corn untouched until

---

[3] **Michaelmas:** The feast of St. Michael the Archangel (September 29), which coincides with the harvest season and the beginning of autumn.

[4] **quarters:** A quarter is a unit of measurement equal to 8 bushels (291 liters).

you hold in reserve the corn of one year, not more (it might deteriorate), or at least of half a year. . . .

The seventh rule teaches you how you may learn by the comparison of the accounts with the estimates the diligence or negligence of your servants and bailiffs of manors and lands.

At the end of the year, when all the accounts of all the manors have been rendered and heard, concerning all the lands, yields, and expenses, collect all the rolls. Then in great secrecy, by one or two of the most discreet and faithful men you have, compare the account rolls with the rolls containing the estimates of corn and stock which you had compiled after the previous harvest. According to how far they agree you will see the good intentions or shortcomings of your servants and bailiffs and you will be able to put things right, when necessary. . . .

The twenty-fifth rule teaches you the two rules concerning the selling and the threshing of your corn.

Follow these two rules concerning the sale and threshing of corn: There should not be any sale of corn unless the straw is kept back for strewing your sheep-folds every day, and for making compost in the yard. And you can be sure that the straw which is thus retained will always be worth as much as half the corn sold. Also, do not permit that on any manor oats are threshed, anywhere, before Christmas, be it fodder or for sale; before that date all should be bought if you can. And after Christmas, when the sowing of oats is commencing have your oats threshed; their freshly threshed straw, if mixed with some hay, will then be worth as much as hay by itself and will give great strength to your oxen and stamina for work. And you should well understand, that if you want to sell oats you will be able to sell better and take more for them later on in the year when everyone is forced to sow.

The twenty-sixth rule teaches you how you ought to arrange at Michaelmas the sojourn for the whole year.

Every year at Michaelmas when you will know the estimate of all your corn then plan your sojourn for the whole of the coming year and how many weeks in each place, according to the seasons of the year and the advantages of the land in flesh and fish. And in no way burden the places where you stay with debts or with too long a residence, but arrange your sojourn in such a way that the place at your departure does not remain in debt; that something is left on the manor so that it can continue to increase yields, especially of cows and sheep, until in the end your stock will pay for your wine, your robes, your wax, and all your wardrobe. And this will be in a short time if you hold by and act according to this treatise, as you can plainly see in this way: wool of 1,000 sheep in good pasture ought to yield at least 50 marks yearly, the wool of 2,000 sheep 100 marks and so on, counting by thousands. The wool of 1,000 sheep in medium pasture ought to yield at least 40 marks and in coarse and feeble pasture 30 marks.

The twenty-seventh rule teaches you that the return from your cows and sheep is worth much.

The return of cows and sheep in cheese is worth much money, daily throughout the season and this without the calves, lambs, and manure which all help to produce corn and thereby profit.

Examining the Evidence

1. Based on this document, what were the principal sources of income and forms of expenditure on an English landed estate at this time?
2. To what extent was the landowner expected to assume direct management of his or her properties?
3. In Grosseteste's view, what were the principal challenges involved in the management of an estate?

11.2 THE MARKET INSPECTOR AT SEVILLE

Ibn Abdun, *The Markets of Seville* (c. 1100)

During the commercial expansion of the twelfth and thirteenth centuries, the ports of the Mediterranean Sea operated much like a free-trade zone. Merchants traveled wherever the lure of profit drew them, and Jews, Muslims, and Christians intermingled in the marketplaces. Upon arriving in a foreign port, however, merchants also became subject to the laws and customs of local rulers. The following selections are excerpted from a manual for market inspectors (*muhtasib*) written by Ibn Abdun (d. 1134), who served as a local administrator in Seville in the early twelfth century, when the city was the capital of the Almoravid dynasty. The Almoravids, Berber nomads from North Africa, had seized Seville in 1091 and launched a fundamentalist reform of Islamic rule in Spain. Ibn Abdun's treatise reflects the ideological spirit of Almoravid rule.

The *muhtasib* must arrange the crafts in order, putting like with like in fixed places. This is the best and most orderly way.

There must be no sellers of olive oil around the mosque, nor of dirty products, nor of anything from which an irremovable stain can be feared.

Rabbits and poultry should not be allowed around the mosque, but should have a fixed place. Partridges and slaughtered barnyard birds should only be sold with the crop plucked, so that the bad and rotten can be distinguished from the good ones. Rabbits should only be sold skinned, so that the bad ones may be seen. If they are left lying in their skins, they go bad. . . .

Bread should only be sold by weight. Both the baking and the crumbs must be supervised, as it is often "dressed up." By this I mean that they take a small quantity of good dough and use it to "dress up" the front of the bread which is made with bad flour. . . .

The glaziers [glassmakers] must be forbidden to make fine goblets for wine; likewise the potters.

The *ratl* weights for meat and fish and *harisa* [a spicy paste used in cooking] and fritters and bread should be made of iron only, with a visible seal on them. The *ratl* weights of the shopkeepers should always be inspected, for they are bad people.

The cheese which comes from al-Mada'in [an area south of Seville] should not be sold, for it is the foul residue of the curds, of no value. If people saw how it is made, no one would ever eat it. Cheese should only be sold in small leather bottles, which can be washed and cleaned every day. That which is in bowls cannot be secured from worms and mold. . . .

No slaughtering should take place in the market, except in the closed slaughterhouses, and the blood and refuse should be taken outside the market. Animals should be slaughtered only with a long knife. . . . No animal which is good for field work may be slaughtered, and a trustworthy and incorruptible commissioner should go to the slaughterhouse every day to make sure of this; the only exception is an animal with a defect. Nor should a female still capable of producing young be slaughtered. No animal should be sold in the market which has been brought already slaughtered, until an owner establishes that it is not stolen. The entrails should not be sold together with the meat and at the same price. . . .

Fish, whether salt or fresh, shall not be washed in water, for this makes it go bad. Nor should salted fish be soaked in water, for this also spoils and rots it. . . .

If someone assays gold or silver coins for a person, and later it emerges that there is base metal in them, the assayer must make good, for he deceived and betrayed the owner of the coins, who placed his trust in him. Swindlers when detected must be denounced in all crafts, but above all in assaying coin, for in this case the swindler can only be a person who is expert in matters of coin.

Bernard Lewis, ed. and trans., *Islam: From the Prophet Muhammad to the Capture of Constantinople*, vol. 2 (New York: Harper & Row, 1974), 158–161, 163–165.

Women should be forbidden to do their washing in the gardens, for these are dens for fornication.

Women should not sit by the riverbank in the summer if men appear there.

No barber may remain alone with a woman in his booth. He should work in the open market in a place where he can be seen and observed. . . .

No one may be allowed to claim knowledge of a matter in which he is not competent, especially in the craft of medicine, for this can lead to loss of life. The error of a physician is hidden by the earth. Likewise a joiner [a carpenter who does not use nails]. Each should keep to his own trade and not claim any skill of which he is not an acknowledged master—especially with women, since ignorance and error are greater among them.

Only a skilled physician should sell potions and electuaries [medicinal pastes mixed with honey or syrup] and mix drugs. These things should not be bought from the grocer or the apothecary whose only concern is to take money without knowledge; they spoil the prescriptions and kill the sick, for they mix medicines which are unknown and of contrary effect. . . .

Only good and trustworthy men, known as such among people, may be allowed to have dealings with women in buying and in selling. The tradespeople must watch over this carefully. The women who weave brocades must be banned from the market because they are nothing but harlots. . . .

Muslim women shall be prevented from entering their [Christian and Jewish] abominable churches, for the priests are evil-doers, fornicators, and sodomites. Frankish [Christian] women must be forbidden to enter the church except on days of religious services or festivals, for it is their habit to eat and drink and fornicate with the priests, among whom there is not one who has not two or more women with whom he sleeps. This has become a custom among them, for they have permitted what is forbidden and forbidden what is permitted. The priests should be ordered to marry, as they do in the eastern lands. If they wanted to, they would.

No women may be allowed in the house of a priest, neither an old woman nor any other, if he refuses marriage. They should be compelled to submit to circumcision, as was done to them by al-Muy'tadid 'Abbad.[1] They claim to follow the rules of Jesus, may God bless and save him. Now Jesus was circumcised . . . yet they themselves do not practice this. . . .

A Jew must not slaughter meat for a Muslim. The Jews should be ordered to arrange their own butcher's stalls. . . .

The curriers and silk dyers must be ordered to ply their trades outside the city only. . . .

A garment belonging to a sick man [leper], a Jew, or a Christian must not be sold without indicating its origin; likewise, the garment of a debauchee. Dough must not be taken from a sick man for baking his bread. Neither eggs nor chickens nor milk nor any other foodstuff should be bought from him. They should only buy and sell among themselves. . . .

Prostitutes must be forbidden to stand bareheaded outside the houses. Decent women must not bedeck themselves to resemble them. They must be stopped from coquetry and party making among themselves, even if they have been permitted to do this [by their husbands]. Dancing girls must be forbidden to bare their heads.

No contractor, policeman, Jew, or Christian may be allowed to dress in the costume of people of position, of a jurist, or of a worthy man. They must on the contrary be abhorred and shunned and should not be greeted with the formula, "Peace be with you," for the devil has gained mastery over them and has made them forget the name of God. . . .

Catamites [homosexuals] must be driven out of the city and punished wherever any one of them is found. They should not be allowed to move around among the Muslims nor to participate in festivities, for they are debauchees accursed by God and man alike.

Examining the Evidence

1. Apart from the marketplaces, what other public spaces were included within the market inspector's jurisdiction?

2. In what ways do Ibn Abdun's instructions reflect Islamic religious beliefs and commandments?

3. In Ibn Abdun's view, which groups of people posed the greatest threats to public health and morals? Why?

---

[1] **al-Muy'tadid 'Abbad:** Emir of Seville, 1040–1069. This assertion is not confirmed by other sources.

11.3 SPLENDORS OF HANGZHOU

A Memoir of the Splendors of the Capital (c. 1235)

In 1127, Jurchen steppe invaders from Manchuria conquered northern China, forcing the Song (960–1276) court to flee to the south and establish a new capital at Hangzhou. Despite the greatly reduced size of their empire and its precarious military situation, the Southern Song emperors ruled over a prosperous society enjoying unprecedented economic growth. Hangzhou, in the heart of a fertile rice-growing region, flourished as the commercial as well as political center of the empire. Hangzhou's population swelled to more than a million people by 1200, and the city became a hub of domestic and international trade. The following excerpts are taken from a memoir of life in Hangzhou published in 1235. The unknown author barely mentions the court and the imperial government. Instead, he lavishes attention on the city's marketplaces, restaurants, teahouses, entertainment quarters, social clubs, religious life, and pastimes.

Marketplaces

During the morning hours, pearls and jades, rare and exotic goods, newly picked flowers and fruits, fresh fish and wild game, and marvelous items found nowhere else in the empire all are gathered for sale in New Street, which runs northward from the imperial palace's Gate of Peace and Tranquility. From there to Heaven-Gazing Gate, Pure Stream Ward, Central Mall,[1] Ba Creek Landing, Government Lane, Canopy Square, and Contented Populace Bridge throngs of people overflow the food stalls and commercial shops.

At night the markets continue to hum in all of these places—except in front of the imperial palace—but none more so than the Central Mall, where exquisite porcelains and lacquer dishes as well as a hundred kinds of merchandise are set out for sale, just as in daytime. Other marketplaces throughout the lanes and alleys of the city echo with the calls of shopkeepers and peddlers hawking their wares. Taverns and music halls quiet down only after the fourth watch [2 a.m.]. By the fifth watch [4 a.m.], the officials are astir, hastening to the morning audience at the court, and the shopkeepers getting ready for the early morning business have already opened their shutters. All year round it is like this. . . .

The liveliest time of year comes during the Lantern Festival.[2] Row upon row of businesses and homes are gaily decorated, and tents are set up for various displays and spectacles too numerous to describe in full. During the Longxing era [1163–1164], the Imperial Ancestral Temple and the Six Palaces of the imperial harem were located at the Central Mall, directly opposite the present dyeworks of the Imperial Workshops. Once, after performing the New Year's sacrifices to his ancestors, Emperor Xiaozong [r. 1162–1189] stopped to see the lantern displays and sample the rare foodstuffs. Columns of imperial attendants stood in order of rank before the emperor's carriage. They spent piles of cash to purchase fancy delicacies, and with shouts and huzzahs handed out coins and gifts to onlookers. Some were fortunate enough to get gold and silver coins. At that time one could still find some of the gourmet shops—such as Mama Li's Porridges and Zhang's Rice Pastries in the South Mall—of merchants who had come to Hangzhou from the old capital at Kaifeng.

---

[1] **Central Mall:** Hangzhou was famous for its malls or entertainment quarters where the brothels were located and opera troupes, puppet masters, storytellers, and other entertainers plied their trades.

[2] **Lantern Festival:** Occurring on the fifteenth day of the first lunar month, it marks the end of the New Year season.

Translation by Richard von Glahn.

On occasions of imperial processions or the spring and autumn religious festivals the carriages are lined up in long files with their canopies overlapping each other, like rows of fish scales. . . .

In the vacant plaza beneath the capital magistrate's hall various kinds of entertainers and actors are always performing and great crowds gather to watch. The same is true of the boulevard in front of the offices of the imperial constabulary. During the summer months, acrobats also put on amazing performances at the army training ground outside the Tide-Facing Gate. In other market places and anywhere where there is sufficient open space—such as the meat market in the Great Mall, the medicine market at Coal Bridge, the booksellers' lane at the Orange Grove Pavilion, the vegetable market on the east side, and the rice market on the north side—you will also see people engaged in all kinds of entertainments. There are many other popular gathering places like the shops of the Fujian candied fruit sellers at the Five Span Tower, but I cannot name them all.

Guilds

Commercial establishments are grouped into "guilds," a name given to them because each trade is required to provide the government with goods and services. Whether they are petty shopkeepers or great merchants, all must pool their resources to meet the officials' demands, and thus they are organized into guilds. Even physicians and fortunetellers must share this duty. Some trades that are not designated guilds by the government nonetheless refer to themselves as guilds, such as the wine guild and the food vendors' guild. Some merchant groups are called "circles," such as the south side flower circle, the fresh fruit circle of Muddy Street, the Riverbank dried-fish circle, and the Back Street Market tangerine circle. Artisans and craftsmen sometimes refer to themselves as "crafts," such as the comb and cutlery craft, the belt and sash makers' craft, and the gold-and-silver plating craft.

Some trades also have unusual names: dealers in the seven kinds of treasures [antiques] call themselves the "Bone Brokers Guild,"[3] while the bathhouses have taken the name "Fragrant Waters Guild."

In general, the capital attracts goods of every variety and the finest quality. In the flower market of Government Lane, for example, one finds caps, combs, hairpins, and bracelets of exquisite craftsmanship surpassing anything that existed in past times. Among the famous shops of the capital known far and wide one can mention the honey locust soaps sold in the Central Mall; the sweet bean soup vendors of the Sundry Goods Bazaar; Ge Family Pickled Dates; Guang Family Porridges in Government Lane; the fruit vendors of the Great Mall; the cured meats sold in front of the Temple of Perpetual Mercy; Fifth Sister Song's Fish Broth outside the Qian River Gate; the juicy gizzards of Gushing Gold Gate; Zhi Family Lamb Stew and Peng Family Boots in the Central Mall; Xuan Family Tailors and Zhang Family Rice Pastries in the South Mall; Gu the Fourth's Piccolos at Tide-Facing Gate; and Qiu Family Flutes at the Great Mall. . . .

Teahouses

Larger teahouses commonly display paintings and calligraphy by famous artists. In the old capital of Kaifeng, only restaurants hung paintings on their walls for the enjoyment of their patrons waiting for their meal to be prepared. Now the teahouses all do the same.

The teahouses sell powdered tea and salted soybean soup in the winter and plum flower wine in the summer. During the Shaoxing era [1131–1162], musicians would play the plum flower wine tunes and tea was served with a ladle just as the wine shops do. The teashops sold tea by the pint, just like the tavern-keepers of Kaifeng.

The capital's young fops often gather at teahouses to practice singing or playing musical instruments; these amateur performances are called "giving notice."

A hospitable teahouse is more of a cozy gathering spot than a place that merely sells tea. Tea drinking is just an excuse for a get-together; but the customers spend money liberally on tea.

---

[3] **Bone Brokers Guild**: "Bone" is a pun; the word rhymes with a rare word for "antiques."

There is a certain class of teahouses where pimps and hustlers gather to solicit customers. Another sort of teahouse is used by various tradesmen to hire help, find apprentices, and hold meetings of the guild elders. These places are called "business exchanges."

"Plain water teahouses" are merely façades for brothels, the tea being merely a cover. The younger generation gladly squanders their money there. This type is also known as a "dry" teahouse.

A "teakettle carrier" is slang for someone who delivers tea and wine to private homes and takes advantage of his frequent visits to pass messages back and forth and act as a go-between for lovers. There is also another group of dubious characters known as "tea squeezers"—they are the ruffians who are employed as street watchmen and thus can bully the residents and cadge money and gifts from them. . . .

Associations

For men of letters there is the West Lake Poetry Club, which has no peer among Hangzhou's other associations. It draws its members from scholars and officials residing in the capital and visiting poets from other parts of the country; over the years many famous scholars have emerged from its ranks. There are salons for anyone seeking to hone their skills at poetry. Those fond of verse riddles might join the North and South Salons; the West Salons cater to those who favor the word games popular in Jiangxi province.

For the sports-minded, there are clubs for football, polo, and archery.

For devotees of Buddhism, the Upper Tianzhu Monastery has a lay society known as the Radiant Light Assembly, whose members all come from wealthy families in the city and its suburbs. They make donations of incense, lanterns, candles, and alms to assist the monks with their annual expenses. Whenever any of the Buddhist monasteries or temples holds services, the Tea Society provides tea for all the devout believers who attend. The Dharma Propagation Temple in the city has a Pure Land Assembly, whose male members gather on the seventeenth day of each month and female members on the eighteenth to chant sutras and listen to sermons. At the end of the year it also holds a festival in honor of the Medicine Buddha that lasts for seven days and nights. At West Lake during the fourth month of each year the temple sponsors a Release Living Creatures Assembly to free the fishermen's catch and put them back into the lake. The sutra assemblies of various other temples hold their own "release living creatures" ceremonies in different places on specified days.

Annual festivals are held on the feast days of the gods at temples across the city. The inhabitants greet the icons of the gods carried in processions through the streets and present offerings. The groups that participate in these processions include the Embroidered Body Society;[4] the Eight Saints Society; "The Fisherman at Work and Leisure" Troupe;[5] the Demons and Spirits Society; the Girls and Boys Pantomime Chorus; the Puppeteers Club; the Exotic Food and Drink Club; the Flower-and-Fruit Society; the Seven Treasures Antiquarian Society—which displays marvelous treasures and exotic goods from China and foreign lands; the Fine-Groomed Horse Society—whose members come from the rich and noble families, dressed in all their finery; and the Pure Music Society—the group that counts the greatest number of rakes among its members.

Examining the Evidence

1. What social and economic functions did Hangzhou's teahouses serve?
2. How were individual firms and groups of businesses organized in Hangzhou?
3. Did the types of associations and public gathering places in Hangzhou encourage mixing of different social classes, or did they tend to reinforce existing social, religious, and economic identities?

---

[4] **Embroidered Body Society:** Religious devotees who tattooed their bodies (tattooing was a common punishment for criminals) as marks of penance.

[5] **"The Fisherman at Work and Leisure" Troupe:** A troupe specializing in the popular opera of the same name.

11.4 ANGKOR AND JAVA: LANDS ACROSS THE SEA

Zhao Rugua, *A Gazetteer of Lands Across the Sea* (1225)

During the Song dynasty (960–1276), China's maritime trade with Japan, Southeast Asia, and the Indian Ocean world flourished, while the overland Silk Road across Central Asia declined. Foreign merchants flocked to the ports of South China, especially Quanzhou in Fujian province. In 1225, Zhao Rugua, the imperial commissioner for maritime trade at Quanzhou, compiled a geography of overseas lands and peoples, copying liberally from earlier Chinese records while adding information he had acquired from merchant acquaintances. At that time, the Cambodian kingdom of Angkor was at its height as the dominant state in mainland Southeast Asia, having recently defeated Champa, its bitter enemy. Zhao's entry for Java is mostly devoted to the kingdom of Kediri (1045–1222). Zhao suggests that Buddhism was still widespread in Java at this time, but the Kediri kings were firmly devoted to Brahmanism and Hindu gods such as Vishnu.

Angkor

1. Cambodia lies on the southern border of Champa. To the east lies the sea; to the west, Pagan [Burma]; to the south, Grahi [Chaiya on the Malay Peninsula, part of the Srivijaya confederation]. Voyaging from Quanzhou by sea, with favorable winds one can reach Cambodia in a little over a month. The land measures 7,000 leagues around. Its capital is called Angkor. All year round there is no cold season.

2. In dress and hairstyle the king largely resembles the ruler of Champa, but the king's comings and goings are conducted with far more elaborate ceremony. He rides in a stately carriage drawn by a pair of horses, or sometimes by oxen. The cities and fortifications likewise resemble those of Champa. The officials and common folk dwell in houses made of bamboo matting and thatched roofs, while the king alone resides in a palace of hewn stone. The palace has a magnificent pond lined with granite and teeming with lotus flowers; it is spanned by a golden bridge 30 *zhang* [280 feet] long. The palace buildings are stout and majestic, and very richly ornamented. The king sits on a throne of five aromatic and seven precious woods enclosed by ivory screens; above him a canopy bedecked in jewels is raised on carved ebony pillars. When the officials gather for a royal audience they first approach the dais and prostrate themselves three times. Then they ascend the dais and kneel, hands crossed on their breasts, in a circle around the king to discuss affairs of state. When they have finished, the officials again prostrate themselves before retiring.

3. In the southwest corner of the capital stands a bronze tower surmounted by twenty-four bronze pagodas and guarded by eight bronze elephants, each weighing 4000 *jin* [2500 kg]. The king has some 200,000 war elephants; he also has many horses, although they are small in stature. He is reverent and solemn in his devotion to Buddhism. Each day troupes of more than 300 women perform dances and present food offerings to the Buddhist icons. These women are called *ausram*, or slave dancing girls.

4. Their customs are lewd. Fornication is not considered a crime, but thieves are punished by cutting off a hand and a foot and burning a tattoo on their chest. The spells and rituals of their priests have miraculous powers. The yellow-robed monks have wives and families, whereas the red-robed monks dwell in temples and scrupulously obey their ascetic vows. There are also priests [brahmans] who clothe themselves in tree leaves; they have a god named Bhadra [Shiva], whom they worship diligently. They consider the right hand as pure but the left hand unclean; at meals they mix meat and sauces together with rice and eat it with the right hand only.

Translation by Richard von Glahn.

5. The soil here is rich and fertile. Cambodians do not mark off their fields with boundaries; each person plows and sows as much land as his strength will allow. Rice and other grains are invariably cheap. An ounce of lead money buys two bushels of rice. The native products include ivory; fine and coarse varieties of gharu wood; yellow wax; king-fisher feathers, which this country has in the greatest abundance; foreign oils; ginger peel; gold-colored incense; sappan wood; raw silk; and cotton cloth. Merchants from abroad offer gold and silver, porcelain wares, satins, parasols, skin-covered drums, wine, sugar, vinegar, and pickled condiments in exchange for these goods.

6. The following countries pay homage to the king of Angkor: . . . [13 countries are listed]. Formerly Angkor had neighborly relations with Champa and submitted an annual tribute of gold. But in the summer of 1177 the ruler of Champa sent a fleet to attack Angkor. When his terms for peace were refused, the Champa ruler massacred the population. Because of this a bitter enmity ensued and the king of Angkor vowed to exact vengeance. In 1199 Angkor raised a great army and invaded Champa, taking the ruler captive and executing his ministers and servants. The slaughter nearly annihilated the whole population. A Cambodian was installed as ruler, and today Champa too has become one of the countries subject to Angkor's dominion.

Java

1. Java also is known as Pekalongan [a port city on Java's north coast]. From Quanzhou it lies in the compass direction of south-south-east. Ships usually set sail in the winter months to take advantage of the monsoon winds from the north. Sailing night and day with favorable winds the voyage takes a little more than a month. . . . Sailing northwest from Java for 15 days brings you to Brunei [in Borneo]; in another ten days you can reach the land of Srivijaya [Sumatra]; in another seven days, Kedah [in Malaysia]; and in another seven days, Negeri Selat [Singapore]. From there one can travel to Tonkin [northern Vietnam] and finally to Guangzhou.

2. In the kingdom of Java there are two types of temples: those dedicated to the holy Buddha, and those of the ascetics [brahmans]. . . . The king of Java ties his hair in a mallet-shaped knot and wears a headdress like a golden bell. He dresses in robes of silk brocade, wears leather shoes on his feet, and sits upon a square throne. After their daily audiences with the king the ministers and officers bow three times before retiring. When the king goes forth he rides an elephant or is carried in a palanquin [a carriage carried by porters], accompanied by 500 or 700 stout soldiers bearing arms. Upon seeing their king his subjects all sit down and wait for him to pass before rising to their feet again. Three of the king's sons are appointed as royal deputies. Among his officials are a pair known as *rakryan* who jointly administer the affairs of state, like the chief councilors of state in China.[1] These ministers do not receive a monthly salary. Instead, from time to time they are given a portion of the tribute goods the king receives from his subjects. Junior to them are some 300 civil officials who share authority over the capital city, the treasuries and storehouses, and the armed forces. Army commanders receive an annual salary of 20 ounces of gold. The soldiers, a full 30,000 in number, also receive payments in gold in accordance with their rank.

3. It is customary in this land to contract marriages without the services of a matchmaker. The man merely offers a present of gold to the woman's family in order to take her as his bride. The king does not inflict corporal punishment on criminals. Those who violate the laws must pay a fine in gold according to the gravity of their crime; but robbers and thieves are put to death. In the fifth month the people of this land take excursions in boats; in the tenth month they enjoy roaming in the mountains—some riding hill ponies, others carried in a litter. They make music with pipes, drums, and a gamelan [wooden xylophone], and are also skilled dancers.

---

[1] **who jointly . . . in China:** The Song emperors generally appointed two chief councilors of state who shared the responsibility of prime minister.

4. The mountains of Java are full of monkeys. They do not fear men. If you whistle for them they will emerge from the forest. Throw them fruits and nuts and the largest monkey will approach first. The locals call this one "King of the Monkeys." He eats his fill, and only then will the other monkeys gobble up the leftovers. In this country there are bamboo arenas where the people make sport of cockfighting and boar fighting.

5. The dwellings are grand and beautifully decorated with gold and green marble. When merchants arrive they are lodged in a guesthouse and supplied with plentiful food and fine drink. The natives wear their hair loose and hanging down their backs. For clothing they wrap themselves in sheaths that reach from the chest to the knees. When sick they take no medicine, but only pray to the gods and buddhas to invoke their aid. The people have personal names, but no surnames. They are hot-tempered and pugnacious. Whenever one of them has a grievance with a Malay they quickly come to blows. Once, in the year 435, the Javanese entered into communication with China. But after that intercourse was broken off until the year 993, under our August Dynasty, when they resumed the protocols of sending tribute to Our Court.

6. The land is broad and flat, well suited to agriculture. They grow rice, hemp, millet, and beans, but no wheat. The fields are plowed with oxen. The people pay a tenth of their harvest to the ruler. They also boil seawater to obtain salt. The country abounds in fish, turtles, fowl, and goats. They also slaughter horses and oxen for food. Among their fruits are large melons, coconuts, bananas, sugar cane, and taro. Other local products include ivory, rhinoceros horns, pearls, camphor, tortoise shells, sandalwood, anise seed, cloves, cardamoms, laka wood, mats, foreign swords, pepper, betel nut, sulfur, saffron, sappan wood, and white parrots. They also raise silkworms and weave silk. In addition, they have multicolored embroidered silks, cotton fabrics, and damask cloths. The land does not produce tea. Wine is made from coconut and the pith of the gomuti palm—a tree the likes of which has never been seen by Chinese—or else by fermenting the fruit of the sago palm together with betel nut. All of these liquors are clear and fragrant. The crystallized sugar obtained from sugar cane comes in brown and white varieties; they are exceedingly sweet and delicate in flavor.

7. The Javanese cast coins made of copper, silver, white copper, and tin. Sixty of these coins are worth an ounce of gold, and thirty-two are worth half an ounce of gold. When foreign merchants come to trade they barter with lumps of gold and silver in varying degrees of fineness, gold and silver vessels, colored batik-dyed fabrics, black damask, medicinal plants, cinnabar, copperas, alum, borax, arsenic, lacquer wares, iron tripods, and celadon and white porcelain wares. Pepper is available here in great quantities. Merchant vessels, anticipating earning several-fold profits, often risk defying imperial prohibitions and smuggle bronze coin out of China to trade for goods here. Our Court has repeatedly forbidden trade with the Javanese, but foreign merchants use the ruse of claiming to come from Sukadana [in western Java] instead.

Examining the Evidence

1. What features of Southeast Asian societies and cultures appeared most exotic to Zhao Rugua?
2. Based on Zhao's reports, were Song government officials principally concerned with the political, military, religious, or economic aspects of foreign countries?
3. From the evidence of Zhao's lists of imported and exported goods, how did the economies of Southeast Asian countries differ from that of China?

11.5 BUSINESS PARTNERSHIPS IN FLORENCE

Gregorio Dati, *Diary* (1375–1406)

Gregorio Dati (1362–1435), a Florentine silk merchant, kept a diary detailing his business activities. Dati invested the profits from his silk business in various undertakings, notably trading ventures to Valencia, which then was part of the kingdom of Aragon in Spain. His business affairs in Valencia were managed by his brother Simone, whose ill-chosen investments and the ensuing lawsuits cost Dati substantial losses. By the 1420s, Dati's fortunes had improved, however, and he served in several important offices in Florence's republican government. Dati was a self-made entrepreneur: his grandfather had been a pursemaker, and his father had modest success as a wool merchant. His first marriage, in 1388, was to a woman of equally undistinguished background. After Dati's first wife died in 1390 following a miscarriage, he remarried three times. Dati fathered twenty children—only eight of whom were still alive when he ceased writing his diary in 1431.

On 15 April 1375, when I had learned enough arithmetic, I went to work in the silk merchant's shop belonging to Giovanni di Giano and his partners. I was thirteen years old and I won their esteem. . . .

I left Giovanni di Giano on 2 October 1380, spent fifteen months with the Wool Guild, and returned to him on 1 January 1382. . . .

On 1 January 1385 Giovanni di Giano and his partners made me a partner in their silk business for as long as it may please God. I am to invest 300 gold florins which I have not got, being actually in debt to the business. However, with God's help, I hope to have the money shortly and am to receive two out of every twenty-four shares, in other words, a twelfth of the total profit. We settled our accounts on 8 June 1387, on Giovanni di Giano's death. May he rest in peace. My share of the profits

for the two years and five months I had been a partner came to 468 gold florins, 7 soldi. . . .[1] We formed a new partnership on the following terms: Buonaccorso Berardi is to invest 8,000 florins and have eleven shares; Michele di SerParente is to invest 3,500 florins and have eight shares; I am to invest 500 florins and have three shares; Nardo di Lippo is to invest 500 and have two shares. Thus the capital of the company shall amount to 12,500 gold florins. And if any partner invests additional money in the company, that investment will earn one-half of the percentage of the profit earned by the regular shares.

On 1 January 1389 we settled our accounts, and my share of the profits for the nineteen months came to 552 gold florins, 6 soldi. . . .

My beloved wife, Bandecca, went to Paradise after a nine-month illness started by a miscarriage in the fifth month of pregnancy. It was eleven o'clock at night on Friday, 15 July 1390, when she peacefully returned her soul to her Creator in Buonaccorso Berardi's house. The next day I had her buried in S. Brancazio; she had received the last sacraments.

I went to Valencia on 1 September 1390, taking Bernardo with me. I came back on 30 November 1392, having suffered much hardship during my stay, both in mind and body. We were still owed 4,000 Barcelona pounds by Giovanni di Stefano, who acknowledged this debt in a notarized deed which I brought back with me to Florence. In Valencia I had an illegitimate male child by Margherita, a Tartar slave whom I had bought. He was born on 21 December 1391 in Valencia on St. Thomas's Day and I named him after that saint. I sent him to Florence in March on Felicedel Pace's ship. God grant that he turn out well. . . .

[1] **soldi:** 29 soldi equaled 1 gold florin.

Gene Brucker, ed., *Two Memoirs of Renaissance Florence: The Diaries of Buonaccorso Pitti and Gregorio Dati*, trans. Julia Martines (New York: Harper & Row, 1967), 108–112, 114–115, 117, 120–124, 129.

On 1 January 1393, we dissolved the company and Michele di Ser Parente withdrew all his investments. My profit was reckoned as 1,416 florins, 21 soldi, and 60 florins were paid for Simone's salary.

Recommending ourselves to God and good fortune, we set up a new company for a year, starting on 1 January 1393, on the following terms: Buonaccorso Berardi shall invest 4,000 florins and receive eleven shares; I shall invest 1,000 florins and receive five shares; Nardo di Lippo shall invest 500 florins and receive three and one-half shares; Bernardo di Giovanni shall invest 500 florins and receive three and one-half shares. The capital shall amount to 6,000 florins. . . .

I did not actually have the money, but was about to get married—which I then did—and to receive the dowry which procured me a larger share and more consideration in our company. Yet we achieved little that year.

I set out for Valencia in September 1393 in order to wind up matters there but did not get beyond Genoa. When I reached the Riviera, I was set upon and robbed by a galley from Brigazone and returned to Florence on 14 December, having lost 250 florins' worth of pearls, merchandise, and clothes belonging to myself, and 300 gold florins' worth of the company's property.

On 1 January 1394 we drew up our balance sheet and my profit came to 162 florins, 2 soldi. We renewed our partnership for another year and made a few changes. . . .

On January 1396 I found that I had made 600 florins on my own, independently of any partnership, on goods sent to and received from Valencia and elsewhere. My expenditure, however, of which I have kept no account, came to about 250 florins, leaving a balance of 350. . . . Altogether I found myself in 1395 with little cash in hand, as a result of the great expenses to which I had gone in the hope that they would yield greater profits than they did. In addition, there were the expenses I was put to by our brother Don Jacopo [a priest], my losses over Giovanni Stefani [a bankrupt former business partner] in Valencia, and the money which was stolen from me near Genoa. It is fitting to give praise to God for all things. Altogether, having reckoned my profits, the two dowries received and my

outlay for the half-share in the farm in S. Andrea, bought from Monna Tita, I have about 200 florins in hand. God grant that henceforth we prosper in soul and body. . . .

I married my second wife, Isabetta, the daughter of Mari Vilanuzzi, on Sunday, 22 June [1393]. . . .

Her first cousins, Giovanni and Lionardo di Domenico Arrighi, promised that she should have a dowry of 900 gold florins and that, apart from the dowry, she should have the income on a farm in S. Fiore a Elsa, which had been left her as a legacy by her mother, Monna Veronica. It was not stated at the time how much this amounted to, but it was understood that she would receive the accounts. We arranged our match very simply indeed and with scarcely any discussion. God grant that nothing but good may come of it. On the 26th of that same June, I received a payment of 800 gold florins from the bank of Giacomino and Company. This was the dowry. I invested it in the shop of Buonaccorso Berardi and his partners. . . . At the same time I received the trousseau which my wife's cousins valued at 106 florins, in the light of which they deducted six florins from another account, leaving me the equivalent of 100 gold florins. But from what I heard from her and what I saw myself, they had overestimated it by 30 florins or more. However, from politeness, I said nothing about this. . . .

Our Lord was pleased to call to himself the blessed soul of Isabetta, known as Betta, on Monday, 2 October [1402]. . . . Betta and I had eight children, five boys and three girls. . . .

When the partnership with Michele di Ser Parente expired [in 1402], I set up shop on my own under the name of Goro Stagio and Company. My partners are Piero and Jacopo di Tommaso Lana who contribute 3,000 [florins], while I contribute 2,000, and Nardo di Lippo who contributes his services. The partnership is to start on 1 January 1403 and to last three years. The clauses and articles of agreement and the amounts invested by each partner will be entered in a secret ledger covered with white leather belonging to our partnership. . . .

As already stated, I have undertaken to put up 2,000 florins. This is how I propose to raise them: 1,370 florins and 25 soldi are still due to me from my old partnership with Michele di Ser Parente. . . . The rest I expect to obtain if I marry again this year, when I hope to find a woman with a dowry as large as God may be pleased to grant me. If I do not marry, I will find the money some other way. . . .

[O]n 8 May 1403, I was betrothed to Ginevra, daughter of Antonio di Piero Piuvichese Brancacci, in S. Maria sopra Porta. The dowry was 1,000 florins: 700 florins in cash and 300 in a farm at Campi. . . . On 4 July 1403, I invested Ginevra's dowry in our company. . . . It came to 671 florins. At the beginning of January 1404, I examined my accounts and found that I had made excellent profits. However, I did not close our accounts as a large shipment of goods was at sea on its way to Simone.

In that year, 1404, Simone and the King of Castile became involved in the business of the Venetian customs. He needed a great deal of goods from us and much of what we sent him we had to buy. Later, as a result of the King of Aragon's laws directed against anyone shipping goods to the King of Castile, the merchandise was held up in Barcelona [in Aragon]. Antonio Gucci, who was there for the Serristori[2] and was also looking after our interests, had a run of bad luck and tried to make us suffer for losses which were not ours, so that we found ourselves involved in litigation over this with the Serristori in Florence. . . .

1 January 1404: I know that in this wretched life our sins expose us to many tribulations of soul and passions of the body, that without God's grace and mercy which strengthens our weakness, enlightens our mind and supports our will, we would perish

daily. I also see that since my birth forty years ago, I have given little heed to God's commandments. Distrusting my own power to reform, but hoping to advance by degrees along the path of virtue, I resolve from this day forward to refrain from going to the shop or conducting business on solemn Church holidays, or from permitting others to work for me or seek temporal gain on such days. Whenever I make exceptions in cases of extreme necessity, I promise, on the following day, to distribute alms of one gold florin to God's poor. I have written this down so that I may remember my promise and be ashamed if I should chance to break it. . . .

I began proceedings against Messer Giovanni Serristori and Company on the . . . of September [1405] before the Merchants' Court. I was reluctant to do this but had no choice. I had suffered grievous harm in spirit and pocket and was likely to be ruined if I did not defend myself. God bring me safely out of this! The partnership with Piero and Jacopo Lana and Nardo di Lippo expired on 31 December 1406. We did not renew it because of the risks we had run in connection with what had happened in Spain. It is advisable for us to lie low for a while and wait and pay our creditors and put our trust in God.

Examining the Evidence

1. What were the principal means by which Dati raised capital for his business ventures?
2. With whom did Dati form partnerships? Explain the relatively short duration of the partnerships.
3. What were the main obstacles and risks faced by entrepreneurial merchants such as Dati?

---

[2] **Serristori:** A prominent Florentine merchant family.

MAKING CONNECTIONS

1. How important were family connections in the types of business organizations described in this chapter?
2. Were the principles for managing a landed estate similar to those for undertaking commercial ventures? How did they differ?
3. Do the readings in this chapter describe merchants and the world of commerce in positive terms? Why or why not? Explain the differences in attitudes toward merchants.
4. In what ways did urban life, economic livelihood, and social interactions in Seville differ from those in Hangzhou?

CHAPTER 12

Centers of Learning and the Transmission of Culture, 900–1300

Thriving economic growth and urban prosperity from the tenth to the thirteenth centuries nourished the spread of literacy and the proliferation of new educational institutions throughout Eurasia. The rediscovery of Greek philosophy in the Islamic world and Latin Christendom and the rise of Neo-Confucianism in East Asia fostered intellectual renaissances. The infusion of all these new ideas posed challenges to established religious traditions. As we can see in the controversy surrounding Peter Abelard and in the debate between al-Ghazali and Ibn Rushd, fierce disputes erupted among Muslims and Christians alike over efforts to reconcile philosophical questioning and religious faith. In both Islam and Christianity, mystical traditions that advocated a direct and personal experience of the divine threatened to undermine the authority of the clergy and learned scholars. In China, the traditional esteem for education was enhanced by the civil service examinations, which made mastery of Confucian learning essential to political power and social success. Women also assumed new roles in religious and literary culture, as the strikingly different examples of Margery Kempe and Sei Shōnagon show.

12.1   A CONTROVERSIAL CHRISTIAN THEOLOGIAN

Peter Abelard, *The Story of My Misfortunes* (c. 1132)

Peter Abelard (1079–1142) was one of the most influential intellectual figures of medieval Europe. Abelard arrived in Paris as a student around 1100 and quickly distinguished himself as a bold thinker and brilliant debater. In 1115, after studying theology with the renowned Anselm of Laon, he became master at the cathedral school of Notre Dame in Paris. It was there that Abelard's love affair with one of his students, the seventeen-year-old Heloise, caused a great scandal. After Heloise became pregnant, she retired to a convent, where she spent the remainder of her life. Abelard became a monk, entering the monastery of St. Denis outside Paris, but later established his own school near Troyes. Abelard's insistence on subjecting the articles of Christian faith to Aristotelian logical proof provoked heated controversy. His *Theologia*, a study of Christian doctrine, was banned at a council convened at Soissons in 1121. In 1141, the church denounced his teachings as heresy, and the pope condemned Abelard to perpetual silence.

One day, after the exposition of certain texts, we scholars were jesting among ourselves, and one of them, seeking to draw me out, asked me what I thought of the lectures on the Books of Scripture. I, who had as yet studied only the sciences, replied that following such lectures seemed to me most useful in so far as the salvation of the soul was concerned, but that it appeared quite extraordinary to me that educated persons should not be able to understand the sacred books simply by studying them themselves, together with the glosses thereon, and without the aid of any teacher. Most of those who were present mocked at me, and asked whether I myself could do as I had said, or whether I would dare to undertake it. I answered that if they wished, I was ready to try it. Forthwith they cried out and jeered all the more. "Well and good," said they; "we agree to the test. Pick out and give us an exposition of some doubtful passage in the Scriptures, so that we can put this boast of yours to the proof." And they all chose that most obscure prophecy of Ezekiel.[1]

I accepted the challenge, and invited them to attend a lecture on the very next day. Whereupon they undertook to give me good advice, saying that I should by no means make undue haste in so important a matter, but that I ought to devote a much longer space to working out my exposition and offsetting my inexperience by diligent toil. To this I replied indignantly that it was my wont to win success, not by routine, but by ability. I added that I would abandon the test altogether unless they would agree not to put off their attendance at my lecture. In truth at this first lecture of mine only a few were present, for it seemed quite absurd to all of them that I, hitherto so inexperienced in discussing the Scriptures, should attempt the thing so hastily. However, this lecture gave such satisfaction to all those who heard it that they spread its praises abroad with notable enthusiasm, and thus compelled me to continue my interpretation of the sacred text. When word of this was bruited about [made known publicly], those who had stayed away from the first lecture came eagerly, some to the second and more to the third, and all of them were eager to write down the glosses which I had begun on the first day, so as to have them from the very beginning.

* * *

I returned to Paris, and there for several years I peacefully directed the school which formerly had

---

[1] The Book of Ezekiel, included in the Hebrew Bible and the Christian Old Testament, records the visions of the sixth-century B.C.E. prophet Ezekiel.

Peter Abelard, *The Story of My Misfortunes: The Autobiography of Peter Abelard*, trans. Henry Adams Bellows (Glencoe, IL: Free Press, 1958), 11–12, 14–15, 36–38, 42–43, 51–52, 54–55.

been destined for me, nay, even offered to me, but from which I had been driven out. At the very outset of my work there, I set about completing the glosses on Ezekiel which I had begun at Laon. These proved so satisfactory to all who read them that they came to believe me no less adept in lecturing on theology than I had proved myself to be in the field of philosophy. Thus my school was notably increased in size by reason of my lectures on subjects of both these kinds, and the amount of financial profit as well as glory which it brought me cannot be concealed from you, for the matter was widely talked of. But prosperity always puffs up the foolish, and worldly comfort enervates the soul, rendering it an easy prey to carnal temptations. Thus I, who by this time had come to regard myself as the only philosopher remaining in the whole world, and had ceased to fear any further disturbance of my peace, began to loosen the rein on my desires, although hitherto I had always lived in the utmost continence. And the greater progress I made in the lecturing on philosophy or theology, the more I departed alike from the practice of the philosophers and the spirit of the divines in the uncleanness of my life. For it is well known, methinks, that philosophers, and still more those who have devoted their lives to arousing the love of sacred study, have been strong above all else in the beauty of chastity.

* * *

At the outset I devoted myself to analyzing the basis of our faith through illustrations based on human understanding, and I wrote for my students a certain tract on the unity and trinity of God. This I did because they were always seeking for rational and philosophical explanations, asking rather for reasons they could understand than for mere words, saying that it was futile to utter words which the intellect could not possibly follow, that nothing could be believed unless it could first be understood, and that it was absurd for any one to preach to others a thing which neither he himself nor those whom he sought to teach could comprehend. . . .

Now, a great many people saw and read this tract, and it became exceedingly popular, its clearness appealing particularly to those who sought

information on this subject. And since the questions involved are generally considered the most difficult of all, their complexity is taken as the measure of the subtlety of him who succeeds in answering them. As a result, my rivals became furiously angry, and summoned a council to take action against me, the chief instigators being my two intriguing enemies of former days, Alberic and Lotulphe. . . . While they were directing the school at Rheims, they managed by repeated hints to stir up their archbishop, Rodolphe, against me, for the purpose of holding a meeting, or rather an ecclesiastical council, at Soissons. . . .

Before I reached Soissons, however, these two rivals of mine so foully slandered me with both the clergy and the public that on the day of my arrival the people had come near to stoning me and the few students of mine who had accompanied me thither. The causes of their anger was that they had been led to believe that I had preached and written to prove the existence of three gods. No sooner had I reached the city, therefore, than I went forthwith to the legate [pope's representative]; to him I submitted my book for examination and judgment, declaring that if I had written anything repugnant to the Catholic faith, I was quite ready to correct it or otherwise to make satisfactory amends. . . .

These three [men], then, took my book and pawed it over and examined it minutely, but could find nothing therein which they dared to use as the basis of a public accusation against me. Accordingly they put off the condemnation of the book. . . .

But my rivals, perceiving that they would accomplish nothing if the trial were held outside of their own diocese and in a place where they could have little influence on the verdict, and in truth having small wish that justice should be done, persuaded the archbishop that it would be a grave insult to him to transfer this case to another court, and that it would be dangerous for him if by chance I should thus be acquitted. They likewise went to the [papal] legate, and succeeded in so changing his opinion that finally they induced him to frame a new sentence, whereby he agreed to condemn my book without any further inquiry, to burn it forthwith in the sight of all, and to confine me for a year in another monastery. The argument that they used was that it sufficed for the condemnation of my book that I presumed to read it in public without the approval either of the Roman pontiff or of the Church, and that, furthermore, I had given it to many to be transcribed. Methinks it would be a notable blessing to the Christian faith if there were more who displayed a like presumption. . . .

Straightaway upon my summons I went to the council, and there, without further examination or debate, did they compel me with my own hand to cast that memorable book of mine into the flames. . . .

* * *

[Upon release from the monastery of St. Denis] they granted me permission to betake myself to any solitary place I might choose, provided only I did not put myself under the rule of any other abbey. This was agreed upon and confirmed on both sides in the presence of the king and his counselors. Forthwith I sought out a lonely spot known to me of old in the region of Troyes, and there, on a bit of land which had been given to me, and with the approval of the bishop of the district, I built with reeds and stalks my first oratory in the name of the Holy Trinity. . . .

* * *

No sooner had scholars learned of my retreat than they began to flock thither from all sides, leaving their towns and castles to dwell in the wilderness. In place of their spacious houses they built themselves huts; instead of dainty fare they lived on the herbs of the field and coarse bread; their soft beds they exchanged for heaps of straw and rushes, and their tables were piles of turf. . . .

And as their numbers grew ever greater, the hardships which they gladly endured for the sake of my teaching seemed to my rivals to reflect new glory on me, and to cast new shame on themselves. Nor was it strange that they, who had done their utmost to

hurt me, should grieve to see how all things worked together for my good, even though I was now, in the words of Jerome,[2] afar from cities and the marketplace, from controversies and the crowded ways of men. . . .

The thing which at that time chiefly led me to undertake the direction of a school was my intolerable poverty, for I had not strength enough to dig, and shame kept me from begging. And so, resorting once more to the art with which I was so familiar, I was compelled to substitute the service of the tongue for the labor of my hands. The students willingly provided me with whatsoever I needed in the way of food and clothing, and likewise took charge of the cultivation of the fields and paid for the erection of buildings, in order that material cares might not keep me from my studies. Since my oratory was no longer large enough to hold even a small part of their number, they found it necessary to increase its size, and in so doing they greatly improved it, building it of stone and wood. Although this oratory had been founded in honor of the Holy Trinity, and afterwards dedicated thereto, I now named it the Paraclete [Holy Spirit], mindful of how I had come there a fugitive and in despair, and had breathed into my soul something of the miracle of divine consolation.[3]

Examining the Evidence

1. In Abelard's view, why was he condemned for heresy?
2. To what does Abelard attribute his popularity as a teacher?
3. What does Abelard reveal about his personal weaknesses?

---

[2] **Jerome:** St. Jerome (d. 420), a renowned Christian theologian, spent several years living in the desert as an ascetic hermit.
[3] **. . . in honor of the Holy Trinity . . . divine consolation:** The Holy Spirit was especially associated with consolation of the soul.

12.2   SPIRITUAL QUEST OF A FEMALE MYSTIC

The Book of Margery Kempe (c. 1436–1438)

Margery Kempe (c. 1373–1440) was born into a prosperous family in Lynn, one of England's major commercial towns. At age twenty she married a local townsman, with whom she bore fourteen children. Kempe's visions of Jesus Christ, in which they engaged in long and intimate conversations, initially were triggered by the trauma of childbirth. Unlike most Christian female mystics, Kempe did not withdraw into the solitary life of a nun or recluse. Instead, she traveled widely, spending much time in the company of men and engaging in fervent discussions about church doctrines and proper Christian life. Though illiterate, Kempe displays familiarity with writings about other pious women, especially St. Bridget of Sweden (1303–1373), who had acquired a devoted following in England. Kempe dictated her life story to several scribes; the book that bears her name is written from a third-person perspective and refers to Kempe as "this creature."

Then on a Friday before Christmas Day, as this creature, kneeling in a chapel of Saint John within a church of Saint Margaret in N., wept wonder sore, asking mercy and forgiveness for her sins and her trespasses, our merciful Lord Jesus Christ, blessed may he be, ravished her spirit and said unto her, "Daughter, why weep you so sorely? I am come to you, Jesus Christ, who died on the cross, suffering bitter pains and passions for you. I, the same God, forgive you your sins to the utterest point. And you shall never come into hell nor into purgatory, but, when you shall pass out of this world, within the twinkling of an eye you shall have the bliss of heaven, for I am the same God who has brought your sins to your mind and made you to be shriven [forgiven] thereof. And I grant you contrition to your life's end. Therefore I bid you and command you, boldly call me Jesus, your love, for I am your love and shall be your love without end.

And, daughter, you have a hair cloth upon your back. I want you to take it away, and I shall give you a hair cloth in your heart that shall please me much better than all the hair cloths in the world. Also, my worthy daughter, you must forsake what you love best in this world, and that is eating of meat. And instead of that flesh you shall eat my flesh and my blood, that is the very body of Christ in the sacrament of the altar. This is my will, daughter, that you receive my body every Sunday, and I shall flow so much grace into you that all the world shall marvel thereof. You shall be eaten and gnawed by the people of the world as any rat gnaws the stockfish. Dread you not, daughter, for you shall have the victory of all your enemies. I shall give you grace enough to answer every clerk in the love of God. . . ."

* * *

This creature was sent by our Lord to diverse places of religion, and among them she came to a place of monks where she was right welcome for our Lord's love, save there was a monk who bore great office in that place who despised her and set her at naught. Nevertheless, she was set at table with the abbot, and many times during the meal she said many good words as God would put them in her mind, the same monk who had so despised her being present, and many others, to hear what she would say. And through her dalliance his affection began greatly to incline toward her and he began to have great savor in her words. So that afterward the aforesaid monk came to her and said, she being in church and he also at that time, "Damsel, I hear said that God speaks unto you. I pray you tell me whether I shall be saved or not and in what sins I have most displeased God, for I will not believe you unless you can tell me my sin."

The creature said to the monk, "Go to your Mass, and if I may weep for you, I hope to have grace for you."

Lynn Staley, trans. and ed., *The Book of Margery Kempe* (New York: W. W. Norton, 2001), 13–14, 20–21, 29–31.

He followed her counsel and went to his mass. She wept wonderfully for his sins. When Mass was ended, the creature said to our Lord Christ Jesus, "Blessed Lord, what answer shall I give to this man?"

"My worthy daughter, say in the name of Jesus that he has sinned in lechery, in despair [pride], and in the keeping of worldly goods."

"Ah, gracious Lord, this is hard for me to say. He shall cause me much shame if I tell him any lie."

"Dread you not, but speak boldly in my name, in the name of Jesus, for these are not lies."

And then she said again to our Lord Jesus Christ, "Good Lord shall he be saved?"

"Yes," said our Lord Jesus, "if he will forsake his sin and work after your counsel. Charge him that he forsake his sin and be shriven [absolved] thereof and also forsake the outside duties he has."

Then came the monk again, "Margery, tell me my sins."

She said, "I pray you, sir, ask not thereafter, for I am surety for your soul. You shall be saved if you will work after my counsel."

"Forsooth, I will not believe you unless you tell me my sin."

"Sir, I understand that you have sinned in lechery, in despair, and in the keeping of worldly goods."

Then stood the monk still, somewhat abashed, and afterward he said, "Whether have I sinned—with wives or with single women?"

"Sir, with wives."

Then said he, "Shall I be saved?"

"Yes sir, if you will work after my counsel. Sorrow for your sin, and I shall help you to sorrow; be shriven thereof, and forsake it voluntarily. Leave the outside duties that you have, and God shall give you grace because of my love."

The monk took her by the hand and led her into a fair building, made her a great dinner, and afterward gave her gold to pray for him. . . .

* * *

On a day long before this time, while this creature was bearing children and she was newly delivered of a child, our Lord Christ Jesus said to her she should bear no more children, and therefore he bade her go to Norwich. And she said, "Ah, dear Lord, how shall I go? I am both faint and feeble."

"Dread you not, I shall make you strong enough. I bid you go to the vicar of Saint Stephen's and say that I greet him well and that he is a high chosen soul of mine and tell him he pleases me much with his preaching and show him your secrets and my counsels such as I show you."

Then she took her way toward Norwich and came into his church on a Thursday a little before noon. And the vicar went up and down with another priest who was his ghostly father, who was alive when this book was made. And this creature was clad in black clothing at that time. She saluted the vicar, praying him that she might speak with him an hour or else two hours in the afternoon, when he had eaten, about the love of God.

He, lifting up his hands and blessing himself, said, "Benedicite! [Bless you!] How could a woman occupy an hour or two hours in the love of our Lord? I shall never eat a meal until I learn what you can say of our Lord God for the time of one hour."

Then he set himself down in the church. She, sitting a little beside, showed him all the words which God had revealed to her in her soul. Afterward, she showed him all her manner of living from her childhood as nearly as it would come to her mind: how unkind she had been against our Lord Jesus Christ, how proud and vain she had been in her bearing, how obstinate against the laws of God, and how envious against her fellow Christians, then, when it pleased our Lord Christ Jesus, how she was chastised with many tribulations and horrible temptations, and afterward she was fed and comforted with holy meditation, especially in the mind of our Lord's Passion.

And, while she dallied in the Passion of our Lord Jesus Christ, she heard so hideous a melody that she could not bear it. Then this creature fell down as if she had lost her bodily strength and lay still a great while, desiring to put it away, and she might not. Then knew she well by her faith that there was great joy in heaven, where the least point of bliss passes without any comparison all the joy that ever might be thought or felt in this life. She was greatly strengthened in her faith and more bold to tell the vicar her feelings, which she had by revelations, both of the quick and of the dead and of his own self. She told him how sometimes the Father of heaven dallied in her soul as plainly and as verily as one friend speaks to another by bodily speech; sometimes the Second Person in Trinity; sometimes all three Persons in Trinity and one substance in Godhead dallied in her soul and informed her in her faith and in his love how she should love him, worship him, and dread him—so excellently that she heard never a book, neither Hilton's book, nor Bridget's book, nor *Stimulus Amoris*, nor *Incendium Amoris*,[1] nor any other than ever she had heard read that spoke so highly of love of God but that she felt as highly about the working in her soul if she could or else might have showed what she felt.

Sometimes Our Lady spoke to her mind. Sometimes Saint Peter, sometimes Saint Paul, sometimes Saint Katherine [a fourth-century virgin martyr], or what saint in heaven she had devotion for appeared to her soul and taught her how she should love our Lord and how she should please him. Her dalliance was so sweet, so holy, and so devout that this creature might not oftentimes bear it but fell down and twisted with her body and made wondrous faces and countenance with violent sobbings and plenty of tears, sometimes saying "Jesus, mercy," sometimes "I die." And therefore many people slandered her, not believing it was the work of God but that some evil spirit vexed her in her body or else that she had some bodily sickness.

---

[1] **Hilton's book . . . *Incendium Amoris***: Walter Hilton's *Scale of Perfection*, St. Bridget's *Book of Celestial Revelations*, *The Prick of Love* (a mystical text falsely attributed to St. Bonaventure), and Richard Rolle's *The Fire of Love* were all popular devotional texts.

Notwithstanding the rumor and grudging of the people against her, this holy man, the vicar of Saint Stephen's church of Norwich, who God had exalted and through marvelous works showed and proved as holy, ever held with her and supported her against her enemies, as he had power, after the time that she by the bidding of God had showed him her manner of governance and living, for he trustfully believed that she was well learned in the law of God and endowed with grace from the Holy Ghost, to whom it belongs to inspire wherever he will. And, though his voice be heard, it is not known by the world from whence it comes or whither it goes. This holy vicar after this time was always confessor to this creature when she came to Norwich and houseled her [gave her communion] with his own hands. And, when she was on a time admonished to appear before certain officers of the bishop to answer to certain articles which would be put against her by the stirring of envious people, the good vicar, preferring the love of God before any shame of the world, went with her to hear her examination and delivered her from the malice of her enemies.

Examining the Evidence

1. Why were the clergymen whom Kempe encountered persuaded that her visions were genuine?
2. How did Kempe's identity as a woman shape her religious experiences?
3. In what ways might Kempe's contemporaries have regarded her activities as subversive?

12.3 THE EDUCATION OF IBN SINA

Ibn al-Qifti, *The Life of Ibn Sina,* from *The History of Learned Men* (c. 1227)

Ibn Sina (Latin name, Avicenna; 980–1037) was the son of a Persian official in service to Nuh ibn Mansur (r. 977–997), the Samanid emir of Bukhara (in modern Uzbekistan). The emir also employed Ibn Sina as a physician and adviser, but the fall of the Samanid regime in 1004 forced Ibn Sina to flee Bukhara and wander in search of safety and patronage. He spent most of his adulthood in Iran, writing more than 150 books—including his monumental *Canon of Medicine*—spanning virtually every branch of learning. In this memoir, Ibn Sina

Bernard Lewis, ed. and trans., *Islam from the Prophet Muhammad to the Capture of Constantinople*, vol. 2 (New York: Harper & Row, 1974), 177–181.

recounts his early education in Bukhara. As Ibn Sina tells us, his intellectual awakening occurred when he read the works of the Persian scholar Abu'l Nasr al-Farabi (d. 950), whose commentaries on Aristotle opened up the world of Greek philosophy to him.

My father was from Balkh and moved from there to Bukhara during the reign of Nuh ibn Mansur. He was employed as an official and administered a village called Kharmaythan, a dependency of Bukhara and an administrative center. Nearby was a village called Afshana, where he married my mother, who came from there, and settled down. I was born to her there, as was my brother. Later we all moved to Bukhara, where I was given teachers of Qur'an and polite letters. By the time I was ten years old, I had mastered the Qur'an and so much of polite letters as to provoke wonderment.

My father was one of those who had responded to propaganda for the Egyptians and was counted among the Isma'ilis.[1] He had accepted their teachings on the soul and the mind, as had my brother. They often discussed it with one another. I listened to them and understood what they said, and they tried to win me over to this doctrine. Sometimes they also used to discuss philosophy, geometry, and Indian arithmetic,[2] and my father decided to send me to a certain grocer who knew Indian arithmetic so that I could learn it from him.

Then Abu Abdallah al-Natili, who claimed to be a philosopher, came to Bukhara. My father lodged him in our house in the hope that I would learn something from him. Before he came, I was studying under Isma'il al-Zahid, and I was one of his best pupils. I became proficient in the different methods of questioning and of objection to the respondent, in accordance with the customary procedures. Then, under the guidance of al-Natili, I began to read the *Isagoge* [an introduction to Aristotelian logic by the Greek philosopher Porphyry]. When he told me the

definition of *genus*, that is, that which is said of a number of things which differ in species in answer to the question "What is it?" I began to give greater precision to this definition in a way the like of which he had never heard before. He was full of admiration for me and persuaded my father to let me devote myself entirely to learning. Whatever problem he put to me, I resolved better than he could himself. Thus I learned from him the broad principles of logic, but he knew nothing of the subtleties.

Then I began to read books and study commentaries on my own until I mastered logic. I also read the geometry of Euclid, from the beginning to the fifth or sixth figure, under the guidance of al-Natili, and was then able to cope with the rest of the book on my own. Then I passed to the *Almagest* [an astronomical treatise by Ptolemy]. When I had finished with the preliminaries and came to the geometrical figures al-Natili said to me, "Read it on your own and solve the problems yourself, and then explain to me what you have read so that I may show you what is right and what is wrong." The man was not capable of handling this book himself. I therefore began to explain the book by myself. There were many difficult problems which al-Natili had not known until the time when I explained them to him and made him understand them.

Eventually al-Natili left me and went to Urganch. For my part, I busied myself with the study of *The Seals of Wisdom*[3] and other commentaries on physics and metaphysics, and then the doors of knowledge opened before me. Then I took up medicine and began to read books written on this subject. Medicine is not one of the difficult sciences, and in a very short time I undoubtedly excelled in it, so that physicians of merit studied under me. I also attended the sick, and doors of medical treatments based on experience opened before me to an extent that cannot be described. At the same time I carried on debates and controversies in jurisprudence. At this point I was sixteen years old.

Then, for a year and a half, I devoted myself to study. I resumed the study of logic and all parts of

---

[1] **Isma'ilis:** A branch of Shi'a Islam that had won favor among the Fatimid rulers of Egypt and North Africa at this time.

[2] **Indian arithmetic:** The Indians were the first to conceive of zero and positional notation. This system was introduced to Europe by Muslims, hence the common but inaccurate term "Arabic numerals."

[3] *The Seals of Wisdom*: A work by al-Farabi (d. 950), who played the crucial role in helping Ibn Sina to comprehend Greek philosophy.

philosophy. During this time I never slept a whole night through and did nothing but study all day long. I acquired great knowledge. For every problem which I considered, I established firmly the premises of its syllogisms and arranged them in accordance with this knowledge. Then I considered what might be deduced from these premises, and I observed their conditions until the true solution of the problem was demonstrated. Whenever I was puzzled by a problem or unable to establish the middle term of a syllogism, I would go to the mosque, pray, and beg the Creator of All to reveal to me that which was hidden from me and to make easy for me that which was difficult. Then at night I would return home, put a lamp in front of me, and set to work reading and writing. Whenever sleep overcame me or when I felt myself exhausted, I would drink a modest cup to restore my strength and then go on reading. When I dozed, I would dream of the same problem, so that for many problems the solution appeared to me in my sleep. I went on like this until I was firmly grounded in all the sciences and mastered them as far as was humanly possible. What I learned then is what I know now, and I have not added to it to this day. Thus I mastered logic, physics, and mathematics.

Then I returned to the study of the divine science. I read [Aristotle's] book called *Metaphysics*, but could not understand it, the aim of its author remaining obscure to me. I read the book forty times, until I knew it by heart, but I still could not understand its meaning or its purpose. I despaired of understanding it on my own and said to myself, "There is no way to understand this book." Then one afternoon I happened to be in the market of the booksellers, and a crier was holding a volume in his hand and shouting the price. He offered it to me, and I rejected it impatiently, believing there was no profit in this science. He persisted and said, "Buy this book from me, it is cheap. I will sell it to you for three *dirhams* because the owner needs the money." I bought it and found it was Abu'l Nasr al-Farabi's book, explaining the meaning of the *Metaphysics*. I returned to my house and made haste to read it. Immediately the purposes of the book became clear to me because I already knew it by heart. I gave much alms to the poor in thanksgiving to Almighty God.

The sultan of Bukhara at that time was Nuh ibn Mansur. He was stricken by an illness that baffled the physicians. My name was well-known among them because of the extent of my studies. They mentioned me to the sultan and asked him to summon me. I appeared before him and joined them in treating him and distinguished myself in his service.

One day I asked his permission to go into their library, look at their books, and read the medical ones. He gave me permission, and I went into a palace of many rooms, each with trunks full of books, back-to-back. In one room there were books on Arabic and poetry, in another books on jurisprudence, and similarly in each room books on a single subject. I read the catalogue of the books of the ancients and asked for those I needed. Among these books I saw some the very names of which many people do not know, books which I had never seen before and never saw again.

I therefore read these books, made use of them, and thus knew the rank of every author in his own subject. When I reached the age of eighteen, I had completed the study of all these sciences. At that point my memory was better, whereas today my learning is riper. Otherwise, my knowledge is the same and nothing has been added.

In my neighborhood there lived a man called Abu'l-Hasan al-Arudi who asked me to write him an encyclopedic work on science. I wrote *Prosodic Wisdom* for him and named it after him. In it I dealt with all sciences other than mathematics. I was then twenty-one years old. There was another man in my neighborhood who was called Abu Bakr al-Baraqi and was born in Khwarazm. He was unique in jurisprudence, Qur'anic exegesis [textual explanation], and asceticism, with an inclination toward these sciences. He asked me to explain books on these sciences for him and I therefore wrote for him a book called *The Sum and Substance* in about twenty sections. I also wrote him a book on ethics, which I called *The Saintly and the Sinful*. These two books are only to be found with him, since he did not lend them to anyone to make copies.

Then my father died, and my situation was transformed. I had to enter the service of the emir, and necessity obliged me to leave Bukhara and move to

Urganch, where Abu'l-Husayn al-Suhayli, a lover of these sciences, was the vizier. I was presented to the ruler Ali ibn al-Ma'mun [r. 997–1009, known as a patron of scholars]. I was then wearing the costume of a jurist—a hood and a chin-flap. They assigned me a monthly salary suited to one such as myself. Then necessity obliged me to move to Nasa, thence to Baward, thence to Tus, to Samarkand, to Jajarm on the frontier of Khurasan, and thence to Jurjan. My objective was the emir Qabus, but it happened that at this time Qabus was captured and imprisoned in a fortress where he died [in 1013]. I therefore went toward Dihistan, where I was taken seriously ill and later returned to Jurjan, where Abu Ubayd al-Juzjani joined me. I composed an ode on my situation, of which here is a verse:

> When I grew great no city could contain me,
> When my price rose I lacked a buyer.

Examining the Evidence

1. In Islam, oral instruction from a teacher was regarded as superior to book learning. Would Ibn Sina agree?
2. In Ibn Sina's view, what was the foundation of learning?
3. What role did the Islamic faith play in Ibn Sina's education?

CONTRASTING VIEWS

REASON VERSUS REVELATION IN ISLAMIC LEARNING

12.4   ABU HAMID MUHAMMAD AL-GHAZALI, *DELIVERANCE FROM ERROR* (c. 1110)

Abu Hamid Muhammad al-Ghazali (1058–1111) became a renowned teacher and the most influential Muslim philosopher apart from Muhammad. Son of a cotton merchant, al-Ghazali was appointed to a prestigious professorship in Baghdad in 1091, when he was only thirty-three years old. Despite his great success as a teacher, in 1095 al-Ghazali suffered a spiritual crisis that led to a nervous breakdown. He resigned his post, gave away all of his wealth apart from an allowance for his family, and devoted himself to the study of Sufi mystical practices. In 1106, the Saljuq sultan ordered al-Ghazali to resume public teaching at Nishapur. During his final years at Nishapur, al-Ghazali compiled several theological works and his autobiographical *Deliverance from Error*, in which he spells out the limitations of Aristotelian philosophical reasoning.

I proceeded from the study of scholastic theology to that of philosophy. It was plain to me that, in order to discover where the professors of any branch of knowledge have erred, one must make a profound study of that science; must equal, nay surpass, those who know most of it, so as to penetrate into secrets of it unknown to them. Only by this method can they be completely answered, and of this method I can find no trace in the theologians of Islam. In theological writings devoted to the refutation of philosophy I have only found a tangled mass of phrases full of contradictions and mistakes, and incapable of deceiving, I will not say a critical mind, but even the common crowd. Convinced that to dream of refuting a doctrine before having thoroughly comprehended it was like shooting at an object in the dark, I devoted myself zealously to the study of philosophy; but in books only and without the aid of a teacher. I gave up to this work all the leisure remaining from teaching and from composing works on law. There were then attending my lectures three hundred of the students of Baghdad. With the help of God, these studies, carried on in secret, so to speak, put me in a condition to thoroughly comprehend philosophical systems within a space of two years. I then spent about a year meditating on these

Claud Field, trans., *The Confessions of Al Ghazzali* (London: John Murray, 1909), 23–24, 51–57.

systems after having thoroughly understood them. I turned them over and over in my mind till they were thoroughly clear of all obscurity. In this manner I acquired a complete knowledge of all their subterfuges and subtleties, of what was truth and what was illusion in them. . . .

When the human being can elevate himself above the world of sense, toward the age of seven, he receives the faculty of discrimination; he enters then upon a new phase of existence and can experience, thanks to this faculty, impressions, superior to those of the sense, which do not occur in the sphere of sensation.

He then passes to another phase and receives reason, by which he discerns things necessary, possible, and impossible; in a word, all the notions which he could not combine in the former stages of his existence. But beyond reason and at a higher level a new faculty of vision is bestowed upon him, by which he perceives invisible things, the secrets of the future and other concepts as inaccessible to reason as the concepts of reason are inaccessible to mere discrimination and what is perceived by discrimination to the senses. Just as the man possessed only of discrimination rejects and denies the notions acquired by reason, so do certain rationalists reject and deny the notion of inspiration. It is a proof of their profound ignorance; for, instead of argument, they merely deny inspiration as a sphere unknown and possessing no real existence. . . .

In the same way as reason constitutes a particular phase of existence in which intellectual concepts are perceived which are hidden from the senses, similarly, inspiration is a special state in which the inner eye discovers, revealed by a celestial light, mysteries out of the reach of reason. . . .

To prove the possibility of inspiration is to prove that it belongs to a category of branches of knowledge which cannot be attained by reason. It is the same with medical science and astronomy. He who studies them is obliged to recognize that they are derived solely from the revelation and special grace of God. Some astronomical phenomena only occur once in a thousand years; how then can we know them by experience?

We may say the same of inspiration, which is one of the branches of intuitional knowledge. Further, the perception of things which are beyond the attainment of reason is only one of the features peculiar to inspiration, which possesses a great number of others. The characteristic which we have mentioned is only, as it were, a drop of water in the ocean, and we have mentioned it because

people experience what is analogous to it in dreams and in the sciences of medicine and astronomy. These branches of knowledge belong to the domain of prophetic miracles, and reason cannot attain to them.

As to the other characteristics of inspiration, they are only revealed to adepts in Sufism and in a state of ecstatic transport. The little that we know of the nature of inspiration we owe to the kind of likeness to it which we find in sleep; without that we should be incapable of comprehending it, and consequently of believing in it, for conviction results from comprehension. . . .

When we have ascertained the real nature of inspiration and proceed to the serious study of the Qur'an and traditions [*hadith*], we shall then know certainly that Muhammad is the greatest of prophets. After that we should fortify our conviction by verifying the truth of his preaching and the salutary effect which it has upon the soul. We should verify in experience the truth of sentences such as the following: "He who makes his conduct accord with his knowledge receives from God more knowledge"; or this, "God delivers to the oppressor him who favors injustice"; or again, "Whosoever when rising in the morning has only one anxiety (to please God), God will preserve him from all anxiety in this world and the next."

When we have verified these sayings in experience thousands of times, we shall be in possession of a certitude on which doubt can obtain no hold. Such is the path we must traverse in order to realize the truth of inspiration. . . .

For those whose faith has been undermined by philosophy, so far that they deny the reality of inspiration, we have proved the truth and necessity of it, seeking our proofs in the hidden properties of medicines and of heavenly bodies. It is for them that we have written this treatise, and the reason for our seeking for proofs in the sciences of medicine and astronomy is because these sciences belong to the domain of philosophy. All those branches of knowledge which our opponents boast of—astronomy, medicine, physics, and divination—provide us with arguments in favor of the Prophet.

As to those who, professing a lip-faith in the Prophet, adulterate religion with philosophy, they really deny inspiration, since in their view the Prophet is only a sage whom a superior destiny has appointed as guide to men, and this view belies the true nature of inspiration. To believe in the Prophet is to admit that there is above intelligence a sphere in which are revealed to the inner vision truths beyond the grasp of intelligence.

(continued)

CONTRASTING VIEWS *(continued)*

12.5 | IBN RUSHD, *ON THE HARMONY OF RELIGION AND PHILOSOPHY* (c. 1190)

Ibn Rushd (Latin name Averroes; 1126–1198) spent most of his career as a judge in Seville and Córdoba, the intellectual capital of Islamic Spain. He wrote commentaries on Aristotle as well as treatises on medicine, astronomy, and law. His major theological work, *On the Incoherence of Incoherence*, is a detailed refutation of al-Ghazali's critique of philosophy. *On the Harmony of Religion and Philosophy*, in contrast, was intended as a gesture of reconciliation toward Islamic theologians. In this book, Ibn Rushd insisted that the ancient Greek philosophers, like good Muslims, were seekers of truth; the methods of logic and dialectical reasoning developed by philosophers are no less valuable because their authors had not received the benefits of revelation. Although Ibn Rushd's arguments were rejected by nearly all Islamic (and Christian) theologians, he gained lasting renown within Latin Christendom as the leading interpreter of Aristotle.

We maintain that the business of philosophy is nothing other than to look into creation and to ponder over it in order to be guided to the Creator—in other words, to look into the meaning of existence. For the knowledge of creation leads to the cognizance of the Creator, through the knowledge of the created. The more perfect becomes the knowledge of creation, the more perfect becomes the knowledge of the Creator. The Law encourages and exhorts us to observe creation. Thus, it is clear that this is to be taken either as a religious injunction or as something approved by the Law. But the Law urges us to observe creation by means of reason and demands the knowledge thereof through reason. This is evident from different verses of the Qur'an. For example, the Qur'an says: "Wherefore take example from them, you who have eyes." That is a clear indication of the necessity of using the reasoning faculty, or rather both reason and religion, in the interpretation of things. Again it says: "Or do they not contemplate the kingdom of heaven and earth and the things which God has created?" This is in plain exhortation to encourage the use of observation of creation. . . .

Now, it being established that the Law makes the observation and consideration of creation by reason obligatory—and consideration is nothing but to make explicit the implicit—this can only be done through reason. Thus we must look into creation with the reason. Moreover, it is obvious that the observation which the Law approves and encourages must be of the most perfect type, performed with the most perfect kind of reasoning. . . .

One cannot maintain that this kind of reasoning is an innovation in religion because it did not exist in the early days of Islam. For legal reasoning and its kinds are things which were invented also in later ages, and no one thinks they are innovations. Such should also be our attitude towards philosophical reasoning. . . . Now, as it is established that the Law makes the consideration of philosophical reasoning and its kinds as necessary as legal reasoning, if none of our predecessors has made an effort to enquire into it, we should begin to do it, and so help them, until the knowledge is complete. For if it is difficult or rather impossible for one person to acquaint himself single-handed with all things which it is necessary to know in legal matters, it is still more difficult in the case of philosophical reasoning. And, if before us, somebody has enquired into it, we should derive help from what he has said. It is quite immaterial whether that man is our co-religionist or not; for the instrument by which purification is perfected is not made uncertain in its usefulness by its being in the hands of one of our own party, or of a foreigner, if it possesses the attributes of truth. By these latter we mean those Ancients [the Greek philosophers] who investigated these things before the advent of Islam.

Now, such is the case. All that is wanted in an enquiry into philosophical reasoning has already been perfectly examined by the Ancients. All that is required of us is that we should go back to their books and see what they have said in this connection. If all that they say be true, we should accept it and if there be something wrong, we should be warned by it. . . .

All things have been made and created. This is quite clear in itself, in the case of animals and plants, as God has said, "Verily the idols which you invoke, beside God, can never create a single fly, though they may all assemble for that purpose." We see an inorganic substance and then

Averroes, *The Philosophy and Theology of Averroes*, trans. Mohammed Jamil-al-Rahman (Baroda, MI: A. G. Widgery, 1921), http://www.fordham.edu/halsall/source/1190averroes.html.

there is life in it. So we know for certain that there is an inventor and bestower of life, and He is God. Of the heavens we know by their movements, which never become slackened, that they work for our benefit by divine solicitude, and are subordinate to our welfare. Such an appointed and subordinate object is always created for some purpose. The second principle is that for every created thing there is a creator. So it is right to say from the two foregoing principles that for every existent thing there is an inventor. There are many arguments, according to the number of the created things, which can be advanced to prove this premise. Thus, it is necessary for one who wants to know God as He ought to be known to acquaint himself with the essence of things, so that he may get information about the creation of all things. For who cannot understand the real substance and purpose of a thing, cannot understand the minor meaning of its creation. . . .

It is evident from the above arguments for the existence of God that they are dependent upon two categories of reasoning. It is also clear that both of these methods are meant for particular people; that is, the learned. . . . The masses cannot understand the two above-mentioned arguments but only what they can grasp by their senses; while the learned men can go further and learn by reasoning also, besides learning by sense. They have gone so far that a learned man has said, that the benefits the learned men derive from the knowledge of the members of human and animal body are a thousand and one. If this be so, then this is the method which is taught both by Law and by Nature. It is the method which was preached by the Prophet and the divine books. The learned men do not mention these two lines of reasoning to the masses, not because of their number, but because of a want of depth of learning on their part about the knowledge of a single thing only. The example of the common people, considering and pondering over the universe, is like a man who looks into a thing, the manufacture of which he does not know. For all that such a man can know about it is that it has been made, and that there must be a maker of it. But, on the other hand, the learned look into the universe, just as a man knowing the art would do; try to understand the real purpose of it. So it is quite clear that their knowledge about the Maker, as the maker of the universe, would be far better than that of the man who only knows it as made. . . .

If you look a little intently it will become clear to you, that in spite of the fact that the Law has not given illustration of those things for the common people, beyond which their imagination cannot go, it has also informed the learned men of the underlying meanings of those illustrations. So it is necessary to bear in mind the limits which the Law has set about the instruction of every class of men, and not to mix them together. . . . Hence it is that the Prophet has said, "We, the prophets, have been commanded to adapt ourselves to the conditions of the people, and address them according to their intelligence." He who tries to instruct all the people in the matter of religion, in one and the same way, is like a man who wants to make them alike in actions too, which is quite against apparent laws and reason.

12.6 SHARAFUDDIN AHMAD YAHYA MANERI, *LETTERS* (1346–1347)

The mystical tradition of Sufism emphasized an intuitive understanding of the divine that is transmitted from masters to disciples. Letters written by masters to their disciples thus became an important means of spiritual instruction, and numerous letter collections by Sufi masters have been preserved. Sheikh Sharafuddin Ahmad Yahya Maneri (d. 1381) spent nearly his whole career in his native region of Bihar, in eastern India. Although Sharafuddin preferred a life of solitude and contemplation, he maintained an active correspondence with those who sought spiritual guidance from him. Several collections of his letters were published during his lifetime. The following letters were written to a local governor in Bihar whose secular duties prevented him from attending the sheikh's public lectures.

The aspiration of the Seeker should be such that, if offered this world with its pleasures, the next with its heaven, and the Universe with its sufferings, he should leave the world and its pleasures for the profane, the next world and its heaven for the faithful, and choose the sufferings for himself. He turns from the lawful in order to

Wm. Theodore de Bary, Stephen N. Hay, Royal Weiler, and Andrew Yarrow, eds., *Sources of Indian Tradition* (New York: Columbia University Press, 1958), 420–422.

(continued)

CONTRASTING VIEWS (*continued*)

avoid heaven, in the same way that common people turn from the unlawful to avoid hell. He seeks the Master and His Vision in the same way that worldly men seek ease and wealth. The latter seek increase in all their works; he seeks the One alone in all. If given anything, he gives it away; if not given, he is content.

The marks of the Seeker are as follows. He is happy if he does not get the desired object, so that he may be liberated from all bonds; he opposes the desire-nature so much that he would not gratify its craving, even if it cried therefore for seventy years; he is so harmonized with God that ease and uneasiness, a boon and a curse, admission and rejection, are the same to him; he is too resigned to beg for anything either from God or from the world; his asceticism keeps him as fully satisfied with his little all—a garment or a blanket—as others might be with the whole world. . . . He vigilantly melts his desire-nature in the furnace of asceticism and does not think of anything save the True One. He sees Him on the right and on the left, sitting and standing. Such a Seeker is called the Divine Seer. He attaches no importance to the sovereignty of earth or of heaven. His body becomes emaciated by devotional aspirations, while his heart is cheered with Divine Blessedness. Thoughts of wife and children, of this world and the next, do not occupy his heart. Though his body be on earth, his soul is with God. Though here, he has already been there, reached the Goal, and seen the Beloved with his inner eye.

This stage can be reached only under the protection of a perfect teacher, the Path safely trodden under his supervision only. . . . It is indispensable for a disciple to put off his desires and protests, and place himself before the teacher as a dead body before the washer of the dead, so that He may deal with him as He likes.

* * *

Intellect is a bondage; faith, the liberator. The disciple should be stripped naked of everything in the universe in order to gaze at the beauty of faith. But thou lovest thy personality, and canst not afford to put off the hat of self-esteem and exchange reputation for disgrace.

All attachments have dropped from the masters. Their garment is pure of all material stain. Their hands are too short to seize anything tainted with impermanence. Light has shone in their hearts enabling them to see God. Absorbed in His vision are they, so that they look not to their individualities, exist not in their individualities, have forgotten their individualities in the ecstasy of His existence, and have become completely His. They speak, yet do not speak; hear, yet do not hear; move, yet do not move; sit, yet do not sit. There is no individual being in their being, no speech in their speech, no hearing in their hearing. Speakers, they are dumb; hearers, they are deaf. They care little for material conditions, and think of the True One alone. Worldly men are not aware of their whereabouts. Physically with men, they are internally with God. They are a boon to the universe—not to themselves, for they are not themselves. . . .

The knowledge that accentuates personality is verily a hindrance. The knowledge that leads to God is alone true knowledge. The learned are confined in the prison of the senses, since they but gather their knowledge through sensuous objects. He that is bound by sense-limitations is barred from supersensuous knowledge. Real knowledge wells up from the Fountain of Life, and the student thereof need not resort to senses and groping. The iron of human nature must be put into the melting-pot of discipline, hammered on the anvil of asceticism, and then handed over to the polishing agency of the Divine Love, so that the latter may cleanse it of all impurities. It then becomes a mirror capable of reflecting the spiritual world, and may fitly be used by the King for the beholding of His Own Image.

COMPARING THE EVIDENCE

1. What did al-Ghazali mean by "inspiration"? What commonalities, if any, are found in the teachings of Ibn Rushd and Sharafuddin?

2. Did these Islamic teachers agree that study and learning were necessary parts of Islamic religious practice? Why or why not?

3. How did al-Ghazali and Ibn Rushd differ in their views of the purpose and value of natural sciences such as astronomy and medicine?

4. In the eyes of these Islamic teachers, what role did revelation play in the quest for truth?

12.7 FATE AND FORTUNE IN CHINA'S CIVIL SERVICE EXAMINATIONS

Hong Mai, *Tales of the Listener* (1160–1180)

During the Song dynasty (960–1276), civil service examinations became the main avenue of recruitment for government office in China, and thus the route to power and wealth as well. Ambitious young men devoted many years to studying in preparation for the exams. However, the intense competition saddled them with weighty anxieties. Examination candidates often visited temples, seeking divine omens about their prospects for success. The following stories about examination prophecies were recorded by the noted scholar Hong Mai (1123–1202) in his *Tales of the Listener*, a vast anthology of anecdotes culled from family members, friends, and contemporary writings. Although many of Hong's tales involve supernatural interventions, they also feature actual persons such as Sun Zhu, whose untimely death was greatly mourned by Emperor Shenzong (r. 1069–1085). Zitong, the deity who figures in the final story, was a popular local god whose oracles were deemed especially trustworthy.

Sun Zhu's Official Appointment

At the age of fourteen Sun Zhu accompanied his father, Sun Xi, upon his appointment to an office in Jingdong. Once, while passing through Dengzhou, Sun paid his respects at the Temple of the Eastern Sea. He secretly prayed to the temple god, hoping to find out whether he would someday pass the civil service examinations, and if so what official rank he might obtain.

That night Sun had a dream in which he was told, "You will make your mark in the examinations in your first try, and your rank will be among the highest academicians." When he awoke Sun was very pleased, but being still young he did not know the rank an academician held. Upon making inquiries he was told, "This is an auspicious omen. Surely you will be appointed an Academician of the Dragon Chart Hall" [the highest rank of academicians, usually given to a councilor of state].

Afterward, the young man indeed passed the civil service examinations and received an appointment at the court. Sun distinguished himself in a succession of government posts and steadily earned the emperor's favor. On a number of occasions he related his dream to others.

In 1079, upon being elevated to the office of Hanlin Academician, Sun was besieged by visitors and well-wishers who congratulated him on his promotion. But Sun responded gloomily: "This is what has been foretold long ago. Members of the Hanlin Academy rank at the top of all the academicians. Will this not be the end of me? The appointment I've received today is an occasion for mourning, not for celebration."

Several months later, while traveling outside the capital city to visit his parents, Sun suddenly fell ill while riding in his carriage. Emperor Shenzong repeatedly dispatched his personal physician to examine Sun and treat his illness, hoping that Sun would get well so that he could appoint him to the council of state. Afterward Sun did indeed recover from his illness. His Highness was greatly pleased and sent a messenger to say, "Whenever you can return to the court I intend to make great use of your services."

Upon hearing of the emperor's message, the other ministers flocked to pay their respects to Sun Zhu. Ceremonial caps and canopied carriages milled about the front gate of his home night and day. Sun confided in his family members, saying, "On the appointed day my office will be raised to the rank of chancellor. Could it be that the god's words deceived me?"

Translation by Richard von Glahn.

When Sun arrived at the court for an imperial audience he said to the palace attendants, "I have been sick for a long time, and fear that I will not be able to perform the kowtow prostrations before His Highness. Please set out a carpet, and practice lifting me up after each prostration." When Sun made the second prostration his illness suddenly returned, and he lost consciousness. The attendants quickly pulled Sun to his feet, but he had already expired.

Huang Shixian Prays at Pear Mountain

In 1138 a man by the name of Huang Shixian traveled from Putian in Fujian province to the capital to take the palace examination. Originally Huang had agreed to make the journey together with his fellow townsman, Chen Yingqiu. But Huang was not able to put his affairs in order by the appointed day of departure and only set out several days afterward.

Upon arriving in Jian'an in northern Fujian, Huang paid his respects at the Temple of Lord Li at Pear Peak in hopes of obtaining a dream omen. That night he dreamed that the god spoke to him saying, "I need say no more—just find out what I have already told Master Chen."

Only after arriving at Hangzhou was Huang able to meet with Chen and learn what had transpired. But Chen adamantly denied having visited the temple and insisted that he knew nothing. Huang nevertheless persisted in pressing him for an answer. Exasperated, Chen blurted out in a loud voice, "Fine! Shixian shall take the first place, and I will rank second. Does that satisfy you?" Elated to hear the prediction in his dream confirmed, Huang told Chen everything that had happened at Pear Mountain. When the results of the examination were posted, the ranking exactly matched Chen's words.

The "Springtime in the Han Palace" Song

In 1134, a special provincial examination was held in Sichuan. At that time a provincial intendant in Chengdu, the capital of Sichuan province, offered a prayer to the deity Zitong seeking to find out the name of the scholar who would place first in the examinations. That night the intendant dreamed of going to the temple and seeing two scholars coming out arm-in-arm and singing a song to the tune of "Springtime in the Han Palace." When they sang the line, "I ask, how can halls of jade compare to a thatch cottage hidden by brambles?" the god's statue pointed at them and said, "This is the one."

The next day the intendant went to the temple to verify his dream. The temple was thronged with scholars who came and went in a never-ending stream. After a long time passed, two men emerged together clasping hands and singing the same tune he had heard in his dream. Scrutinizing their faces, he realized the men looked exactly like the pair in his dream. The intendant rushed up to them, bowed, and said, "One of you surely will take top honors in the exam!" Then he described in detail everything he had seen and heard in his dream. The two men were delighted, but immediately fell to quarreling with each other. One said, "I was the one who began singing this tune." The other replied, "But I was the one who sang that line."

One of the men was a certain Huang Gong from Xianjing. After some hesitation he roused himself to say, "This is an old dream that belongs to my family. How can it have anything to do with you, my dear sir? When my father first sat for the civil service examinations he dreamed that Lord Zitong bestowed a poem on him which read:

The news from the jade hall approaches;
Your name ranks high on the golden tablet.

"When he awoke my father was overjoyed and said to himself, 'Surely I will attain the rank of Hanlin Academician!' But at the time of his death he was merely serving as the school preceptor of Chengdu.[1] Thinking about that now, the poem must have been intended for me. The 'news from the jade hall' of which the poem spoke surely refers to the line in the song we were singing."

That year Huang Gong indeed placed first in the examinations. It took two generations for the omen in the poem to be realized. Although the song had

---

[1] **merely serving as** . . . **Chengdu:** School preceptor generally was an entry-level position in the Song civil service.

been intended as a casual jest, its roots had been planted decades before. Such is the miraculous power of Lord Zitong!

Examining The Evidence

1. How are the prophecies revealed in these stories?

2. In each case, the true meaning of the prophecy at first remains hidden. What message does this narrative technique suggest?

3. What do Hong Mai's stories tell us about Chinese beliefs regarding the relative importance of personal merit, fate, and divine intervention in determining worldly success?

12.8 COURT LIFE IN JAPAN FROM A WOMAN'S PERSPECTIVE

Sei Shōnagon, *The Pillow Book* (c. 1002)

Little is known about Sei Shōnagon (born c. 967) other than what she tells us about herself in *The Pillow Book*, a memoir of her ten years at the Heian court in the service of Empress Sadako. After the empress died in childbirth at age twenty-four in 1000, Shōnagon left the court, and nothing is known of her subsequent life. *The Pillow Book*—the title refers to notebooks kept by the bedside so that the writer can jot down random thoughts—contains hundreds of anecdotes and observations in no topical or chronological order. At first, Shōnagon seems to have compiled her pillow book as a private memoir. But around 996 word of its existence spread throughout the court, and parts of it became public knowledge. Later sections of the book appear to have been written in a more self-consciously literary vein.

When I make myself imagine what it is like to be one of those women who live at home, faithfully serving their husbands—women who have not a single exciting prospect in life, yet who believe that they are perfectly happy—I am filled with scorn. Often they are of quite good birth, yet have had no opportunity to find out what the world is like. I wish they could live for a while in our society, even if it should mean taking service as Attendants, so that they might come to know the delights it has to offer.

I cannot bear men who believe that women serving in the Palace are bound to be frivolous and wicked. Yet I suppose their prejudice is understandable. After all, women at Court do not spend their time hiding modestly behind fans and screens, but walk about, looking openly at people they chance to meet. Yes, they see everyone face to face, not only ladies-in-waiting like themselves, but even Their Imperial Majesties, . . . High Court Nobles, senior courtiers, and other gentlemen of rank. In the presence of such exalted personages the women in the Palace are all equally brazen, whether they be the maids of ladies-in-waiting, or the relations of court ladies who have come to visit them, or housekeepers, or latrine-cleaners, or women who are of no more value than a roof tile or a pebble. Small wonder that the young men regard them as immodest! Yet are the gentlemen themselves any less so? They are not exactly bashful when it comes to looking at the great people in the Palace. No, everyone at Court is much the same in this respect. . . .

* * *

A good lover will behave as elegantly at dawn as at any other time. He drags himself out of bed with a look of dismay on his face. The lady urges him on: "Come, my friend, it's getting light. You don't want anyone to find you here." He gives a deep sigh, as if to say that the night has not been nearly long enough

Ivan Morris, ed. and trans., *The Pillow Book of Sei Shōnagon* (New York: Columbia University Press, 1991), 39, 49, 69, 71, 123–125, 138, 237–238, 263–264.

and that it is agony to leave. Once up, he does not instantly pull on his trousers. Instead he comes close to the lady and whispers whatever was left unsaid during the night. Even when he is dressed, he still lingers, vaguely pretending to be fastening his sash.

Presently he raises the lattice, and the two lovers stand together by the side door while he tells her how he dreads the coming day, which will keep them apart; then he slips away. The lady watches him go, and this moment of parting will remain among her most charming memories.

Indeed, one's attachment to a man depends largely on the elegance of his leave-taking. . . .

* * *

Elegant things:
   A white coat worn over a violet waistcoat.
   Duck eggs.
   Shaved ice mixed with liana syrup and put in a
      new silver bowl.
   A rosary of rock crystal.
   Wisteria blossoms. Plum blossoms covered
      with snow.
   A pretty child eating strawberries.

* * *

Unsuitable things:
   A woman with ugly hair wearing a robe of
      white damask.
   Hollyhock worn in frizzled hair.
   Ugly handwriting on red paper. . . .
   It is unpleasant to see a woman of a certain age
      with a young husband; and it is most unsuit-
      able when she becomes jealous of him be-
      cause he has gone to visit someone else. . . .
   A woman of the lower classes dressed in a scar-
      let trouser-skirt. The sight   is all too
      common these days. . . .

* * *

When it is raining, I feel absolutely miserable. I en-
tirely forget how beautiful the weather was earlier in the day and everything seems hateful, whether I am in one of the beautiful galleries in the Palace or in a very ordinary house. Nothing gives me the slightest pleasure, and I can think of one thing only: when will the rain stop?

When the moon is shining I love to receive a visi-
tor, even if it is someone who has not come to see me for ten days, twenty days, a month, a year, or perhaps seven or eight years, and who has been inspired by the moonlight to remember our previous meetings. Even if I am in a place where it is hope-
lessly difficult to receive visitors and where one is constantly in fear of being seen, I will allow the man to speak with me, though we may have to stand up all the time. And then, if it is at all possible, I will keep him with me for the night.

Moonlight makes me think of people who are far away and also reminds me of things in the past—sad things, happy things, things that de-
lighted me—as though they had just happened. I do not like *The Tale of Komano*[1] in the slightest, for its language is old fashioned and it contains hardly anything of interest. Yet I am always moved by the moonlight scene in which one of the characters recalls past events and, producing a moth-
eaten fan, recites the line, "My horse has come this way before."

* * *

[Addressing Her Majesty the Empress] I [said], "I have decided to give up writing poetry for good and all. If each time there is a poem to be composed you call on me to do it, I don't see how I can remain in Your Majesty's service. After all, I don't even know how to count the syllables correctly. How can I be expected to write winter poems in the spring and spring poems in the autumn and poems about chrysanthemums when the plum blossoms are in bloom? I realize that there have been many poets in my family, and of course it's a great satisfaction if one of my verses turns out well and people say, 'Of everything written on that day Shōnagon's was the best. But that's what one would expect considering who her father was.' The trouble is that I have no particular talent and, if I push myself forward and turn out some doggerel as though I thought it was

---

[1] *The Tale of Komano:* Now lost. Nothing is known of this book, other than the suggestion here that it was a romance tale.

a masterpiece, I feel I am disgracing the memory of my ancestors."

I was speaking quite seriously, but the Empress laughed and said, "In that case you must do exactly as you wish. I shan't ask you to write any more poems."

Late one evening, not long after this incident, His Excellency the Minister of the Center, Korechika, who was making elaborate preparations for the Night of the Monkey, gave out subjects on which the Empress's ladies-in-waiting were to write poems. They were all very excited and eagerly set themselves to the task. Meanwhile I stayed with the Empress and talked to her about various things. Presently Korechika caught sight of me. "Why don't you join the others and write a poem?" he asked. "Pick your subject."

"Her Majesty has excused me from poetry," I said, "and I don't have to worry about such things any more."

"How odd!" said Korechika. "I can hardly believe she would allow that. Very well, you may do as you like at other times, but please write something tonight."

But I did not pay the slightest attention. When the poems of the other women were being judged, the Empress handed me the following little note:

Surely it is not you,
You whom we know as Motosuke's heir,[2]
That will be missing from this evening's round
    of verse.

I laughed delightedly and, when Korechika asked me what had happened, I replied with this verse:

Were I not known as the daughter of that man,
I should have been the very first
To pen a poem for this night of verse.

And I added to Her Majesty that, if my father were anyone else, I should have written a thousand poems for her without even waiting to be asked.

* * *

Things that lose by being painted:
    Pinks, cherry blossoms, yellow roses. Men or
        women who are praised in   romances as
        being beautiful.
Things that gain by being painted:
    Pines. Autumn fields. Mountain villages and
        paths. Cranes and deer. A very cold winter
        scene; an unspeakably hot summer scene.

* * *

A man's heart is a shameful thing. When he is with a woman whom he finds tiresome and distasteful, he does not show that he dislikes her, but makes her believe she can count on him. Still worse, a man who has the reputation of being kind and loving treats a woman in such a way that she cannot imagine his feelings are anything but sincere. Yet he is untrue to her not only in his thoughts but in his words; for he speaks badly about her to other women just as he speaks badly about those women to her. The woman, of course, has no idea that she is being maligned, and hearing his criticism of the others she fondly believes he loves her best. The man for his part is well aware that this is what she thinks. How shameful!

* * *

One day Lord Korechika, the Minister of the Center, brought the Empress a bundle of notebooks. "What shall we do with them?" Her Majesty asked me. "The Emperor has already made arrangements for copying the *Records of the Historian*."[3]

Let me make them into a pillow," I said.[4]

"Very well," said Her Majesty, "You may have them."

I now had a vast quantity of paper at my disposal, and I set about filling the notebooks with odd facts, stories from the past, and all sorts of other things, often including the most trivial material. On the whole I concentrated on things and people that I

---

[2] **Motosuke's heir:** Shōnagon's father, Kiyowara no Motosuke (d. 990), was a renowned poet and scholar.

[3] **Records of the Historian:** The lengthy history of ancient China by the Chinese historian Sima Qian (145–87 B.C.E.).

[4] **"Let me . . . a pillow":** In other words, use them to compose her pillow book.

found charming and splendid; my notes are also full of poems and observations on trees and plants, birds and insects. I was sure that when people saw my book they would say, "It's even worse than I expected. Now one can really tell what she is like." After all, it is written entirely for my own amusement and I put things down exactly as they came to me. How could my casual jottings possibly bear comparison with the many impressive books that exist in our time? Readers have declared, however, that I can be proud of my work. This has surprised me greatly; yet I suppose it is not so strange that people should like it, for, as will be gathered from these notes of mine, I am the sort of person who approves of what others abhor and detest the things they like.

Whatever people may think of my book, I still regret that it ever came to light.

Examining the Evidence

1. What did Shōnagon consider to be the chief failings of men and women? Did she regard men and women as equals?
2. What do Shōnagon's observations about nature tell us about her aesthetic values?
3. What was Shōnagon's purpose in writing? Do you think she saw writing as a means to achieve immortality?

MAKING CONNECTIONS

1. Did advocates of Aristotelian learning and logic, such as Abelard and Ibn Sina, share similar ideas about the purpose of philosophy and its place in the quest for knowledge?
2. Margery Kempe and Sharafuddin Ahmad Yahya Maneri both personified mystical approaches to achieving union with the divine and leading a moral life. To what extent were Kempe and Sharafuddin similar in their personal piety and the spiritual guidance they offered to others?
3. Did the figures encountered in this chapter's readings believe that all human beings had equal intellectual and spiritual capacities? Why or why not?
4. Both Margery Kempe and Sei Shōnagon were women who—in contrast to most women of their time—led public lives in the company of men. Did they envision themselves as role models for other women? To what extent would other men and women of their day have regarded them as role models?

CHAPTER 13

Crusaders, Mongols, and Eurasian Integration, 1050–1350

Eurasia in the twelfth and thirteenth centuries was marked by violent struggles and bloody conquests, as well as by an unprecedented surge of cross-cultural interactions. The Crusades escalated the tensions between Christians and Muslims into holy war, yet at the same time shredded the fragile unity between the Roman and Orthodox Christian churches. After the final expulsion of the crusaders from Jerusalem and the Christian reconquest of most of Muslim-ruled Iberia, the political as well as religious boundaries between the Christian and Islamic worlds strengthened. The Mongols, in contrast, fostered the movement of people, goods, and ideas across vast territories through religious tolerance and encouragement of commerce. To settled peoples from the Christian and Islamic lands, the customs and lifestyle of the nomadic Mongols appeared utterly alien. However, the Mongol khans who brought China, Persia, and Russia under their heel also invited comparison with Alexander and Caesar, the most renowned world conquerors of the past.

13.1 THE GREAT SCHISM IN THE CHRISTIAN CHURCH

Reciprocal Excommunications (1054)

After the collapse of the unified Roman Empire, relations between the Latin Christian church based at Rome and the Greek church based at Constantinople became increasingly strained. In 1054, Pope Leo IX (r. 1049–1054) sent a delegation to Constantinople to attempt a reconciliation. But the pope's representative, Cardinal Humbert, clashed bitterly with Michael Cerularius, the Orthodox patriarch, over issues such as the doctrine of *filioque*—the belief that the Holy Spirit proceeds not only from God the Father but also from the Son (Jesus)— which the Orthodox church rejected. Consequently, Humbert drew up a charge of anathema (excommunication) against Cerularius. In response, Cerularius hastily convened a synod (council) that issued its own excommunication of the papal delegation. Although the breach was not irreparable, historians trace the Great Schism between the Roman and Orthodox churches to the mutual excommunications of 1054.

Humbert's Anathema of Michael Cerularius

Humbert, by the grace of God cardinal-bishop of the Holy Roman Church; Peter, archbishop of Amalfi; Frederick, deacon and chancellor, to all sons of the Catholic Church:

The holy Roman, first, and Apostolic See, toward which, as toward the head, belongs the special solicitude of all churches, for the sake of the peace and benefit of the church, has deigned to appoint us legates to this city, in order that, according to our instructions, we might come over and see whether in fact the clamor still continues which, without ceasing, comes to [Rome's] ears or, if that is not so, in order that the Holy See might find out about it. Therefore, above all else, let the glorious emperors, the clergy, the Senate, and the people of this city of Constantinople, and the entire Catholic church,

know that we have noted here a great good, on account of which we deeply rejoice in the Lord, but also we have perceived a very great evil because of which we are extremely saddened.

For, with respect to the pillars of the empire and its wise and honest citizens, the City is most Christian and orthodox. However, with regard to Michael, falsely called patriarch, and his followers in folly, too many tares [weeds] of heresies are daily sown in its midst. For as the Simoniacs sell God's gifts; as the Valesians castrate their guests and promote them not only to the priesthood but even to the episcopate; as the Arians rebaptize people already baptized (especially Latins in the name of the Holy Trinity); as the Donatists affirm that, excepting the Greek church, Christ's church and the true sacrifice [of the Mass] and baptism have perished from the whole world; as the Nicolaites permit and defend [carnal] marriage for ministers of the holy altar; as the Severians maintain that the law of Moses is accursed; . . . as the Manichaeans declare, among other things, that anything fermented is alive; as the Nazarenes maintain the bodily cleanliness of the Jews to such a point that they deny baptism to infants who die before the eighth day after birth and [deny] communion to menstruating women or those about to give birth or if they [the women] were pagan they forbid them to be baptized; also, they [the Nazarenes], preserving their hair and beards, do not receive into communion those who, according to the custom of the Roman Church, cut their hair and shave their beards.[1] Although admonished by our Lord Pope Leo regarding these errors and many of his deeds, Michael [Cerularius] himself has with contempt disregarded these warnings. Moreover, to

---

[1] **Simoniacs . . . Nazarenes:** All of the groups mentioned here were deemed heretics because of their deviations from the official doctrines of the Christian church.

Deno Geanakoplos, ed., *Byzantium: Church, Society, and Civilization Seen Through Contemporary Eyes* (Chicago: University of Chicago Press, 1984), 207–212.

us his [Leo's] ambassadors who are seeking faithfully to stamp out the cause of such great evils, he denied his presence and any oral communication, and he forbade [us the use of] churches to celebrate Mass in, just as earlier he had closed the Latin churches [in Constantinople], . . . he hounded them everywhere in word and deed. Indeed, in the person of its sons, he cursed the Apostolic See, in opposition to which he signed himself "ecumenical patriarch." Wherefore, not putting up with this unheard-of slander and insult to the first, holy Apostolic See, and seeing the Catholic faith assaulted in many ways, we, by the authority of the undivided and Holy Trinity and that of the Apostolic See, whose embassy we constitute, and by the authority of all the orthodox fathers of the seven [ecumenical] councils and that of the entire Catholic church, whatever our most revered lord the pope has denounced in Michael and his followers, unless they repent, we declare to be anathematized:

"May Michael, false neophyte patriarch, who only out of human fear assumed the monastic habit, now known notoriously to many because of his extremely wicked crimes, and with him Leo the archdeacon called bishop of Ochrida, and his treasurer Michael, and Constantine [IX, the reigning Byzantine emperor] who with profane feet trampled upon the Latins' sacrifice [the Eucharist], and all their followers in the aforesaid errors and presumptions, be anathematized. . . ."

Michael Ceralarius and the Standing Synod Anathematize the Papal Legation

Decree in response to the bull of excommunication cast before the holy altar by the legates of Rome against the most Holy Patriarch Michael in the month of July of the 7th indiction [1054]:

When Michael, our most holy despot and ecumenical patriarch was presiding [over the Orthodox Church] certain impious and disrespectful men (what else, in fact, could a pious man call them?) — men coming out of the darkness (they were begotten of the West) — came to this pious and God-protected city from which the springs of orthodoxy flow as if from on high, disseminating the teachings of piety to the ends of the world. To this city [Constantinople] they came like a thunderbolt, or an earthquake, or a hailstorm, or to put it more directly, like wild wolves trying to defile the Orthodox belief by the difference of dogma. Setting aside the Scriptures, they deposited [an excommunication] on the holy order according to which we, and especially the Orthodox church of God, and all those who are not in accord with their impiety (because we Orthodox want to preserve what is Orthodox and pious) are charged with, among other things, the fact that unlike them we do not accept the shaving of our beards. Nor did we want to transform what is natural for men into the unnatural [i.e., we favor marriage for the lower clergy, rather than celibacy]. In addition, we do not prohibit anyone from receiving communion from a married presbyter. In addition to all this, we do not wish to tamper with the sacred and holy creed, which holds its authority inviolate from synodal and ecumenical decrees, by the use of wrongful arguments and illegal reasoning and extreme boldness. And unlike them we do not wish to say that the Holy Spirit proceeds from the Father and the Son — O what artifice of the devil! — but rather we say that the Holy Spirit proceeds from the Father. But we declare that they do not follow the Scripture which says "Do not shave your beards." Nor do they want to fully understand that God the Creator in an appropriate way created woman, and he decreed that it was improper for men to be alone. But they dishonor the fourth [canon] of the Synod of Gangra, which says to those who despise marriage: "If one would hesitate to receive communion from a married presbyter, let him be anathematized." In addition they respect and honor the sixth synod which says . . . that those who are about to become deacons or to be worthy of being ordained presbyters should not have relations with their wives. And we, who continue to observe inviolate the ancient canons of the apostolic perfection and order, wish to affirm that the marriage of ordained men [priests] should not be dissolved and they should not be deprived of having sexual relations with their wives which from time to time is appropriate. So if anyone is found to be worthy of the office of deacon or subdeacon, he could not be kept from this office and he should be restored to his lawful wife, in order that what God has himself ordained and blessed should not be dishonored by us, especially since the Gospel declares, "Those whom God has joined together, let not man put asunder. . . ."

Moreover, they [Latins] do not wish to comprehend, and insist that the Holy Spirit proceeds not only from the Father but also from the Son, although they have no evidence from the Evangelists [the Gospels] nor from the ecumenical councils for this blasphemy against the holy doctrine. For the Lord Our God speaks of "the spirit of the Truth, [which] proceeds from the Father." But the fathers of this new impiety speak of "the Spirit which proceeds from the Father and the Son." But if the Holy Spirit proceeds from the Father, then this property of his is affirmed. And if the Son is generated from the Father, then this property of the Son is likewise affirmed. But if, as they foolishly maintain, the Holy Spirit proceeds from the Son, then the Spirit which proceeds from the Father has more properties than even the Son. . . .

[The papal envoys] insisted further that they had even more to say than what had been written [in the document] against our faith and would prefer to die rather than to come to face us and the synod. These things were reported to us and to the synod by the powerful and sacred emperor. . . . Because it would be improper and completely unworthy for such impiety against our faith to go unpunished, the emperor found a perfect solution for the matter by sending an honorable and respectful letter to Our Mediocrity [a humble title of the Byzantine patriarch] . . . which read as follows:

"Most holy lord, Our Majesty, after examining what has happened, has found that the root of the evil was committed by the interpreters and by the party of Argyrus [the Latin commander of the Byzantine army in Italy, a political enemy of

Cerularius]. And concerning those who are alien and foreign and have been influenced by others we can do nothing. But those responsible we have sent to Your Holiness in order that they might be instructed properly and through their example others may not do such foolishness. Let the document with the anathema be burned in the presence of all including those who have counseled, published, and written it, and even those who have some idea about it. . . ."

So read the imperial and sacred decree. And in accordance with the foresight of our most pious emperor, that impious document and those who deposited it or gave an opinion on its composition were placed under anathema in the great *secretum* in the presence of the legates sent to the emperor. . . . The original of the impious document . . . was not burned, but was placed in the depository of the *chartophylax* [the officer in charge of official church records] in order that it be to the perpetual dishonor of those who have committed such blasphemies against us and as permanent evidence of this condemnation.

Examining the Evidence

1. According to Humbert, what were the principal errors of the Orthodox church?
2. In what ways did the Orthodox clergy's view of the nature of the doctrinal dispute differ from that of the Roman delegation?
3. How did the authority of the Orthodox patriarch in matters of church doctrine differ from that of the Roman pope?

13.2 THE CRUSADERS IN CAPTIVITY

John of Joinville, *The Life of Saint Louis* (1309)

John of Joinville (c. 1225–1317) was a French nobleman who, in 1248, joined the crusade (known as the Sixth Crusade) led by the French king Louis IX (r. 1226–1270).

Louis intended to strike at Egypt, the heartland of the Ayyubid sultanate. After capturing the Mediterranean port of Damietta in June 1249, Louis's army bogged down trying to cross the Nile Delta and the king was taken prisoner. During Louis's month of captivity, the Mamluks, the sultan's elite bodyguard, revolted and

Caroline Smith, ed. and trans., *Joinville and Villehardouin: Chronicles of the Crusades* (London: Penguin Books, 2008), 220, 222–223, 225–226, 228–229, 234–237, 244–245.

deposed the sultan, leading to the founding of the Mamluk sultanate (1250–1517). Louis's family paid the Mamluks a heavy ransom for his release. After returning to France in 1254, Joinville became one of Louis's closest advisers. Joinville gave testimony in the proceedings that led to the king's canonization as St. Louis in 1297 and compiled a biography of his friend, *The Life of Saint Louis*.

The king's council and the sultan's council fixed a date to reach an agreement. The terms of the agreement were these: Damietta would be returned to the sultan, while the sultan would return the kingdom of Jerusalem to the king. The sultan was also bound to protect the sick people who were in Damietta, along with the salted meats (since they did not eat any pork) and the king's siege engines, until such time as the king could send for all these things. . . . The Saracens[1] said they would do nothing unless the king's own person was left as surety. And to this my lord Geoffrey of Sergines, the good knight, said that he would rather the Saracens captured and killed them all than that they should be reproached for having left the king as surety. . . .

Meanwhile, a great misfortune struck our people: a treacherous sergeant named Marcel began to call out to our men, "Lord knights! Surrender your-selves — the king commands you to do so. Do not let the king be killed." Everyone believed that this order came from the king, and they surrendered their swords to the Saracens. The emir saw that the Saracens were leading our people away prisoner, and he told my lord Philip that there was no need for him to make a truce with our people, since he could see clearly that they had already been captured. . . .

While the misfortune of being captured befell our people who were on land, so too were those of us on the water captured, as you will hear shortly. The wind was coming at us from the direction of Damietta and this deprived us of the benefit of the current. The knights whom the king had set in his small boats to protect the sick had fled. Our soldiers lost their course on the river and ended up in

a backwater, which meant we had to turn back towards the Saracens. A little before the crack of dawn those of us who were going by water arrived at the stretch of the river where lay the sultan's galleys that had prevented the arrival of provisions coming from Damietta. There was a great commotion there because they were firing such a great number of bolts [arrows] charged with Greek fire[2] at us and at our people who were riding along the riverbank that it seemed as if the stars were falling from the sky. . . .

When I saw that we could not avoid being taken captive, I took my casket and my jewels and threw them into the river, along with my relics. Then one of my sailors said to me, "My lord, unless you allow me to tell the Saracens you are the king's cousin, they'll kill you all, and us sailors with you." And I said that I was quite willing for him to say what he wanted. . . .

The chief admiral of the galleys sent for me and asked me if I was the king's cousin. I said that I was not, and told him how and why the sailor had said that I was. And he said that I had acted wisely because otherwise we would all have been killed. He asked me whether I was in any way related to Emperor Frederick of Germany, who was still alive at that time, and I replied that I understood my lady my mother to be his first cousin. He told me that he liked me the better for this. . . .

The sultan sent his councilors to talk to us, and they asked to whom they should address the sultan's message. We told them they should speak to the good Count Peter of Brittany. There were people there called dragomans [interpreters] who knew the Saracen language and French, and they translated the Saracen into French for Count Peter. And these were their words: "My lord, the sultan has sent us to you to know if you wished to be released." The count replied, "Yes." "And what will you give to the sultan in return for your release?" they asked. "Whatever is possible and bearable for us, within reason," said the count. "Will you," they asked "give any of the castles in the possession of the barons of Outremer [i.e., the Teutonic Knights]?" The count replied that he did not have the power to do so, because the barons held

---

[1] **the Saracens:** By the time of the Crusades, Latin Christians regularly used the word *Saracen* — originally coined by the Romans as a name for tribal peoples in Syria and Arabia — to refer to Muslims.

[2] **Greek fire:** An incendiary weapon used in naval warfare; its actual composition remains unknown.

their castles from the emperor of Germany, who was still alive at that time. They asked whether we would give any of the castles of the Temple or Hospital in return for our release. And the count responded that this was impossible, since when the guardians of these castles were installed, they were made to swear on relics that they would not hand over any of the castles in return for any man's freedom. They said it seemed to them that we had no desire to be released, and that they would leave and send men in who would indulge in some swordplay with us, as they had done with the others. And then they left.

As soon as they left, a large body of men came into our pavilion: young Saracens with swords at their belts. They brought with them a man of great old age, completely white-haired, who had asked us whether it was true that we believed in a God who had been taken prisoner for us, was wounded and killed for us, and came back to life on the third day. And we replied, "Yes." Then he told us that we should not be disheartened if we had suffered these persecutions for him. "Because," he said, "you have not yet died for him as he died for you. And if he had the power to bring himself back to life, you can be certain that he will free you when he pleases." Then he went away, and all the other young men after him. I was very glad about this because I had been quite convinced that they had come to cut off our heads. And it was not long after this that the sultan's men came who told us that the king had negotiated our release. . . .

[At this point the Mamluks, disgruntled by the sultan's favor toward a rival group of Turks, over-threw and killed him. Negotiations continued between the crusaders and the Mamluks, whom Joinville refers to as "the emirs."]

[The king's representatives] reached agreement with the emirs on condition that as soon as Dami-etta had been surrendered to them, they would re-lease the king and the other great men who were there. . . . The king also had to swear to pay them 200,000 *livres* before leaving the river, and another 200,000 *livres* once he had reached Acre. . . .

The oaths that the emirs had to swear to the king were formulated thus: if they did not keep the agree-ment made with the king, they would be as dishon-ored as he who, because of his sinfulness, goes on pilgrimage to Muhammad at Mecca with his head uncovered, and as dishonored as those who leave their wives and then take them back afterwards. (In such cases, according to the law of Muhammad, no man can leave his wife and ever be able to take her back, unless he sees another man sleep with her before he does so.) The third oath was this: that if they did not keep the agreement made with the king they would be as dishonored as the Saracen who eats pig's flesh. The king willingly accepted from the emirs the oaths just described, because Master Nicholas of Acre, who knew the Saracen language, said that they could not swear a more powerful oath according to their law.

When the emirs had sworn, they had the oath they wished the king to take written down. It was drawn up on the advice of priests who had converted to their faith. The text said this: that if the king did not keep the agreement he had made with the emirs, he would be as dishonored as the Christian who denies God . . . and his Mother, and is barred from the fellowship of his twelve companions and of all the saints. The king agreed readily to this. The last point of the oath said that if he did not keep terms with the emirs, he would be as dishonored as the Christian who denies God and his law and who, scorning God, spits and tramples on the cross.[3] When the king heard this he said that, please God, he would never take this oath. The emirs sent Master Nicholas, who knew the Saracen language, to the king. He said to him, "My lord, the emirs are deeply outraged that they swore an oath precisely as you asked, and yet you refuse to swear the oath they ask of you. You may be certain that if you do not swear it they will behead you and all your people." The king replied that they could do as they wished, for he would rather die a good Christian than live with the anger of God, his Mother, and his saints. . . . I do not know how the oath was finalized, only that the emirs felt themselves satisfied by the oaths of the king and the other great men who were there. . . .

At sunrise my lord Geoffrey of Sergines went into Damietta and surrendered the city to the emirs; the sultan's banners were raised on the towers. The

---

[3] **spits . . . the cross:** The cross on which Jesus was crucified, considered by Christians to be the holiest of relics.

Saracen knights entered the city and started to drink the wine. They were soon all drunk. One of them came to our galley and drew his bloodied sword, saying that for his part he had killed six of our people. Before Damietta was surrendered, the queen and all our people inside the city, except those who were sick, were brought on board our ships. The Saracens were under oath to protect the sick, but they killed them all. The king's engines, which they were also supposed to protect, were hacked to pieces, and they did not keep the salted meats, which they were meant to look after since they do not eat pork. Instead they made one pile of salt pork and other of dead people and they set fire to both; there was such a large blaze that it lasted throughout Friday, Saturday, and Sunday. . . .

When the king came aboard his ship he found that his people had not prepared anything for him, no bed and no clothes. Until we reached Acre he had to sleep on the bedding the sultan had provided

him, and he had to wear the clothes the sultan had ordered to be made for him and had presented to him. . . . I sat with the king throughout the six days we were at sea, despite my sickness. He told me then how he had been captured and how, with God's aid, he had negotiated his ransom and ours. He had me tell him how I was captured on the river, and afterwards he told me I should be most grateful to Our Lord for having delivered me from such great dangers.

Examining The Evidence

1. Based on the oaths each side is asked to swear, how did Muslims and Christians differ in their core religious beliefs?
2. What does Joinville's narrative tell us about the role of holy relics in Christian religious belief and practice?
3. What is Joinville's assessment of the character of his Muslim enemies?

13.3 THE CHRISTIAN CONQUEST OF VALENCIA

The Chronicle of Jaime I of Aragon (1238) and the Charter Issued by Jaime I (1242)

After the capture of Toledo by Castile in 1085, the Muslim rulers of Iberia ceded authority to North African Muslim regimes—first the Almoravids (1070–1145) and then the Almohad dynasty (1145–1212)—that stymied the Christian advance for more than a century. Following the victory of Christian armies at the battle of Navas de Tolosa in 1212, however, the Almohad regime collapsed. The remaining Muslim city-states fell to Christian armies in quick succession. With the capture of Valencia in 1238 by King Jaime I (r. 1213–1276) of Aragon, the Christian *Reconquista* ("Reconquest") essentially came to completion. The first selection describes the surrender of

Valencia. Although narrated in the first-person voice of the king, the chronicle was not actually written by Jaime. The second selection is a charter issued by Jaime in 1242 to the Muslim inhabitants of six towns in the newly conquered territories.

On the third day the Rais [Muslim governor] sent me word that if I would give him an escort he would come out to me. I sent one of my barons to him, and he came immediately. He told me that the King of Valencia, Zaen [Zayyan ibn Mardanish], had considered the thing, and that he knew that the town could not hold out in the end; wherefore, that he might not cause the Valencians to bear more ill than they had already borne, he would surrender the city on this condition: that the Saracens, men

Olivia Remie Constable, ed., *Medieval Iberia: Readings from Christian, Muslim, and Jewish Sources* (Philadelphia: University of Pennsylvania Press, 1997), 209–215.

and women, might take away all their effects; that they should not be searched, nor should any outrage be done to them, and they all, himself and they, should go under escort to Cullera [a coastal town south of Valencia]. Since it was the will of God I should have the city, he had to will it so. On that I said that I would consult the Queen, who alone was in the secret. He said that he thought that was good, and he went out of the house, where I and the Queen remained. I then asked her what she thought of Zaen's proposal. She said, that if it seemed right to me to take those terms, she thought it right also; for Valencia was not a thing that a man who could have it should risk from one day to another. I felt that she gave me good advice, and I told her that I agreed with what she said, but I would add what I thought a very good reason for accepting Zaen's terms, namely, that should the town be taken by force, it would go hard for me if a wrangling over it arose in the army. Not for base lucre nor for apparel of any sort ought I put off what my ancestors and myself had so long desired to take and have; and even yet, if I were wounded or fell ill before the town could be taken by force, the whole thing might still be lost. Wherefore, so good a work as that should not be put to risk, and one should follow it up well, and end it.

After saying that, I sent for Rais Abnalmalet, and answered him in this wise — "Rais, you know well that I have made a great outlay in this business of mine; yet notwithstanding the outlay that I and my people have made and the ills we have suffered, for all that it shall not be but that I will agree to your terms, and have you escorted to Cullera, with all the goods that the Saracens, men and women, may be able to carry. For love of the King and of you, who have come here, will I do your people that grace, that they may go safely and securely with their apparel and with what they can carry."

When the Rais heard that, he was content; and he said he gave me great thanks, though their loss was to be great; withal he thanked me much for the grace I did them. After a time, I asked him on what day it should be. He said they needed ten days for clearing out. I told him that he asked too much, that the army was growing weary of the delay, for nothing was being done, and it was not for their good nor from mine. And so after a long discourse we agreed

that on the fifth day they would surrender the town, and begin to depart. . . .

The Saracens busied themselves about departing within the five days I had agreed on with them, so that on the third day they were all ready to quit; and I myself, with knights and armed men about me, brought them all out into the fields between Ruzafa and the town. I had, however, to put some of my own men to death because of their attempting to take goods from the Saracens, and carry off some women and children. So it was, that though the people who came out of Valencia were so numerous — there being between men and women well fifty thousand — by the grace of God they did not lose between them one thousand *sols*, so well did I escort, and have them escorted, as far as Cullera.

When that was done I made my entrance into the city, and on the third day began the division of the houses among the Archbishop of Narbonne, the bishops, and the barons who were with me, as well as the knights who were entitled to heritages in the district. I also gave shares to the corporations of the cities [of Aragon and Catalonia], according to the number of men-at-arms each had there.

At the end of three weeks I appointed partitioners to divide the lands of the district of Valencia. I made the "yoke" [*jouvada*] to be of six *caficades*.[1] I had the whole land of the district measured, and the grants I made carefully examined. When this was done, I found that, in consequence of the grants made to some of the men, the charters came to more *jouvadas* than the land itself. Many men there were who had asked for a small portion of land, and I found afterwards that, through their cheating, it was twice or three times as much as they ought to have had. As there was not enough land for the grants, I took away from those who had too much, and redistributed it, so that all had some, as was fitting.

* * *

This is a charter of favor and protection that Jaime, by the grace of God king of the Aragonese, the Mallorcas, and Valencia, count of Barcelona and

---

[1] "yoke" [*jouvada*] to be of six *caficades*: *Jouvada* ("yoke") was the amount of land a pair of oxen could plow in a day. A *caficade* is another unit of measurement.

Urgell, and lord of Montpellier, makes to the entire community of Saracens who are in Eslida and in Ahin, in Veo, in Senquier, in Pelmes and Sueras, who placed themselves in his power and became his vassals.

Therefore he granted them that they may keep their homes and possessions in all their villages with all their districts, income and profits, in both dry-farming and irrigated lands, cultivated and un-worked, and all their farms and plantings.

And they may make use of the waters just as was their custom in the time of the Saracens, and may divide the water as was customary among them.

And they may pasture their stock in all of their districts as was customary in the time of the pagans [Muslims].

And Christians or anyone of another Law [religio-ethnic group] are not to be sent to settle in their districts without their permission.

Nor may anyone bother their pasturage or stock. And they are to be safe and secure in their persons and things. And they can travel over all their districts, for tending to their affairs, without Christian [interference].

And the castellans of the castles, or the bailiffs, may not demand castle-provisioning of wood and pack animals and water or any service for the castles. Nor are [Christians] to bother them in their houses or vineyards and trees and produce.

Nor may they forbid preaching in the mosques or prayer being made on Fridays and on their feasts and other days; but they [the Muslims] are to carry on according to their religion. And they can teach students the *Qur'an* and all the books of the *hadith* [words and deeds of Muhammad]; and the mosque endowments are to belong to the mosques.

And they are to judge legal cases under the control of their *qadi* [law judges] for those Saracens who are in Eslida, about marriages, and inheritance shares, and purchases and all other cases, according to their Law.

And Saracens who are now outside the villages of said castles, whenever they come back, can recover their properties forever. And Saracens who want to go away from there can sell their properties and other things to Saracens living there, and the bailiffs cannot stop them; nor are they to pay any fee for that purpose to the castellan of the castle.

And they are to be secure in going about by land or sea, in person and possessions and family and children. And they are not to pay any military-exemption fee, or army substitute, or tally upon their properties except the [civil or rental] tenth on wheat, barley, panic-grass [used as hay to feed livestock], millet, flax, and vegetables; and the tenth is to be paid on the threshing floor. And they are to give from mills, public ovens, shops, merchants' inns, and baths that portion which they used to give in the time of the pagans.

And when they wish, they can go to visit relatives, wherever they may be.

And the dead may be buried in their cemeteries, without interference or fee. And fines are to be given according to their Law.

And they are not to pay on any produce, such as onions, cucumbers or other fruits of the land except the aforesaid. On trees and their fruits and on climbing vines they are not to give a tenth, but they give a tenth on vineyards and they give the *zakat* [Islamic alms tax] on livestock according as they are accustomed.

And Christians may not be housed in their homes and properties unless the Saracens wish. And Christians are not to bring charges against Saracens except with a proper Saracen witness.

And the Saracens of the said castle are to recover their properties, wherever they may be in the kingdom except in Valencia city and Burriana.

And on beehives and domestic animals they are not to have anything except what has been said.

And if a Saracen dies, his heirs are to inherit the property. And Saracens who want to marry outside their village may do so, without opposition from the castellan or a fee.

And those of Eslida, Ahin, Veo, Pelmes, and Senquier are tax-free on all things from the day on which the lord king granted this charter up through one year. And when that year is finished, they are to discharge the services as above. And the lord king receives them and theirs under his protection and safeguard.

Done at Artana, on the fourth kalends of June, in the year of our Lord 1242.

Examining the Evidence

1. What considerations prompted Jaime to accept the Muslim governor's terms for surrendering Valencia?

2. To what extent did Jaime grant the defeated Muslims legal, religious, and economic autonomy in return for their surrender?

3. How did Jaime's treatment of Muslims living in rural villages differ from those living in the city of Valencia? How can this difference be explained?

CONTRASTING VIEWS

EUROPEAN AND MUSLIM DEPICTIONS OF THE MONGOL KHANS

13.4 | ALA-AD-DIN ATA-MALIK JUVAINI, *THE HISTORY OF THE WORLD CONQUEROR* (c. 1252–1260)

Juvaini (1226–1283) was born into a distinguished Persian family in Khorasan, in northeastern Iran, with a long history of service to the Seljuk Turk rulers. His father was taken captive by the Mongols in 1233 but soon found himself appointed as deputy to the Mongol governor of Khorasan. Juvaini, too, entered the entourage of the Mongol governor and accompanied him on a journey to the Mongol capital of Qaraqorum in 1252, shortly after Mongke's election as Great Khan. During his year-long stay in Qaraqorum, Juvaini began writing his chronicle of the Mongol conquests from the time of Chinggis Khan. Subsequently, Juvaini served under the Mongol leader Hulegu, brother of Qubilai Khan, during his conquest of Baghdad and overthrow of the Abbasid caliphate in 1258. Juvaini spent the remainder of his life as governor of Baghdad under the Mongol Ilkhan regime.

God Almighty in wisdom and intelligence distinguished Chinggis Khan from all his coevals [contemporaries] and in alertness of mind and absoluteness of power exalted him above all the kings of the world; so that all that has been recorded touching the practice of the mighty Khosros of old[1] and all that has been written concerning the customs and usages of the Pharaohs and Caesars was by Chinggis Khan invented from the page of his own mind without the toil of perusing records or the trouble of conforming with tradition; while all that pertains to the method of subjugating countries and relates to the crushing of the power of enemies and the raising of the station of the followers was the product of his own understanding and the compilation of his own intellect. And indeed, Alexander, who was so addicted to the devising of talismans and the solving of enigmas, had he lived in the age of Chinggis Khan, would have been his pupil in craft and cunning, and of all the talismans for the taking of strongholds he would have found none better than blindly to follow in his footsteps: whereof there can be no clearer proof nor more certain evidence than that having such numerous and powerful foes and such mighty and well-accoutered enemies, whereof each was the *faghfur*[2] of his time and the Khosros of his age, he sallied forth, a single man, with few troops and no accoutrement, and reduced and subjugated the lords of the horizons from the East unto the West; and whoever presumed to oppose and resist him, that man, in enforcement of the *yasas* [Mongol law codes] and ordinances which he imposed, he utterly destroyed, together with all his followers, children, partisans, armies, lands, and territories. There has been transmitted to us a tradition of the traditions of God which says: "Those are my horsemen; through them shall I avenge me on those that rebelled against me," nor is there a shadow of a doubt but that these

1 **the mighty Khosros of old:** Khosros I (r. 531–579), the Sasanid king of Iran.

2 *faghfur:* "Son of Heaven," a reference to the title of the emperor of China.

'Ala-ad-Din 'Ata-Malik Juvaini, *Genghis Khan: The History of the World Conqueror*, translated from the text of Mizra Muhammad Qazvini by J. A. Boyle (Manchester, UK: Manchester University Publishing, 1997), 23–26.

words are a reference to the horsemen of Chinggis Khan and to his people. And so it was that when the world by reason of the variety of its creatures has become a raging sea, and the kings and nobles of every country by reason of the arrogance of pride and the insolence of vainglory had reached the very zenith of "Vainglory is my tunic, and pride my cloak," then did God, in accordance with the above-mentioned promise, endow Chinggis Khan with the strength of might and the victory of domination—"Verily, the might of the Lord is great indeed"; and when through pride of wealth, and power, and station the greater part of the cities and countries of the world encountered him with rebellion and hatred and refused to yield allegiance (and especially the countries of Islam, from the frontiers of Turkestan to uttermost Syria), then wherever there was a king, or a ruler, or the governor of a city that offered him resistance, him he annihilated together with his family and followers, kinsmen, and strangers; so that where there had been a hundred thousand people there remained, without exaggeration, not a hundred souls alive; as a proof of which statement may be cited the fate of the various cities, whereof mention has been made in the proper place.

In accordance and agreement with his own mind he established a rule for every occasion and a regulation for every circumstance; while for every crime he fixed a penalty. And since the Tartar peoples had no script of their own, he gave orders that Mongol children should learn writing from the Uighur; and that these *yasas* and ordinances should be written down on rolls. These rolls are called the *Great Book of Yasas* and are kept in the treasury of the chief princes. Wherever a khan ascends the throne, or a great army is mobilized, or the princes assemble and begin to consult together concerning affairs of state and the administration thereof, they produce these rolls and model their actions thereon; and proceed with the disposition of armies or the destruction of provinces and cities in the manner therein described.

At the time of the first beginnings of his dominion, when the Mongol tribes were united to him, he abolished reprehensible customs which had been practiced by those peoples and had enjoyed recognition amongst them; and established such usages as were praiseworthy from the point of view of reason. There are many of these ordinances that are in conformity with the *shari'a* [Islamic law]. . . .

Being the adherent of no religion and the follower of no creed, he eschewed bigotry, and the preference of one faith to another, and the placing of some above others; rather he honored and respected the learned and pious of every sect, recognizing such conduct as the way to the Court of God. And as he viewed the Muslims with the eye of respect, so also did he hold the Christians and idolaters in high esteem. As for his children and grandchildren, several of them have chosen a religion according to their inclination, some adopting Islam, others embracing Christianity, others selecting idolatry and others again cleaving to the ancient canon of their fathers and forefathers and inclining in no direction; but these are now a minority. But though they have adopted some religion they still for the most part avoid all show of fanaticism and do not swerve from the *yasa* of Chinggis Khan, namely, to consider all sects as one and not to distinguish them from one another.

13.5   WILLIAM OF RUBRUCK, *THE JOURNEY OF FRIAR WILLIAM OF RUBRUCK* (c. 1255)

William of Rubruck (c. 1210–c. 1270) was a Franciscan friar, probably originally from Flanders, whose account of his travels across Asia provided Europeans with a first-hand glimpse of the Mongols. At the instigation of King Louis IX of France, then at Acre in Palestine after being released by his Muslim captors (see Document 13.2), William set out in 1253 on an expedition to the camp of the Mongol chief Sartaq in southern Russia. Sartaq reportedly had converted to Christianity. William's mission was to determine whether Sartaq could be enlisted in the Christian struggle to recapture Jerusalem. The rumor proved false, and Sartaq dispatched William and his companions to his father, Batu, the khan of the Golden Horde. Batu in turn sent William to the Great Khan Mongke. Having failed to make headway in converting the Mongol leaders, William returned home, arriving at Acre in the summer of 1255.

Christopher Dawson, ed., *The Mongol Mission: Narratives and Letters of the Franciscan Missionaries in Mongolia and China in the Thirteenth and Fourteenth Centuries* (London: Sheed and Ward, 1955), 148, 150, 153–156, 160, 183–184, 194–195.

(continued)

CONTRASTING VIEWS (continued)

At last on St. Stephen's Day [December 26th] we entered upon a plain as vast as the sea and such that not even the smallest hill was to be seen, and on the following day, the feast of St. John the Evangelist, we reached the *orda* [camp] of the great lord [Mongke]. . . .

On the octave of the Holy Innocents [January 4th] we were taken to the court. . . . Near the entrance was a bench with some *kumiss* [fermented mare's milk] on it, and they made the interpreter stand near this while we were made to sit on a stool in front of the ladies. The whole dwelling was completely covered inside with cloth of gold and in the middle in a little hearth was a fire of twigs and roots of wormwood, which grows to a great size there, and also the dung of oxen. The Khan was sitting on a couch wearing a speckled and shiny fur like seal-skin. He is a flat-nosed man of medium height, about forty-five years old; a young wife was sitting next to him and a grown-up daughter, who was very ugly, Cirina by name, was sitting on a couch behind them with some little children. For that dwelling had belonged to one of his wives, a Christian, whom he had loved deeply and by whom he had the said daughter. Although he had introduced in addition the young wife, nevertheless the daughter was mistress of all that court which had belonged to her mother. . . .

[William addressed the Khan]: "You are a man to whom God has given great dominion on earth, we therefore beg Your Puissance [Powerful One] to grant us leave to stay in your country to carry out the service of God on behalf of you, your wives and your children. We have neither gold nor silver nor precious stones which we could present to you; we have but ourselves and we offer ourselves to serve God and pray to Him for you. . . ."

Then the Khan began to reply: "Just as the sun spreads its rays in all directions, so my power and the power of Batu [khan of the Golden Horde] is spread everywhere. Therefore we have no need of your gold or silver." . . . I begged him not to be offended at what I had said about gold and silver, for I had said it not because he had need of or desired such things, but rather because we would gladly have honored him with both temporal and spiritual gifts.

He then told us to get up from our knees and sit down again and after a short time we took leave of him and went out, and his secretaries and his interpreter, who is bringing up one of his daughters, went with us. They began to ask a great many questions about the kingdom of France, whether there were many sheep and oxen and horses

there, as if they were about to march in at once and take everything, and many other times I had to do great violence to myself to hide my indignation and anger, and I replied: "There are many good things there, which you will see if it falls to your lot to go there." . . .

[Upon returning] to our lodging, the interpreter came to meet us and said, "Mongke Khan has pity on you and grants you permission to stay here for the space of two months, by which time the intense cold will be over, and he informs you that ten days' journey from here is a fine city called Qaraqorum; if you wish to go there he will have you provided with all that you need." . . .

As for the city of Qaraqorum, I can tell you that, not counting the Khan's palace, it is not as large as the village of Saint Denis [outside Paris], and the monastery of Saint Denis is worth ten times more than that palace. There are two districts there: the Saracens' quarter where the markets are, and many merchants flock thither on account of the court which is always near it and on account of the number of envoys. The other district is that of the Cathayans [Chinese] who are all craftsmen. There are twelve pagan temples belonging to the different nations, two mosques in which the law of Muhammad is proclaimed, and one church for the Christians at the far end of the town. The town is surrounded by a mud wall and has four gates. At the east gate are sold millet and other grain, which is however seldom brought there; at the west sheep and goats are sold; at the south oxen and carts; at the north horses. . . .

On the day of Epiphany . . . Mongke Khan had made a great feast; and it is his custom to hold court on such days as his soothsayers tell him are feast days or the Nestorian priests[3] say are for some reason sacred. On these days the Christian priests come first with their paraphernalia, and they pray for him and bless his cup; when they retire the Saracen priests come and do likewise; they are followed by the pagan priests who do the same. [An Armenian] monk told me that the Khan only believes in the Christians; however, he wishes them all to come and pray for him. But he was lying, for he does not believe in any of them. . . .

---

[3] **Nestorian priests:** The Nestorian tradition of Christianity, which emphasized the humanity of Jesus, had been deemed heresy by both the Greek and Roman churches since the fourth century. However, the Nestorian church attracted many followers in Iran and Central Asia.

On the day of Pentecost Mongke Khan summoned me. . . . He then began to make a profession of faith to me. "We Mongols," said he, "believe there is but one God, by Whom we live and by Whom we die and towards him we have an upright heart." I said, "God Himself will grant this for it cannot come about but by His gift." He asked what I had said and the interpreter told him. Afterwards the Khan continued: "But just as God gave different fingers to the hand so has He given different ways to men. To you God has given the Scriptures and you Christians do not observe them. You do not find in the Scriptures that a man ought to disparage another, now do you?" "No," I replied, "but from the beginning I made it clear to you that I had no wish to wrangle with anyone." "My words do not apply to you," said he. "Similarly, you do not find that a man ought to turn aside from justice for the sake of money?" "No, my Lord," I said, "and for a truth I have not come to these parts in order to gain money, rather have I refused that which was offered to me." There was a scribe present, who bore witness to the fact that I had refused a iascot[4] and some pieces of silk. "My words do not apply to you," he said. "As I was saying, God has given you the Scriptures and you do not keep them; to us, on the other hand, He has given soothsayers, and we do what they tell us, and live in peace." He drank four times, I believe, before he finished saying these things.

And while I was listening closely to hear if there was still more he wished to declare concerning his faith, he began to speak of my return saying, "You have stayed here a long time, it is my wish that you go back. . . ." From then onwards I had neither the opportunity nor the time to put the Catholic Faith before him. . . .

[The Mongols] are so much puffed up with pride that they believe the whole world is anxious to make peace with them. But indeed, if I were given leave, I would preach war against them throughout the whole world with all my strength.

4 *iascot:* The common currency of the Mongol Empire was a silver ingot—called *yastuq* in Mongolian—weighing 2 kg.

13.6   MARCO POLO, *THE DESCRIPTION OF THE WORLD* (c. 1307)

Marco Polo (1254–1324), a Venetian merchant, accompanied his father and uncle on their return journey to the Mongol realm, arriving at Shangdu, the summer capital of Qubilai Khan (r. 1260–1294) in 1275. At that time, Qubilai already ruled over north China ("Cathay," in Polo's account). In 1276, he conquered the southern Song territories ("Mangi"), bringing all of China under his dominion. Polo remained in China until 1290, finally returning to Venice in 1295. It was during his imprisonment in a Genoese jail in 1298–1299—the reason for his incarceration is unknown—that Polo narrated his travels to a fellow prisoner and professional writer named Rustichello. Despite the book's instant popularity, Polo had many detractors who reacted to his enthusiastic glorification of the pagan Mongol khan with skepticism and disbelief.

Now I wish to begin to tell you in this part of our book all the very great doings and all the very great marvels of the very great lord of the Tartars, namely the great Khan who now reigns, who is called Qubilai Khan, which Khan means to say in our language the great lord of lords, emperor, and this lord who now reigns indeed he really has this name of lord of lords by right because everyone knows truly that this great Khan is the most powerful man in people and in lands and in treasure that ever was in the world or that now is from the time of Adam our first father till this moment; and under him all the peoples are set with such obedience as has never been done under any other former king. . . .

In all of the provinces of Cathay [northern China], of Mangi [southern China], and in all the rest of his dominion are found many unfaithful and disloyal persons who would rebel against their lord if they could; and therefore it is necessary in every province where there are large cities and many people to keep armies there, which stay in the country four or five miles away from the city, which cannot have gates or walls to prevent them from entering in whenever they please. And the great Khan makes these armies change every two years, and he does the same with the captains who command them; and with this curb the people stay quiet, and cannot move nor make any change. Besides the pay which the great Khan always gives them

Marco Polo, *The Description of the World*, ed. A. C. Moule and Paul Pelliot (London: George Routledge & Sons, 1938), 192, 195, 203, 207–209, 221–222.

(continued)

CONTRASTING VIEWS (*continued*)

from the revenues of the provinces, these armies live on an infinite number of flocks which they have and on the milk which they send to the cities to sell, and so buy the things which they need. . . .

The great Khan has twelve wise barons who have charge of learning and informing themselves of the operations which the captains and soldiers carry out particularly in the expeditions and battles where they are; and those then report to the great Khan. I tell you that to those captains who prove themselves well in war and in battle, him who at first was lord, that is head, of a hundred men he makes him lord of a thousand, and him who at first was lord of a thousand he makes them lord of ten thousand and thus he gave to each according to his rank as he saw that they deserved; and with all this he makes him a great gift of gold and fair silver vessels and of many fair jewels, and a superior tablet having or denoting authority, that is with orders of authority. . . . For they had deserved it very well, for never afterwards were men seen who did so much in arms for the love of their lord as those did on the day of the battle. . . .

You may know quite truly that the great Khan stays in the capital town which is in the province of Cathay, which is the great city called Khanbaliq [modern Beijing], . . . three months of the year, that is December and January and February. And in this town he has his great palace near the new city on the side toward midday, in this form; and I will describe its likeness to you. The palace is square in every way. First there is a square circuit of wall, and each face is eight miles long, round which is a deep moat; and in the middle of each side is a gate by which all the people enter who gather there from every side. Then there is the space of a mile all round, where the soldiers are stationed. After that space is found another circuit of wall, of six miles for a side, which has three gates on the midday face and another three on the side facing the mountains, of which the one in the middle is larger and stays always locked and is never opened except when the great Khan wishes to come in or go out; and the other two smaller, which are on one side of it and the other on the other, always stand open, and by them all the people come in. And at each angle of this wall, and in the middle of each of the faces, is a beautiful and spacious palace, so that all round about the wall are eight palaces, in which are kept the munitions of the great Khan, that is one kind of trappings in each; as bridles, saddles, stirrups and other things which belong to the equipment of horses. And in another bows, strings, quivers, arrows, and other things belonging to archery. In

another cuirasses, corslets, and similar things of boiled leather; and so with the rest. . . .

And in the middle of this space . . . is the great palace of the great lord, . . . which is made in such a way as I shall tell you. Know that it is the greatest and most wonderful that ever was seen. . . . The walls of the halls and of the rooms inside are all covered with gold and with silver and blue, and there are portrayed very finely in carved work lions & dragons and beasts and birds and fair stories of ladies and knights and many other different kinds of beautiful things and stories of wars; & the roof also is made so that nothing else is seen there but gold and silver and paintings. On each quarter of the palace is a great flight of marble steps which go up from the ground to the top of said wall of marble which surrounds the palace. . . . The hall is so great and so broad that it is a great marvel, and more than six thousand men would well feed there at once, sitting at table together. And in that palace there are four hundred rooms, so many that it is a marvel to see them. It is so beautiful and so large and so rich and so well made that there is not a man in the world who should have the power to know how to plan it better nor make it. . . .

On this same day of [the Khan's] birth all the Tartars of the world, all the kings & princes and barons who are subject to his jurisdiction, and all the provinces and regions and cities which hold land of him make great feast and give him very great presents, each as is suitable to him who brings it. . . . And there come many other men also, each with great presents on that day, to ask favors of the lord; and they are those who wish to ask him to give them some domain. And the great lord has chosen twelve barons who are set over this affair, to give the domains to men like these according as is fitting to each. And again on this day all people of whatever faith they are, all the idolaters and all the Christians or the Jews and all the Saracens and all the other races of the Tartar peoples make great petitions and great prayers, each to the idols and to their God with great chants, and great lights, and great incense, that he may be pleased to save and protect their lord, and that they give him long life and good and joy and health, and safety and prosperity.

COMPARING THE EVIDENCE

1. Juvaini and Marco Polo portray the Mongol khans (Chinggis and Qubilai, respectively) as the greatest rulers of all time. Did they use similar criteria to measure the greatness of the Mongol rulers?

2. Why did the Muslim Juvaini regard Chinggis, a pagan, as the legitimate ruler of the peoples he conquered? Would the Christian friar William of Rubruck agree? Why or why not?

3. How do these authors portray the attitude of the Mongol rulers toward religion?

4. How and why did William of Rubruck and Marco Polo differ in their impressions of the Mongol rulers, their capitals, and their courts?

13.7 MONGOL RULE IN RUSSIA

Medieval Russian Chronicles (c. 1257–1409)

The khans of the Golden Horde—descended from Jochi, Chinggis Khan's eldest son—ruled much of Russia from the 1230s to circa 1500. The Mongol conquests of 1237–1240 caused widespread destruction in Russia. By the fourteenth century, however, the Russian princes were enjoying the benefits of Mongol protection. The Grand Prince of Muscovy (modern Moscow) gradually emerged as the dominant figure among the Russian princes. Our major sources of information about Mongol rule in Russia are anonymous chronicles compiled under the auspices of the Orthodox Church. The final document below is a letter by the Mongol chief Edigei—a lieutenant of Timur, the upstart Mongol khan in Central Asia—sent to Grand Prince Vasilii I (r. 1389–1425) in 1409. Timur had deposed the Golden Horde khan Tokhtamysh (r. 1376–1395), and Edigei demanded that Vasilii accept Timur's appointees as the new leaders of the Golden Horde.

Mongol Census, c. 1257 [from the Nikonian Chronicle]

That same winter [1257] census takers came from the Tatar land and took a census of the entire land of Suzal, Riazan, and Murom, and posted chiefs of 10, 100, 1,000, and 10,000, and having made all the arrangements, returned to the [Golden] Horde,

enumerating all except archimandrites,[1] abbots, monks, priests, deacons, church servitors, and the entire church retinue, whosoever obeys the Lord God and the most pure Virgin and lives in the house of the Lord and serves the Churches of God.

Opposition to Muslim Tax-Farmers, 1262 [from the Voskresensk Chronicle]

God delivered the people of the Rostov land from the savage torture of the Muslims through the prayers of the Holy Virgin and instilled fury in the hearts of Christians, unable to endure any longer the oppression of the pagans; and they convoked a *veche* [town meeting] and drove them from the towns: from Rostov, from Vladimir, from Suzdal, from Iaroslavl, from Pereiaslavl; these accursed Muslims had farmed tribute from the Tatars and had brought much ruin upon men thereby, enslaving Christian men for [nonpayment of] interest [on loans], and many men were taken to various places; but God, who loves mankind, in his mercy delivered his people from great misfortune. . . . That same summer Grand Prince Aleksandr [Nevskii, of Moscow] decided to go to the tsar in the Golden Horde, so that his entreaties might avert misfortune from the people.

---

[1] **archimandrites:** In the Greek and Russian Orthodox churches, the archimandrite was an honorific rank for a priest, one level below a bishop.

A Source Book for Russian History from Early Times to 1917, Volume 1, edited by George Vernadsky (New Haven, CT: Yale University Press, 1972), 48–50, 113. Copyright © 1972 by Yale University. Used by permission of the publisher.

A Decree on Free Trade in the Mongol Realm, c. 1267–1272

The word of [Khan] Mongke-Temur [r. 1267–1280] to Prince Iaroslav [of Novgorod]: give foreign merchants passage into your domain. From Prince Iaroslav to the people of Riga [on the Baltic coast], and to the great and the small, and to those who come to trade, and to everyone: you shall have free passage through my domain; and if anyone comes to me with arms, him I shall deal with myself; but the merchant has free passage through my domain.

A Mongol Charter Concerning Protection of the Russian Church, c. 1308

And this third charter Tsar [Khan] Mongke-Temur[2] gave to the Metropolitan [patriarch of the Russian Orthodox Church] Peter, in the year 1308:

Tsar [Khan] Chinggis ordered that in the future, in exacting tribute or *korm* [subsistence for officials], do not touch the clergy; may they pray to God with righteous hearts for us and for our tribe, and give us their blessing. . . . And past tsars [khans] have granted privileges to priests and monks by the same custom. . . . And we who pray to God have not altered their charters and, in keeping with the former custom, say thus: let no one, whoever it may be, demand tribute, or tax on land, or transport, or *korm*, or seize what belongs to the church: land, water, orchards, vineyards, windmills. . . . And if anything has been taken, it shall be returned; and let no one, whoever he may be, take under his protection what belongs to the church: craftsmen, falconers, huntsmen; or seize, take, tear, or destroy what belongs to their faith: books, or anything else; and if anyone insults their faith, that man shall be accused and put to death. Those who eat the same bread and live in the same house with a priest — be it a brother, be it a son — they shall likewise be granted privileges by the same custom, so long as they do not leave them; if they should leave them, they shall give tribute, and everything else. And you priests, to whom we granted our previous charter, keep on praying to God and giving us your blessing! And if you do not pray to God for us with a righteous heart, that sin shall be upon you. . . . Saying thus, we have given the charter to this metropolitan; having seen and heard this charter, the *baskaki* [tax inspectors], princes, scribes, land-tax collectors and customs collectors shall not demand or take tribute, or anything else from the priests and from the monks; and if they should take anything, they shall be accused and put to death for this great crime.

Edigei's Letter to Vasilii I, 1409 [from the *Nikonian Chronicle*]

The prince of the Golden Horde, Edigei, sent a letter to Grand Prince Vasilii Dmitrievich, saying thus: "We have heard that the children of Tokhtamysh are with you, and for this reason we have come in war; and we have also heard that you act wrongfully in the towns: the tsar's [khan's] envoys and merchants come from the Horde to you, and you ridicule the envoys and merchants, and moreover they are subjected to great injury and persecution from you. This is not good; for in the past this was part of the tsar's domain and he held power; you respected the ancient customs and the tsar's envoys, and merchants were treated without persecution and without injury; and you should ask the old men how this was done in the past. Now you do not do this; but is this change good? Temur-Kutlui[3] became tsar, and you became sovereign of your domain, and since that time you have not visited the tsar in the Horde; you have not seen the tsar with your own eyes, nor have you dispatched any princes, or elder boyars, or younger boyars, or anyone else, nor have you sent a son or a brother with any message. Then Shadibek[4] ruled for eight years, and you did not visit him either, or send anyone with any message. And the reign of Shadibek likewise came to an end, and now Bulat-Saltan [Pulad] has become tsar, and this

---

[2] **And this . . . Tsar [Khan] Mongke-Temur:** Mongke-Temur died in 1280; it is unclear whether this charter was originally given by Mongke-Temur or by Togta (r. 1291–1312), then the reigning khan of the Golden Horde.

[3] **Temur-Kutlui:** Timur appointed Temur-Kutlui as tsar in place of Tokhtamysh, whose sons now had taken shelter with Vasilii.

[4] **Shadibek:** After Temur-Kutlui's death in 1399, Edigei set up his brother Shadibek in his place as khan.

is already the third year of his rule, and you have likewise failed to visit him yourself, or send a son, or brother, or elder boyar. You are the eldest, the grand prince, over such a great domain, but all your deeds are evil and wrongful. . . . It would be well for you . . . to observe the ancient customs, and then you will live safely and rule in your domain. Whenever you suffer any harm either from Russian princes or from Lithuania, each year you send complaints to us against them, and you give us no respite on this account; and you say that your domain is destitute and that there is no means of paying tribute. Heretofore we have never seen your domain with our own eyes, but only heard reports of it; but as for your messages and letters which you have sent to us in the Horde, you have lied to us everywhere; and as for the tribute of one ruble per two *sokhi* [plows — taxation units] which you have collected from each region of your realm, where is that silver? It would be well for you to acknowledge this, to give over what was given over honestly in the past, lest evil befall your domain, and Christians meet their final doom, and our anger and war be upon you."

Examining the Evidence

1. What were the economic consequences of the Golden Horde's conquests in Russia?
2. What impact did the policies of the khans of the Golden Horde have on Orthodox Christianity in Russia?
3. What does Egidei's letter reveal about the changes in the political relationship between the Golden Horde khanate and the Russian princes?

MAKING CONNECTIONS

1. Based on these accounts, what were the positive results and negative consequences of the Mongol conquests?
2. Compare how the policies of King Jaime of Aragon toward the Muslim inhabitants of Valencia differ from those adopted by the Mongol conquerors. What do these policies tell us about their conceptions of the relationship between ruler and subject?
3. How did the Mongol khans' attitudes toward religious belief and practice differ from those of Christian and Islamic clerics and rulers?
4. To what extent did the authors represented in this chapter agree on the qualities that made a ruler great?

CHAPTER 14

Collapse and Revival in Afro-Eurasia, 1300–1450

The Black Death pandemic disrupted the social order of Latin Christendom, as we see in Buonaiuti's account of the plague in Florence. The widespread, devastating disease exposed deep social fissures that erupted into violent conflicts such as the English Peasant Revolt of 1381. As Sanudo's praise of Venice shows, however, by the fifteenth century the Italian city-states had regained their former prosperity. The devastation wrought by the Black Death lingered much longer in the central Islamic lands. Despite the plague's effects, the Islamic world continued to expand, sometimes through conquest—notably in the Ottoman conquest of the Byzantine Empire—but more commonly through conversion, for example, in Mali in West Africa. With the passing of the Mongol empires, commercial and cultural traffic across Central Asia ebbed. The founder of the Ming dynasty, Emperor Hongwu, was determined to eradicate all Mongol influences from Chinese culture and society. However, in the European and Muslim imagination, China remained the fabled land of majesty and mystery evoked in the popular Persian tale of Prince Humay.

THE PLAGUE IN FLORENCE AND ITS ECONOMIC EFFECTS

Marchionne di Coppo Buonaiuti, *Florentine Chronicle* (c. 1370–1380)

Marchionne di Coppo Buonaiuti (1336–1385) was born into a wealthy patrician family, probably bankers, in Florence. He was active in Florentine politics in the 1360s and 1370s, when he became a member of the city's executive council and frequently represented Florence on diplomatic missions. His *Florentine Chronicle*, written after his retirement from politics, glorifies the history and accomplishments of his native city. Buonaiuti's account of the effects of the Black Death on Florence was written three decades after the event. His description of the devastation caused by the pandemic draws perhaps on his own eyewitness observations—he was twelve at the time. It also draws on the inherited memory of the Black Death shared by his contemporaries and on literary accounts such as Boccaccio's *Decameron*, completed in 1351.

Concerning the deadly outbreak of disease which happened in the city of Florence, where many people died

In the year of our lord 1348 there occurred in the city and *contado* [county] of Florence a great pestilence, and such was its fury and violence that in whatever household it took hold, whosoever took care of the sick, all the caregivers died of the same illness, and almost nobody survived beyond the fourth day, neither doctors nor medicine proving of any avail, and there appeared to be no remedy, either because those illnesses were not yet recognized, or because doctors had never previously had cause to study them properly. Such was the fear that nobody knew what to do: when it caught hold in a household, it often happened that not a single person escaped death. And it wasn't just men and women: even sentient [capable of feeling] animals such as dogs and cats, hens, oxen, donkeys and sheep, died from that same disease and with those symptoms, and almost none who displayed those symptoms, or very few indeed, effected a recovery. Those symptoms were as follows: either between the thigh and the body, in the groin region, or under the armpit, there appeared a lump, and a sudden fever, and when the victim spat, he spat blood mixed with saliva, and none of those who spat blood survived. Such was the terror this caused that seeing it take hold in a household, as soon as it started, nobody remained: everybody abandoned the dwelling in fear, and fled to another; some fled into the city and others into the countryside. No doctors were to be found, because they were dying like everybody else; those who could be found wanted exorbitant fees cash-in-hand before entering the house, and having entered, they took the patient's pulse with their heads turned away, and assayed the urine samples from afar, with aromatic herbs held to their noses. Sons abandoned fathers, husbands wives, one brother the other, one sister the other. The city was reduced to bearing the dead to burial; many died who at their passing had neither confession nor last sacraments, and many died unseen, and many died of hunger, for when somebody took ill to his bed, the other occupants in panic told him: "I'm going for the doctor"; and quietly locked the door from the outside and didn't come back. The victim, abandoned by both people and nourishment, yet kept constant company by fever, wasted away. Many were those who begged their families not to abandon them; when evening came, the relatives said to the patient: "So that you don't have to wake up the people looking after you at night, asking for things, because this is going on day and night, you yourself can reach for cakes and wine or water, here they are on the shelf above your bed, you can get the stuff you want." And when the patient fell asleep, they went away and did not return. If,

Jonathan Usher, trans., *Florentine Chronicle of Marchionne di Coppo di Stefano Buonaiuti (1216–1385)*, http://www.brown.edu/Departments/Italian_Studies/dweb/plague/perspectives/marchionne.php.

through good fortune the victim had been strengthened by that food, the next morning alive and still strong enough to get to the window, he would have to wait half an hour before anybody came past, if this was not a busy thoroughfare, and even when the odd person passed by, and the patient had enough voice to be heard a little, if he shouted, sometimes he would be answered and sometimes not, and even if he were to be answered, there was no help to be had. For not only none or very few wished to enter a house where there were any sick people, but they didn't even want to have contact with those who issued healthy from a sick person's house, saying "He's jinxed, don't speak to him," saying: "He's got it because there's the '*gavocciolo*' in his house"; and "*gavocciolo*" was the name they gave to these swellings. Many died without being seen, remaining on their beds till they stank. And the neighbors, if any were left, having smelled the stench, did a whip round and sent him for burial. Houses remained open, nobody dared to touch anything, for it seemed that things remained poisoned, and whoever had anything to do with them caught the disease.

At every church, or at most of them, pits were dug, down to the water-table, as wide and deep as the parish was populous; and therein, whosoever was not very rich, having died during the night, would be shouldered by those whose duty it was, and would either be thrown into this pit, or they would pay big money for somebody else to do it for them. The next morning there would be very many in the pit. Earth would be taken and thrown down on them; and then others would come on top of them, and then earth on top again, in layers, with very little earth, like garnishing lasagna with cheese. The gravediggers who carried out these functions were so handsomely paid that many became rich and many died, some already rich and others having earned little, despite the high fees. The female and male sick-bay attendants demanded from one to three florins a day, plus sumptuous expenses. The foodstuffs suitable for the sick, cakes and sugar, reached outrageous prices. A pound of sugar was sold at between three and eight florins, and the same went for other confectionery. Chickens and other poultry were unbelievably expensive, and eggs were between 12 and 24 *denari* each: you were lucky to find three in a day, even searching through the whole city. Wax

was unbelievable: a pound of wax rose to more than a florin, nevertheless an age-old arrogance of the Florentines was curbed, in that an order was given not to parade more than two large candles. The churches only had one bier apiece, as was the custom, and this was insufficient. Pharmacists and grave-diggers had obtained biers, hangings and laying-out pillows at great price. The shroud-cloth apparel which used to cost, for a woman, in terms of petticoat, outer garment, cloak and veils, three florins, rose in price to thirty florins, and would have risen to one hundred florins, except that they stopped using shroud-cloth, and whoever was rich was dressed with plain cloth, and those who weren't rich were sewn up in a sheet. The benches placed for the dead cost a ludicrous amount, and there weren't enough of them even if there had been a hundred times more. The priests couldn't get enough of ringing the bells: so an order was passed, what with the panic caused by the bells ringing and the sale of benches and the curbing of spending, that nobody should be allowed the death-knell, nor should benches be placed, nor should there be a public announcement by the crier, because the sick could hear them, and the healthy took fright as well as the sick. The priests and friars thronged to the rich, and were paid such great sums that they all enriched themselves. And so an ordinance was passed that only one rule [of religious houses] and the local church could be had, and from that rule a maximum of six friars. All harmful fruit, such as unripe plums, unripe almonds, fresh beans, figs and all other inessential unhealthy fruit, was forbidden from entering the city.

Many processions and relics and the painting of Santa Maria Impruneta were paraded around the city, to cries of "Mercy," and with prayers, coming to a halt at the rostrum of the Priori.[1] There peace was made settling great disputes and questions of woundings and killings. Such was the panic this plague provoked that people met for meals as a *brigata* [assembly] to cheer themselves up; one person would offer a dinner to ten friends, and the next evening it would be the turn of one of the others to offer

---

[1] **the Priori:** The nine members of Florence's chief governing body—also known as the Signoria—chosen from the city's chief merchant guilds.

the dinner, and sometimes they thought they were going to dine with him, and he had no dinner ready, because he was ill, and sometimes the dinner had been prepared for ten and two or three less turned up. Some fled to the country, and some to provincial towns, to get a change of air; where there was no plague they brought it, and where it already existed they added to it. No industry was busy in Florence; all the workshops were locked up, all the inns were closed, only chemists and churches were open. Wherever you went, you could find almost nobody; many rich good men were borne from their house to church in their coffin with just four undertakers and a lowly cleric carrying the cross, and even then they demanded a florin apiece. Those who especially profited from the plague were the chemists, the doctors, the poulterers, the undertakers, and the women who sold mallow, nettles, mercury plant and other poultice herbs for drawing abscesses. And those who made the most were these herb sellers. Woolen merchants and retailers when they came across cloth could sell it for whatever price they asked. Once the plague had finished, anybody who could get hold of whatsoever kind of cloth, or found the raw materials to make it, became rich; but many ended up moth-eaten, spoilt and useless for the looms, and thread and raw wool lost in the city and the *contado*. This plague began in March as has been said, and finished in September 1348. And people began to return to their homes and belongings. And such was the number of houses full of goods that had no owner, that it was amazing. Then the heirs to this wealth began to turn up. And someone who had previously had nothing suddenly found himself rich, and couldn't believe it was all his, and even felt himself it wasn't quite right. And both men and women began to show off with clothes and horses.

The quantity of people who died during the plague outbreak of the year of our lord 1348

The bishop and the Signoria in Florence having ordered a careful count of how many were dying of plague in the city of Florence, and seeing finally at the beginning of October that nobody was dying of that pestilence any more, it was discovered that putting together men and women, children and adults, from March to October, ninety-six thousand had died.

Examining the Evidence

1. Many Christians attributed the Black Death to divine wrath and punishment. Does Buonaiuti seem to share this view?

2. According to Buonaiuti's account, what were the economic consequences of the plague in Florence?

3. In what ways did the extensive mortality resulting from the Black Death affect the social order in Florence?

14.2 THE ENGLISH PEASANT REVOLT

Jean Froissart, *Chronicles of England, France, Spain, and the Adjoining Countries* (1400)

Jean Froissart (c. 1337–c. 1410) was born in Valenciennes, in the duchy of Hainault in Flanders, on the eve of the outbreak of the Hundred Years' War (1339–1453) between England and France. Froissart enjoyed a long career as a poet and court historian. He began to compile his *Chronicles*, which cover the years from 1326 to 1400, after arriving in England in 1361, during a truce declared by the English and French monarchs. In England, he gained the patronage of Queen Philippa, who, like Froissart, was a native of Hainault. In 1369, after the war resumed and his benefactress died, Froissart returned to the Continent but continued to work on his voluminous history. The following passages from Froissart's *Chronicles* describe the Peasant Revolt of 1381, which was triggered by a new head tax that King Richard II (r. 1377–1399) had imposed on his subjects.

Jean Froissart, *Chronicles of England, France, Spain, and the Adjoining Countries* (London: William Smith, 1839), 652–653, 657–662, 664.

It is customary in England, as well as in several other countries, for the nobility to have great privileges over the commonalty, whom they keep in bondage; that is to say, they are bound by law and custom to plough the lands of gentlemen, to harvest the grain, to carry it home to the barn, to thrash and winnow it; they are also bound to harvest the hay and bring it home. All these sources they are obliged to perform for their lords, and many more in England than in other countries. The prelates and gentlemen are thus served. In the counties of Kent, Essex, Sussex, and Bedford these services are more oppressive than in all the rest of the kingdom.

The evil-disposed in these districts began to rise, saying, they were too severely oppressed; that at the beginning of the world there were no slaves, and that no one ought to be treated as such, unless he had committed treason against his lord, as Lucifer had done against God; but they had done no such thing, for they were neither angels nor spirits, but men formed after the same likeness with their lords, who treated them as beasts. This they would no longer bear, but had determined to be free, and if they labored or did any other works for the lords, they would be paid for it.

A crazy priest in the county of Kent, called John Ball, who, for his absurd preaching, had been thrice confined in the prison of the archbishop of Canterbury, was greatly instrumental in inflaming them with those ideas. He was accustomed, every Sunday after mass, as the people were coming out of the church, to preach to them in the marketplace and assemble a crowd around him; to whom he would say: "My good friends, things cannot go on well in England, nor ever will until every thing shall be in common; when there shall neither be vassal nor lord, and all distinctions leveled; when the lords shall be no more masters than ourselves. How ill have they used us! And for what reasons do they thus hold us in bondage? Are we not all descended from the same parents, Adam and Eve? And what can they show, or what reasons give, why they should be more the masters than ourselves? Except, perhaps, in making us labor and work, for them to spend. They are clothed in velvets and rich stuffs, ornamented with ermine and other furs, while we are forced to wear poor cloth. They have wines, spices, and fine bread, when we have only rye and the refuse of the straw; and, if we drink, it must be water. . . . Let us go to the king, who is young, and remonstrate with him on our servitude, telling him we must have it otherwise, or that we shall find a remedy for it ourselves. . . . "

On Corpus Christi day King Richard heard mass in the Tower of London, with all his lords, and afterwards entered his barge, attended by the earls of Salisbury, Warwick, and Suffolk, with other knights. He rowed down the Thames toward Rotherhithe, a manor belonging to the crown, where were upwards of ten thousand men, who had come from Blackheath to see the king and to speak to him. When they perceived his barge approach, they set up such shouts and cries as if all the devils in hell had been in their company. . . .

When the king and his lords saw this crowd of people, and the wildness of their manner, there was not one among them so bold and determined, but felt alarmed: the king was advised by his barons not to land. . . ."What do ye wish for?" demanded the king, "I am come hither to hear what you have to say." Those near him cried out with one voice, "We wish thee to land, when we will remonstrate with thee, and tell thee more at our ease what our wants are." The Earl of Salisbury then replied for the king and said, "Gentlemen, you are not properly dressed, nor in a fit condition for the king to talk with you."

Nothing more was said, for the king desired to return to the Tower of London. When the people saw they could obtain nothing more, they were inflamed with passion, and went back to Blackheath, where the main body was, to relate the answer they had received, and how the king was returned to the Tower. They all then cried out, "Let us march instantly to London." They immediately set off, and in their road thither, they destroyed the houses of lawyers, courtiers, and monasteries. Advancing into the suburbs of London, which were very handsome and extensive, they pulled down many fine houses. In particular they demolished the prison of the king called the Marshalsea, and set at liberty all those confined within it. They did much damage to the suburbs, and menaced the Londoners at the entrance of the bridge for having shut the gates of it, saying, they would set fire to the suburbs, take the city by storm, and afterwards burn and destroy it.

With respect to the common people of London, numbers were of their opinions, and on assembling together said, "Why will you refuse admittance to these honest men? They are our friends, and what they are doing is for our good." It was then found necessary to open the gates, when crowds rushed in, and ran to those shops which seemed well stored with provision. If they sought for meat or drink, it was placed before them, and nothing refused, but all manner of good cheer offered, in hopes of appeasing them. . . .

On Friday morning those lodged in the square before St. Catherine's, near the Tower, began to make themselves ready; they shouted much, and said that if the king would not come out to them, they would attack the Tower, storm it, and slay all in it. The king was alarmed at these menaces, and resolved to speak with them; he therefore sent orders for them to retire to a handsome meadow at Mile-end, where, in the summertime, people go to amuse themselves, and that there the king would grant them their demands. . . .

On the king's arrival, attended by the barons, he found upwards of sixty thousand men assembled from different villages and counties of England; he instantly advanced into the midst of them, saying in a pleasant manner, "My good people, I am your king and your lord. What is it you want? And what do you wish to say to me?" Those who heard him answered, "We wish thou wouldst make us free forever: us, our heirs, and our lands, and that we should no longer be called slaves, nor held in bondage." The king replied, "I grant your wish; now, therefore, return to your homes and the places from whence you came, leaving behind two or three men from each village, to whom I will order letters to be given sealed with my seal. . . . " The people were thus quieted, and began to return towards London.

On the Saturday morning . . . all the rabble were again assembled, under the conduct of Wat Tyler, Jack Straw, and John Ball, to parley at a place called Smithfield. . . . These reprobates wanted to pillage the city this same day, their leaders saying, ". . . The pardons which the king has granted us will not be of much use to us. . . . If we now plunder the city of the wealth that is in it, we shall have been beforehand, and shall not have repent of so doing; but if we wait for their arrival, they will wrest it from us." To this opinion all had agreed, when the king appeared in sight, attended by sixty horse. . . .

Wat Tyler, seeing the king, said to his men, "Here is the king. I will go and speak with him; do not stir from hence until I give you a signal." . . . On saying this he spurred the horse on which he rode and, leaving his men, galloped up to the king, and came so near that his horse's head touched the crupper of that of the king. The first words he said, when he addressed the king, were, "King, dost thou see all those men there?" "Yes," replied the king, "why dost thou ask?" "Because they are all under my command, and have sworn by their faith and loyalty to do whatever I shall order." "Very well," said the king, "I have no objections to it." Tyler, who was only desirous of a riot, answered, "And thinkest thou, king, that those people and as many more who are in the city, also under my command, ought to depart without having had thy letters? Oh no, we will carry them with us." "Why," replied the king, "so it has been ordered, and they will be delivered out one after the other. But friend, return to thy companions, and tell them to depart from London. Be peaceable and careful of yourselves, for it is our determination that you shall all of you have your letters by villages and towns, as it had been agreed upon."

As the king finished speaking, Wat Tyler, casting his eyes around him, spied a squire attached to the king's person bearing his sword. Tyler mortally hated this squire; formerly they had had words together, when the squire ill-treated him. . . . [Tyler demanded:] "Give me that sword." "I will not," replied the squire, "for it is the king's sword, and thou are not worthy to bear it, who art but a mechanic; and if only thou and I were together, thou wouldst not have dared to say what thou hast for as large a heap of gold as this church." "By my troth," answered Tyler, "I will not eat this day before I have thy head." At these words the mayor of London, with about twelve more, rode forward, armed under their robes. . . . "Truly," [said] the mayor, who found himself supported by the king, "does it become such a stinking rascal as thou art to use such speech in the presence of the king, my natural lord? I will not live a day, if thou pay not for it." Upon this, he drew a kind of scimitar he wore, and struck Tyler such a blow on the head as felled him to his horse's feet. When he was down, he was surrounded on all sides, so that his men could not see him; and one of the king's squires, called John Standwich, immediately leaped from his horse and, drawing a handsome sword which he bore, thrust it into his belly, and thus killed him. . . .

[The king's men quickly routed the insurgents.]

A proclamation was made through all the streets, that every person who was not an inhabitant of London, and who had not resided there for a whole year, should instantly depart. . . . After this proclamation had been heard, no one dared to infringe it; but all departed instantly to their homes, quite

discomfited. John Ball and Jack Straw were found hidden in an old ruin, thinking to steal away; but this they could not do, for they were betrayed by their own men. The king and the lords were well pleased with their seizure; their heads were cut off, as was that of Tyler, and fixed on London Bridge.

Examining the Evidence

1. How do the leaders of the rebellion justify their demands for social equality?
2. Does Froissart portray King Richard as a hero?
3. Do Froissart's sympathies lie with the rebels or the nobles? Why?

14.3	THE MING EMPEROR'S RULES FOR VILLAGE GOVERNMENT

Emperor Hongwu, *The Placard of the People's Instructions* (1398)

In 1368, Zhu Yuanzhang, a general of peasant birth who had taken up arms against the Mongol rulers of China, founded his new Ming (1368–1644) dynasty. During his reign as Emperor Hongwu (r. 1368–1398), China's new sovereign dedicated himself to reasserting Chinese culture by restoring Confucian values and traditions. But Hongwu also was deeply skeptical about the scholar–official elite who traditionally dominated Chinese government and society. Therefore, he created a system of village self-government that would protect ordinary people from abuses of power by imperial officials. Shortly before his death, Hongwu issued the "Placard of the People's Instructions" in forty-one articles to set down rules that he hoped would preserve his principles of civil governance—and his dynasty—for all time.

Since ancient times, rulers have represented Heaven in managing human affairs by setting up separate offices to order the various affairs and bring peace to the lives of the people. Worthies and

gentlemen of bygone times feared only that they would not be employed by their rulers. All who were employed exerted the utmost diligence to serve the rulers, thus bringing glory to their parents, wives and children, and to establish fine reputations in the world. How could there have been any lawbreaking conduct? Therefore, the officials were competent for their posts and the people were content in their livelihoods. Since the world was unified I have set up the cardinal principles, promulgated laws and established offices according to ancient rules: in the capital, the six ministries and the Censorate; in the provinces, the provincial administration commissions, the provincial surveillance commissions, prefectures, subprefectures, and districts. Although the titles are different from previous dynasties the system of government is the same.

That most of the appointed officials are from among the common people could not be helped. For some time it has been difficult to tell whether they were virtuous or wicked. Scholars are not real scholars and the officials are all cunning. They often take bribes and break the law, turn benevolence and

---

Edward L. Farmer, *Zhu Yuanzhang and Early Ming Legislation: The Reordering of Chinese Society Following the Era of Mongol Rule* (Leiden The Netherlands: Brill, 1995), 197–201, 204–206.

righteousness upside down, and injure the good people, so that the common people bring all of their complaints to the capital. So it has been for years without cease. Now this order is promulgated to declare to the people of the realm that all minor matters concerning households and marriage, land, and disputes involving assault and battery shall be judged by the elders and the community headmen. Serious matters involving sexual crime, robbery, fraud, or homicide shall be reported to the officials. After this order is promulgated, any officials or functionaries who dare to confound it shall be sentenced to the death penalty. For those commoners who dare to confound it, their entire families shall be banished to the frontiers. . . .

1. In all minor matters involving household and marriage, land, assault and battery, and disputes among the people, it is not permitted to bring lawsuits directly to government offices. These matters must go through the local community headmen and elders for judgment. Those who do not go to the community headmen and elders, regardless of the merits of the cases, shall be sentenced to beating with sixty strokes of the heavy stick and the cases sent back to the community headmen and elders for judgment.

2. The elders and community headmen live close to and have fields side by side with the common people of the village . . . so that matters of right and wrong, good and evil, are all known to them. Whenever there is an accusation from the people, a meeting shall be held immediately and the case judged fairly. The bamboo or thorn stick may be used for appropriate torture. If the case cannot be settled, causing the people to go bother the government offices, the community headmen and elders shall each be sentenced to sixty strokes of the heavy stick. Those who are over seventy years of age shall not be beaten, but redeem the punishment according to the [statutes of the *Ming Law*] *Code*. They shall still make an appropriate judgment in the case. If they act wrongly out of personal consideration and confound right and wrong, the community headmen and elders shall be punished for the crimes of judges implicating the innocent and exonerating the guilty.

The litigations which shall be judged by the elders and community headmen are as follows: household and marriage, land, assault and battery, suits over ownership, fires, theft, abusive language, money lending, gambling, eating fruits of gardens and orchards without permission, illegal killing of plowing oxen, discarding or destroying utensils or crops, animals biting and killing people, unauthorized use of property by junior or younger members of the family, dishonoring the spirits, son or grandson violating instructions, witchcraft and heterodoxy, domestic animals trampling or eating crops, equally dividing irrigation water. . . .

12. After a case among the common people has been settled by the elders and community headmen, if crafty persons disagree with the judgment and repeatedly appeal to the officials by fabricating evidence and making false accusations, they shall be sentenced to capital punishment and their families banished to the frontier. If the officials fail to check the reasons for accepting appeals, thereby taking bribes and practicing fraud, they shall all be punished.

13. Elders and community headmen, when judging suits, shall not establish a jail. Regardless of [what crimes] men or women commit, they shall not be imprisoned. The interrogation takes place during the day and the accused shall be released at night. If the case is not settled they shall return the next day for questioning. . . .

17. The elders of each [village] shall send reports of the facts of good conduct of filial sons, obedient grandsons, virtuous husbands, chaste widows, or even persons having only a single praiseworthy virtue to the Imperial Court, and to the officials who shall then forward them to the Court. . . .

25. Villagers are not equal in wealth. No family is without the happy and sad events of marriages and funerals. From now on, the households of the community shall help one another whenever these events occur. For example, in case the marriage of the child of a certain poor family cannot be managed temporarily, if every household of the community contributes one *guan* of paper currency and there are a hundred households, there will be

one hundred *guan*; if every household contributes five *guan*, there will be five hundred *guan*. With help like this, could it not be accomplished? From now on when a family has a marriage this rule shall be used to take turns giving help. If the father or the mother of a family dies and has to be buried, each family shall contribute some amount of money or some rice to help the family with the inner and outer coffins, or rites performed by Buddhist or Daoist priests to secure a good destiny for the deceased. . . .

27. The purpose of the community wine drinking ceremony is to rank the elder and younger and distinguish the worthy from the unworthy. This is a good way to improve customs. The people have already been ordered to carry it out. Now it is declared again: it must be carried out in accordance with the regulations previously issued; elder and younger are to be seated in ranked order, the worthy and unworthy are to be seated separately. When this is done for a long time, will not the people pursue good and avoid evil? The customs will be pure and honest and every individual will become a good subject. . . .

29. Now the realm is at peace. Except for paying taxes and performing corvée [compulsory] labor service, the people do not have other obligations. Everyone shall be attentive to his livelihood so as to have sufficient clothing and food. It is essential that every household follow the regulations in planting mulberries, dates, persimmons, and cotton. Every year silkworms shall be reared. The production of silk and cotton will be sufficient to provide clothing. The dates and persimmons during the prosperous years can be exchanged for money, and during the lean years they can be used for food. Such activity is beneficial to you people. The community headmen and the elders shall oversee and inspect as usual. If any dare to disobey, their families shall be banished to the frontier. . . .

31. From the ancient times, the purpose of the people's paying taxes and performing corvée service is essentially to secure peace. In recent years, those in office are incompetent, officials and functionaries are unable to teach people to do good and are bent solely on taking bribes. When the time comes for tax collection and corvée service, they always receive money in return for extending the time limit, exempting the duties of the rich and sending the poor to perform them instead. This causes the ignorant people to follow their example: to refuse to pay their allocated taxes punctually, to claim to have sold grain which they actually still have, to refuse to perform their share of corvée service. From now on, when paying taxes and performing corvée service, the people shall not bribe the officials. The allocated taxes shall be paid punctually, and their corvée service shall be performed on time. If taxes have already been paid and the corvée service performed but the officials, functionaries, tax captains, and community headmen collect them again the suffering families may gather a number of people to tie up the offenders and send them to the capital for severe punishment. . . .

33. The favor which our parents bestow in giving us birth is extremely great. Their toilsome labors of nurture are recorded in detail in the *Grand Pronouncements*. Now it is declared again that among the people those who have living agnatic [related through male kin] grandparents and parents shall unstintingly support them in accordance with their families' means. Those whose agnatic grandparents and parents are dead shall sacrifice to them at the appointed times to show their filial respects. Parents shall instruct their children; children shall be filial to their agnatic uncles; wives shall encourage their husbands to do good. In this way the clans will become harmonious, no one will break the law, and parents, wives, and children will care for one another day and night. Will this not lead naturally to the enjoyment of peace?

Examining the Evidence

1. What are the chief responsibilities that the emperor delegated to village leaders, and what powers did he reserve for government officials?
2. In what ways was the emperor's conception of village self-government modeled on the family institution?
3. What seem to have been the most common sources of dispute and social conflict in Chinese villages? Why might this have been the case?

14.4 RELIGIOUS ALLEGORY IN PERSIAN MANUSCRIPT ILLUMINATIONS

Prince Humay Meets the Lady Humayun in Her Garden by Moonlight (Early Fifteenth Century)

"Persian miniature painting" is a conventional term for manuscript illuminations that embellished Persian-language books composed throughout the eastern half of the Islamic world, from Istanbul to Delhi. Persian miniature painting reached its height of accomplishment during the heyday of the Ottoman, Safavid, and Mughal empires in the fifteenth and sixteenth centuries. In addition to its eclectic blend of Islamic motifs, Persian miniature painting also reflects the influence of Chinese paintings that circulated throughout Asia during the Mongol era.

One of the major inspirations for Persian miniature painting was "The Romance of Humay and Humayun," an allegorical tale of the quest of the human soul to achieve mystical union with God. The poem was written in Persian by Khwaju Kirmani (1290–1353), who dedicated it to the Ilkhan ruler Abu Said (r. 1316–1335). It describes the pilgrimage undertaken by Humay, a Syrian prince, after a dream in which he is transported to an enchanted castle where he sees an image of the Chinese princess Humayun. The vision arouses the prince's desire, and upon awakening he sets out for China. His journey and his eventual meeting with the Chinese princess, conveyed in romantic and at times erotic imagery, was intended to symbolize the mystical pursuit and apprehension of the divine associated with the Sufi tradition of Islam. The prince's journey from Syria (the Persian word for Syria also means "dusk" or "misfortune") to China (the dawning east) also signifies the spiritual awakening of the soul aroused by contemplation of divine beauty.

The illustration shown here [*See next page*] was composed by an unknown artist in Iran in the early fifteenth century. In this scene Humay in his dream sees Humayun in her fairyland garden. Enchanted by the beauty of the Chinese princess, Humay calls out to her in the verses from Khwaju's poem that appear in the upper right-hand corner:

> Your waist is fine and finer than a single hair,
> From grief I waste and thinner wax
> Than a single hair in a ringlet twisted
> Upon a pyre:
> Like a Hindu prince casting himself into my sati's[1]
>   flame
> Before the ringlet
> Of Your sun-like Face, I fall into my flame
> And never saw an icon like unto your Face—
> No! Not a trace! What icon here?
> Nor ever did I hear the like of You!

Examining the Evidence

1. How does the painter portray the Chinese setting through motifs that would seem exotic to a Muslim audience?

2. In what ways do the painting and Khwaju's poem reflect the cultural synthesis that emerged in Islamic Central Asia in the aftermath of Mongol conquests?

3. Why would Muslims deem feminine beauty and romantic courtship appropriate metaphors for a spiritual quest? Why might some Muslims object?

---

[1] **Sati:** The Hindu practice whereby a widow casts herself onto the burning pyre of her deceased husband to accompany him in death.

Poem translation, Michael Barry, *Figurative Art in Medieval Islam and the Riddle of Bihzad of Herat (1465–1535)* (Paris: Flammarion, 2004), 130.

The Persian Price Humay Meeting the Chinese Princess Humayun in a Garden, c. 1450 (gouache on paper) by Islamic School (fifteenth century). Musée des Arts Decoratifs, Paris, France/ Giraudon/Bridgeman Images.

14.5 THE FALL OF CONSTANTINOPLE TO THE OTTOMAN TURKS

Nestor-Iskander, *Tale of the Capture of Constantinople* (c. 1500)

Nestor-Iskander's "Tale of the Capture of Constantinople" purportedly is an eyewitness account of the Ottoman Turks' conquest of the Byzantine capital in 1453. The author, who wrote in Russian, claimed to have been taken captive by the Turks as a boy and forced to fight on their side. However, his version of events contains several glaring inaccuracies. Most likely, this account was compiled from various Greek and Russian sources by an educated person, probably an Orthodox monk. At the conclusion of his narrative Nestor-Iskander cites an old Byzantine prophecy, predicting that the "red-haired" people (*rhusios*) would become masters of Constantinople. In Nestor-Iskander's telling, however, *rhusios* is rendered as "the Rus," that is, the Russians. He takes this prophecy to mean that Moscow would succeed Constantinople as "the Third Rome," and that Moscow's metropolitan would replace Constantinople's patriarch as the head of the Orthodox Christian Church.

The godless Sultan Mohammed [Mehmed II, r. 1451–1481], son of Murad [Murad II, r. 1421–1451], who at that time ruled the Turks, took note of all the problems that plagued Constantinople. And, although he professed peace, he wanted to put an end to Emperor Constantine XI [r. 1449–1453]. Towards that end he assembled a large army and, by land and by sea, suddenly appeared with that large force before the city and laid siege to it. The Emperor, his nobles, and the rest of the population did not know what to do. . . . The Emperor . . . sent his envoys to Sultan Mehmed in order to discuss peace and past relations. But Mehmed did not trust them, and as soon as the envoys departed, he ordered cannons and guns to fire at the city. Others were commanded to make ready wall-scaling equipment and

build assault structures. Such city inhabitants as Greeks, Venetians, and Genoese left because they did not want to fight the Turks. . . .

When the Emperor saw this exodus, he ordered his nobles and high officials to assign the remaining soldiers to each sector of the city's wall, to main gates, and to windows. The entire population was mobilized and alarm bells were hoisted throughout the city. Each person was informed of his assignment and each was told to defend his country. . . . Meanwhile, day and night, the Turks bombarded all parts of the city without stopping, and gave its defenders no time to rest. They also made preparations for the final assault. This activity went on for thirteen days.

On the fourteenth day, after they had said their heathen prayers, the Turks sounded trumpets, beat their drums, and played on all other of their musical instruments. Then they brought many cannons and guns closer to the walls and began to bombard the city. They also fired their muskets and thousands of arrows. Because of continued heavy shooting, city defenders could not stand safely on the wall. Some crouched down awaiting the attack; others fired their cannons and guns as much as they could, killing many Turks. The Patriarch, bishops, and all clergy prayed constantly, pleading for God's mercy and for His help in saving the city.

When the Turks surmised that they had killed all the defenders on the wall, they ordered their forces to give a loud shout. Some soldiers carried incendiary devices, others ladders, still others wall-destroying equipment, and the rest many other instruments of destruction. They were ordered to attack and capture the city. City defenders, too, cried out and shouted back and engaged them in fierce battle. The Emperor toured the city, encouraging his people, promising them God's help and ordering the ringing of church

A. Stender-Petersen, ed., *Anthology of Old Russian Literature* (New York: Columbia University Press, 1954), 214–220.

bells so as to summon all the inhabitants to defend their city. When the Turks heard the ringing of church bells, they ordered their trumpets, flutes, and thousands of other musical instruments to sound out. And there was a great and terrible slaughter! . . .

Deploying all of these forces the Turks concentrated their assault on the Poloe Mesto. When city defenders retreated from the Poloe Mesto, Turkish foot soldiers hurriedly cleared the way for other units to advance. Turkish units broke through and their light cavalry units overwhelmed city defenders. All city inhabitants came to the rescue of city commanders, dignitaries, and the regular forces, and they engaged the Turks. The Emperor joined the battle with all of his nobles, his special cavalry units, and his foot soldiers. They attacked the Turks inside the city, engaged them in fierce hand-to-hand combat, and drove them away from the Poloe Mesto. . . .

When Mehmed learned about the death of his eastern military commander, he wept profusely because he admired the commander's bravery and wisdom. He also became very angry and led all of his forces to the Sublime Porte. He ordered that the Emperor's positions be bombarded with cannons and guns, being concerned that the Emperor's forces might attack him. Then, the godless Mehmed appeared opposite the Poloe Mesto and ordered his forces to fire cannons and guns at defenders in order to induce them to retreat. He also instructed the Turkish admiral Balta-Oghlu, in charge of many regiments and a select force of 3,000, to capture the Emperor dead or alive.

When they noticed the determination of the godless Mehmed, the Byzantine military commanders, officials, and nobles joined the battle and implored the Emperor to leave in order to escape death. He wept bitterly and told them, "Remember the words I said earlier! Do not try to protect me! I want to die with you!" And they replied, "All of us will die for God's church and for you!" . . .

The impious Mehmed then ordered all of his forces to occupy all city streets and gates in order to capture the Emperor. In his camp he retained only the Janissaries,[1] who readied their cannons

and guns in fear of a sudden attack by the emperor. Sensing God's command, the Emperor went to the Great Church [Hagia Sophia], where he fell to the ground pleading for God's mercy and forgiveness for his sins. Then he bade farewell to the Patriarch, the clergy, and the Empress, bowed to those who were present and left the church. Then all the clergy, indeed the entire people, countless women and children, cried and moaned, hoping that their plea would reach heaven. As he left the church the Emperor said, "If you want to suffer for God's church and the Orthodox faith, then follow me!"

Then he mounted his horse and went to the Golden Gate, hoping to encounter there the godless. He was able to attract some 3,000 soldiers. Near the Gate they met a multitude of Turks whom they defeated. The Emperor wanted to reach the Gate but could not on account of many corpses. Then he encountered another large Turkish force and they fought till darkness. In this manner the Orthodox Emperor Constantine suffered for God's churches and for the Orthodox faith. On May 29, according to eyewitnesses, he killed more than 600 Turks with his own hand. And the saying was fulfilled: "It started with Constantine, and it ended with Constantine." . . .

[After the capture of the city, the sultan, accompanied by his high officials,] went from the Sublime Porte to the Gate of St. Romanus to a church where the Patriarch, his clergy, and a multitude of people, including women and children, were assembled. He came to the square before the church, dismounted his horse, prostrated himself on the ground, put a handful of dust on his head, and thanked God. And, as he admired the wonderful structure, he said, "Truly no one can transcend the people who are here and who were here before!"

Then he went inside the church. The holy place resembled a wasteland. He stopped at a place reserved for the highest dignitaries. The Patriarch, his clergy, and all who were present there cried, sobbed, and knelt before him. With his hands he motioned for them to rise and then said, "Athanasius! I am telling you, your suite and all of your people: From now on, do not fear my anger. Henceforth neither killing nor enslavement will be permitted!" . . .

---

[1] **Janissaries:** An elite corps of slave–soldiers who served as the Ottoman sultan's household troops and bodyguards.

Then [the sultan] went to the imperial palace. There he met a certain Serb who handed him the Emperor's [Constantine's] head. Mehmed was pleased with it and called Byzantine nobles and military commanders and asked them to verify whether or not the head was really the Emperor's. Because they were afraid, they all said, "It is the Emperor's head!" He examined it and said, "It is clear that God is the creator of all, including emperors. Why then does everyone have to die?"

Then he sent the head to the Patriarch, instructing him to inlay it with gold and silver and to preserve it the best he knew how. The Patriarch placed it in a silver chest, gilded it, and hid it under the altar of the great church. I have heard from others that the survivors of the battle at the Golden Gate where the Emperor was killed took the Emperor's corpse that night and buried it in Galati. . . .

---

[2] **Methodius of Patera . . . Leo the Wise:** Methodius was a third-century church father and martyr; Leo the Wise (Leo VI), emperor of Byzantium from 886 to 912, was said to have been the author of several prophetic books.

All of this happened as a consequence of our sins, that the godless Mehmed ascended the imperial throne. . . . Yet, those who know history also know that all of this was prophesied by Methodius of Patera and by Leo the Wise[2] concerning the destiny of this city. Its past has been fulfilled and so will be its future. For it is written: "A nation of Rus, as has been prophesied in the vision of St. Daniel, will triumph. And they will inherit the traditions of the seven hills [Rome], as well as its laws, and will disseminate them among five or six nations that comprise Rus, and they will implant seeds among them and will harvest many benefits."

Examining the Evidence

1. In Nestor-Iskander's account, how and why did the Turks succeed in capturing Constantinople?
2. In what ways does the author depict Emperor Constantine as a hero?
3. Does Nestor-Iskander portray the Ottoman conquest of Constantinople as a catastrophe for the Christian religion? Why or why not?

14.6   THE SULTAN OF MALI

Ibn Battuta, *Rihla* (1356)

A native of Morocco, Ibn Battuta (1304–1368) set out on a pilgrimage to Mecca in 1325 that extended into a series of journeys lasting nearly thirty years, taking him to every corner of the Muslim world. He made his final journey, an expedition across the Sahara Desert to the sultanate of Mali in West Africa—known among Arabs as the Sudan, "the country of the blacks"—in 1352–1353. Upon his return to Morocco, Ibn Battuta composed a *rihla*, or travel diary. As a literary genre, *rihla* flowered among North African Muslims during this time. Most were written by pilgrims to Mecca who surveyed the places, people, and customs they visited. Ibn Battuta's more ambitious work drew both on his personal experiences

and on other writings and legendary lore. His account of Mali seems to have been based on his personal experiences.

The Sultan of Mali

He is the sultan Mansa Sulayman. *Mansa* means "sultan" and Sulayman is his name. He is a miserly king from whom no great donation is to be expected. It happened that I remained for this period without seeing him on account of my illness. Then he gave a memorial feast for our lord Abu'l-Hasan [sultan of Morocco, r. 1331–1348] (may God be content with him) and invited the emirs and *faqihs* [jurists] and the *qadi* [chief judge] and the

Nehemia Levtzion and Jay Spaulding, eds., *Medieval West Africa: Views from Arab Scholars and Merchants* (Princeton, NJ: Markus Wiener, 2003), 72–73, 75, 78–83.

khatib [prayer leader], and I went with them. They brought copies of the Qur'an and the Qur'an was recited in full. . . .

Their trivial reception gift and their respect for it

When I departed the reception a gift was sent to me and dispatched to the *qadi*'s house. The *qadi* sent it with his men to the house of Ibn al-Faqih. Ibn al-Faqih hastened out of his house barefooted and came in to me saying, "Come! The cloth and gift of the sultan have come to you!" I got up, thinking that it would be robes of honor and money, but behold! It was three loaves of bread and a piece of beef fried in *gharti* and a gourd containing yogurt. When I saw it I laughed, and was long astonished at their feeble intellect and their respect for mean things.

My speaking to the Sultan after this and his kindness toward me

After this reception gift I remained for two months during which the sultan sent nothing to me and the month of Ramadan came in. Meanwhile I frequented the *mashwar* [council-place] and used to greet him and sit with the *qadi* and *khatib*. I spoke with Dugha the interpreter, who said, "Speak with him, and I will express what you want to say in the proper fashion." So when he held a session at the beginning of Ramadan I stood before him and said, "I have journeyed to the countries of the world and met their kings. I have been four months in your country without your giving me a reception gift or anything else. What shall I say of you in the presence of other sultans?" He replied, "I have not seen you or known about you." The *qadi* and Ibn al-Faqih rose and replied to him saying, "He greeted you and you sent to him some food." Thereupon he ordered that a house be provided for me to stay in and an allowance be allotted to me. Then, on the night of 27 Ramadan, he distributed among the *qadi* and the *khatib* and the *faqihs* a sum of money that they call *zakah* and gave

to me 33-1/3 *mithqals* [of gold].[1] When I departed he bestowed on me 100 *mithqals* of gold. . . .

The self-debasement of the Sudan before their king

The Sudan are the humblest of people before their king and the most submissive towards him. They swear by his name, saying *"Mansa Sulayman ki."* When he calls to one of them at his sessions in the pavilion, the person called takes off his clothes and puts on ragged clothes, and removes his turban and puts on a dirty *shashiyya* [cap], and goes in holding up his garments and trousers half-way up his leg, and advances with submissiveness and humility. He then beats the ground vigorously with his two elbows, and stands like one performing a *rak'a* [prayer cycle] to listen to his words.

If one of them addresses the sultan and the latter replies, he uncovers the clothes from his back and sprinkles dust on his head and back, like one washing with water. I used to marvel how their eyes did not become blinded.

An amusing story about the poets' reciting to the sultan

On the feast day, when Dugha has finished his performance, the poets come. They are called *jula*, of which the singular is *jali*. Each of them has enclosed himself within an effigy made of feathers, resembling a bird called *shaqshaq*, on which is fixed a head made of wood with a red beak as though it were the head of the *shaqshaq*. They stand in front of the sultan in this comical shape and recite their poems. I was told that their poetry was a kind of exhortation in which they say to the sultan, "This *banbi* [dais] on which you are sitting was sat upon by such-and-such a king and among his good deeds were so-and-so; and such-and-such a king, and among his good deeds were so-and-so, so you too do good deeds which will be remembered after you." Then the chief of the poets mounts the steps of the *banbi* and places his head in the lap of the sultan. Then he mounts to the top of the *banbi* and places his head on the sultan's right shoulder, then upon his left shoulder, talking in their language. Then he descends. I was

---

[1] *mithqal*: A unit of measurement (4.25 grams) mostly used to weigh precious metals.

informed that this act was already old before Islam, and they had continued with it. . . .

Anecdote

It happened during my sojourn at Mali that the sultan was displeased with his chief wife, the daughter of his maternal uncle, called Qasa. The meaning of *qasa* with them is "queen." She was his partner in rule according to the custom of the Sudan, and her name was mentioned with his from the pulpit. He imprisoned her in the house of one of the *farariyya* [chiefs] and appointed in her place his other wife Banju, who was not of royal blood. People talked much about this and disapproved of his act. His female cousins went in to congratulate Banju on her queenship. They put ashes on their forearms and did not scatter dust on their heads. Then the sultan released Qasa from her confinement. His cousins went in to congratulate her on her release and scattered dust over themselves according to the custom. Banju complained about this to the sultan and he was angry with his cousins. They were afraid of him and sought sanctuary in the mosque. He pardoned them and summoned them into his presence. The women's custom when they go into the sultan's presence is that they divest themselves of their clothes and enter naked. This they did and he was pleased with them. They proceeded to come to the door of the sultan morning and evening for a period of seven days, this being the practice of anyone whom the sultan has pardoned.

Qasa began to ride every day with her slave girls and men with dust on their heads and to stand by the council face veiled, her face being invisible. The emirs talked much about her affair, so the sultan gathered them at the council place and said to them through Dugha: "You have been talking a great deal about the affair of Qasa. She has committed a great crime." Then one of her slave girls was brought forth bound and shackled and he said to her, "Say what you have to say!" She informed them that Qasa had sent her to Jatil, the sultan's cousin who was in flight from him at Kanburni, and invited him to depose the sultan from his kingship, saying, "I and all the army are at your service!" When the emirs heard that they said, "Indeed, that is a great crime and for it she deserves to be killed!" Qasa was fearful at

this and sought refuge at the house of the *khatib*. It is their custom there that they seek sanctuary in the mosque, or if that is not possible then in the house of the *khatib*.

The Sudan disliked Mansa Sulayman on account of his avarice. Before him was the king Mansa Magha, and before Mansa Magha, Mansa Musa. Mansa Musa was generous and virtuous. He liked white men and treated them kindly. It was he who gave to Abu Ishaq al-Sahili in a single day 4,000 *mithqals*. Reliable persons have informed me that he gave to Mudrik b. Faqqus 3,000 *mithqals* in a single day. His grandfather Sariq Jata embraced Islam at the hands of the grandfather of this Mudrik. . . .

What I approved of and what I disapproved of among the acts of the Sudan

One of their good features is their lack of oppression. They are the farthest removed of people from it and their sultan does not permit anyone to practice it. Another is the security embracing the whole country, so that neither the traveler there nor dweller has anything to fear from thief or usurper. Another is that they do not interfere with the wealth of any white man who dies among them. They simply leave it in the hands of a trustworthy white man until the one to whom it is due takes it. Another is their assiduity [diligence] in prayer and their persistence in performing it in congregation and beating their children to make them perform it. If it is Friday and a man does not go early to the mosque he will not find anywhere to pray because of the press of people. It is their habit that every man sends his servant with his prayer-mat to spread it for him in a place that he thereby has a right to until he goes to the mosque. Their prayer-carpets are made from the fronds of a tree resembling the palm that has no fruit. Another of their good features is their dressing in fine white clothes on Friday. If any one of them possesses nothing but a ragged shirt he washes it and cleanses it and attends the Friday prayer in it. Another is their eagerness to memorize the great Qur'an. . . .

One of their disapproved acts is that their female servants and slave girls and little girls appear before men naked, with their privy parts uncovered.

During Ramadan I saw many of them in this state, for it is the custom of the *farariyya* to break their fast in the house of the sultan, and each one brings his food carried by twenty or more of his slave girls, they all being naked. Another is that their women go into the sultan's presence naked and uncovered, and that his daughters go naked. . . . Another is their sprinkling dust and ashes on their their heads out of good manners. . . . Another is that many of them eat carrion, and dogs, and donkeys.

Examining the Evidence

1. What is Ibn Battuta's initial opinion of the Mali sultan Sulayman? Does his assessment of the sultan's character change over the course of his stay in Mali?
2. What features of West African society does Ibn Battuta approve of, and what features does he find offensive?
3. What does Ibn Battuta's account reveal about the place of women in Mali society?

14.7 GLORIOUS VENICE

Marin Sanudo, *In Praise of the City of Venice* (1493)

In the fifteenth century, Venice reached its height as the dominant mercantile empire of the Mediterranean. Venice's commercial success, however, stemmed more from its military power and economic strength than from the entrepreneurial savvy of its seagoing traders. Thus, the well-being of the Venetian state became the chief priority of government and citizens alike. "In Praise of the City of Venice" was written in 1493 by a humanist scholar, Marin Sanudo (1466–1536), in homage to the wealth and power of his native city. Sanudo traced the founding of Venice in the fifth century to mainlanders who fled to this island refuge to escape the Huns and other barbarian invaders. However, he insisted that from its beginning Venice was blessed by liberty, wealth, and, above all, Christian piety.

This city of Venice is a free city, a common home to all men, and it has never been subjugated to anyone, as have been all other cities. It was built by Christians, not voluntarily but out of fear, not by deliberate decision but from necessity. Moreover it was founded not by shepherds as Rome was, but by powerful and rich people, such as have ever been since that time, with their faith in Christ, an obstacle to barbarians and attackers. . . .

David Chambers and Brian Pullan, eds., *Venice: A Documentary History, 1450–1630* (Oxford: Blackwell, 1992), 4–7, 11–13, 16–17, 20–21.

This city, amidst the billowing waves of the sea, stands on the crest of the main, almost like a queen restraining its force. It is situated in salt water and built there, because before there were just lagoons, and then, wanting to expand, firm ground was needed for the building of palaces and houses. These are being constructed all the time; they are built above the water by a very ingenious method of driving piles, so that the foundations are in water. Every day the tide rises and falls, but the city remains dry. At times of very low tides, it is difficult to go by boat to wherever one wants. The city is about 7 miles in circumference; it has no surrounding walls, no gates which are locked at night, no sentry keeping watch as other cities have for fear of enemies; it is so very safe at present, that no one can attack or frighten it. As another writer has said, its name has achieved such dignity and renown that it is fair to say Venice merits the title "Pillar of Italy"; "deservedly it may be called the bosom of Christendom." For it takes pride of place before all others, if I may say so, in prudence, fortitude, magnificence, benignity, and clemency; everyone throughout the world testifies to this. To conclude, this city was built more by divine than human will. . . .

The population of the city, according to a census which was made, is about 150,000 souls. There are three classes of inhabitants: gentlemen [nobles] who govern the state and republic, whose families will be mentioned below; citizens; and artisans or the lower class. The gentlemen are not distinguished from the citizens by their clothes, because they all dress in much the same way, except for the senatorial office-holders, who during their term of office have to wear the colored robes laid down by law. . . . The majority are merchants and all go to do business on Rialto. . . .

Venice is divided into six *sestieri* [districts]. . . . In [the sestier of San Polo] is the island of Rialto, which I would venture to call the richest place in the whole world. First of all, overlooking the [Grand] Canal, is the grain warehouse, large and well stocked, with two doorways and many booths; there are two lords appointed to supervise it, as I shall relate below. Then you come to Riva del Ferro, so called because iron is sold there; where it ends at the Rialto Bridge is the public weighhouse, where all the merchandise for sale has to be weighed, and the reckonings are made of customs and excise duty. Here is the Rialto itself, which is a piazzetta, not very large at all, where everyone goes both morning and afternoon. Here business deals are made with a single word "yes" or "no." There are a large number of brokers, who are trustworthy; if not they are reprimanded. There are four banks: the Pisani and Lippomani, both patricians, and the Garzoni and Augustini, citizens. They hold very great amounts of money, issue credits under different names, and are called authorized bankers; their decisions are binding. They have charge of the moneys of the Camerlenghi [Treasurers of the Republic]. Furthermore, throughout the said island of Rialto there are storehouses, both on ground level and above, filled with goods of very great value; it would be a marvelous thing were it possible to see everything at once, in spite of the fact that much is being sold all the time. Every year goods come in from both east and west, where galleys are sent on commission from the Signoria [Venice's chief governing body]; they are put in the charge of whoever wants this [responsibility], provided he is a patrician, by public auction. It should be noted that the Venetians, just as they were merchants in the beginning, continue to trade every year; they send galleys to Flanders, the Barbary Coast, Beirut, Alexandria, the Greek lands, and Aigues-Mortes. All the [galley] fleets have a captain elected by the great Council, and the Signoria

appoints the galley patrons by auction at Rialto, i.e., according to whoever bids highest for the galleys. . . .

On the island of Rialto, these stores and warehouses, of which there are such a great number, pay rent for the most part to [the Procurators of] St. Mark's [the public treasury]; a high rent is paid for every small piece of space on Rialto, not only for these properties, but for those belonging to various private persons who rent out shops. Such a shop at Rialto may cost about 100 ducats in rent and be scarcely two paces wide or long. Property here is very expensive. Our own family, the Sanudi, can bear witness to this, having an inn called the Bell at the New Fishmarket. The ground floor is all let out as shops; it is a small place, but from this one building we get about 800 ducats a year in rent, which is a marvelous thing and a huge rent. This is because it is on such a good site; the inn itself brings in 250 ducats, more than the foremost palace in the city; I daresay it is the best property of its sort in Venice. On Rialto, moreover, there are all the skilled crafts; they have their separate streets, as I shall write below.

Here, on the Canal, there are embankments where on one side there are barges for timber, and on the other side for wine; they are rented as though they were shops. There is a very large butchery, which is full every day of good meat, and there is another one at St. Mark's. The Fishmarket overlooks the Grand Canal; here are the most beautiful fish, high in price and of good quality. The fish are caught in the Adriatic Sea by fishermen, for there is a neighborhood in Venice called San Niccolo where only fishermen live, and they speak an ancient Venetian dialect called *nicoloto*. . . . In this city nothing grows, yet whatever you want can be found in abundance. And this is because of the great turnover in merchandise; everything comes here, especially things to eat, from every city and every part of the world, and money is made quickly. . . . And on Rialto the prices of some things are controlled so that those who buy are not cheated. Mutton, sold at the butchery, cannot be sold for more than 3 *soldi* a pound, and if short weight is given the butchers are penalized by the lords in charge of them, because there are officials who weigh the meat which has been sold. . . . Oil is fixed at 4 *soldi* to the pound weight, candles at 4 *soldi* a pound; a barber's charge for hairdressing is the standard 3 *soldi*; a cartload of wood at all times cannot be more than 28 *soldi*, and there are loading-officials of the commune so that justice is done fairly to everyone. And for other goods the saying is "right weight and high price." Other comestibles are sold as they want, but the Guistizia Vecchia, who are lords with special responsibility, are free to fix a just price on things to eat. Thus the city is governed as well as any city in the world has ever been; everything is well ordered, and this is why the city has survived and grown. . . .

It only remains to mention the Ducal Palace, where our most serene Prince resides. It is at St. Mark's and is a most beautiful and worthy building. . . . The outside walls are all worked over and inlaid with white marble and with stones from all over the world. Inside, the walls on the ground floor are gilded and inlaid with paneling so that it is a very beautiful sight. There are four gilded chambers—I never saw any more beautiful—which took a very great time and elaborate workmanship apart from the gold and the labor. Excellent rooms are the Hall of Public Audience and the Hall of the Senate, which they are working on at present and will be very worthy. One can therefore compare the Venetians to the Romans . . . on account of the buildings, both private and public, being erected at the present

time. Indeed it can be said, as another writer has done, that our republic has followed the Romans in being as powerful in military strength as in virtue and learning. . . .

To conclude about the site of Venice: it is a marvelous thing, which must be seen to be believed; its greatness has grown up only through trade, based on navigation to different parts of the world. It is governed by its own statutes and laws, and is not subject to the legal authority of the [Holy Roman] Empire as everywhere else is. . . . And the order with which this holy Republic is governed is a wonder to behold; there is no sedition from the non-nobles [*populo*], no discord among the patricians, but all work together to [the Republic's] increase.

Examining the Evidence

1. According to Sanudo, in what ways did Venice surpass the achievements of ancient Rome? What seems to impress Sanudo the most about Venice?
2. How does Sanudo define the social hierarchy in Venice? Was the Venetian Republic a democracy?
3. What role did the state play in the city's economic life? Would you say that free enterprise prevailed in Venice?

MAKING CONNECTIONS

1. Compare the social turmoil caused by the Black Death in Florence—which experienced its own popular insurrection, the Ciompi revolt, in 1378—with the conflict between the upper and lower classes in England described by Froissart. Why was it unlikely that an uprising like the English Peasant Revolt would occur in the immediate aftermath of the Black Death?
2. Compare and contrast the vision of social order expressed by the Ming emperor Hongwu with Marin Sanudo's depiction of a harmonious society in Venice. Do they share any common principles?
3. Based on his assessment of Islamic practices in West Africa, would Ibn Battuta be likely to approve of the religious sentiments expressed in the painting "Prince Humay Meets the Lady Humayun in Her Garden by Moonlight"?
4. Compare the images of the Byzantine king and the Ottoman sultan in Nestor-Iskander's account of the capture of Constantinople with Ibn Battuta's depiction of the king of Mali. Do they share similar conceptions of the ideal king? Why or why not?

The Early Modern World, 1450–1750

CHAPTER 15

Empires and Alternatives in the Americas, 1430–1530

The native peoples of the Americas adapted to diverse environments over the course of thousands of years, and in Mesoamerica (roughly Mexico and part of Central America) and the Andes (the western spine of South America), they developed complex empires that flourished in early modern times. Because only the Maya developed a decipherable writing system, however, most documents relating to the era before the arrival of the Europeans and Africans were composed soon after contact and conquest in the sixteenth and seventeenth centuries. The following selections offer glimpses of key concerns in religious, political, and everyday life from the Aztec, Inca, and Eastern Woodlands regions.

15.1 AZTEC SACRIFICE

Florentine Codex (c. 1540–1560)

One of the most comprehensive sources on Aztec life and history is known as the *Florentine Codex*. Now housed in a museum in Florence, Italy, it is a series of manuscripts compiled by the Spanish Franciscan priest Bernardino de Sahagún several decades after the Spanish Conquest. Despite Sahagún's oversight role, the codex was largely composed and entirely illustrated by a team of Aztecs and former Aztec subjects. Beginning in the 1520s, Aztec boys were trained by Franciscan missionaries to adapt Spanish phonetics and the Latin alphabet to Nahuatl, making it a true written language for the first time. The following selection, translated directly from courtly Nahuatl, describes the sacrificial feast of Toxcatl, in which a captive warrior impersonated the god Tezcatlipoca for an entire year.

In the time of Toxcatl there was Tezcatlipoca's great festival. At that time he was given human form; at that time he was set up. Wherefore died his impersonator, who for one year had lived [as Tezcatlipoca].

And at that time was appointed his [new] impersonator, who would again live [as Tezcatlipoca] for a year.

For many impersonators were living, whom stewards in various places guarded; whom they maintained. About ten [so] lived. These were indeed selected captives; they were selected when captives were taken. There one was chosen if he was seen to be suitable, if he was fair of body. Then he was taken. They entrusted these to stewards. But one destined to be a slave, him the captor slew.

Indeed he who was thus chosen was of fair countenance, of good understanding, quick, of clean body, slender, reed-like, long and thin, like a stout cane, like a stone column all over, not of overfed body, not corpulent, nor very small, nor exceedingly tall. . . .

For him who was thus, who had no flaw, who had no [bodily] defects, who had no blemish, who had no mark, who had on him no wart, [no such] small tumor, there was taken the greatest care that he be taught to blow the flute, that he be able to play his whistle; and that at the same time he hold all his flowers and his smoking tube. At the same time he would go playing the flute, he would go sucking [the smoking tube], he would go smelling [the flowers].

So [his flute], his flowers, his smoking tube went together when he followed the road.

And while yet he lived, while yet he was being trained in the home of the steward, before he appeared [in the presence of the people], very great care was taken that he should be very circumspect in his discourse, that he talk graciously, that he greet people agreeably on the road if he met anyone.

For he was indeed much honored when he appeared, when already he was an impersonator. Since he impersonated Titlacauan, he was indeed regarded as our lord. There was the assigning of lordship; he was importuned; he was sighed for; there was bowing before him; the commoners performed the earth-eating ceremony before him.

And if they saw that already his body fattened a little, they made him take brine; with it they thinned him; they thinned him with salt. Thus he became thin; he became firm; his body became hard.

And for one year he [thus] lived; at the time of Toxcatl he appeared [before the people], and at that time died the man who had been impersonator for one year, who had been led along the road, who had waited for one year, who had [thus] passed one year. Just then he went being substituted; one was set in his place [from among] all whom the various stewards were guarding, were maintaining, at the time that [the first impersonator] appeared [before the people].

Thereupon he began his office. He went about playing the flute. By day and by night he followed whatever way he wished.

Fray Bernardino de Sahagún, *The Florentine Codex*, 2d ed., vol. 2, ed. and trans. Arthur Anderson and Charles Dibble (Santa Fe: School of American Research and University of Utah, 1981), 66–71.

His eight servitors went following him. Four [of them] had fasted for a year. Their hair was shorn as if they were one's pages; their hair was cut; their hair was clipped; they were not clipped smooth like a gourd; they were not clipped bald like a gourd; their heads were not smooth like pots; they did not stick [hair] to the head.

And also there were four constables, masters of youths. They cut their hair similarly; their hair arrangement was similar. It was arranged upright for them on their foreheads.

At this time Moctezuma adorned [the impersonator]; he repeatedly adorned him; he gave him gifts; he arrayed him; he arrayed him with great pomp. He had all costly things placed on him, for verily he took him to be his beloved god. [The impersonator] fasted; hence it was said: "He fasteth in black," [for] he went with his face smoke-black. His head was pasted with feathers, with eagle down. They only covered his hair for him; it fell to his loins.

And when he was attired, he went about with popcorn flowers laid upon his head; they were his crown of flowers. And he was dressed in these same on both sides; they drew them out to his armpits. This was called "the flowery stole."

And from his ears on both sides went hanging curved golden shell pendants. And they fitted [his ears with] ear plugs made of turquoise, turquoise mosaic. And a shell necklace was his necklace. Moreover, his breast ornament was of white seashells.

And then his lip pendant, his slender lip pendant, was of snail shell. And down his back went hanging what was like a cord bag called *icpatoxin*.

Then on both sides, on his upper arms, he placed golden bracelets, and on both sides, on his wrists, he went placing turquoise bracelets taking up almost all his forearms. And he went putting on only his net cape like a fish net of wide mesh with a fringe of brown cotton thread. And his costly breechclout reached to the calves of his legs.

And then he went placing his bells on both sides, on his legs. All gold were the bells, called *oyoalli*. These [he wore] because they went jingling, because they went ringing; so did they resound. And his obsidian sandals had ocelot skin ears. Thus was arrayed he who died after one year.

When [the feast of] Toxcatl went drawing near, when it approached him, when already it went reaching him, first he married; he looked upon a woman; he was married at the time of Uey toçoztli.

And he shed, he put in various places, he abandoned what had been his ornaments in which he had walked about fasting in black. His hair was shorn; he was provided a tuft of hair upon his forehead, like that of a seasoned warrior. They bound it; they wound it round and round. They bound it with [brown cotton thread] called *tochyacatl*; it was tied with a slipknot. And his forked heron feather ornament with a quetzal feather spray they bound to his warrior's hairdressing.

It was for only twenty days that he lived lying with the women, that he lived married to them. The four women in whose company he lived had also lived for a year guarded in the steward's establishment.

The name of the first one was Xochiquetzal; the second was Xilonen; the third was Atlatonan; the fourth was Uixtociuatl.

And when it was already the eve of [the feast of] Toxcatl, still five [days] from it, on the fifth day [from it], five days before the feast of Toxcatl would pass, they began each to sing [and dance].

At this time, in all these days, one knew nothing more of Moctezuma. They who yet had been his companions provided people with food, provided people with favors.

On the first day they sang [and danced] at a place called Tecanman. On the second day it was in the place where was guarded the image of Titlacauan, in the home of him who was the steward who guarded it. On the third day it was at Tepetzinco, in the middle of the lagoon. The fourth time it was at Tepepulco, which is also quite near Tepetzinco.

When they had sung [and danced], thereupon he embarked in a boat. The women went, going with him. They went consoling him; they went encouraging him. The boat proceeded to a place called Acaquilpan or Caualtepec; there it proceeded to the shore; there it landed them.

For here they were left, rather near Tlapitzauhcan. The women then returned. And only they who for the time had become [and] were his servitors went following him while yet he lived.

Thus was it said: when he arrived where [the impersonators of Titlacauan] used to die, [where] a small temple called Tlacochcalco stood, he ascended by himself, he went up of his own free will, to where he was to die. As he was taken up a step, as he passed one [step], there he broke, he shattered his flute, his whistle, etc.

And when he had mounted all the steps, when he had risen to the summit, then the offering priests seized him. They threw him upon his back on the sacrificial stone; then [one of them] cut open his breast; he took his heart from him; he also raised it in dedication to the sun.

For in this manner were all [these] captives slain. But his body they did not roll down; rather, they lowered it. Four men carried it.

And his severed head they strung on the skull rack. Thus he was brought to an end in the adornment in which he died. Thus his life there ended; there they terminated his life when he went to die there at Tlapitzauayan.

And this betokened our life on earth. For he who rejoiced, who possessed riches, who sought, who esteemed our lord's sweetness, his fragrance — richness, prosperity — thus ended in great misery. Indeed it was said: "No one on earth went exhausting happiness, riches, wealth."

Examining the Evidence

1. According to the *Florentine Codex*, what characteristics were required of this sacrificial war captive?
2. What was life like for the captive during the long preparation for the Aztec sacrifice?
3. How might this deity impersonation and sacrifice be explained?

15.2 AZTEC CHILD REARING

Codex Mendoza (c. 1540)

The painted manuscript known as the *Codex Mendoza* was produced by former Aztec scribes around 1540, approximately two decades after the Spanish Conquest of Mexico (1519–1521). Even though it is a post–Conquest document, the codex was clearly informed by prominent elders who lived before the arrival of Hernando Cortés and other conquistadors. Aztec pictographic symbols, somewhat like modern computer icons, are explained with Spanish and Nahuatl text, translated into English below. In the following selection, stages of Aztec child rearing, from birth to marriage, are described in terms of ideal types.

After the mother gave birth, they placed the infant in its cradle. . . . And at the end of four days after the infant's birth, the midwife carried the infant, naked, and took it to the courtyard of the house of the one who has given birth. And in the courtyard they had placed a small earthen tub of water on rushes or reeds [as a mat] called *tule*, where the said midwife bathed the said infant. And after the bath three boys, who are seated next to the said rushes eating toasted maize rolled up with cooked beans, the food they called *yxicue*, purposefully put the food in the little earthen jug so they might eat it. And after the said bath, the said midwife ordered the said boys to call out loudly the new name of the infant who had been bathed. And the name they gave it was that which the midwife wished. And at the beginning, when the infant was taken to be bathed, if it was a boy, they carried him with his symbol in his hand; and the symbol was the tool used by the infant's father, whether of the military or professions like metalworker, woodcarver, or

The Codex Mendoza, Volume 4, edited by Frances F. Berdan and Patricia Rieff Anawalt, 118–127. © 1992 by the Regents of the University of California. Published by the University of California Press. Used by permission of the publisher.

whatever other profession. And after having done this, the midwife handed the infant to its mother. And if the infant was a girl, the symbol they gave her for bathing was a distaff with its spindle and its basket, and a broom, which were the things she would use when she grew up. And they offered the male infant's umbilical cord, along with the little shield and arrows symbol used in bathing, in the place where they warred with their enemies, where they buried it under the ground. And likewise for the girl, they buried her umbilical cord under the *metate*, a stone for grinding tortillas.

And after that, at the end of twenty days, the infant's parents took the infant to the temple or *mezquita* [literally, "mosque," from the Spanish], called *calmecac*. And, with offerings of cloaks, loincloths, and some food, they presented the infant to the priests. And after the infant had been reared by its parents and had reached [a proper] age, they delivered him to the head priest of the said temple to be trained there for priesthood.

And if the infant's parents decided that, upon coming of age, he would serve in the military, then they offered the infant to the master, promising him [to service]. The master of boys and youths was called *teachcauh* or *telpuchtlato*. They made the offering with presents of food and other things for the dedication. And when the infant was of age, they delivered him to the said master.

[This explains] . . . the time and means . . . [they] used in instructing their children in how they should live. . . . Parents corrected their children when they were three years old, by giving good advice. And the ration they gave them at each meal was a half a tortilla.

. . . Parents . . . likewise instructed their children when they were four years old. And they began to teach them to serve in minor and light tasks. The ration they gave them at each meal was one tortilla.

. . . The parents of five-year-old children . . . engaged them in personal services, like toting light loads of firewood and carrying light bundles to the *tiangues*, or marketplace. And they taught the girls of this age how they had to hold the spindle and distaff in order to spin. Ration: one tortilla.

. . . The parents of six-year-old children . . . instructed and engaged them in personal services,

from which the parents benefited, like, for the boys, [collecting] maize that has been spilled in the marketplace, and beans and other miserable things that traders left scattered. And they taught the girls to spin and [to do] other advantageous services. This was so that, by way of the said services and activities, they did not spend their time in idleness, and to avoid the bad vices that idleness tends to bring. The ration they gave the children at each meal was one and a half tortillas.

[For older children, the *Codex Mendoza*] deals with the time and means of the Mexican *naturales* used in instructing and correcting their children, to avoid all idleness, ensure that they pursue and engage in advantageous activities. . . .

. . . The parents of seven-year-old children [are to give] the boys nets for fishing, and the mothers taught their daughters to spin; and they gave them good advice so they would always apply themselves and spend their time in something to avoid all idleness. The ration they gave their children at each meal was one and a half tortillas.

. . . [As for] the parents of eight-year-old children: They punished them by putting before them the fear and terror of maguey thorns, so that being negligent and disobedient to their parents would be punished with the said thorns. And also the children wept from fear. . . . The ration per meal that they gave them was set at one and a half tortillas.

. . . [As for] the parents of nine-year-old children: For being incorrigible and rebellious toward them, the parents punished their children with the said maguey thorns, tying the stark-naked boy hand and foot and sticking the said thorns in his shoulders and body. And they pricked the girls' hands with the thorns. . . . The ration per meal they gave them was one and a half tortillas.

. . . [Then for] the parents of ten-year-old children: Likewise they punished them for being rebellious, beating them with sticks and offering other threats. . . . The set rate and ration per meal that they gave them was one and a half tortillas.

. . . They punished the eleven-year-old boy or girl who disregarded verbal correction by making them inhale chili smoke, which was a serious and even cruel torment; and they would chastise them so they not go about in vice and idleness but that they employ their time in gainful activities. They gave the children of that age the bread that is tortillas at the rate of only one and a half tortillas at each meal to teach them not to be gluttons.

. . . If a twelve-year-old boy or girl ignored their parents' corrections and advice, his father took the boy and tied him hand and foot and laid him stark naked on the damp ground, where he stayed an entire day, so that with his punishment he would be chastised and fearful. And for the girl of the same age, her mother made her [rise] before dawn to sweep the house and street, and always be occupied in personal services. Likewise the parents gave them to eat a set amount of one and a half tortillas at every meal.

. . . For the thirteen-year-old boy or girl, the parents engaged [the boys] in carrying firewood from the hills and in transporting sedges and other grasses for household services. And the girls would grind [maize] and make *tortillas* and other cooked foods for their parents. They gave the children a set rate of two tortillas to eat at each meal, etc.

. . . For the fourteen-year-old boy or girl, the parents occupied and engaged the boy in fishing with a canoe in the lakes, and they instructed the girl in weaving cloth. They gave them a set rate of two tortillas to eat, etc.

. . . The father having boys of a youthful age, took them to [one of] two houses . . . , either to the house of the master who taught and instructed youths or to the temple, according to how the youth was inclined. And he delivered him to the chief priest or the master of boys so the youths might be taught from the age of fifteen years.

. . . [The following are] the means and custom they had in making legitimate marriages. The ceremony began when the bride, just after dark, was carried on the back of an *amanteca*, who is a physician. They were accompanied by four other women carrying ignited pine torches, who went lighting their way. And when they arrived at the groom's house, the groom's parents led her to the patio of the house to receive her, and they put her in a room or house where the groom was waiting. And the bride and bridegroom sat on a mat with its seats, next to a burning hearth, and they tied their clothes together, and offered copal incense to their gods. And then two old women and two old men who were present as witnesses gave food to the bride and bridegroom, and then the elders ate. And when the old men and old women finished eating, each one individually addressed the bride and bridegroom, offering them good advice on how they ought to behave and live, and on how they ought to perform the responsibility and position they had acquired, in order to live in peace.

Examining the Evidence

1. As described in the *Codex Mendoza*, what rituals accompanied Aztec childbirth?
2. How were Aztec girls and boys raised differently?
3. According to the *Codex Mendoza*, what were the various steps in an Aztec marriage ceremony?

15.3 THE INCA HUAYNA CAPAC'S FINAL DAYS

Juan de Betanzos, *Narrative of the Incas* (1557)

Juan de Betanzos was a Spanish conquistador who married an Inca princess from Cuzco. Betanzos learned the courtly Quechua language spoken by the nobles of the imperial capital and wrote a bilingual conversion manual for Spanish priests. He also collected spoken histories of past rulers from his wife's mother-in-law and other elder women. Betanzos translated these oral testimonies into Spanish in hopes of publishing a book he called *Narrative of the Incas*. The manuscript was sent to Spain but was

Juan de Betanzos, *Narrative of the Incas*, ed. and trans. Roland Hamilton and Dana Buchanan (Austin: University of Texas Press, 1996), 182–185.

subsequently lost until the 1980s, when Spanish scholars discovered it in an archive on the Mediterranean island of Mallorca. The following passage relates the last deeds of the Inca Huayna Capac, the uncle of Betanzos's wife. Huayna Capac died in Quito, the northern Inca capital, around 1527 from what many scholars suspect was small-pox. The disease apparently spread into the Andes from the coastal regions where Spaniards had been recon-noitering for several years.

Since Huayna Capac had already decided to go to the province of Quito, he put his plan into action and, leaving the instructions he felt necessary to protect and preserve his city, he left it, taking with him fifty thousand warriors. He also took with him his son Atawalpa, who was at that time thirteen years old. When Huayna Capac left Cuzco to make this journey, he was sixty years old and he left his son Huascar in Cuzco with the rest of his sons and daughters. He took with him Huascar's mother, who was pregnant and gave birth on the road to a daughter whom they called Chuquihuipa.

Huayna Capac went through his provinces doing much good for all those he met. He was accustomed to doing this for the poor, the widows, and orphans. Even today they love him for the great familiarity that he displayed to all. They say that his solemn demeanor was the same with everyone, the most important and the least important. He answered all who brought him questions and pleased them. No one who came before him left unhappy.

Traveling through his provinces in the above-described way, he reached Tomebamba [modern Cuenca, Ecuador], the province of the Cañares, where Huayna Capac himself had been born. He spent a month there resting and then left for Quito, where he marshaled his forces.

After having rested for some time in the city of Quito and leaving it well guarded, he left in search of the province and the lake that they call Yaguar-cocha, sending his son Atawalpa ahead with twenty thousand warriors.

When the men of Yaguarcocha learned that war-riors were coming against them, they came out on the road to resist their enemies. When they met the men that Atawalpa was bringing ahead of the others, they offered battle. The men of Yaguarcocha defeated him and Atawalpa returned in flight.

When Huayna Capac learned that his son was re-treating, he hurried his warriors, which at that point numbered more than one hundred thousand men. When he saw the soldiers that his son had taken fleeing, he tore his clothes, ripping them in front. He rebuked them, calling them cowards and saying that women were worth more than they. He asked from what they were fleeing; was it from unseen animals, since those from whom they fled were not men like they; why did they flee?

Saying these things to them, he forced them to return and ordered Atawalpa to go at their head with Huayna Capac himself. The men he had with him attacked their enemies with great energy. Since the enemies were spread out in pursuit of Atawalpa, Huayna Capac met them with great strength. He vanquished and captured them.

Pressing his victory, Huayna Capac himself en-tered a town which contained the house of that leader who was his enemy. He entered these houses intending to capture him. When he entered he found a pile of many blankets one on top of another. Think-ing that the enemy leader he was chasing was hiding under them, he began with his hands to remove the blankets. He took down the mound of them and found a very small Indian dwarf underneath.

When Huayna Capac uncovered him, the dwarf said: "Who has uncovered me? I wanted to sleep!" When Huayna Capac heard these words and saw the height of the dwarf, he was so amused that finding the dwarf pleased him as much as the victory that they had achieved over their enemies.

Later he told all his men that since he had cap-tured that dwarf in that battle all should regard him as his eldest son. Thus from that point on they all called the dwarf the eldest son of the Inca. And the dwarf called the children of the Inca brothers and sisters.

After having conquered and subjected these Indi-ans of the province of Yaguarcocha, Huayna Capac returned to Quito with his victory. According to their custom, he entered the city triumphantly be-cause of the victory he had achieved. He remained for six years in the city of Quito, resting and amusing himself as he had in Cuzco.

At the end of those six years in Quito, he fell ill and the illness took his reason and understanding and gave him a skin irritation like leprosy that greatly weakened him. When the nobles saw him so far gone they came to him; it seemed to them that he had come a little to his senses, and they asked him to name a lord since he was at the end of his days.

To them he replied that he named as lord his son Ninancuyochi, who was barely a month old and was in the province of the Cañares. Seeing that he had named such a baby, they understood that he was not in his right mind and they left him and went out. They sent for the baby Ninancuyochi, whom he had named as lord.

The next day they returned and entered and asked him again whom he named and left as ruler. He answered that he named as lord Atawalpa his son, not remembering that the day before he had named the above-mentioned baby. The nobles went immediately to the lodgings of Atawalpa, whom they told was now lord, and they gave him their respects as such. He told them that he had no wish to be the ruler even though his father had named him. The next day the nobles returned to Huayna Capac and in view of the fact that Atawalpa did not wish to be ruler, without telling him anything of what happened the day before, they asked him to name a lord and he told them it would be Huascar his son.

The nobles immediately placed Ragua Ocllo, the mother of Huascar, and her daughter Chuquihuipa in a room so that they might fast according to their usage and custom when some noble was named and the woman who was to be his principal wife.

Two nobles of Cuzco who were brothers of this Ragua Ocllo, called Xauxigualpa and Amurimachi, learned that Huascar had been named Inca and that Atawalpa did not wish to be. They sent the news to the nobles who were in Cuzco and to Huascar via the post service [i.e., running messengers using the Inca roads].

Huascar retired for a period of fasting after he heard the news in Cuzco. Here we will leave him

and return to Huayna Capac, who was in his final days. After having named Huascar as ruler in the way we have described, he died in four days. After he died, the messengers who had gone for the baby who had been named as ruler by Huayna Capac returned. The baby had died the same day they arrived of the same leprous disease as his father.

A short time after these messengers arrived, others sent by the leaders of Tumbes arrived to see Huayna Capac. These messengers gave news of how some white and bearded men had arrived at the port of Tumbes. They came in a *ganbo*, which means a ship. It was like a building, so large that no one would get sick on it. They themselves had entered it and found them to be men who did no evil to anyone. They gave them those things that the messengers brought. These were *chaquira* [beads], diamonds [cut glass], combs, knives, and things from bartering, all of which the leaders sent to Huayna Capac. They found that he was dead and had died at that moment. . . .

When he died, the nobles who were with him had him opened and took out all his entrails, preparing him so that no damage would be done to him and without breaking any bone. They prepared and dried him in the Sun and air. After he was dried and cured, they dressed him in costly clothes and placed him on an ornate litter well adorned with feathers and gold.

When the body was prepared, they sent it to Cuzco. All the rest of the nobles who were there went with it, including the mother of Huascar and her daughter. Atawalpa remained in Quito with 100 nobles from the city of Cuzco, all kinsmen of his.

Examining the Evidence

1. In de Betanzos's account, what kind of ruler was the Inca Huayna Capac in his last days?
2. How does this passage treat the problem of Inca succession?
3. According to de Betanzos, what is made of the arrival of Europeans on Pacific shores at the time of Huayna Capac's death?

15.4 ANDEAN RELIGION

Huarochirí Manuscript (c. 1600)

Unlike Mexico and Guatemala, where many native-language writings have survived from the pre-Columbian and colonial periods, Andean documents in languages other than Spanish are rare. A remarkable exception is the *Huarochirí Manuscript*, composed in Quechua some time around 1600 by a native speaker trained by a Spanish priest to render the language phonetically. The manuscript was composed during a search for alleged idolaters in and around the village of Huarochirí, high in the Andes Mountains east of Lima and thus demonstrates a clear interest in locating shrines and other sacred places and objects. Although some post–Conquest elements such as Roman Catholic notions of sin and guilt creep into the narrative from time to time, the following passage relates the adventures of the deity Huayta Curi in a way that probably would not have differed much from precolonial oral narratives. In treating shamanism and relations between the sexes in a humorous and frank manner, for example, it is clearly Andean in tone and content.

These people, the ones who lived in that era, used to spend their lives warring on each other and conquering each other. For their leaders, they recognized only the strong and the rich. We speak of them as the Purum Runa, "people of desolation."

It was at this time that the one called Paria Caca was born in the form of five eggs on Condor Coto mountain.

A certain man, and a poor friendless one at that, was the first to see and know the fact of his birth; he was called Huayta Curi, but was also known as Paria Caca's son.

Now we'll speak of this discovery of his, and of the many wonders he performed.

They say that fellow called Huayta Curi subsisted at the time just by baking potatoes in earth pits, eating the way a poor man does, and people named him "Baked Potato Gleaner."

At that time there was another man named Tamta Ñamca, a very rich and powerful lord.

Both his own house and all his other [wives' and servants'] houses looked like *cassa* and *cancho* feather weavings, for they were thatched with wings of birds. His llamas were yellow llamas, red and blue llamas; he owned llamas of every hue.

Seeing that this man lived so well, people who came from all the villages paid him homage and worshiped him.

For his part, he pretended to be very wise and spent his life deceiving a whole lot of people with the little that he really knew.

Then this man called Tamta Ñamca, who pretended to be so wise, even to be a god, contracted a really horrible disease.

His illness went on for many years, and in time people talked. "How can a man who knows so much, who's so powerful, be so sick?" they said.

Just like the Spaniards who, on such occasions, summon experts and doctors, Tamta Ñamca, hoping to recover, summoned all sorts of shamans and wise men. But no one at all could diagnose that disease of his.

Just then Huayta Curi was coming from the vicinity of Ura Cocha, and he went to sleep on the mountain by which we descend to Sieneguilla. . . .

While he was sleeping, a fox who'd come up from down below and one who'd come from up above met face to face there. One fox asked the other, "Brother, how are things in Upper Villca?"

"What's good is good. But a lord in Anchi Cocha, a *villca* [literally "priest"] as a matter of fact, one who claims to know a whole lot, to be a god himself, is terribly ill. All the wise men who found their way to him are wondering, "Why's he so ill?" No one can identify his sickness. But his disease is this: while

Frank Salomon and George Urioste, eds. and trans., *The Huarochirí Manuscript: A Testament of Ancient and Colonial Andean Religion* (Austin: University of Texas Press, 1991), 54–57.

his wife was toasting maize, a grain of *muro* [speckled] maize popped from the griddle and got into her private part.

"She picked it out and served it to a man to eat. Because of having served it, she became a sinner in relation to the man who ate it." . . .

"As a result of this fault," he told the fox who'd come from down below, "a snake has made its dwelling on top of that magnificent house and is eating them up. What's more, a toad, a two-headed one, lives under their grinding stone. And nobody is aware of these devouring animals."

And then he asked, "And how are people doing in Lower Villca, brother?"

The other fox answered similarly, saying, "There's a woman, the offspring of a great lord and a *villca*, who almost died because of a penis." . . .

As the foxes were telling each other these tidings, the man called Huayta Curi heard that the great lord who pretended to be a god was ill.

This great man had two daughters. He had joined the elder daughter to a fellow *ayllu* [community] member who was very rich. He married her.

The poor man called Huayta Curi came to the lord while he was still ill. When he arrived, he went around asking surreptitiously, "Isn't someone sick in this town?"

"It's my father who's sick," replied the younger daughter.

Huayta Curi answered, "Let's get together. For your sake I'll cure your father." . . .

The young woman didn't agree right away.

She told her father, "Father, there's a poor man here. He came and said to me, 'I'll cure your father.' "

All the wise men who were sitting there burst into laughter when they heard these words, and said, "If we ourselves can't cure him, how can this nobody make him well?"

But that lord wanted a cure so badly that he called for Huayta Curi. "Let him come, never mind what sort of man he is," he said.

When the great lord summoned him, Huayta Curi entered and said, "Father, if you want to get well, I'll make you well. But you'll have to give me your daughter."

Overjoyed, Tamta Ñamca replied, "Very well then!"

But when his older daughter's husband heard this proposition he flew into a rage. "How dare he join her, the sister-in-law of such a powerful man as me, to a nobody like that?" . . .

Huayta Curi began his cure by saying, "Father, your wife is an adulteress. Because she's an adulteress, a sinner, she's made you ill. As for what's eating you, it's the two snakes that dwell on top of this magnificent house of yours. And there's a toad, a two-headed one, that lives under your grinding stone."

"Now we'll kill them all. Then you'll get well. After you recover, you must worship my father [Paria Caca] above all things. He'll be born tomorrow or the day after. And as for you, you're not such a powerful man. If you were really powerful, you wouldn't be sick."

The rich man was astonished when Huayta Curi said this.

And when Huayta Curi said, "Now I'll take apart this gorgeous house of his," he became distraught. And his wife said, "This nobody, this crook, is slandering me! I'm no adulteress!"

Nonetheless the sick man wanted his health back very badly, and he let his house be dismantled. Then Huayta Curi removed the two snakes and killed them. Next he clearly explained the facts to the rich man's wife: just how a grain of *muro* maize had popped out and gotten in her private part, and how she, after picking it out, had served it to a man.

After that, the woman confessed everything. "It's all true," she said.

Next he had the grinding stone lifted. A toad, a two-headed one, came out from under it and fled to Anchi Cocha ravine.

It exists as a spring there to this day.

When the people come to that spring, it either makes them disappear or else drives them crazy.

Once Huayta Curi finished all these deeds the ailing man got well.

After Tamta Ñamca's recovery, on the day that had been foretold, Huayta Curi went for the first time to Condor Coto mountain.

It was there that the one called Paria Caca dwelled in the form of five eggs. All around him a wind rose up and began to blow.

In earlier times no wind had been observed.

Just before he went there on the appointed day, the man who'd recovered his health gave him his unmarried daughter.

While the two of them were traveling in the vicinity of that mountain they sinned together.

Examining the Evidence

1. Who are the main characters in this folk tale, and what is the central problem?
2. How is disease explained in this story from the *Huarochiri Manuscript*?
3. What is the resolution of this tale, and what does it tell us about Andean religious beliefs in the time of the Incas?

15.5 JESUIT VIEWS ON HURON SOCIETY

Jesuit Relations (1632–1637)

The native peoples of North America's Eastern Woodlands lacked a written language, but like most cultures worldwide, they possessed rich oral traditions and respected the men and women who memorized and recited mythical and historical narratives. As with most of the Mesoamerican and Andean sources included in this chapter, the earliest written sources date to the early post–Conquest era rather than pre-Columbian times and often were recorded by highly opinionated foreign soldiers or missionaries. In the case of the Huron of eastern Canada, it was French Jesuit missionaries who proved interested enough in their Native American cultural tradition to collect and translate what today would be regarded as ethnographic research. As can be seen in the selections in this document on shamanism and youthful sexuality, the Jesuits were unable to withhold moral judgments derived from their own Roman Catholic upbringing and training.

Variety of Huron Shamans

[The Hurons] say that the Sorcerers [i.e., shamans] ruin them; for if anyone has succeeded in an enterprise, if his trading or hunting is successful, immediately these wicked men bewitch him, or some member of his family, so that they have to spend it all in Doctors and Medicines. Hence, to cure these

and other diseases, there are a large number of Doctors whom they call *Arendiouane*. These persons, in my opinion, are true Sorcerers, who have access to the Devil. Some only judge of the evil, and that in diverse ways, namely, by Pyromancy, by Hydromancy, Necromancy, by feasts, dances, and songs; the others endeavor to cure the disease by blowing, by potions, and by other ridiculous tricks, which have neither any virtue nor natural efficacy. But neither class does anything without generous presents and good pay.

There are some Soothsayers [conjurers], whom they call also *Arendiouane* and who undertake to cause the rain to fall or to cease, and to predict future events. The Devil reveals to them some secrets, but with so much obscurity that one is unable to accuse them of falsehood; witness one of the village of *Scanonaenrat* . . . who, a little while before the [accidental] burning of the villages before mentioned, had seen in a dream three flames falling from the Sky on those villages. But the Devil had not declared to him the meaning of this enigma; for, having obtained from the village a white dog, to make a feast with it and to seek information by it, he remained as ignorant afterward as before.

Lastly, when I was in the house of [Amantacha, a Huron convert], an old woman, a sorceress, or female soothsayer of that village, said she had seen those who had gone to the war, and that they were

James Axtell, ed., *The Indian Peoples of Eastern America: A Documentary History of the Sexes* (New York: Oxford University Press, 1981), 73–75, 190.

bringing back a prisoner. We shall see if she has spoken the truth. Her method is by pyromancy. She draws for you in her hut the lake of the Iroquois; then on one side she makes as many fires as there are persons who have gone on the expedition, and on the other as many fires as they have enemies to fight. Then, if her spell succeeds, she lets it be understood that the fires from this side have run over, and that signifies that the warriors have already crossed the lake. One fire extinguishing another marks an enemy defeated; but if it attracts it to itself without extinguishing it, that is a prisoner taken at mercy.

It Takes a Village

We read that Caesar praised the Germans highly for having in their ancient savage life such continence as to consider it a very vile thing for a young man to have the company of a woman or girl before he was twenty years old. It is the reverse with the boys and young men of Canada, and especially with those of the Huron country, who are at liberty to give themselves over to this wickedness as soon as they can, and the young girls to prostitute themselves as soon as they are capable of doing so. Nay even the parents are often procurers of their own daughters; although I can truthfully say that I have never seen a single kiss given, or any immodest gesture or look, and for this reason I venture to assert that they are less prone to this vice than people here [in France]. This may be attributed partly to their lack of clothing, especially about the head, partly to the absence of spices and wine, and partly to their habitual use of tobacco, the smoke of which deadens the senses and ascends to the brain.

Many young men, instead of marrying, often keep and possess girls on terms of supplying food and fire, and they call them not wives, *Aténonha*, because the ceremony of marriage has not been performed, but *Asqua*, that is to say, companion, or rather concubine; and they live together for as long as it suits them, without that hindering the young man or the girl from going freely at times to see their other friends, male or female, and without fear of reproach or blame, such being the custom of the country.

But their preliminary marriage ceremony is this: when a young man wishes to have a girl in marriage he must ask her parents for her, without whose consent the girl cannot be his (although most frequently the girl does not accept their consent and advice, only the best and most sensible doing so). The lover who would make love to his mistress and obtain her good graces will paint his face and wear the finest adornments he can get, so as to appear more handsome; then he will make a present to the girl of some necklace, bracelet, or earring made of wampum [shell]. If the girl likes this suitor she accepts the present, whereupon the lover will come and sleep with her for three or four nights, and so far there is still no complete marriage nor promise of one made, because after they have slept together it happens quite often that the kindness is not maintained, and that the girl, who in obedience to her father has allowed this unauthorized favor, has in spite of it no affection for this suitor, and he must then withdraw without further steps. This happened in our time to a savage in regard to the second daughter of the great chief of Quieunonascaran, as the father of the girl himself complained to us, in view of the girl's obstinacy in not wishing to go on to the last marriage ceremony, because she did not like the suitor.

When the parties are agreed and the consent of the parents given, they proceed to the second marriage ceremony in the following manner. A feast is served of dog, bear, moose, fish, or other meat prepared for them, to which all the relations and friends of the espoused couple are invited. When all are assembled and seated, each according to his rank, all round the lodge, the father of the girl, or the master of ceremonies deputed to the office, announces before the whole gathering, pronouncing his words aloud and clearly, that such and such are being married and that it is for that reason the company is assembled and this feast of bear, dog, fish, etc., prepared for the enjoyment of all and to complete so worthy a proceeding. All meeting with approval, and the kettle cleaned out, everyone withdraws. Then all the women and girls bring the newly married wife a load of wood for her store, if she is married at the season when she cannot do it easily herself. . . .

If in course of time husband and wife like to separate for any reason whatever, or have no children, they are free to part, it being sufficient for the husband to say to the wife's relations and to herself that she is no good and may provide elsewhere for herself, and after that she lives in common with the rest until some other man seeks her out; and not only the men procure this divorce when their wives have given them some cause for doing so, but the wives also leave their husbands with ease when the latter do not please them. Hence it often happens that some woman spends her youth in this fashion, having had more than a dozen or fifteen husbands, all of whom nevertheless are not the only men to enjoy the woman, however much married they be; for after nightfall the young women and girls run about from one lodge to another, as do the young men for their part on the same quest, possessing them wherever it seems good to them, yet without any violence, leaving all to the wishes of the woman. The husband will do the like to his neighbor's wife and the wife to her neighbor, no jealousy intervening on that account, and no shame, disgrace, or dishonor being incurred.

But when they have children begotten from the marriage they rarely separate and leave one another except for some important reason, and when that does happen they are not long without being married again to someone else, notwithstanding their children, as to the possession of whom they come to an agreement.

Examining the Evidence

1. In the descriptions provided by the Jesuit observer in these selections, in what activities did male and female Huron shamans participate?
2. According to the Jesuit's observations, how did the Huron decide on mates and marriage partners, and how did they separate?
3. Given the opinions of the Jesuit author, how accurately do these passages reflect Huron life in the early modern period?

MAKING CONNECTIONS

1. What do these selections reveal about warfare and captive taking in the Americas?
2. How do these documents portray childhood and mating or marriage practices?
3. What insights do these readings offer on Native American humor and imagination?

ACKNOWLEDGMENTS

Chapter 1 [1.1] Pg. 5: Rick Groleau, "Neanderthals on Trial," *NOVA Online*, last modified January 2002, www.pbs.org/wgbh/nova/neanderthals/mtdna.html. © 2002-2018 WGBH Educational Foundation. **[1.2a]** Pg. 8: From *Lucy: The Beginnings of Humankind* by Donald Johanson and Maitland A. Edey. Copyright © 1981 by Donald Johanson and Maitland A. Edey. Reprinted with the permission of Simon & Schuster, Inc. All rights reserved. **[1.2b]** Pg. 10: Jamie Shreeve, "Oldest Skeleton of Human Ancestor Found," *National Geographic Magazine*, October 1, 2009. Reprinted with permission of National Geographic Creative. **[1.3]** Pg. 13: Reprinted with permission of Zone Books.

Chapter 2 [2.1] Pg. 19: Martha T. Roth, *Law Collections from Mesopotamia and Asia Minor. Writings from the Ancient World*, Vol. 6. (Atlanta, GA: Society of Biblical Literature, 1995), 71–140. Reprinted with permission of the Society of Biblical Literature. **[2.2]** Pg. 21: *The Literature of Ancient Egypt*, Third Edition, edited by William K. Simpson (Yale University Press, 2003), 438–441. Used by permission of the publisher. **[2.3]** Pg. 23: Republished by permission of Johns Hopkins University Press. William L. Moran, ed. and trans., *The Amarna Letters* (Baltimore, MD: Johns Hopkins University Press, 1992), 8–9. Permission conveyed through Copyright Clearance Center, Inc. **[2.5a]** Pg. 27: Excerpts from *The Epic of Gilgamesh: The Babylonian Epic and Other Texts in Akkadian and Sumerian*, translated and with an introduction by Andrew George. Copyright © 1999 Andrew George. Used by permission of Penguin Random House LLC. All rights reserved. **[2.5b]** Pg. 28: Excerpts from *The Epic of Gilgamesh: The Babylonian Epic and Other Texts in Akkadian and Sumerian*, translated and with an introduction by Andrew George. Copyright © 1999 Andrew George. Used by permission of Penguin Random House LLC. All rights reserved.

Chapter 3 [3.2] Pg. 33: Excerpts from *The Rig Veda: An Anthology*, translated by Wendy Doniger O'Flaherty. Copyright © 1981 Wendy Doniger O'Flaherty. Used by permission of Penguin Random House LLC. All rights reserved. **[3.4]** Pg. 38: Reprinted with permission of The Society for the Study of Early China. **[3.5]** Pg. 40: From *Chinese Civilization: A Sourcebook*, 2nd Edition, by Patricia Buckley Ebrey. Copyright ©1981 by The Free Press, a Division of Simon & Schuster, Inc. Copyright ©1993 by Patricia Buckley Ebrey. Reprinted with the permission of The Free Press, an imprint of Simon & Schuster, Inc. All rights reserved.

Art Pg.32, © J.M. Kenoyer/Harappa.com

Chapter 4 [4.3] Pg. 48: Reprinted by permission of Brill Publishers. Translation from Ann Guinan in *The Context of Scripture, Vol. 1, Canonical Compositions from the Biblical World*, ed. William W. Hallo, (Leiden: Brill, 1997), 423–426. Permission conveyed through Copyright Clearance Center, Inc. **[4.4]** Pg. 50: Reprinted with kind permission of Stanley Insler. **[4.7]** Pg. 56: Reprinted with permission of Hackett Publishing Company, Inc. All rights reserved.

Chapter 5 [5.2] Pg. 59: Reprinted by permission of Columbia University Press. Ainslee T. Embree, ed. and trans., "The Thirteenth Rock Edict," in *Sources of Indian Tradition*, 2d ed., vol. 1 (New York: Columbia University Press, 1988), 142–143. Permission conveyed through Copyright Clearance Center, Inc. **[5.3]** Pg. 60: Reprinted by permission of Columbia University Press. Ainslee T. Embree, ed. and trans., "The Book of Good Conduct," in *Sources of Indian Tradition*, 2d ed., vol. 1 (New York: Columbia University Press, 1988), 142–143. Permission conveyed through Copyright Clearance Center, Inc. **[5.6]** Pg. 67: Translation by Richard von Glahn. **[5.7]** Pg. 71: Copyright © 1954 University of Chicago Press. Reprinted with permission.

Chapter 6 [6.2] Pg. 77: Excerpt(s) from *The Aeneid* by Virgil, translated by Robert Fitzgerald, translation copyright © 1980, 1982, 1983 by Robert Fitzgerald. Used by permission of Random House, an imprint and division of Penguin Random House LLC. All rights reserved. **[6.3]** Pg. 79: Republished with permission of Catholic University of America Press. Saint Augustine, *City of God*, Books 8–16, Demetrius Zema, trans. (Catholic University Press, 2008). Permission conveyed through Copyright Clearance Center, Inc. **[6.4]** Pg. 82: *Historia Augusta: Vol. III*, translated by David Magie, Loeb Classical Library Volume 263 (Cambridge, MA: Harvard University Press). First published 1932. Loeb Classical Library® is a registered trademark of the President and Fellows of Harvard College. **[6.5]** Pg. 85: Iain Gardner and Samuel N. C. Lieu, *Manichaean Texts from the Roman Empire* (Cambridge, UK: Cambridge University Press, 2004). Copyright © 2004 Iain Gardner and Samuel N. C. Lieu. Published by Cambridge University Press, reproduced with permission.

Chapter 7 [7.3] Pg. 92: From *The Huarochiri Manuscript: A Testament of Ancient and Colonial Andean Religion*, translated and edited by Frank Salomon and George L. Urioste, Copyright © 1991. By permission of the University of Texas Press. **[7.4a]** Pg. 96: © The East Asian Library and the Gest Collection, Princeton University. **[7.4b]** Pg. 97: From *Chinese Civilization: A Sourcebook*, 2nd Edition, by Patricia Buckley Ebrey. Copyright © 1981 by The Free Press, a Division of Simon & Schuster, Inc. Copyright © 1993 by Patricia Buckley Ebrey. Reprinted with the permission of The Free Press, an imprint of Simon & Schuster, Inc. All rights reserved. **[7.5a]** Pg. 98: Stuart Lyons, *Horace's Odes and the Mystery of Do-Re-Mi* (Liverpool, UK: Liverpool University Press, 2007), 174. Copyright © 2007 Liverpool University Press. Reproduced with permission of the Licensor through PLSclear. **[7.5b]** Pg. 98: Reprinted with permission of The British Museum.

Art Pg. 91, Brooklyn Museum 38.121; Pg. 92, Brooklyn Museum Libraries (NK8839.1_B79). Drawings and text by Lois Martin.

Chapter 8 [8.2] Pg. 106: Republished by permission of the Pontifical Institute of Mediaeval Studies at the University of Toronto. **[8.3]** Pg. 109: Excerpts from *The Secret History of Procopius*, translated and with an introduction by G. A. Williamson. Copyright © 1966. Permission conveyed through David Higham Associates Ltd. **[8.4]** Pg. 112: Deno John Geanakoplos, *Byzantium: Church, Society, and Civilization Seen*

Through Contemporary Eyes (Chicago: University of Chicago Press, 1984), 153–154. Copyright © 1984 University of Chicago Press. Reprinted with permission. [8.6] Pg. 115: © 1956 Dumbarton Oaks Research Library and Collection, Trustees for Harvard University. Originally published in *Dumbarton Oaks Papers*, 9–10. [8.7] Pg. 116: Selections from A. Guillaume, trans. and ed., *The Life of Muhammad: A Translation of Ishaq's Sirat Rasul Allah* (Oxford, UK: Oxford University Press, 1955), 117–119, 130, 133–135. Reprinted with permission of Oxford University Press Pakistan.

Chapter 9 [9.2] Pg. 124: Copyright © 2005 by Richard N. Frye. All rights reserved. [9.3] Pg. 127: Republished with permission of Brill Academic Publishers. Yen Chih-T'ui, *Family Instructions for the Yen Clan*, trans. Têng Ssu-Yü (Leiden: E. J. Brill, 1968). Permission conveyed through Copyright Clearance Center, Inc. [9.4] Pg. 130: Republished with permission of Brill Academic Publishers. Yen Chih-T'ui, *Family Instructions for the Yen Clan*, trans. Têng Ssu-Yü (Leiden: E. J. Brill, 1968). Permission conveyed through Copyright Clearance Center, Inc. [9.5] Pg. 132: Republished with permission of Columbia University Press. Wm. Theodore de Bary, Wing-tsit Chan, and Burton Watson, eds., *Sources of Chinese Tradition* (New York: Columbia University Press, 1960). Permission conveyed through Copyright Clearance Center, Inc. [9.6] Pg. 133: Republished with permission of Princeton University Press. "Buddhism and the State in Early Japan," translated by William E. Deal, in *Buddhism in Practice*, ed. Donald S. Lopez (Princeton, N.J.: Princeton University Press, 1995). Permission conveyed through Copyright Clearace Center, Inc. [9.7] Pg. 135: Text from *The Complete Kama Sutra* by Alain Danielou ©1993. Reprinted by permission of Inner Traditions International and Bear & Company. www.innertraditions.com.

Art Pg. 139, Wolfgang Kaehler/LightRocket via Getty Images; Pg. 140, Julio Etchart/ullstein bild via Getty Images.

Chapter 10 [10.1] Pg. 143: Republished with permission of University of California Press Books. Dennis Tedlock, *2000 Years of Mayan Literature* (Berkley: University of California Press, 2010). Permission conveyed through Copyright Clearance Center, Inc. [10.2] Pg. 145: Reprinted with permission of University of Oklahoma Press and O-Books/John Hunt Publishing. All rights reserved. [10.3] Pg. 149: Republished with permission of University of Oklahoma Press. *The Incas of Pedro de Cieza de León*, Harriet de Onis, trans., ed. Victor Wolfgang von Hagen (Norman: University of Oklahoma Press, 1976). Permission conveyed through Copyright Clearance Center, Inc.

Art Pg. 144, Drawing by Linda Schele © David Schele; Pg. 156, © The Trustees of the British Museum; Pg. 157: © The Trustees of the British Museum; Pg. 158, Sandwich Islands: View of the Morai of the King, at Kayakakoua on the Island of Owhyhi, from 'Voyage Autour du Monde sur les Corvettes de L'Uranie 1817–29' engraved by Lejeune, published 1825 (engraving), Arago, Jacques Etienne Victor (1790–1855) (after)/Private Collection/Bridgeman Images.

Chapter 11 [11.2] Pg. 164: *Islam: From the Prophet Muhammad to the Capture of Constantinople, Volume 2: Religion and Society*, by Bernard Lewis (1974/1987)-1.249 words (pp. 158–161 & 163–165) © 1974 by Bernard Lewis. By Permission of Oxford University Press USA. [11.3] Pg. 166: Translation by Richard von Glahn. [11.4] Pg. 169: Translation by Richard von Glahn. [11.5] Pg. 172: *Two Memoirs of Renaissance Florence: The Diaries of Buonaccorso Pitti and Gregorio Dati*. Gene Brucker, ed. Excerpt translated by Julia O'Faolain (as Julia Martinez). Published by Harper & Row, 1967. Copyright © Julia O'Faolain. Reproduced by permission of the estate of the translator c/o Rogers, Coleridge & White Ltd., 20 Powis Mews, London W11 1JN.

Chapter 12 [12.2] Pg. 179: From *The Book of Margery Kempe, A Norton Critical Edition* by Margery Kempe, translated by & edited by Lynn

Staley. Copyright © 2001 by W. W. Norton & Company, Inc. Used by permission of W. W. Norton & Company, Inc. [12.3] Pg. 181: *Islam: From the Prophet Muhammad to the Capture of Constantinople, Volume 2: Religion and Society* by Bernard Lewis (1974/1987)-1.249 words (pp. 158–161 & 163–165) © 1974 by Bernard Lewis. By Permission of Oxford University Press USA. [12.6] Pg. 187: Republished with permission of Columbia University Press. Wm. Theodore de Bary, Stephen N. Hay, Royal Weiler, and Andrew Yarrow, eds., *Sources of Indian Tradition* (New York: Columbia University Press, 1958). Permission conveyed through Copyright Clearance Center, Inc. [12.7] Pg. 189: Translation by Richard von Glahn. [12.8] Pg. 191: Republished with permission of Columbia University Press. *The Pillow Book of Sei Shonagon*, Ivan Morris ed. and trans. (New York: Columbia University Press, 1991). Permission conveyed through Copyright Clearance Center, Inc.

Chapter 13 [13.1] Pg. 196: *Byzantium: Church, Society, and Civilization Seen Through Contemporary Eyes*, Deno Geanakoplos, ed. (Chicago: University of Chicago Press, 1984). Copyright © 1984 The University of Chicago. All rights reserved. [13.2] Pg. 198: Excerpts from *Chronicle of the Crusades*, by Jean de Joinville and Geoffroy de Villehardouin. Caroline Smith, trans. Copyright © 2008 Caroline Smith. Used by permission of Penguin Random House LLC. All rights reserved. [13.3] Pg. 201: *Medieval Iberia: Readings from Christian, Muslim, and Jewish Sources*, Olivia Remie Constable, ed. (Philadelphia: University of Pennsylvania Press, 1997), 209–215. Reprinted with permission of the University of Pennsylvania Press. [13.4] Pg. 204: © UNESCO 1958. [13.5] Pg. 205: © Christopher Dawson, 1955, *The Mongol Mission: Narratives and Letters of the Franciscan Missionaries in Mongolia and China in the Thirteenth and Fourteenth Centuries*, Sheed and Ward, used by permission of Bloomsbury Publishing Plc. [13.7] Pg. 209: *A Source Book for Russian History from Early Times to 1917*, Vol. 1, George Vernadsky, ed. (Yale University Press, 1972). Copyright © 1972 by Yale University. Used by permission of the publisher.

Chapter 14 [14.3] Pg. 218: Republished with permission of Brill Academic. Edward L. Farmer, *Zhu Yuanzhang and Early Ming Legislation: The Reordering of Chinese Society Following the Era of Mongol Rule* (Leiden: Brill, 1995). Permission conveyed through Copyright Clearance Center, Inc. [14.6] Pg. 225: From *Corpus of Early Arabic Sources for West African History*, J. F. P. Hopkins and N. Levtzion, eds., J. F. P. Hopkins, trans. Copyright © 1981 J. F. P. Hopkins and N. Levtzion. Published by Cambridge University Press. [14.7] Pg. 228: Republished with permission of John Wiley and Sons Inc. *Venice: A Documentary History, 1450–1630*, David Chambers and Brian Pullan, eds., (Oxford, UK: Blackwell, 1992). Permission conveyed through Copyright Clearance Center, Inc.

Art Pg. 222, The Persian Prince Humay Meeting the Chinese Princess Humayun in a Garden, c.1450 (gouache on paper), Islamic School, (15th century)/Musee des Arts Decoratifs, Paris, France/Bridgeman Images

Chapter 15 [15.1] Pg. 234: Reprinted with permission of the University of Utah Press. [15.2] Pg. 236: Republished with permission of University of California Press. *The Essential Codex Mendoza*, Frances F. Berdan and Patricia Reiff Anwalt, eds. (Berkeley: University of California Press, 1992). Permission conveyed through Copyright Clearance Center, Inc. [15.3] Pg. 238: Republished with permission of University of Texas Press. Juan de Betanzos, *Narrative of the Incas*. Roland Hamilton and Dana Buchanan, eds. and trans. (Austin: University of Texas Press, 1996). Permission conveyed through Copyright Clearance Center, Inc. [15.4] Pg. 241: From *The Huarochiri Manuscript: A Testament of Ancient and Colonial Andean Religion*, translated and edited by Frank Salomon and George L. Urioste. Copyright © 1991. By permission of the University of Texas Press. [15.5] Pg. 243: Father Gabriel Sagard, *The Long Journey to the Country of the Hurons*, edited by George M. Wrong, translated by H. H. Langton (The Champlain Society, 1939): 121–125. Reprinted with permission.